D1738315

Continued on back

CALIFORNIA SCHOOL OF PROFESSIONAL PSYCHOLOGY
LOS ANGELES

ADOLESCENT SEXUALITY IN A
CHANGING AMERICAN SOCIETY

Adolescent Sexuality in a Changing American Society

*Social and Psychological Perspectives
for the Human Services Professions*

Second Edition

CATHERINE S. CHILMAN

with contributions by   MARGARET FELDMAN
LEWAYNE D. GILCHRIST
LORRAINE V. KLERMAN
JAMES F. JEKEL
PETER SCALES
STEVEN PAUL SCHINKE

A WILEY-INTERSCIENCE PUBLICATION
JOHN WILEY & SONS
New York · Chichester · Brisbane · Toronto · Singapore

Library of Congress Cataloging in Publication Data:

Chilman, Catherine S.
   Adolescent sexuality in a changing American society.

   (Wiley series on personality processes, ISSN 0195-4008)
   "A Wiley-Interscience publication."
   Includes index.
   1. Youth—United States—Sexual behavior—Addresses,
essays, lectures. 2. Youth—United States—Attitudes—
Addresses, essays, lectures. 3. Adolescent psychology—
Addresses, essays, lectures. 4. Youth—Service for—
United States—Addresses, essays, lectures. I. Title.
II. Series.

HQ27.C48   1983   306.7'088055   82-20185
ISBN 0-471-09162-6

Printed in the United States of America

10 9 8 7 6 5 4 3 2 1

To my three beloved daughters, who long ago taught me so much about the funny, worrisome, tender, heart-breaking, fulfilling task of mothering daughters as they grew from childhood to maturity as young women: as wives, mothers, community workers, and part-time professionals in the human services fields. To Margaret C. Carpenter, Jeanne C. Klovdahl, and Cathy C. Brown and their own daughters and sons.

Series Preface

This series of books is addressed to behavioral scientists interested in the nature of human personality. Its scope should prove pertinent to personality theorists and researchers as well as to clinicians concerned with applying an understanding of personality processes to the amelioration of emotional difficulties in living. To this end, the series provides a scholarly integration of theoretical formulations, empirical data, and practical recommendations.

Six major aspects of studying and learning about human personality can be designated: personality theory, personality structure and dynamics, personality development, personality assessment, personality change, and personality adjustment. In exploring these aspects of personality, the books in the series discuss a number of distinct but related subject areas: the nature and implications of various theories of personality; personality characteristics that account for consistencies and variations in human behavior; the emergence of personality processes in children and adolescents; the use of interviewing and testing procedures to evaluate individual differences in personality; efforts to modify personality styles through psychotherapy, counseling, behavior therapy, and other methods of influence; and patterns of abnormal personality functioning that impair individual competence.

IRVING B. WEINER

University of Denver
Denver, Colorado

Preface

This work is written primarily for human services professionals who work with adolescents. It combines research-based knowledge and theory from the behavioral and social sciences with well-tested guidelines for direct services and program development. It is hoped that this material will be useful in promoting competent professional practice in a field that particularly calls for scientific objectivity, human empathy, steady courage, and sensitive appreciation of the joys and griefs experienced by young people as they grow toward mature womanhood or manhood.

A comprehensive approach is used to promote an understanding of the many social and psychological aspects of adolescent sexuality. This sexuality is defined as including all the facets of development, experience, feelings, attitudes, and values that together shape adolescent sexual (including sex role) behaviors.

The first 10 chapters provide a foundation of knowledge and theory concerning such topics as adolescent growth, recent societal trends affecting adolescent sexual attitudes and behaviors, development of sexuality from infancy through the teenage years, factors associated with early intercourse and contraceptive use, and the so-called causes and consequences of adolescent childbearing.

Much of the material in these chapters is adapted from the 1978 edition, *Adolescent Sexuality in a Changing American Society: Social and Psychological Perspectives,* which was written under contract with the Center for Population Research, National Institute of Child Health and Development, and was intended primarily for researchers. It contained an analytic summary of all available social and psychological research (through early 1976) concerning the many facets of adolescent sexuality. The current volume, written in less technical terms, condenses the research summary and adds studies that appeared between 1976 and 1981.

Chapters concerned with professional practice with adolescents and their families have also been added. Written by well-known specialists in their fields, these chapters cover the following topics: sexuality education and counseling, family planning services for young people, comprehensive programs for pregnant and parenting adolescents, and implications of research for public policies. The book closes with case illustrations of many of the different ways individual adolescents feel and behave in respect to their developing sexuality.

As an author-editor, I am first indebted to the writers of the professional practice chapters: Margaret Feldman, Ph.D., Ithaca College; Lewayne D. Gilchrist, Ph.D., University of Washington; James F. Jekel, M.D., M.P.H., Yale University; Lorraine V. Klerman, Dr.P.H., Brandeis University; Peter Scales, Ph.D., Planned Parenthood Federation of America; Steven Paul Schinke, Ph.D., University of Washington.

Wendy Baldwin, Ph.D., Chief of the Behavioral Sciences Branch, the Center for Population Research, N.I.C.H.D., was a constant source of scholarly assistance in the development of the first edition and has continued to provide resource materials for the present edition. Other important reviewers have included psychologists Elizabeth Douvan, George Cvetkovich, and M. Brewster Smith. My thanks go also to Mary Ann Riggs, word processor operator extraordinary.

Most profoundly, I wish to express appreciation to the many thousands of young women and men who took part in the numerous research projects that furnish the foundation of this book. And it is for the enhancement of their well-being that the book is basically written. May it serve its purpose, at least in part.

CATHERINE S. CHILMAN, PH.D.

University of Wisconsin—Milwaukee
Milwaukee, Wisconsin
February 1983

Contents

CHAPTER 1

Introduction: Purposes, Methods, and Basic Concepts

PURPOSES

The major purposes of this book are to encourage a comprehensive, humane understanding of adolescent sexuality and to provide a foundation of social and psychological knowledge and practice useful to professionals in the human services.

If we are to help adolescents realize their potential as whole human beings, then we need to help them integrate the biological, social, and psychological aspects of their sexuality into all aspects of their lives. We need to deal with adolescent sexuality in the context of whole, young human beings in interactions with their personal selves, their peers, their families of the past and of the future, and all the institutions of the larger society. These are *people* we are talking about, not simply owners of ovaries and testicles, vaginas and penises.

Since a central purpose of this book is to achieve an admittedly difficult blend of the rational–scientific and the humanistic–individualistic and to encourage a broader than usual view of adolescents and their sexuality, an unusually wide-ranging effort has been made to bring together large bodies of research, theory, and practice suggestions as a guide to the perceived goal. Perhaps the goal is overly ambitious; in all probability a number of topics are inadequately developed, skimmed over too lightly. The sought-for integration of the numerous topics is incomplete. Nevertheless, it is hoped that the underlying concepts, as well as the specific subject matter, will be helpful and stimulating to human service professionals, policymakers, and, to a lesser extent, researchers.

METHODS

This book includes an analytic overview and summary of the available research related to the social and psychological aspects. It also includes chapters on education in respect to adolescent sexuality, counseling of adolescents regarding the sexual aspects of their lives, the development and implementation of family planning programs, programs for adolescent parents and their children, and suggestions for further policy and program development.

BASIC CONCEPTS

Adolescence

Adolescence is defined as that period of time in a person's life that stretches from the onset of puberty to young adulthood. Puberty refers to the first phase of adolescence, when sexual maturation becomes evident. Entrance into young adulthood is less easily defined. For the purposes of this book, however, the behaviors and needs of young people between age 11 or so and age 19 will be stressed. This is largely because young women and men in this age group tend to be especially misunderstood and underserved in respect to the many aspects of their sexuality.

Adolescence is often seen as consisting of two major stages. The first stretches from the onset of puberty to about ages 14–16. Psychologically, it is characterized by a push for independence from parents and attempts to resolve conflicts between the continuing needs for childish dependence and the desire for a separate identity. The second stage is marked by the search for a mature identity, the quest for a mate, and the exploration of different sets of values and of occupational and other life goals. Throughout adolescence, sexuality is *the* major theme, a concept we will return to later.

Human Sexuality

Human sexuality is often described as including the physical characteristics and capacities for specific sex behaviors, together with psychological learning, values, norms, and attitudes about these behaviors. This definition is broadened here to include a sense of both gender and sex identity and related concepts, behaviors, and attitudes about the self and others as masculine or feminine persons in the context of society. Gender pervades virtually every aspect of the person's life. It is affected by the totality of what it means to be a male or female person; by one's past and present experiences and anticipation of the future; by one's stage of development and life situation; by one's physical–constitutional capacities and characteristics; and by the kind of society and period of time in which one lives. Sex identity is more specific to one's self-definition as a sexual person: a bisexual, homosexual, or heterosexual person, for instance; or, for another example, a virgin or nonvirgin.

The past few centuries, particularly, have been characterized by a proliferation of specialized knowledge and resultant programs and policy. Specialization has brought with it an awesome blooming of information and enrichment of many, but not all, human lives. It has also brought with it a deeply disturbing fragmentation of the self and society. Fragmentation has occurred in the field of sexuality as well as in other aspects of the human condition. Specialized knowledge has made magnificent contributions to our understandings of genetics, human reproduction, the childbirth process, birth control techniques, the nature of the human sex responses, specific aspects of human sex behavior, the formation of gender and sex identity, and the sexual behavior of various species and various human societies. Researchers in the field are far too numerous to detail here. Their contributions have been tremendously useful in helping people reach more richly rewarding lives.

However, these knowledge developments have tended to create an overly mechanistic, technical view of sexuality, focused on intercourse, reproduction, and contraception. This view often fails to include the needs and feelings of the whole masculine or feminine person in relationship to others and to the larger society at this particular period of social history. Combined with other social trends, the new knowledge of and attitudes toward sexuality have played into the breakdown of previously held traditions and values that provided a certain amount of stability and wholeness to life for most people in many parts of the Western industrialized world. Such stability and wholeness exacted a price that included repression and denial of sexual interests, limited sexual fulfillment, difficulties in controlling family size, and high rates of infant and maternal death. Now that this price can be sharply reduced, other costs are appearing. Broadly speaking, they involve a specialized, rational, value-free approach to human sexual behavior and functioning. Basically, this approach is largely genital—a complaint often raised by females concerning the male's conception of sexuality. Perhaps because females have a more complex reproductive function, women may be more likely to view sexuality in interpersonal, less genital-specific terms than men do—a concept to be explained in greater depth in Chapter 2.

The dictum that some would give to people, including adolescents, "Have any sex experiences you want, but don't get pregnant or become infected with a venereal disease," is essentially dehumanizing. It implies that we do not care what happens to the psychological or social person as long as his or her physical problems do not burden society.

By attempting to remove reproductive outcomes, ignorance, and repressive moralizing from human sexuality, we have left it only partially human. To fully humanize sexuality, we need to gain further knowledge about its meaning and effects for the social-psychological, as well as physical, person. We need to recognize more fully the power of sexuality for helping or hurting the human personality. We need to evolve new values, appropriate to our times, that provide the protection of constraints as well as the exhilaration of freedom for the guidance of males and females. This is especially true for those who are young and therefore tender and easily hurt but somewhat less easily helped.

The interpersonal aspects of sexuality require particularly serious consideration. Unlike such other basic human functions as breathing, eating, sleeping, and eliminating or such less fundamental ones as working and playing, sexual behavior (aside from masturbation) inevitably involves an interpersonal relationship. It offers the maximum possible exposure of the self to another. This exposure can be intensely validating to one's sense of self-worth or, at the other end of the continuum, intensely destructive of that sense. In this writer's view, sexual relationships offer the potential of a unique and enormously valuable opportunity for a deeply intimate, loving, shared partnership, which is linked to the most fundamental biological, social, and psychological aspects of life. It involves the individual's total life history: past, present, and future. It is possible to engage in such a relationship in a constricted way, seeking only sensations and denying its multiple meanings. By doing so, however, one risks being dehumanized and alienated, alone with hidden vulnerabilities that become more sensitive because they have not been explored and shared with another trusted person.

Although males and females each have their special vulnerabilities and strengths and although sexuality has somewhat different meanings for each sex, research about adolescent sexuality and resultant policies and programs rarely consider both sexes and rarely take into account their likenesses as well as their differences. An overemphasis is placed on female needs and characteristics. An unfortunate aspect of this tendency is to underrate the importance and the responsibilities of males in sexual partnerships and to underplay the importance of interpersonal partnerships between the two sexes. This lack of sufficient attention to males can create difficulties for any age group; it is particularly apt to do so for impressionable adolescents.

Adolescent Sexuality

All aspects of adolescent development may be viewed as primarily sexual, in the broader sense sketched above. The primary fact about adolescence is that the young person becomes capable of reproduction. This fact marks him or her as no longer being a child and as being launched on the way to adulthood. As frequently pointed out in the literature, adolescence is an invention of complex industrial societies—societies that demand longer periods of growth and preparation for the adult capacities required for self-support and self-management. Earlier onset of adolescence in recent times [e.g., it has been estimated that there has been a downward trend in age of menarche of about 4 months per decade since 1850 (Tanner, 1970)] and the constraints imposed by society have created this special period of life.

It is customary to view this period as having biological, social, and psychological components, but these components are usually treated discretely by writers in the field, especially with respect to sexuality. Sexuality is not generally recognized as being the major basic concern of, and about, adolescents. However, an argument can be made that this is the case, albeit somewhat differently for females and males.

At the biological level, it is clear that the central feature of adolescent development is sexual. Males and females are being prepared for reproductive and parental functions. Aside from the specifically sexual aspects of this development, adolescents also are becoming larger and stronger so that they can carry out parental and other adult roles. Physically, males and females are becoming more differentiated in numerous ways, including their body contours and appearance. This differentiation creates tensions and attractions between them, at least in the context of our culture.

Biological changes, quite naturally, interact with psychological ones. Psychological changes have their cognitive, personal—emotional, and attitudinal–value aspects. Large bodies of research and theory concerning the psychology of adolescence lead in a bewildering variety of directions, with only limited views of its underlying sexual nature. However, if we recognize that the cognitive, motivational, social, and emotional aspects of adolescence are all basically directed toward becoming an adult and that human sexuality (importantly including its gender aspects) is a central feature of adulthood, then it becomes clear that the adolescent is primarily a sexual person pushing toward a full flowering of masculinity or femininity.

Young people develop their sexuality in response to their own unique personalities: their own temperament, feelings, and attitudes about the self and others; abilities and interests; fears and wishes; memories and goals. They bring the total experiences of their lives, especially experiences within their families, to the task of becoming mature women and men. They bring their capacities for and values about interpersonal relationships as males and females to their developing sexuality. These capacities and values, shaped by their family, neighborhood, school, and other community experiences during childhood, affect how they relate, and to whom they relate, as masculine or feminine persons during their adolescent years. As they seek their adult identity, they try different kinds of relationships with people of both sexes who have a variety of social-psychological characteristics.

In adolescence, personal relationships are particularly variable and tenuous as young people move from immersion in the family and simple social systems toward greater independence, distinctive selfhood, and involvement in complex social systems. Although gaining and keeping self-assurance is difficult in many life stages, it is probably especially difficult during adolescence because young people are so much in the process of becoming separate individuals. They lack the support of intimate relations with others who are accepting and acceptable and who can provide validation that they are valued, competent, uniquely significant masculine or feminine persons.

Adolescent sexuality is also shaped by sociocultural forces; by the overall values and norms of the larger society concerning adolescent sexuality, masculinity, and femininity; by the adolescent's particular place in that society as determined by the socioeconomic status of his or her parents and by the young person's race, ethnicity, and religion; by the particular community in which the individual lives and the cultural patterns of that special place; and by the social institutions that serve adolescents.

Development and expression of sexuality is also affected by the point in time in which one has grown up and is now living. For example, it is quite different to have reached adolescence in the 1950s, 1960s, 1970s, or 1980s because of the differing social conditions and attitudes in these various decades.

Clearly, economic conditions and employment opportunities for males and females also have a profound effect on the adolescent's sense of male or female identity, goals, values, and behaviors. Family formation and structure are affected by economic conditions in a number of obvious and not so obvious ways, as we shall see later. So, too, are attitudes of self-esteem and of the sexes toward each other.

Political and related conditions also affect adolescent sexuality in a number of spheres, including conditions of war or peace; age requirements for voting, working, and marriage; equal rights legislation; laws governing contraceptives, sterilization, and abortion; domestic relations and child custody laws; laws and procedures and official attitudes toward various forms of deviant behavior; and the structure and functioning of the police and court system vis-à-vis male and female youths.

As adolescent sexuality is conceptualized in the framework of contemporary society, it seems important to recognize that the life goals for teenagers are far less clear today than they used to be. Not long ago, girls primarily prepared for marriage and parenthood; they protected their virginity because it was seen as important to attracting a "good" husband and basic to being a respectable mother. If they also prepared for employment, they usually saw this as supplementary to their larger purpose. Boys also prepared for marriage and parenthood, primarily through acquiring occupational competence so they could support a family. Clear differences were seen between the sexes in traits, roles, and functions; gender identity was plainly mapped. Young people were fairly sure about where they were headed in the future. By the late 1960s and on into the 1970s and 1980s, there was far less clarity about the roles and functions of men and women, of traditional families, and of life itself. (See also Chapter 3.)

LIMITATIONS

This book has a number of limitations. Secondary sources have been used for discussions of the following topics: physical aspects of adolescent sexuality; the social and psychological aspects of adolescent development in general (such as social, cognitive, moral, and ego development); and current trends in society. Moreover, a number of books and articles that discuss adolescent sexuality have been read but are not discussed in this book because they do not meet criteria of an adequate research basis.

Primary sources have been reviewed and analyzed in depth with respect to the social and psychological aspects of sex behaviors of American adolescents, use or nonuse of contraception and abortion, illegitimacy, early marriage, and the causes and consequences of adolescent parenthood.

Chapters on education, counseling, and program development are based on the best information currently available, although evaluative research is still in its infancy in respect to most of these topics. In general, there are numerous gaps and deficiencies in the research regarding all aspects of adolescent sexuality. Though much has been learned about the topic, especially since the early 1970s, our knowledge base is still frail and partial. Despite this less than satisfactory situation, it seems important to proceed with what is known to further develop professional understanding and skills in provision of services to adolescents in their hazardous voyage from childhood to sexual maturity.

CHAPTER 2

A Bio-Social-Psychological View of Adolescent Sexuality

SOME BIOLOGICAL ASPECTS OF ADOLESCENCE

Introduction

This chapter describes some of the major social and psychological theories regarding the development of adolescent sexuality. Knowledge about the chief aspects of the physical development of adolescents also is given here, but with no attempt to review and analyze related research. Social and psychological research findings about the development of adolescent hetero-sexual relationships are reviewed in Chapter 5.

Biological Determinants of Gender and Some Differences between the Sexes

One pair of the 23 pairs of chromosomes in the cell that marks the beginning of a new human being contains the determinants of genetic sex. This pair is either an XX (female) or XY (male). The composition of this chromosome is determined by whether an X- or Y-carrying sperm of the father fertilized the ovum of the mother. For the first 6 weeks of life, the embryo is sexually undifferentiated. At the end of that time, a male embryo begins to develop testicles; somewhat later, the female embryo begins to develop ovaries packed with egg cells—the total supply for a lifetime.

The testicles soon manufacture sex hormones: first progesterone (the so-called pregnancy hormone); then androgen, the masculinizing hormone; and finally, estrogen, the feminizing hormone. Both males and females contain these hormones within their bodies but in different proportions. Testicles produce enough androgen to dominate the estrogen in the male, while ovaries produce enough estrogen to dominate the androgen in the female. Individuals differ in their exact amount of hormone mix and vary in this mixture at different points of their lives.

The female embryo does not need an extra hormonal push for sex development, as does the male. Without the action of the XY chromosome, development proceeds along female lines. The estrogens of the mother help support the prenatal development of the XX (female) embryo, so that added female sex-determining push is not needed. As reported by Money and Tucker (1975), "Unless there is a sufficient push in the male direction, the fetus will take the female turn at any subsequent fork (of embryonic development). Whether there is a female push or not, nature's first choice is to make Eve. . . . Development as a male requires effective propulsion in the male direction at each critical stage" (p. 73).

The finding that "nature's first choice is to make Eve" is a stunning discovery, revising the age-old myth that she came from Adam's rib. In effect, males, rather than females, are derivative from the basic life form. This finding, together with trends in contemporary society, adds spark to the "sex role revolution" (Sherfey, 1966).

But back to biology—males and females have basically similar physical structures; however, those related to reproduction evolve in different ways. This includes the genitalia, of course. One aspect of this differentiation is that the female clitoris is a "rudimentary penis" and has the same kind of sensitivity to stimulation.

Money and his associates have studied particularly chromosomal irregularities that create "sexual errors of the body" (Money, 1968; Money & Ehrhardt, 1972; Money et al., 1955). These errors are not detailed here, aside from a few remarks. Such errors (which are rare) can cause problems in infertility or inadequate development of the genitalia. Research with people whose sex is in question at birth has lead Money and his colleagues to many important findings, including methods of hormonal, surgical, and psychotherapeutic intervention, as well as further insights into the processes of gender identity formation.

Inadequate supplies of androgen, or androgen insensitivity, can create serious developmental hazards for males. Females do not suffer in their early development from similar problems with respect to estrogen. However, a female may receive an oversupply of androgen. This overdose does not affect a female's internal structures, but it tends to masculinize the molding of the external genitals. Some anomalies can be treated with surgery or hormones in early life.

These findings explain why males are generally more vulnerable than females to sexual differentiation errors at birth. This is one reason that there are higher miscarriage rates with male babies. Although males lead at conception at about 140 to 100, at birth 105 boy babies are born to 100 girl babies. By the time age 40 is reached, the sexes are about equally divided; by age 65, there are only 70 males to 100 females.

A word about people who are born with XXX or XYY chromosomes. In the female case (XXX), no problems seem to appear (except for rare cases of mental retardation), but males (XYY) tend to be slow to mature in self-regulation of behavior and to be especially impulsive in their reactions. However, they do not have a special tendency to become criminals, as was originally thought.

There is emerging evidence that sex hormones affect the developing brain. Research with animals shows, for example, that female monkeys who are injected with heavy doses of androgen in critical periods of their pregnancy bear female offspring who are more boisterous in their play and assertive in their mating behavior than other female monkeys.

Money and Ehrhardt have done intensive, long-range follow-up studies on a group of girls who were prenatally androgenized in the 1950s by the synthetic progestins given to their mothers to prevent miscarriages. (This type of therapy has now been discontinued, owing to discovery of its effects.) The internal organs and hormonal functioning of these girls were not affected, but some were born with masculinized genitalia. This condition was corrected by early surgery. Although these girls have developed like normal females and have a clear sense of feminine identity, they do tend to behave like tomboys, quite different from the control group of nonandrogenized females to which they are matched. These tomboys prefer active rough games, prefer playing with boys, and have little interest in feminine toys or clothes. Although they hope to marry, they also plan active future careers.

In a similar vein, underandrogenized boys tend to be quieter than most boys and less interested in competitive sports but, as in the case of the girls, clear about their masculine identity. (See also Chapter 4 regarding the apparently important effects of early passivity of males on their later sex activity.)

On the basis of his own research and that of others, Money postulates that hormonal differences between males and females create differences in the brain that lead to different levels of responsiveness to stimuli. Bardwick (1971) also summarized a number of animal research studies. She reported that there was emerging evidence that sex hormones seem to exert an action of the central nervous system during fetal or neonatal life to organize it into a male type or female type of brain. This affects predispositions to perceive and respond to stimuli (Bardwick, 1971). This viewpoint is also supported by Gagnon (1965). Females tend to respond more quickly to the nurturant needs of the young, and males respond to stimuli for dominant, active behavior. This is not to say that the sexes behave in radically different ways. Males can and do respond to the needs of the young; females can and do respond to situations that call for activity and dominance. Strong stimuli are needed to elicit these "cross sex" behaviors. Once these behaviors occur, they tend to persist if they are reinforced and supported by the culture.

In part these findings are similar to those obtained by Maccoby and Jacklin in their 1974 exhaustive review of large bodies of related research. They conclude that, on the average, males are inherently more aggressive than females. They fail, however, to find firm evidence that human females are more likely than males to be nurturant in their behavior, though they do not conclude that this may *not* be true.

Moreover, Maccoby and Jacklin did not find differences between the sexes that previously had been proclaimed either by popular assent or by some researchers who drew their conclusions from a small number of studies. According to Maccoby and Jacklin, aside from stronger masculine tendencies toward aggression, the only other trait that appears to clearly involve innate biological factors is that of the superior visual–spatial ability of the average male (Maccoby & Jacklin, 1974). However, Block (1976) raises cogent questions about the validity of many of Maccoby and Jacklin's conclusions. She points to numerous weaknesses in the research on which these conclusions are based. These weaknesses include problems in statistical analysis, small sample size, inadequacy of basic theories and hypotheses, lack of specific research focused on sex differences, problems in research instruments used, and the overrepresentativeness of younger age groups in the research with no allowance made for differences that may emerge later as a result (at least in part) of maturational–biological changes. Block also points out that a number of important studies were omitted from the Maccoby and Jacklin review, and she takes issue with the ways in which some of the findings are interpreted.

As Block sees the evidence from the Maccoby and Jacklin review, she concludes, in part, that boys are inherently more dominant, active, impulsive, curious, and exploring than girls and that they have a more potent self-concept. She also concludes that girls are inherently more likely to express fear, are more susceptible to anxiety, are more lacking in self-confidence, seek more help and reassurance, maintain greater proximity to friends, and score higher on social desirability.

Of course, it is extremely difficult to learn to what extent observed differences between the sexes are biologically based and to what extent they are a product of socialization. As Money points out, biological differences affect individual sensitivity to stimuli and, hence, the individual response to socialization experiences. Also, his research serves as a reminder that there are numerous individual biological differences and that findings about differences between the sexes refer to averages.

Other biological differences between the sexes are frequently overlooked by behavioral scientists in discussion of this topic. For instance, the female's more complex reproductive system leads her to a less genital-specific view of sex than that usually held by males.

Dual female structures and functions are those of conception, pregnancy, childbirth, and breast-feeding and the capacity for sexual response. Although contemporary values, necessities, and methods create the possibility of reproduction-free coitus, the differences in male and female structures remain. These differences probably have more pervasive effects than some "social learning is all" enthusiasts would have us think. Although these effects may largely be ones of social learning, cultural norms are deeply linked to biological differences in the structures and functioning of the two sexes. For example, in coitus, the male enters the woman; he must have an erection to do so; he "loses" his seed to the woman (or the condom); unlike the woman he cannot "fake" an orgasm; and he is generally less able to have multiple orgasms. This tends to create performance anxiety in males to a more basic and pervasive extent than is generally the case for females. The male's need to prove himself sexually is enhanced by a culture that, despite the feminist equal rights movement, still tends to equate adequate masculinity with many forms of active achievement on the part of the male.

Although current "expert" advice to females is that they, too, can and should be sexually aggressive and "take responsibility" for their own sexual fulfillment (Katchadourian & Lunde, 1975), the fact remains that coitus centrally involves aggressive male penetration and female receptivity. Fulfillment for the female depends more on the active behaviors of the male than vice versa. Particularly because of differences in physical structure and partly because of differences in socialization, males tend to be more readily orgasmic than females. Intercourse for males almost always results in sexual climax; this is far less true for females. Moreover, the male is almost always physically stronger than the female, and she is vulnerable to his strength. Then, too, if both partners are fertile, there is the continual possibility that the female can become pregnant. The female is constantly reminded of her reproductive potentialities by the monthly menstrual flow, from puberty through menopause. This flow has negative connotations in almost all cultures. It is generally viewed as being unclean and, in some societies, dangerous or even a curse on women for their sexual sins of being temptresses to men. The loss of blood is often associated with being wounded.

Most adolescent girls and older women have ambivalent views toward menstruation. It is seen as positive evidence that one is a mature, normal female who can become pregnant but is not. It is also seen, at the minimum, as a nuisance that makes life more difficult for females than for males. Until recently the female could console herself about the adverse aspects of menstruation with the thought that this was a sign of fertility. Because she was socialized to believe that having children was a supreme accomplishment and the larger society put a high value on her reproductive abilities, she could feel proud of her own body and its potentialities. In one area, at least, she was clearly superior to men.

Although intercourse often gave little pleasure (and sometimes pain), although menstruation was unpleasant, and although pregnancy and childbirth had attendant burdens, her ability to create and give birth signified a unique and important accomplishment. Now that a variety of demographic and economic forces have combined to question the validity of reproduction as women's central life function, the female can no longer assume that her reproductive capacities are of important value to herself and others. Menstruation can no longer be viewed calmly as a small price to pay for the eventual joys of motherhood.

Menstruation presents further difficulties for women. The energy and mood fluctuations that tend to occur in response to endocrine changes during the menstrual cycle often have profound effects on the female's sexual feelings, her levels of passivity and aggression, and her feelings of depression and life satisfactions (Bardwick, 1971). A full discussion of this topic is beyond the scope of this chapter. Suffice it to say that menstruation is one of many factors that cause females to view their sexuality in more complex, ambivalent terms than males view their sexuality.

It also is important to recognize that females are less likely than males to readily experience sexual arousal in the everyday course of their lives or to be easily aware of arousal when it occurs. Because the penis has an exterior position, it is naturally stimulated by clothing, and because of its obvious erectile capacities, the male is clearly aware of his arousal. The more interior position of the clitoris and its lack of ready visibility creates less frequent sexual stimulation of females and less overt recognition of sexual excitement. The greater tendency toward dual sexuality in women is further exemplified by a fundamental difference between the clitoris and the penis. The sole function of the clitoris is its sensitivity to sexual stimulation, while the ovaries contain the ova which are transported through the oviducts (or fallopian tubes). The penis, however, is both sensitive to stimulation and serves as a conduit for semen and sperm.

All in all, there are many reasons that females are more likely to view sexuality in dualistic, ambivalent, self-protective, and emotionally dependent terms than males. Males, on the other hand, are more likely to view sexuality in a pleasure-oriented, assertive, achieving, unitary, and less personal fashion.

These are subjects to which we will return later as we consider the development and behaviors of adolescent males and females as sexual persons.

Biological Development during Adolescence: Sexual Maturation

Puberty is a process that takes place within an existing biological system. No new system is suddenly created at puberty. The development of reproductive capacity begins at conception. Puberty is a part of this long process (Peterson & Taylor, 1980).

The first sign of impending sexual maturity in boys (at about age 12) is an increase in the rate of growth of the testes and scrotum, which is usually accompanied by the beginning growth of pubic hair. About a year later, there is both an acceleration in growth of the penis and in body height. The first ejaculation generally occurs at about this time. A definite lowering of the voice occurs fairly late in puberty. It takes 2 more years for boys to become adapted to the related vocal cord changes, and they are frequently embarrassed by resultant problems in their speech, often a subject of unfeeling, comic comment by others. A slight enlargement of the breasts and increased nipple sensitivity for a short period may cause anxiety and fear that feminine characteristics are developing. These changes, as well as the adolescent growth spurt, are triggered by marked increases in hormones released by the endocrine glands. This growth spurt usually occurs at about age 13 and continues for 2–3 years, with a slower rate of growth for several more years. Along with the increased height and weight, there is a rapid gain in muscular strength. Changes in body contour, facial features, and body hair are too familiar to detail here. It is worth remarking, however, that growth is uneven, and boys often have trouble coordinating their movements smoothly, another frequent source of embarrassment (Conger, 1973).

Skin problems related to both physical and psychological factors are common for both males and females in adolescence and another frequent source of anxiety about the self. For girls, as for boys, endocrine shifts are responsible for the many physical changes that accompany puberty. On the average, however, girls start to mature about 2 years earlier than boys do. The beginning elevation of the breast and the gradual appearance of pubic hair are usually the first signs of sexual maturity in girls. Growth of the uterus and vaginal canal and enlargement of the labia and clitoris appear at about the same time. Onset of menstruation (menarche) occurs fairly late in this sequence and usually after the peak of the overall growth spurt, which generally starts around age 11 for girls (Conger, 1973).

Menarche marks a definitive and probably mature stage of uterine development, but it does not usually signify the attainment of full reproductive function. The early menstrual cycles, which in some girls are more irregular than later ones, often occur without an ovum being shed (Tanner, 1970). There is frequently a period following menarche, which may last for a year to a year and a half, in which a girl is not yet physiologically capable of conception. Similarly, boys are able to have intercourse long before the emergence of live spermatozoa (Conger, 1973).

There are striking differences for boys and girls in their emergence into sexual maturity. The great majority of adolescent males have nocturnal emissions, often accompanied by erotic fantasies. Aside from anxiety and guilt some may have about these emissions, the experience is generally a pleasurable one—short in duration and surely not accompanied by pain or any sort of handicap. For girls, menstruation is the main symptom of their sexuality.

Wide age ranges at which physical maturation may occur tend to arouse a good deal of anxiety among adolescents, especially if they are different from the average for their peer groups (Conger, 1973). These differences make it difficult to work with groups of young people between ages 11 and 14 or so, because individuals within the groups are at such different stages of development. Among other considerations, these different stages have implications for difficulties in group sex education at this age.

From the viewpoint of the child, early sex development may cause poor synchronization of his or her overall development, since physical changes may be ahead of the cognitive, moral, and personality aspects of development.

The fact that girls tend to mature earlier than boys frequently sharpens conflicts between the sexes and creates particular insecurities for those males whose socialization has led them to believe that they should be stronger, bigger, and "sexier" than girls. A number of studies (too numerous to detail here) suggest that early-maturing girls tend to suffer a social handicap at ages 11 or 12, but later these handicaps are reversed (Faust, 1960). Later data analyses indicate: (1) variations in effects associated with the socioeconomic status of the girl's family; (2) adverse effects of early maturation on the girl's opportunity for full psychological development during the latency years; or (3) a stormy adolescence followed by a higher level of ego development by age 30.

Early-maturing boys seem to have consistent social advantages at least through high school (Clausen, 1975). However, recent follow-up studies of a white, middle-class group suggest that early-maturing males, by age 38, are less creative and autonomous than their late-maturing counterparts (Livson & Peskin, 1980).

There is considerable argument as to whether a biologically determined sex drive exists. Gagnon and Simon (1973), for instance, hold that the desire for sexual gratification is largely learned and culturally determined. It seems likely that the motivation for masturbation, petting, intercourse, and other forms of sex expression (such as voyeurism and exhibitionism) have biological, social, and psychological bases, with endocrine factors as well as social learning playing important parts.

Kinsey's studies indicated that the male sex drive and orgasmic capacity rises rapidly with the onset of adolescence and reaches a peak at about age 16, with variations in related sex behaviors occurring in association with religiosity and educational and occupational levels of his subjects (Kinsey et al., 1948). The females studied by Kinsey reportedly experienced less specific sex needs, on the average, and perceived sex in more ambiguous and diffuse terms, with their orgasmic response being slower to develop and reaching its (average) peak at age 29 (Kinsey et al., 1953). It is quite possible that these differences between the sexes would be far less extreme today as a result of a sharp decline in the double standard and an increased recognition of the high potential of females for sexual response. In similar fashion, the development of the so-called sex drive in orgasmic response is also affected by the dynamic interaction of these kinds of variables.

As a life course, rather than stage, perspective is taken on human development, one becomes increasingly aware of the complexity and discontinuities, as well as the continuities, of developmental outcomes. There is growing recognition that predictions of these outcomes from one stage to another is hazardous. This is especially true in times of rapid social change, such as the immediate present and recent past (Elder, 1980).

These observations are linked to recent trends in psychosocial theories and research that stress the lifelong character of behavioral development, its multidimensionality, and its plasticity relative to environmental change (Baltes & Schaie, 1973). As we shall see in more detail later, these theories are well illustrated by impressive changes in sexual and sex role adolescent behavior during the late 1960s and into the 1970s.

PSYCHOSOCIAL ASPECTS OF THE DEVELOPMENT OF ADOLESCENT SEXUALITY

Introduction

The topic of the psychosocial aspects of adolescent development is far too large to present in detail here. Rather, some general theories will be sketched briefly, with particular attention paid to their applications to adolescent sexuality. These theories include the sociocultural, the developmental, the psychoanalytic, the historical, and the behavioral.

Although some scholars have seen adolescence as typically being a period of storm and stress, others have found that only a small proportion of adolescents find this a particularly difficult period (Offer & Offer, 1969, 1975). "Maturation in adolescence most often takes place in steady, silent, non-tumultuous ways. Adolescence may appear to be bland but our task is to accept and understand the gradualness of ego growth in respect to the cataclysmic ego changes that hardly make a sound" (Marcia, 1980, p. 190).

There is fairly general agreement that adolescents do not become radically different people during their teen years; how smoothly they make the childhood–youth transition depends to some extent on the processes of their earlier development and the total life situation in which they find themselves both in their childhood and their adolescent years. Until recently, most scholars agreed that youngsters who had serious behavioral, emotional, learning, and health problems in childhood tended to continue to have difficulties that were often exacerbated by the stresses of the teen years; those who had a more favorable development tended to go through this stage rather easily (Joint Commission on Mental Health of Children and Youth, 1972). However, as detailed in Chapter 3, adolescent development and behavior is also heavily affected by the period of time in which the person is living (Dragastin & Elder, 1975).

Then, too, a reexamination of past assumptions and research methods in developmental psychology leads to new perspectives on adolescence as a distinctive period in the person's total development. For instance, Livson and Peskin (1980) write that the adolescent years should not be regarded simply as a bridge between childhood and adulthood, with research questions centering on permanent traits that can be detected over the years. Rather, consideration should be given also to such "adolescent-centered dimensions as pubertal-induced behavioral change, identity formation, parent–offspring separation processes, group processes of youth culture, career choice and other phenomena recognized as peculiar to, or peaking in, adolescence" (p. 63).

Regardless of how stormy or smooth adolescence seems to be, it cannot be denied that it is a period of extremely rapid physical growth and change. Inevitably, these developments have a strong effect on young people; inevitably, these developments call for adjustments within the self and on the part of families and other social reference groups.

As sketched in Chapter 1, some theorists distinguish different characteristics of the early and late adolescent period. In reviewing the research, Gordon (1972) writes that during early adolescence the young person is caught between the pressure to achieve and the drive for acceptance by the peer group. Boys show an increasing deviation of energy to the instrumental area (achievement and independence) and girls to the expressive area of interpersonal skills. There is a drive for autonomy from parents and at least a surface conformity to peer group values. Douvan and Adelson (1966) found that early adolescent boys were concerned with working out problems of identity, eroticism, and autonomy (assertiveness and achievement), whereas girls were concerned with those issues in the interpersonal sphere (security, support, and acceptance).

Late adolescence is often viewed as a period when there is less conformity to the peer group and when dependencies on parents are more nearly resolved. Late adolescence is marked by a search for individual identity, a personal set of values, and a future mate with whom one can establish psychological, as well as physical, intimacy.

Sociocultural Influences on Adolescent Development

The individual's development is strongly affected by sociocultural factors. These include the social status of the person and his or her family, as well as the cultural patterns of the larger society and the smaller reference groups to which the person belongs. Each individual reacts to socialization experiences in his or her individual fashion. Thus, although group tendencies are found, many idiosyncratic variations occur within the various social groups.

Society's definition and view of adolescence play a large part in the way this period is experienced by the young people themselves. If adolescents are viewed as rebellious, irresponsible, delinquency prone, and problem laden, this may become a self-fulfilling prophecy. If they are seen as essentially stable, attractive, idealistic, growing in competence, and full of future promise, this too has pervasive effects. Whether society be largely hostile or benign to the teenager, the fact remains that this is a period in which the young person is called on to "shape up." How he or she is getting along in school, in work, at home, and in the community is regarded much more seriously than in earlier years. As the time for full adulthood approaches, pressures grow for evidence of adult-like competency. Then, too, adolescents can get into much more serious trouble than younger children, partly because of their increasing size and strength and partly because of their maturing reproductive potential.

Thus, social attitudes toward the sexuality of young people become particularly important during adolescence. Until recently, concepts of sex as sinful and as a dangerous primitive drive that had to be kept under strict control (especially for girls) created large problems of repression, denial, anxiety, and secrecy for both young people and the persons considered responsible for them (parents, human service professionals, and religious leaders). These concepts still exist but are countered by others that see sex as healthy, natural, and relatively safe (now that contraceptives and abortions are available).

The late 1960s and the 1970s witnessed radical upheavals in the culture of sexuality. Sex-specific attitudes and behaviors became highly permissive, and the push for equal sex roles at home and abroad became strong and widespread. In a sexually open and stimulating climate, young people as well as older ones were almost forced to take a fairly public stand regarding their sexual identity. This was especially difficult for teenagers because of their incomplete and vulnerable stage of psychosocial sexual development. In general, the absence of clear sexual guidelines provided both freedom and confused anxiety. The culture of sexuality differed somewhat in various regions of the country and for people of differing socioeconomic status.

The extent to which social status makes a difference to the person depends on the degree of social stratification in a society and its meaning to that society. Although American society is less stratified than most and earlier definitions of social class have wavered under the impact of recent socioeconomic upheavals in this country, social status still makes a difference in the person's total development and current life situation. The effects of social status are also mediated by race, ethnicity, religion, and regional origins. All these demographic characteristics tend to affect cultural values—values that influence the way people view themselvs and are viewed by others.

Culture evolves from the life history and experiences of a group and constitutes the group's attempt (over the years) to adapt to its environment. Culture plays an important part in the way the child is reared, from birth through adolescence and youth. The values, norms, beliefs, and expectancies of a group are intricately woven into all aspects of the developing person. They constitute many of the roots of personality, and it is both difficult and sometimes dangerous to try to change them.

Culture affects all aspects of sexuality: attitudes and behaviors concerning gender and sex identities, sexual expression, sex roles, mating, fertility control, and parenthood. Culture is most readily changed when the person's basic life situation is changed; when cultural leaders, with whom the individual can identify and wishes to identify, lead the way to new values and beliefs; and when the tools for change are made available.*

---

* There is considerable disagreement, at present, as to how much difference social status makes in contemporary American society. Class lines and values are not nearly so sharply defined as they were in earlier generations. The whole culture experienced such an upheaval in the 1960s that the country is witnessing pervasive "cultural confusion." The mass media (especially television) reach such an extensive audience that new ideas and beliefs are diffused much more rapidly than they formerly were.

However, the life situation for the various social class and racial groups in the United States has not changed as much as some suppose and as many desire. The distribution of national income for individuals and families has not changed for at least 25 years. About 15 percent or more of the population still lives in poverty. Although the median income of American families has risen, the cost of living has outpaced these increases for most people in recent years. A small number of minority-group people have experienced marked improvements in income, educational opportunities, and employment, but the majority still suffers disproportionately from poverty, unemployment, underemployment, and, in general, access to "the good life" (Chilman, 1973; Rubin, 1976). (See also Chapter 3.)

The social status of adolescents is largely determined by the educational, occupational, and income characteristics of their parents. Those who come from families near the top of the socioeconomic ladder are apt to view themselves and their world in relatively optimistic, positive terms. In times of social change, such families tend to be cultural innovators because they have a basic security that allows them the freedom to be nontraditional. This often applies to their sexual attitudes and behaviors as well as other aspects of their lives.

Persons near the middle of the socioeconomic structure (including white-collar workers and upwardly mobile skilled laborers) are often beset by anxieties about losing the security they have and about failing to achieve the upward mobility to which so many of them aspire. Less secure than those at higher levels and more hopeful than those at lower ones, they tend to be more conventional and conservative because they have so much that may be gained—and so much that may be lost (Kohn, 1969). In the area of sexuality, for example, this middle group tends to be more cautious and traditional with respect to sexual freedoms and contraceptive risk taking than those either at the top of the social heap or near or at the bottom.

Members of the less upwardly mobile blue-collar class and those in the lowest socioeconomic group are often alienated from society and its norms. Feeling little hope for the future and viewing society as essentially hostile and dangerous and themselves as powerless, they tend to react to the situation of the moment and take risks because they find life basically uncontrollable anyway (Chilman, 1966; Komarovsky, 1964; Rainwater, 1970; Rubin, 1976).

The culture largely determines how people are socialized for masculine and feminine sex roles. An enormous literature has developed on this topic in recent years. (See, for instance, Bernard, 1981.) Sociologists have emphasized particularly the part played by socialization for sex roles in dating, marriage, family formation, and the like. For instance, if females are socialized to believe that their major function is childbearing, child care, and homemaking, then, quite naturally, they tend to feel these are their major life functions and seek to fulfill them. On the other hand, socialization for work and community roles outside the home and for roles shared with men tends to promote the desire for no or few children (Bernard, 1975). In a similar vein, socialization of males that emphasizes their functions as father-providers or, in contrast, as role-sharing partners with employed women has a pronounced effect on the male's view of his life functions and goals (David & Brannon, 1980; Komarovsky, 1976).

Role socialization also affects attitudes toward sexual behaviors. Traditionally, more sexual freedom has been allowed to adolescent males because of the double standard of sex morality. This standard holds that males are "naturally sexy" and will "take what they can get." It is up to females to control the situation. There are two kinds of women: those who retain their virginity before marriage and are therefore pure, good, and lovable; and those who have premarital intercourse and are therefore to be sexually exploited, but neither loved nor married. Although these attitudes are changing, they are still prevalent, especially among blue-collar and lower-middle-class groups (Skolnick, 1980).

Role socialization varies by social class, religion, ethnicity, and race. In line with earlier comments, adolescents in the higher social classes are more likely to be socialized in nontraditional ways for fairly equal roles and freedoms between the sexes and for considerable sharing of interests and functions, both within and outside the home. Blue-collar youth, more traditional in their early socialization, are changing rapidly in their expressed attitudes toward more equalitarian sex roles. On the other hand, as Rubin (1976) perceptively points out, expressed attitudes are one thing, but the attempt to change enough to *live* these attitudes and to accept them emotionally is quite another.

The topic of sex role socialization will be discussed at greater length in later chapters and will include an examination of racial and other factors that affect the sex behavior and values of adolescent males and females.

There is growing recognition that life situations and cultural climates can vary enormously for adolescents at different periods of history. For instance, youngsters who entered puberty in the radicalized 1960s were part of a huge population cohort that crowded the schools, created an enormous youth market and a strident youth culture, and, to a large extent, provided further fuel for the liberals in their revolt against all forms of authority, including the military. This is but one example of "times making (or helping to make) the teens." Impressive work by social scientists who are studying periods of social history and the effects of these periods on life course development are providing a broadened perspective of human attitudes and behaviors in the context of the total environment at various periods of time (Elder, 1980; Modell et al., 1976). (For further discussion of the impact of society on adolescents and their families at different periods of time, see Chapter 3.)

Psychosocial Development

"Natural Development"

The development point of view of adolescent psychology is variously interpreted. A now somewhat outmoded concept is that children and adolescents go through more or less "natural" developmental stages, prompted in large part by the gradual flowering of physical and intellectual abilities and mediated to a lesser extent by the social environment. Various kinds of behavior are seen as something children grow into and out of depending on their stage of growth (Gessell et al., 1956). Of late, more emphasis has been placed on environmental influences, sometimes to the neglect of those having to do with "natural" maturation. For instance, as we have seen, the behavior of an adolescent is considerably affected by his or her particular stage of physical growth. Nevertheless, as children move from infancy into childhood and adolescence, they are affected more and more by their life experiences and less and less by physical growth factors.

The stages or phases of child and adolescent development are also viewed somewhat differently by different psychological theorists. These theorists tend to specialize in a particular aspect of development: social, cognitive, moral, or personality (including self-concept or ego). As a result, there is an unfortunate tendency for both research and programs to overlook the whole developing person.

Social Development

Studies of social development of adolescents show that young people experience a broadening of social contacts as they move into junior high and high school. Cliques—small groups of intimate friends—are important. These tend to be single-sex groups in early adolescence and become heterosexual in the later stages, although many teenagers belong to both kinds of groups. Girls, particularly, tend to form cliques around sharply defined social class, racial, and popularity lines. In late adolescence, groups become less important, as people begin to form more permanent couple relationships.

Intense, intimate same-sex friendships are typical among most adolescents, especially girls. In early adolescence, these are more apt to be based on shared activities. During the midteen years, they take on a more deeply interpersonal aspect, again especially for girls. Later these friendships tend to be replaced by close heterosexual attachments. The push of the boy for autonomy tends to make his friendships more diffuse and centered on activities, whereas the girl's sharing, dependent, and nurturant orientation tends to create deeper relationships with friends.

The emphasis on same-sex cliques and friends during early adolescence stems from the need to break free of the family and to form affectional ties with peers who are partners in the perilous quest for independence. Establishing a sense of gender identity, learning about one's sex roles, and developing competence in interpersonal relations are all facilitated by close associations with one's own sex prior to the more risky venture of forming close heterosexual ties (Conger, 1973). (See also Chapter 4.)

The adolescent crush on an older person is also common. This crush can be on a person of the same or opposite sex. It is often experienced as "falling in love" and may take on an intense meaning for the adolescent. The object of the adolescent's affections may serve partially as a substitute parent, partially as an ego ideal, and partially as a fantasied love–sex object. Such attachments usually become less salient in later adolescence as the young person achieves greater self-reliance.

Studies strongly suggest that at about age 15 adolescents are especially vulnerable to deficits that may occur in their relationships with friends. This seems to be especially true for girls, for whom sensitivity, empathy, and acceptance on the part of friends is particularly important. Tensions, jealousies, and conflicts with friends are common for girls at this age, whereas boys are more apt to focus on quarrels and disputes over activities, property, and girlfriends (Coleman, 1980).

Although these differences between the sexes may be due largely to differences in sex role socialization, the boys and girls whom we are currently seeking to understand may well have been subjected to these socialization differentials. These sex differences, found by researchers, on the average, are of special interest in the context of adolescent sexuality. The possibly greater dependence of the average 15-year-old girl on supportive interpersonal relationships may make her particularly vulnerable in early dating relationships. (See also Chapters 5 and 6.) Other vulnerabilities of adolescent girls in their heterosexual interactions are discussed by Hetherington (1972) and Wallerstein and Kelly (1980), who found in their research that daughters of divorced or separated parents had difficulty in being able to interact appropriately with males. Some spent a large proportion of their time seeking male company and engaging in sex-related behaviors. This seems particularly apt to occur among girls whose mothers are actively involved in dating relationships.

Numerous studies have also shown that boys who live for long periods of time in homes in which the father is not present because of divorce, separation, or nonmarriage have difficulties in sex role development and therefore adjustment to their peer groups (Coleman, 1980). However, as Coleman points out, much more research is needed to clarify further these matters as well as many aspects of the effects of family structure, size, and behaviors on the social development of adolescents.

Although it is common to emphasize the extreme importance of peer group pressure on adolescent behavior, it appears that the power of this pressure varies for different kinds of adolescents. Research indicates that the teenagers who need to conform to the peer group are more likely to be under age 15, have low group status, lack self-esteem, have poor communication and low involvement with parents, and be members of a strife-torn family (Coleman, 1980; Conger, 1973).

It has also been found that individuals vary in their tendency to conform to either peers or parents. Important contributing factors include personality traits, level of maturity, quality of family relationships, and other variables yet to be clearly identified through research. These issues of conformity and nonconformity are important to bear in mind when we consider factors that may make an important contribution to the various sexual, contraceptive, and childbearing behaviors of adolescents of both sexes.

Cognitive Development

Intelligence and cognition are related to adolescent sexuality in understanding and dealing with one's own sexual capacities and behaviors; in developing verbal, interpersonal communication skills; and in the capacity to perform effectively in school, work, and society. All these are essential to the eventual formation of stable, secure mate and parent–child relationships. Higher levels of intelligence and cognitive development bring greater ability to grasp and deal with abstract principles and concepts; to handle complex situations with flexibility, adaptability, and speed of response; and to see the relationships between ideas and events. Such abilities increase throughout childhood, but adolescence is generally the time at which the higher levels of cognitive development—formal operations— are reached, although there are marked variations between individuals in this regard (Piaget, 1972). The most basic aspect of formal operations is the ability to move one's thinking from the real to the possible, to hypothesize a number of possibilities, and, through logical thinking, to deduce what potential outcomes are likely.

Formal operations most fundamentally involve propositional thinking. Not all adolescents arrive at this state, either because of their limited abilities or because of the cultural norms of their reference groups. More gifted youngsters tend to arrive at this stage by ages 12–14; those with lower measured intelligence, by ages 14–16 (Conger, 1973).

Adelson (1975), in a study of the development of adolescent ideology, concludes that childish perceptions, which are concrete and narrow, are swept away as the child advances through adolescence. "He is ever more able to transcend the sheer particularity of an act, to place behavior within a web of circumstances . . . by expanding and commanding time, linking past to present and present to future; the act has a history and its effects extend forward in time (p. 67). . . . The young adolescent is locked into the present. His view of the future is constricted: he may grasp the effect of today on tomorrow, but not on the day after tomorrow" (p. 68). Hence, it seems that young (and intellectually limited) adolescents would be unlikely to grasp the full future significance of giving birth to a child during their teen years, either within or outside of marriage. Another relevant finding reported by Adelson is that younger adolescents rarely reason logically in cost–benefit terms regarding a course of action; they are more likely to make a choice arbitrarily, based largely on impulse. They also tend toward simplistic idealism and move toward greater pragmatism and realism as they become older.

Adolescent thought patterns tend to be egocentric (Cvetkovich & Grote, 1975). Adolescents often fail to differentiate self-concerns from the concerns of others. They also tend to see themselves as unique (Elkind, 1967). Cvetkovich and Grote suggest that effective overdifferentiation is often manifested in the form of personal fable. For instance, many adolescents evidently believe that they are immune to death. Elkind (1966) reports that adolescents often believe that they have a special relationship with God. In this relationship, they look to God for guidance and support as one would to a personal confidant. Keeping personal diaries, a widespread practice among adolescents, also reflects a personal fable. Such journals are often kept with the express belief that their contents will have universal significance to posterity.

Elkind (1967) has concluded that egocentrism diminishes by the time adolescents are 15–16 years old. As they begin to apply the operations of formal logic to themselves (that is, to think about themselves objectively), first the imaginary audience and then the personal fable begin to recede as important considerations. The imaginary audience is the adolescents' anticipation of how others will react to them. As they test against reality the hypothesis they have about others' reactions, they gradually learn to distinguish the difference between their own preoccupations and the concerns of others. The personal fable probably lasts longer than does the imaginary audience. Elkind, in fact, suggests that it may never entirely disappear. He states that the personal fable is reduced by the establishment of close relationships with others.

Flavell (1963) conceptualizes the reduction of egocentrism in similar terms:

> Social interaction is the principal liberating factor, particularly social interaction with peers. In the course of his contacts (and especially his conflicts and arguments) with other children, the child increasingly finds himself forced to reexamine his own precepts and concepts in the light of those of others and by so doing gradually rids himself of cognitive egocentrism. (p. 279)

Although the concept of egocentrism is tied to cognitive development by some theorists, it is seen in more psychodynamic terms by others. Clearly, self-centeredness and perceptions of special immunity are more than a matter of intellectual perception. They also have to do with personality development and the emotional narcissistic preoccupation of many teenagers, especially in the early stage of adolescent development.

Moral Development

Moral development is closely linked to cognitive development. This development also has large implications for sex-related values and behaviors. Moral development, like cognitive development, theoretically proceeds by sequential stages from simplistic, present-oriented concepts of concrete rights and wrongs to more abstract, complex principles. According to the research of Kohlberg (often criticized for its small samples consisting only of boys and for its subjective methods of measurement), the formal operation stages of moral development often start at about age 12 and include an orientation of interpersonal mutuality [I'll help you; you help me—or the sexual giving in order to get, which is proposed by Masters and Johnson (1969) as a path to sexual fulfillment] and maintenance of social order through fixed rules and authority. The eventual highest order is Stage 6—an orientation toward universal ethical principles chosen by the individual as having personal meaning rather than a mere adjustment to convention.

At more childish levels of moral development, Kohlberg (1964) proposed Stage 0: The good is what I want and like (quite similar to a recently proposed sex-related value, "If it feels good, do it"). Stage 1 is a punishment–obedience orientation: "You're wrong if you get caught" (or, perhaps, nonmarital coitus is all right so long as you do not get pregnant or a venereal disease). Stage 3 is instrumental hedonism and concrete reciprocity, also somewhat similar to the Masters-Johnson formulation or, on a more concrete level, "What can I gain from having sex with him/ her?" It is likely that relatively few adolescents (or even adults) proceed to Stage 6, which requires an individual search for moral and ethical principles to which the individual can subscribe and to which he or she can hold in spite of pressures for opportunistic or conventional behavior (Kohlberg, 1964).

In the current period of general upheaval in moral values, it seems likely that adolescents would have an especially difficult time in defining even conventional values, let alone arriving at universal principles to which they can personally subscribe. Kohlberg and Gilligan (1972) take a pessimistic view of current youth values. They report findings from their research and that of others concerning shifts that have been observed in moral development of adolescents between the early 1960s and 1970s. In the early 1960s, a small group of college students entered a stage of moral nihilism and relativism; this was seen by them as a shift from conventional to principled morality and as part of an identity crisis in freeing the self from childhood moral expectations and guilt. By the early 1970s, a large proportion of youths, perhaps the majority, had adopted this position. Starting as a "moral revolution" as part of the counterculture, it had now become a conventional position, with "a cultural industry" purveying it.

Kohlberg goes on to say that the adult culture has little to offset the counterculture. The conditions of society create little need for adolescents, and there is a "vested interest in keeping them out of the economy. As moral counterculture, the new culture differs from the conventional one in its extreme relativism and consequent fluidity, not in any positive forms of moral thought different from the conventional . . . what is new is the creation of a questioning culture providing half-answers to which adolescents are exposed prior to their own spontaneous questioning" (Kohlberg & Gilligan, 1972, p. 174). Reactions against this questioning culture have become especially strong since the mid-1970s, with fundamentalist religious groups (sometimes self-termed the Moral Majority) mounting campaigns for a return to traditional concepts of the family and rigidly defined rules concerning right and wrong. (See also Chapter 3.)

Hoffman (1980) raises questions as to whether there actually are such clearly defined stages of moral development as Kohlberg has proposed. Moreover, the kinds of values that adolescents adopt as they grow older are apt to be heavily dependent on the larger cultural climate in which they are living at the time of their adolescent years. Hoffman notes further that, although a number of theories have been proposed concerning moral development during adolescence, there is a serious paucity of research in this important area. (See also comments below concerning superego changes during adolescence.)

Personality Development

According to psychoanalytic and related theories, personality development includes a gradual growth from the complete dependency, narcissism, impulsivity, and feelings of omnipotence of the infant through the increasing independence, social awareness, abilities for self-control, and reality perceptions of the older child. Successful growth in these directions depends, in large part, on the experience of the child within the family and in other social relationships, including the school.

The psychosexual development of the person, in the classical psychoanalytic tradition, begins in the earliest month of life. The first 5 years of a child's experience determines his or her sexual "fate." The chief issue for both sexes is satisfactory progress through the oral and anal stages of development toward the "shining goal" of genital development.

It is held that satisfactory adjustment to the genital stage requires resolution of the Oedipal conflict for boys and the Electra conflict for girls. Boys and girls originally fall in love with their mothers and are sexually attracted to them. This creates a special problem for boys who must face the fantasied jealous wrath of their fathers. Imagined paternal resentment creates fear of castration in the rival son. Boys thus acquire castration fears and, if all goes well, solve this problem by allying themselves with their powerful fathers and giving up the goal of mother as a sex–love object. Being identified with their fathers, they then seek to someday attract women like their mothers. But this process does not free the male from conflicts. The incest taboo, along with fears of the father, may make it difficult in later life to have sex relations with the loved wife–mother.

Boys who do not manage resolution of the Oedipal conflict (especially difficult if father is out of the home, either physically or psychologically) and fail to achieve an identification with their fathers are apt either to identify with their mothers (hence, becoming effeminate) or to be perpetually attracted to their mothers sexually but feel guilty about this attraction because of incest prohibitions. Such males supposedly have an especially difficult time in later life forming close love–sex relationships with other women. They may tend to doubt their own virility and become Don Juans in a perpetual search for sexual conquests that confirm their masculinity but that are quickly terminated because of the guilt involved.

Psychosexual development is also far from easy for girls—some say it is easier than for boys; some say it is harder for girls. Theoretically, girls fall in love with their fathers at about age 3 and also desire them sexually. Then they must cope with the jealous resentments of their mothers as well

as the stringencies of the incest taboo. The impasse is resolved by identification with mother and giving up father as a sex–love object for the
later pleasures of marrying a man like father. As in the case of boys, this
solution may not work for the girl either, because in later life it may be
difficult for her to feel sexually free with the father–husband. The double-
standard concept may make women fear that they will not be lovable,
adequate wives if they are sexually free; in this case, they will become unworthy of love and marriage. These conflicts supposedly lead to "prostitution anxiety" and frigidity in many women.

Freud has won indignant reactions from today's liberated women
through his penis envy theory. According to Freud, females resent their
gender because they feel that their genital equipment is inferior to that of
the male. The little girl, upon seeing the male penis, feels cheated and
thereafter longs to have one, too. (This does seem to be a spectacular example of male chauvinism.) Freud and his followers further theorized
that, in order to make an adequate adjustment to life, the girl needs to
give up her envy of the male and his penis and resolve her jealous longings
by accepting her feminine fate: marrying a penis (male) and subsequently
giving birth to a penis (male). Further, she needs to give up her fixation
on her own small penis (clitoris) as a source of sexual pleasure and shift
to the vagina as an orgasmic source in coitus with a penis (male)
(Deutsch, 1945).

Upon reflection, it seems more likely that the little girl would envy her
mother's sexual equipment more than her father's. The adult female body,
with its breasts and voluptuous curves, is a long way from the small girl's
relatively simple body. Perhaps this is a source of the often noted, continuing anxieties of females about the attractiveness of their own bodies
and their jealousies of other females.

Freud further postulated that fears and wishes such as those sketched
above are repressed from consciousness by males and females because of
strong social prohibitions and the anxieties they arouse. Various psychological defense mechanisms are evolved by the individual to cope with
these repressed feelings. Thus, these feelings are expressed through a variety of indirect means, such as dreams, physical illnesses, rationalization,
substitution, projection, and sublimation. People with strong egos (high
levels of self-esteem) are able to recognize and deal with these unacceptable feelings more realistically and openly than people with weak egos.
They are in less need of strong defense mechanisms.

The personality is seen as comprising three layers: the id (primitive
selfish impulses, including sex and aggression); the ego (self-concept);
and the superego (conscience). A task of both the ego and superego is to
control the unacceptable primitive impulses of the id. The superego (con-

science), acquired through socialization primarily in the early years within the family, varies according to the values, beliefs, and methods of socialization by parents and other closely involved adults. A child might acquire a stern, repressive conscience indoctrinated through severe, authoritarian methods of child rearing, or, at the other extreme, he or she might acquire a highly permissive, weak conscience that provides few controls over primitive feelings. Ego development is affected by superego development and by ways in which children are treated: the extent to which they are seen as lovable, significant, and capable; the extent to which their primitive feelings are accepted as natural but requiring self-control; the extent to which parents help children identify, face, and deal competently with the realities of their lives. The task of the ego is to balance the person's needs for self-centered expression of primitive feelings with the prohibitions and demands of the superego *and* to synthesize these opposing imperatives in ways that are satisfactory both to the self and to the society (S. Freud, 1946).

Freud further theorized that the growing child went through a latency stage from about age 6 to age 12. It was to be hoped that Oedipal conflicts had been resolved and the child was ready to give up the intimate love–sex relationships with parents. The middle years of childhood were seen as relatively calm, allowing a period of integrative growth and gradual separation from close intimacy with parents.

Adolescence, according to Freud and his followers, is a dramatically different story. At this time, endocrine changes trigger rapid growth toward adult sexuality. The adolescent, awakened by these changes, undergoes severe conflicts that supposedly had been solved in the first 5 years of life. Oedipal wishes, castration fears, incest desires, and penis envy (for girls) are reawakened. Repressed earlier in the unconscious, these feelings press for recognition, thereby causing guilt and anxiety in the young person. The resurgence of these wishes plus the pressures of physical growth and the new temptations and demands of the larger society create personality disorganization. The ego needs to be tested and reworked in harmony with adolescent growth; the superego needs to be reexamined and reformulated in accordance with the standards and values of the adolescent and, eventually, adult society. Increased pressures from the id, brought about by sexual reawakening and triggered by endocrine changes, tend to both undermine ego strength and demand superego accommodations for greater tolerance of sexual feelings (S. Freud, 1953; Josselyn, 1968).

Sex relationships in early adolescence are seen as unwise in that the adolescent might be unable to handle their intensity because he or she is in a state of relative personality disorganization. Such relationships, moreover, might inhibit further psychological growth toward greater maturity (Blos, 1970; A. Freud, 1969).

Hypothetically, the conflicts of adolescence are resolved when the person has restructured the concept of himself or herself as a competent, valuable adult who can cope with the real world, accept his or her own sexuality within socially desirable limits, and control, though not deny, primitive sexual feelings.

The above theories have been severely criticized by many behavioral scientists. The concept of innate drives, operating as unchanging streams that need to be controlled, has been strongly questioned. Freudian theories have been seen as growing out of and being especially pertinent to middle-class Viennese society at the turn of the century.

Feminists have scorned Freud's concept that women are jealous of men because of penis envy. Quite logically, they argue that jealousy and anger have arisen because of the huge number of prerogatives that have been accorded males—social, political, economic, and psychological—and the relegation of women to dependent, inferior status.

The findings of Masters and Johnson (1966) that the clitoris, not the vagina, is the central erogenous zone for females has further fanned feminine criticism of Freud. Freud, indeed, was sexist in his assumption that because vaginal penetration was so deeply satisfying to the male it was naturally deeply satisfying to the female and that if it was not, this indicated that she was immature and nonaccepting of her femininity.

Freud's concept of the childhood latency stage also appears not to be sound. There is increasing evidence that children in the middle years have continuing sexual interests; they simply learn to conceal them better from adults (Broderick & Bernard, 1969). The family is not salient, as it was in Freud's time, in the shaping of the child's development: The larger society today plays a far more active role. There is also growing evidence that the incest taboo was not so universal as Freud had assumed.

Clearly, Freud was strongly influenced by the society in which he lived and the patients whom he saw. When he was evolving his concepts, he was also influenced by the philosophies of his time and the stage of development of psychology as a science. This does not mean that the theories of Freud and his followers should be discarded completely. Many of his concepts offer powerful insights that can be adapted to current life conditions. His theories of ego development—the conflicts between primitive selfish feelings and the demands of society, the strong influence of repressed and forgotten fears and wishes, the need to gradually win independence from ties to the family, the use of defense mechanisms to bolster self-esteem, the complexity of intimate sexual relationships, the continuing importance of early childhood experiences—all these ideas still seem to have important implications for understanding human behavior.

It is not necessary to accept Freudian doctrine in toto to appreciate the extreme importance of family relationships to the development of adolescent sexuality. Although there is growing recognition that today's adolescent has been shaped from early infancy partly by the family and partly by the many forces in the larger society, the quality of family relationships, the size and structure of the family, the family's life situation, and the quality and kind of child-rearing methods used all make a deep, lasting impression on the developing child as he or she grows toward maturity.

Children learn their most fundamental lessons about human relationships within their families. Family experiences profoundly affect the capacity for intimacy; for communicating wishes, fears, love, and anger; for sharing and withholding; for giving as well as taking; for accepting or rejecting one's own sexuality and that of others; and for participating in the most awesome of all human experiences—birth and death. Throughout life, all human interactions carry with them ancient (sometimes dimly perceived) memories of relationships with mothers, fathers, brothers, sisters, grandparents, aunts, uncles, and so on (Sheehy, 1976). As Erikson (1968) particularly emphasizes, and as detailed later, the task during adolescence and youth is to differentiate the self from these relationships and find what is personally valid in maturity as distinct from childhood.

Other views of the importance of family life emphasize the strong effects that families (especially parents) have on the physical, cognitive, moral, and attitudinal development of children and adolescents. They also point out the effects of family structure and size on family formation attitudes and expectancies. All this is true: Relationship effects are stressed here because they are so often overlooked by the majority of researchers.

Family Development and Systems Perspectives

Theory and research concerning individual (including adolescent) development has been extensively broadened since the early 1970s. We have already seen that the field has become more and more aware of the impact on human development of the larger social and economic environments at different points in time and of the shifts in personal attitudes and functioning that can occur at different stages of the life span. There is also growing awareness among developmental psychologists of theory and research that has been contributed by their sibling professions: family development scholars (most of whom have been sociologists) and family therapists (most of whom have been psychiatrists).

Knowledge and theories from both the fields of family development and family therapy are important. A few of the major concepts from each of these fields are briefly sketched here and will be referred to in more detail in later chapters. These concepts enrich and, to an extent, provide a firmer research basis for concepts from psychoanalytic and related theory outlined above.

FAMILY DEVELOPMENT. The family development perspective heightens awareness of the impact of the midstage of family life and the lives of both the parents and the adolescents in the family. As shown earlier, major tasks for adolescents are winning relative autonomy from parents and developing an independent sense of identity, including a more mature gender and sex identity. The developmental agenda for parents includes coming to terms with their own approaching middle age; with the granting of greater freedoms to their growing children, who simultaneously continue to need considerable support and protection; and with renegotiation of many aspects of their marital relationship—all too often including either separation or divorce (Sheehy, 1976).

Parenthood brings with it a built-in conflict between self-needs and the needs of one's children. This conflict is apt to be especially acute for mothers, for whom parenthood is usually a particularly intense, demanding experience. According to Fox (1978), the mother of a maturing daughter must serve as both a protector for the daughter as child and a guide for the daughter as woman. Learning to manage the conflict between the two aspects of the mother role is one of the major developmental tasks of this period. "Learning when to let go and when not to yield, when to share information and when not to, when to allow one's child to find her own way and bear the consequences . . . is hard work and takes untold amounts of psychic energy" (Fox, 1978, p. 38). This is energy that many mothers may lack, especially if there are a number of children in the family, if there are strained marital relationships or the mother is a single parent, if there are economic and employment pressures, if the family suffers from the oppression of racism, or if other family problems exist, such as poor health, subtstance abuse, poor housing, or lack of adequate human services.

Fox (1978) writes poignantly of a second developmental task for mothers at midstage in the family life cycle. According to Fox, this so-called midlife crisis is a crisis of being—the need to find meaning beyond one's role as a mother or, alternatively, to find ways to extend the role of mother. A closely allied crisis, that of aging, "pervades this phase of female adulthood; for many women the perceived loss of culturally valued youth with its easy beauty at the same time that their daughters are exercising their youthful attractiveness is a bitter experience, one which some feel can foster an unintentional hostility and competition between mother and daughter" (p. 39).

In very similar fashion, fathers at midstage experience anxiety over entry into middle age, gradually diminishing physical (including sexual) resources, employment pressures, marital strains, and father–son dilemmas of protecting versus freeing, sharing versus withdrawing, and supporting versus competing.

FAMILY THERAPY.   Family therapists particularly emphasize the significance of the family as a dynamic interaction system, a system that is affected by many external and internal factors, including the developmental stage. According to this theory, which was primarily developed through clinical observations in the treatment of schizophrenic patients, anything that happens to one member of the family affects all members in a multitude of ways. As a system, the family strives to maintain balance and unity. Disturbances within and between family members are felt throughout the system. The family, as a group, tends to elect a scapegoat to act out the problems that may actually reside in other family members. In effect, the acting-out scapegoat tends to preserve the system's unity. If this scapegoat should leave the family or "reform," the family's wholeness can be threatened and another scapegoat may be chosen (Napier & Whittaker, 1978).

In short, family therapists find that, when one person in the family is disturbed (e.g., a daughter who is behaving in a sexually promiscuous way), all members of the family are apt to be experiencing stress, often within family subsystems, such as the marital dyad, as well as within individual members. According to family systems theory, as propounded by many family therapists, family members in such a case are not primarily upset because the daughter is misbehaving; rather, she is misbehaving because of stresses in the family subsystems and the total family system. Lack of open and clear communication within the family is a characteristic of such troubled families. Note the observation by Fox (1978) regarding problems of mother–daughter communication on sexual and other topics at family midstage.

At a simpler, less pathology-oriented level of theory, Furstenberg and Crawford's 1978 work in clinical observations and reanalysis of longitudinal data pertaining to several small studies of adolescent parents points to the frequent incorporation of these young parents and their children in the system of their families of origin. For example, the arrival of the young married adolescent daughter's baby often seemed to provide a new and welcome function for the grandparents, especially the maternal grandmother. Also, the unity of the total family system at midstage, threatened by the departure of grown children and by marital stresses, was sometimes restored by the dependency needs of single teenage daughters with their babies. And, in turn, these hitherto angry and rebellious daughters seemed, in some instances, to be virtually transformed with gratitude when their parents provided forgiveness and supporting care to them and their children. On a less cheery note, Furstenberg and Crawford (1978) also observed the jealous reaction of some of the siblings of adolescent mothers. Were these siblings getting the message, as some seemed to, that they should become teenage mothers too?

Recent work by both Fox and Furstenberg particularly points to the critical importance of considering family development as well as family systems factors in both research and practice in the area of adolescent sexuality. Obviously, a similar observation may be made in respect to all aspects of adolescence (or any other life stage for that matter). Important as familial factors may be, their significance varies for different individuals. In attempting to understand and provide services for adolescents, it is essential to view them both within the family context and as separate (or separating) persons.

Ego Development

Turning, then, to the concepts of ego development, we find that, building on Freud's work, numerous theories and definitions about the ego have been proposed. Contemporary ego psychologists continue to see ego strength, as well as the use of defense mechanisms to protect ego vulnerabilities, as being important. However, they part company with Freudian doctrine in many other respects.

Loevinger (1966, 1976), in writing of the processes of ego development, postulates that the person moves from infancy to maturity along the major lines from total dependence and impulsivity, to dependence on external controls, to internalization of rules, to autonomy, and finally to integration.

Following other theorists, this writer has proposed elsewhere (Chilman, 1977) that there is a constant struggle throughout life to achieve a balance between individualistic self-expression and socialized concern for the expressive needs of others. Human beings value their own independence but also need to depend on others. They gradually learn to control their impulsive urges because, without such controls, they are rejected by others. These central issues are reworked over and over in the context of those interpersonal relationships that become salient at different stages of the life cycle. If all goes well and the person is able to grow from one stage of ego development to the next, he or she moves to higher levels of self-socialization. Although there is a sense of coming full circle with basic self–other issues over and over again, continuing personal growth (for those fortunate enough to achieve it) makes it possible to meet these issues at higher levels of personal development.

Adolescents are at a level where they face critical issues in relationships with parents, social reference groups, friends of the same sex, other significant adults, dating partners, and temporary or permanent mates. These critical issues are threatening to self-autonomy. They also revive relationship conflicts experienced in early childhood that need to be reworked again. How well these self–other issues were resolved in childhood affects how well they will be resolved in adolescence. The degree to which adolescents are able to handle the critical relationships of the teen years also affects relationships in later life.

Values of the "narcissistic 1970s" that favored impulsive self-fulfillment and responsibility only for the self probably threatened the person's ongoing ego development at all stages of the life cycle, including the adolescent stage. Although it is unrealistic to attempt to be responsible for what another person does, it seems essential to be responsible toward another person if human relationships are to have the kind of trust and intimacy proposed by Erikson (1968), as outlined later in this chapter.

To return to Loevinger's concept of ego development, many adolescents would be in the self-protective or conformist developmental stage and not yet ready to form stable mate relationships because they have not yet identified their own individuality. Therefore, they would be unable to recognize and value the individuality of another.

Viewed in terms of ego strength, adolescents who are insecure about their own self-worth would tend to be unable to face realities about themselves and others and unable to cope effectively with the many aspects of a mate relationship, including the realistic use of contraceptives. Also, we shall see later that adolescents who are low in ego strength, or self-esteem, appear to have a greater tendency to engage in early nonmarital sex relationships and, eventually, to become unmarried parents.

The development of ego strength during adolescence also requires that young people deal with their superegos, which include the conscience or moral attitudes, beliefs, and goals. An overuse of the superego (a rigid reliance on right and wrong rather than reasoning) can seriously undermine ego strength, and a weak superego (lack of moral guidelines) can fail to provide the controls that the ego needs as a defense against unrestrained impulses. Thus, adolescents welcome experiences that bolster their self-esteem (ego supportive successes) and help with clarification of their own values and those of society. Especially younger adolescents are as upset by too much freedom as they are by too much control.

Before adolescence, youngsters tend to accept the moral teachings of their parents and other adults who are significant in their lives. However, increasing maturity and the necessity to cope more or less independently with the outer world requires that young people develop their own set of beliefs and life goals. To put the matter all too briefly, adolescents who have been brought up in authoritarian homes may react during their teens either by rejecting the severe superego mandates that have been imposed upon them and behaving in an impulse-ridden manner or, conversely, by submitting to an overly demanding, externalized superego and behaving in a constrictive, anxious, self-denying, guilt-ridden fashion. They might also, confusingly and confusedly, alternate between the two courses of behavior.

Of course, not all adolescents are raised in authoritarian homes. Some are raised with overpermissiveness, with little or no guidance or discipline and, therefore, with few limits or goals to guide them. One would expect that such youngsters would be mainly impulsive in their behavior, including their sexual behavior.

Baumrind (1975), among other researchers in child development, advocates that parents adopt an authoritative (not authoritarian) approach to child rearing. That is, parents should see themselves as being able to know what is good and right for their children, to use firm but mild and reasonable methods of discipline, set appropriate standards of achievement, and establish clearly defined behavioral limits. These approaches are to be combined with affectionate family relationships, open communication, and a fundamentally democratic environment. Such an ideal, hard-to-achieve familial style would tend to help children develop a superego (a personal value system) that provides them with the supports they need but that is flexible enough to allow for gradual growth toward self-determination.

The Search for Identity: Personal, Gender, and Sex

According to Erikson (1968), the formation of an individual sense of identity is a central task for the adolescent. Adolescents act upon the universal needs of people to see themselves as individuals, separate from others, although sharing many of their values and interests. This need is closely related to the desire for self-consistency—a feeling of wholeness and integrity, a unity of the self over time. Erikson states, "The young person, in order to experience wholeness, must feel a progressive continuity between that which he has come to be during the long years of childhood and that which he promises to become in the anticipated future; between that which he conceives himself to be and that which he perceives others to see in him" (p. 212).

Erikson proposes his own theory of developmental life stages. He postulates that failure at any stage might be expected to adversely affect later stages. His first six stages are listed below:

Developmental Stages	Basic Components
1. Infancy	Trust vs. mistrust
2. Early childhood	Autonomy vs. shame, doubt
3. Preschool	Initiative vs. guilt
4. School age	Industry vs. inferiority
5. Adolescence	Identity vs. identity confusion
6. Young adulthood	Intimacy vs. isolation

All these stages also have possible applications to adolescent sexuality, as we shall see in later chapters.

In general, it is dubious whether the majority of adolescents actually go through an intensive identity-seeking process. It takes a rather large cushion of affluence, cultural values that support individual development, (probably) a high order of intelligence, a wide range of environmental opportunities, and freedom from such responsibilities as marriage and parenthood to do so. For example, Douvan and Adelson (1966) found that an early foreclosure of personal identity development was the more frequent pattern. Although Erikson and others have regarded this as a serious problem in terms of wasted individual potentialities and denial of parts of the self, this may not be an accurate perception with respect to most young people. For instance, Offer and Offer (1969) found that their sample of middle-class, urban, white boys, for the most part, revealed considerable life satisfaction and little rebellion or identity crisis up-heavals during their high school years. A smaller group of their subjects showed considerable, but not extreme, disturbance, and a few appeared to be deeply troubled. Those who had the most severe difficulties tended to come from troubled homes.

According to the findings of Douvan and Adelson (1966) in a 1958 national study, girls find it more difficult than boys to obtain a separate identity. They tend to seek it first through their families, then through their boyfriends, and eventually through their husbands. Perhaps in to-day's society, with the push for equal sex roles and less socialization of girls for passivity and dependence, females will be more able to work in-dependently toward their own sense of individual identity. Now that mar-riage and motherhood is no longer *the* prescribed pattern in their lives, perhaps girls can establish a more autonomous identity. However, it may be an error to adopt the traditionally masculine model that equates auton-omy and individuality with effective maturity.

There has been increased, and welcome, attention paid to the concept of interpersonal identity (as contrasted to self-focused identity) in recent years (Marcia, 1980; Spence & Helmreich, 1978). According to this con-cept, people define themselves partly in terms of their acquisition of the skills and qualities inherent in emotional sensitivity toward others.

The concept of interpersonal identity formation, as one aspect of in-dividual personality development, broadens the theory of personal iden-tity in important and necessary ways. It provides a more socialized and altruistic dimension to the ideal of the mature adult personality. Among other things, it suggests a revision of attitudes concerning what the "suc-cessfully" developing girl or boy is to become: a separate, self-actualizing person, bent on achieving an individualized identity or a self who is concerned about the feelings and wishes of others as well as his or her own. The focus of self-identity, particularly strong during the 1970s, was rationalized by the statement, "How can I relate to others before I find out who I am?" One can answer this query with "How can you relate to others before you find out who they are, as well?"

In much of the past, it was assumed that girls and women would play supporting, nurturant, other-oriented roles in human relationships. The female half of the population was expected to submerge self-goals to promote the individual goals of the male half. Under these conditions, Erikson and other males were freed to seek their individual identities and write books about the search, thereby producing theories that usually applied better to males than females. Now that females are seeking "complete" equality with males, perhaps both sexes will need to seek personal identity in both autonomous and interpersonal terms. As women seek to take on many of the functions and roles of men, they leave a "nurturance gap" in human relationships: a gap that men, as well as women, will need to fill if we are to have a socialized, humane society.

As Marcia (1980) wisely points out, there is an unfortunate tendency to expect too much psychological growth to occur during adolescence. Further exploration of self-identity and further opportunities for self-integration can take place during the adult years. This is especially true in postindustrialized societies, in which life conditions permit a series of educational, occupational, and familial careers over the now prolonged life span.

The Development of Gender Identity

Although gender is determined by biological factors, as shown earlier, gender identity (self-concept as a male or female) appears to be the result of socialization. According to studies of Money and associates, socialization plays by far the most dominant role in the development of gender identity. As far as can be determined, this sense of identity is largely formed by age 15 months to 5 years or so. Working with children whose physical gender was anomalous at birth, Money's research group has found that it is extremely difficult and hazardous to attempt to change an older child's gender self-concept. It is far easier, in most instances, to change the child's physical structure and functioning through surgery and/or endocrine therapy than to attempt to change his or her psychosocial sense of gender.

Much has been learned through working with transsexuals (Money & Tucker, 1975; Stoller, 1968). According to findings thus far, transsexuals are physically normal males or females who have acquired, through early socialization, a sense of gender identity of the opposite sex. When, through

TABLE 2.1. Outline of a Sexual Career

Stages and ages	Agents	Assemblies
1. Infancy; ages 0–2½–3	Mother to family	Formation of base for conventional gender identity package.
2. Childhood; ages 3–11	Family to peers, increasing media	Consolidation of conventional gender identity package; modesty–shame learning; nonsexually motivated "sex" play; learning of sex words without content; learning of sex activities without naming; learning of general moral categories; mass media through commercials and programming content reinforcing conventional gender, sex, and family roles; media also preparing for participation in youth culture.
3. Early adolescence; ages 11–15	Family, same-sex peers, media	First societal identification as a conventional sexual performer; first overt physical sexual activity with self or others; development of fantasy materials; beginnings of male–female divergence in overt sexual activity; application of gender package to sexual acts; application of moral values to emergent sexual behavior; privitization of sexual activities; same-sex peers reinforce homosocial values; family begins to lose moral control; media reinforces conventional adult content of gender roles; media attaches consumer practices to gender success; basic attachment to youth culture formed.
4. Later adolescence; ages 15–18	Same-sex peers, increasing, cross-sex peers, media, decreasing family	Increased practice of integrating sexual acts with nonsexual social relations; movement to heterosocial values; increased frequency of sexual activity; declining family controls; continuing media reinforcement of sexual–gender roles, and consumer and youth culture values; sexual experience with wider range of peers; common completion of sexual fantasy content; consolidation of gender differences in sexual roles and activity; good girl–bad girl and maternal–erotic distinctions completed.

Gender identity →

Sexual identity →

Stages and ages	Agents	Assemblies
5. Early adulthood; ages 18–23	Same-sex and cross-sex peers, media, minimum family of origin	Mate selection, narrowing of mate choice; increased amount of sexual practice; commitment to love by male, sex by female; linkage of passion to love; dyadic regression; insulation from family judgment and peer judgment; increasing pressure to marry; relief from same-sex competition by stabilization of cross-sex contacts; legitimization of sexual activity by peers and romantic code; media reinforces youth culture values of romance and virtues of marriage; experience with falling in and out of love; termination of protected school-student statuses.
6. Final mate selection— early marriage; ages 20–27	Fiancé(e), spouse, same-sex peers, family of origin increases	Regularizes and legitimizes sexual activity; stable rates of sex activity; variation in kinds of sexual behavior; children born in most cases; increasing sexual anxiety about children; family values reinforced by children and family of origin; declining eroticism, increased maternalism; culmination of purchasing–consumer values in wedding gifts or buying new products; routinization of sexual behavior; decreased contact with cross-sex peers unless they are married; interaction in multiple dyads; sexual activities restricted by pregnancy, children, work.
7. Middle marriage; ages 28–45	Spouse, same-sex peers, family of origin, married peers	Declining sexual activity in marriage; some extramarital sexual experimentation; maturing children; conflict of erotic with maternal; emergence of sexual dissatisfactions; increase in occupational commitments; declines in physical energy and physical beauty; fantasy competition by youth culture; continual multiple dyadic interactions and insulation from cross-sex peers; marriage moving to nonsexual basis for stability and continuity.
8. Post-young children; ages 45+	Spouse, same-sex peers, married peers	Further decline in sexual activity; some extramarital sexual experimentation; substitution of nonsexual commitments other than children as basis of marriage; further decline in physical strength and beauty; further desexualization of gender identity; movement out of public sexual arena.

Source: Gagnon and Simon (1973).

treatment, their physical gender is changed to match their psychosocial gender, the person generally reacts with enormous pleasure and relief, even though a period of adjustment to the new physical self is required.

In these days of confusion over sex roles and appropriate sexual behavior for males and females, it must be exceptionally difficult to establish a clear sense of gender identity. Some would claim that this is no longer very important. They favor 'androgyny'—the ability to behave in both presumably masculine and feminine ways. Androgynous people are thought to be happier and more flexible and competent than those who adhere to more traditional masculine or feminine fashions.

It has been proposed by some writers that there is a sex, as well as a gender, identity. Sex identity refers to the sense of self as a sexually active (or inactive) person. Gagnon and Simon (1973) develop an interesting and imaginative model of gender and sexual development, based on their own theories and research and the studies of others. They show the effects of various influences at different life stages and some of the differences between males and females. (See Table 2.1.)

Gagnon and Simon also propose that young people, responding to dress styles and the like, appear far more erotic and sexual than they actually are and that adult fantasies and anxieties about their probable sex behavior are overblown. This probably has always been true. Adults tend to view adolescents from their own mature level of sexual activity and response and find it hard to realize that adolescents are merely beginners at the art and expectancies of sexual intimacy.

Laws (1970), in writing about female sexual identity, says that it grows out of early development of gender identity, feelings about the self as a feminine person, self-attitudes toward one's own body image and feelings of sexual attractiveness, the experience of the self as a sexual being, and the anticipation and experience of the self as a mother. She correctly emphasizes the importance of feelings of sexual adequacy as a male or female throughout life, with a particular heightening of self-concern about this during adolescence. Clearly, most, if not all, adolescents are busily occupied with improving their body image (and worrying about it), moving toward participation in full sex experiences, and thinking about—or actually acting out—their concerns about their potential reproductive capacities.* Because messages from the mass media today often emphasize that an active sexual life is virtually synonymous with physical and mental health, it is little wonder that so many more of our adolescents are engaging in nonmarital coitus. (See Chapters 3 and 5.)

---

* For an excellent detailed discussion of sex and gender identity among adolescents, see Matteson, 1975.

Learning Theory

Learning theory, as postulated by B. F. Skinner (1938), holds that people behave as they do because they have learned certain behaviors. Those behaviors that have been reinforced by positive experiences or rewards tend to persist. Those that receive little response tend to disappear. Those behaviors that are punished, or negatively reinforced, are avoided. Thus, a person responding to sexual stimuli and previous learning seeks coitus. If he or she finds that it is gratifying and is rewarded by the partner, this behavior will continue. Lack of response tends to extinguish this behavior, at least with that partner. An adverse experience, such as failure to perform adequately, rejection by the partner, or punishment by others, would tend to make the person avoid intercourse. Learning tends to generalize from one experience to another similar situation. For instance, if a mother punishes her son for his sexual interests, he may come to see all older women as sexually dangerous or repressive. These concepts are appealing in their simplicity; they seem to have a certain, but limited, amount of explanatory power. However, they appear to overlook such factors as feelings, values, motivations, capacities, self-concepts, and other particular attributes of the individual.

In general, theories of learning, which are basic to an understanding of any kind of human behavior, including adolescent sexual behavior, are too numerous and complex to discuss adequately here. Aside from Skinner's theories of operant conditioning, leading concepts are those of Bandura and Walters (1963) and Wolpe and Lazarus (1966).

Bandura and Walters have found considerable research support for their concept that much social learning derives from imitation of the behavior of others. People who have significant meaning to the individual serve as behavior models. Thus, for example, adolescents tend to learn gender and sexual behavior from those people with whom they identify—parents, peers, TV stars, and the like.

Wolpe and Lazarus propose that learning is deeply affected by the feelings that a person has at the time an experience occurs. These feelings (or effects) tend to persist beyond the particular experience and are thereafter associated with similar ones. For example, if first intercourse for a young woman is painful and fails to result in an orgasm, she may well become fearful and anxious about intercourse in general. She may then avoid sexual contacts or approach them with tension and anticipation of a negative experience. Through desensitization processes, as a result either of a relationship with a loving, more skilled, and considerate mate or through treatment, she may be able to acquire more positive and relaxed feelings about intercourse.

CHAPTER 3

Adolescent Sexuality in Contemporary American Society*

We saw in Chapter 2 that many factors shape the development and expression of adolescent sexuality. However, the impact of the larger society and its social institutions was mentioned all too briefly. This chapter provides a more adequate treatment of the subject, especially as it examines the enormous social (and, to a lesser extent, economic and political) changes of this period. These changes had profound effects on all social institutions: schools, businesses and industries, governments, religious organizations, human service agencies, and families. Probably every person in the United States felt the effects of these changes to one degree or another.

Children and adolescents felt the impact of shifts occurring within their own families and within such social institutions as schools, religious organizations, and youth serving agencies. Many of the changes reverberated throughout society and its subsystems and heavily affected sexual and familial beliefs, values, attitudes, and behaviors.

The 1960s were years of particularly profound eruption, and 1966–1968 seems to have been a pivotal turnaround time of that decade. The 1960s opened with many young people and adult liberals engaged in an idealistic drive for a renewed society dedicated to peace, social justice, freedom, and equality. This drive took a number of forms: the nonviolent civil rights movement of Martin Luther King's dream, the educational reform and free speech movements at colleges and universities, the federal government's war against poverty, and peace movements that swelled and spread across the land.

By the end of 1963, John F. Kennedy had been assassinated and his assassin murdered. The brief years of Camelot were ended. The counterculture was expanding, and the concept of "God is dead" (so take responsibility for yourself; don't wait for God) emerged. Within the next few

*Much of the material in this chapter is derived from Chilman, 1978; Glick, 1975; O'Neil, 1971; Yankelovich, 1974, 1981.

years, the hippie flower children and drug culture movements had turned toward violence, the Black Power drive strengthened and excluded whites from the push for civil rights, and race riots broke out in inner-city ghettos.

Some of the major events of 1966–1968 are listed:

The Black Panthers emerged as a revolutionary group that excluded white liberals. Race riots broke out in segregated poverty sections of major cities following the 1968 assassination of Martin Luther King.

Other separatist movements of ethnic minority groups grew with a message that the United States had not been a successful melting pot, after all.

The counterculture youth movement, chanting "Don't trust anyone over 30," became more and more violent and less idealistic, with growing emphasis on revolution, autonomy, and sexual freedom. Student strikes at universities demanded curriculum reform, student participation in university governments, and the end of all restrictions on student social life and all university involvement in war-related activity.

The antiwar movement escalated in response to the country's ever deeper involvement in Vietnam. The push for peace increasingly involved people of all ages and backgrounds and culminated in the huge 1968 protest march on the Pentagon.

The war on poverty also became more violent in many locales as its community action program mounted heavier pressure for equal opportunities and full participation of the poor in the administration and staffing of human service programs. The antipoverty war faltered for lack of adequate funding as the war moved, instead, to Vietnam. This resulted in welfare rights protests in a number of cities and the drive to bring the poor people's march to Washington, where its "Resurrection City" gained little popular support.

Despite numerous progressive programs to reduce delinquency, the rates of youth crime continued to increase.

The economy was adversely affected by enlarged war expenditures plus the failure of the Johnson administration to levy higher taxes to offset the inflationary effect of vastly increased military spending. The long inflationary spiral, which began at that time, has continued into the 1980s.

Other increases in federally funded programs included newly passed Medicare and Medicaid legislation as well as other Great Society programs, such as enlarged amounts of aid to public schools that served low-income children.

Many precepts of the hippie counterculture youth movement were adopted more widely by older adults. These precepts included experimental communes, rejection of science and rationalism, use of drugs, and mysticism.

Numerous kinds of therapy arose and continued their popularity, at least till the late 1970s. These methods emphasized quick intimacy, sensuality, free self-expression, an end of the Protestant Ethic, spontaneity, and rejection of repression and sexual hang-ups.

The above developments activated a whole cluster of interrelated changes in respect to values and attitudes associated with human sexuality and family relationships. These changes were part of a much larger societal quest for cultural patterns different from those of a largely agrarian, provincial society that had prevailed in the United States before the two world wars. The society had been dominated by the male white, Anglo-Saxon, Protestant establishment. Reaction against the outdated norms of this society characterized the movement of the 1960s, which called into question all established institutions: familial, governmental, educational, religious, and occupational. An extensive search was launched for norms and values that were better suited to the conditions of a highly technological, urban, consumer society—a society that was perilously poised between the threats of total destruction via a nuclear war and the luxurious promises of an ever more prosperous consumer's paradise.

As sketched above, the idealistic reform movements of the early 1960s failed to fulfill the hopes of a new society dedicated to peace and effective control of the threat of nuclear war. It also failed to spread prosperity to all people, and the quest for a society of equality and social justice had clearly faltered. Depressed by these developments, many young people as well as their elders abandoned their quest for social change and instead sought a psychological utopia primarily within the self. Personal sexual freedom and equality was an important part of this push for individual liberation: for a society of individuals freed from the repressive moral and familial traditions of a now distant past.

Manifestations of the freedom and equality movements of the late 1960s and the 1970s, as they pertain to human sexuality, include the following:

Publication of *The Human Sexual Response* (Masters & Johnson, 1966) and of *Human Sexual Inadequacy* (Masters & Johnson, 1969). Both of these books, continuing in the Kinsey tradition of scientific research about sex, startled the reading public with such information as the finding that women were at least as readily orgasmic as men, given the right understanding and stimulation.

The reemergence of the women's rights movement, which had been in abeyance for some 30 years or more. To a greater extent than in earlier periods, the movement of the 1960s and beyond emphasized equality of women with men in all aspects of life: political, occupational, economic, familial, and sexual. Civil rights legislation passed by the federal government supported better employment for women as well as for racial and ethnic minorities. Women pushed hard for equality within the family, on the job, in schools, in athletics, and in bed. They made impressive gains in all spheres of life, although in the early 1980s they were still in an economically disadvantaged position and the Equal Rights Amendment failed to receive ratification. Women still tend to do the larger share of housework; however, far more husbands are involved in domestic activities, including those of child care, than in the past.

Relationships between adolescent boys and girls became more and more equalitarian. Formal dates seemed to be passé, and girls appeared to assume as much initiative as boys in social activities. The double standard of sex behavior seemed to have largely disappeared, and involvement of teenagers, both boys and girls, in nonmarital intercourse increased markedly, as discussed in Chapter 5.

In recognition of the seriousness of mounting population problems, owing in part to the 1948–1958 baby boom, the U.S. Department of Health, Education and Welfare made federal funds available for nationwide family planning programs in 1966, and funding commitments for these programs were increased during the next 10 years. By the late 1960s, the ZPG (zero population growth) movement became widespread, with its message that the birthrate must be dramatically reduced to save the environment. In actuality, the birthrate had begun to drop in 1958 and continued to do so through 1978, when it rose very slightly and, perhaps, briefly.

Federal funding for family planning services for single teenagers became available in the earlier 1970s, and abortions were legalized for all age groups by action of the U.S. Supreme Court in 1973. (See especially Chapters 7 and 14.)

The divorce rate grew rapidly during the late 1960s until about 1975, when it leveled off somewhat. It rose particularly for black families, especially from 1966–1978 (the last date for which figures are available at this writing). By 1979, almost 40 percent of black families were headed by women, compared to about 12 percent of white families.

Attitudes toward marriage became far less positive during these years. At the end of the 1950s, over 80 percent of the adult population thought that women who did not marry were neurotic, sick, or immoral. By 1976 about the same proportion took a neutral attitude toward marriage for women, seeing it as a purely personal choice. Attitudes toward unmarried parenthood also became far more liberal during these years, with over two-thirds of the population expressing acceptance of this life-style by the mid-1970s. (See Chapter 9.)

Partly because of severe economic needs resulting from marital disruption, partly because of the higher aspiration of women for full equality, and partly because of the rising cost of living, more and more women entered the labor force during this period. By 1967, about 33 percent of the mothers of preschool children were employed outside the home, compared to about 20 percent a few years earlier. By 1978, this was true of almost 50 percent of the mothers of young children and over 66 percent of mothers of teenagers.

Attitudes toward the employment of women outside the home showed a turnaround during this period. National public opinion polls in the mid-1960s showed that the majority of respondents felt that mothers should stay home and care for their children, but by 1978, the majority said that mothers enhanced their womanly status by employment outside the home and priorities for men moved into the realm of warm, human relationships rather than sole financial support of the family.

The gay liberation movement, promoting equal rights for homosexuals and lesbians, appeared toward the end of the 1960s and gained more and more acceptance during the next decade.

In 1960, the Supreme Court took a fairly liberal stand on the public distribution of pornographic materials. Since then, there has been an increase in the public availability of sexually explicit material in books, magazines, the theater, movies, and television programs. Some of this material was rated "restricted to adults" so that parents would be warned to keep their children and teenagers away from "adult materials." This precaution was probably ineffective, for the most part, since these materials were so readily available throughout communities.

Domestic violence and spouse abuse, including incest and rape, appeared to be on the rise by the early 1970s, and these trends seemed to continue throughout the decade. (Such trends are difficult to assess, because they necessarily rely, to a large extent, on familial or self-reports of strongly prohibited behavior.) Violence outside the family was rampant by the close of the 1960s and on into the early 1980s. The nation reeled with the shocking assassinations of such public leaders as Robert Kennedy and Martin Luther King in 1968 and the attempted murders of Ronald Reagan and Pope John Paul II in 1981. Violence was also celebrated and made bloodily explicit in popular books, films, and television shows.

Reading this list of developments from the mid-1960s to the early 1980s can easily give the impression that the period was specially marked by disintegration of traditional familial and sexual morals. It is important to recognize that this apparent disintegration was not peculiar to the familial arena. We also witnessed the breakdown in traditional morality at the highest levels of government, with the corruption in the Nixon White House having been revealed in the Watergate scandals of the early 1970s. Further revelations during the 1970s showed that the FBI had regularly intruded illegally and secretly into private citizen affairs, that the CIA had abused its intelligence gathering and reporting powers abroad and at home, and that members of Congress had accepted bribes from oil-rich countries. Nationally known business executives were accused of misappropriation of funds, various human service professionals were found guilty of abusing medical insurance programs, and some schools were riddled with thievery, beatings, truancy, and vandalism on the part of teenagers who were imitating their "betters."

The liberated society had been liberated from traditional controls, but this liberation had exacted at least as many costs as benefits. Analyses of a series of national opinion polls and attitude surveys during this period revealed that about 80 percent of the American people subscribed to a personal freedom, self-actualization philosophy, with about 15 percent of the population being extremist in their "search for their true selves." (See, e.g., Yankelovich, 1981.) This small group of ardent duty-to-the-self pioneers tended to be under age 35, well educated, children of college-educated parents, employed in the professions, and to a large extent unmarried and childless.

Themes of the narcissistic society became familiar throughout the land: "You owe it to yourself to grow, enjoy, and fulfill your human potential." "Be good to yourself." "You are Number 1; you can't do enough for yourself." "Take control of your own life; take responsibility for only yourself." "You have a *right* to freedom, opportunity, a full sex life, and splendid orgasms." "Join your own support group; spill your guts with those who understand." "Put yourself first and let other persons in your life— spouse, children, parents, friends, and employers—adjust to your need to be yourself as an authentic, growing person. Away with the martyred masochism of an earlier day in which human lives were devastated by duty to others—to family, job, God, and country. Communicate freely; confront openly; learn conflict resolution techniques. Remember that no sin is really a sin so long as you tell everybody about it."

Such prescriptions for "human renewal" were, and are, attractive. To many of their adherents, they posed a serious challenge and opportunity to live a more honest, productive, humane life, freed of oppressive guilt and crippling anxiety. To others, they seemed to be an invitation for unrestrained self-indulgence. In conjunction with these attitudes, a vast congeries of commercial entrepreneurs arose to lead their customers on a happy tour of jet vacations, lavish meals, hot-tub holidays, and exotic shopping trips. The do-it-yourself, self-administered therapies of the 1970s were a poignant symbol of the strivings of people to live better lives by one means or another. Since so many had discarded their former religious beliefs and had entered on a new unchartered course, a large number were eagerly looking for a way to chart the strange territory.

A sobering of attitudes became increasingly apparent by the mid 1970s and later. This sobering was reflected in a number of ways:

A growing interest in the past: in family roots, in history (including family history), in nostalgia for lost and imagined days of innocence.

A strengthening of new religious groups with a focus on mysticism and the occult and frequently the magnetism of a powerful authoritarian leader. A resurgence, too, of nationally disseminated evangelical fundamentalist religions, such as those of the so-called Moral Majority. Active recruitment of adolescents and youths to these religions through appeals to their needs for personal significance, security, belonging, and assured guidance.

By 1980, many traditional religious groups had become politically active nationwide and played an influential part in the election of Ronald Reagan to the presidency on a conservative "profamily" platform. To the conservatives, profamily meant a return to the traditional sex roles and opposition to legalized abortion, gay rights, sex education in the schools, lack of parental censorship of educational materials for children and youths, and availability of contraceptives for teenagers independent of parental knowledge and consent. (See also Chapters 6–14.)

In 1981, the Reagan administration called for a vast reduction in the public funding of social programs that provide basic supports for poor families: income assistance for low-income families, food stamps and school lunches, physical and mental health services (including abortion and family planning), subsidized housing, job training and employment programs, social security, and many other social services.

Conservative attitudes held that families ought to support themselves and if they were not able to do this their needs should be met by volunteers and private funding despite the fact that unemployment, in general, was about 9 percent and rates for inner-city youths were 40 percent or higher. It was clearly impossible for individual families or private agencies to meet the growing economic needs of many people suffering the corrosive effects of both unemployment and runaway inflation. The swing toward more conservative attitudes and programs promised to have severe effects for many teenagers and their families. These effects would be felt most acutely by poor people and members of racial and ethnic minority groups. (See especially Chapter 9.)

Liberals as well as conservatives were reassessing their personal and familial values and attitudes by the end of the 1970s. A number had found that recreational (as contrasted to procreational) sex in uncommitted relationships tended to result in loneliness and feelings of depression. Many people found out through personal experience that divorce was painful and single parenthood was costly and strenuous. People also learned that an exclusive focus on one's rights and self-actualization often resulted in the loss of friends and loved ones. The concept of keeping one's options open began to give way to concern about commitment, altruism, and love. Perhaps these are some of the reasons, along with increasing economic constraints, that sexual and familial attitudes become somewhat more conservative, that marriage and birthrates rose somewhat, while divorce rates leveled off slightly. (Then, too, the purveyors of the youthful counterculture of the late 1960s were well over the distrusted age of 30 by 1981.)

By the mid-1970s, the family was found to be relevant, after all, in contrast to earlier challenges to the contrary. Even though families had changed in many respects between 1958 and 1980 (e.g., becoming smaller and more equalitarian), they were still highly favored by the vast majority of people. A national survey showed in 1976 that almost 90 percent of the respondents yearned for the intimate, stable family of another day but were still unwilling to surrender their new-found sex roles and sexual freedoms in service to this memory (Yankelovich, 1981). Various studies in the mid-1970s also showed that over 66 percent of adults rated their marriages as very happy and that the vast majority of people saw their families as being of first importance to them (Campbell, Converse & Rodgers, 1976; Chilman, 1978; Yankelovich, Skelly & White, 1977). Although by 1980 there had been sharp increases in cohabitation, divorce, single parenthood, never-married parenthood, and remarriage, the majority of children (about 66 percent) still lived with both of their biological parents in intact first marriages.

Schools were also becoming more conservative after 1975. "Back to basics" movements followed the discovery that many high school graduates and college students read, wrote, and reasoned at an eighth-grade level or less. Disillusionment with the limited immediate effectiveness of racial integration in the schools led to a vastly diminished public commitment to such integration by 1981. In general, there was reduced public enthusiasm for public education. This was motivated by both its apparent limited effectiveness and by a growing tax-payers' revolt. The reduced citizen support for the public schools resulted in a movement toward private, often parochial, schools. This shift added to the funding problems of the schools, which were already threatened by their much lower student population, a population that had dropped alarmingly because of the rapid decline in the birthrate. Although the adolescents of the 1960s and early 1970s went to greatly overcrowded high schools (crowded because of the high birthrates of 1948–1958), the teenagers of the late 1970s were attending schools that often had too few students.

Although there were many cross-currents in social and sexual attitudes and behaviors in the late 1970s, the major streams of opinion seemed to be in a conservative direction. Along with concerns about such problems as family breakdown, crime and delinquency, illegitimate births to adolescents and older women, poor school performance, family violence, corruption in government as well as business and industry, went other even more fundamental anxieties. These included worries about ever-rising inflation and unemployment; a drop in the real income of families for the first time since the late 1940s; the apparent inability of many American industries to compete with those of Germany and Japan; severe shortages and rising costs of energy, plus dangerous dependence on the oil-rich nations of the Middle East; threats to the nation's natural resources through air, food, and water pollution; an apparent rise in the military strength of the Soviet Union; and international tensions in many parts of the world. All these developments presented critical survival issues to the nation's citizens—a point surely not missed by the nation's youths. The liberal approach to solutions of the country's social, economic, and international problems apparently had not worked to any impressive extent during the 1960s, nor had the liberating approach to the nation's psychological malaise brought clear gains during the 1970s.

All in all, or so it seemed to many, by the presidential elections of 1980, it was time to turn back the clock to the seemingly safe and sane 1950s or even earlier. But how many woes and injustices of those years had been forgotten? Then, too, seeming solutions to personal and societal problems of an earlier period could not be expected to work effectively in the vastly changed local and national conditions of the late twentieth century. However, an adequate examination of this point is far beyond the limits of this book.

CHAPTER 4

Sexual Behaviors Preceding Heterosexual Relationships among Adolescents— A Brief Overview

DEVELOPMENT OF SEXUALITY IN CHILDHOOD

As discussed in Chapter 2, the development of sexuality is a basic part of the totality of human development, starting even before birth. From virtually any theoretical perspective, most children gradually move from self-centered dependency toward a more socialized independence; from understanding and knowing almost nothing toward the ability to comprehend and deal more or less realistically with the outer world; from a deep attachment to parents (or parent substitutes) to attachment to others outside the family; from uninhibited expression of sexual interests to at least some control over these interests; from no sense of gender and sex identity to an increasingly clear sense of both.

A Longitudinal Study

There is no large-scale longitudinal research that adequately examines the development of human sexuality from infancy through adolescence and on into the adult years. One study (Kagan & Moss, 1962), however, followed a small group of largely middle-class boys and girls from birth through age 14; the same group was interviewed and tested when the members were adults. This careful, intensive study included an attempt to assess differences between the sexes with respect to such personality characteristics as dependency, passivity, anxiety, withdrawal, achievement drive, and sexual interests. Because the subjects were studied as children primarily during the 1930s and 1940s, many of the findings may not apply today. Moreover, there is a danger in making generalizations from such a small group in a particular time and place (an Ohio college town) to the larger population. Then, too, the researchers did not ask about specific sexual behaviors but used incidence of dating, for those 14 or younger,

53

as a criterion of sexual activity for the first phase of the study and reported heterosexual behaviors for the adult phase.

Despite these limitations, Kagan and Moss report a host of interesting findings. For instance, many behaviors, interests, and personality traits during the preschool years appeared to persist in overt or covert form into early adolescence and adulthood. A sense of gender was developed by age 3, along with recognition by young children of many male–female physical and sex role differences. Both boys and girls showed a strong desire to conform to ideal masculine or feminine typologies.

A number of early personality tendencies of males tended to persist from one developmental stage to the next. Passivity, fear of harm, and low muscular activity in early childhood were found to be predictive of low sexual activity, social and sexual anxiety, dependence on love objects, conformity, avoidance of competition, and nonmasculine interests in later childhood, adolescence, and the adult years.

Early passivity among females had less pervasive effects, although it did predict adult tendencies toward dependency on love objects and families and withdrawal from difficult situations. According to the authors, it was impossible to predict adult heterosexual behavior of females from data obtained about them in childhood and early adolescence. This may be because males generally take (or took) the sexual initiative and because the culture requires (or required) repression of female sexuality.

Beyond this obvious interpretation, Kagan and Moss hypothesize that passivity in males may be partly related to physical–constitutional factors, such as energy level and body build. It should be recalled, as shown in Chapter 2, that male sex characteristics are particularly susceptible in their development to prenatal factors.

Early aggression among males was associated with later high levels of heterosexual activity and choice of a typically masculine occupation. Early aggression among girls was found to have less clear-cut outcomes, aside from the fact that such girls tended to channel their drives into high levels of academic achievement and to reject traditional feminine roles.

In general, measured personality tendencies (except for dependence and withdrawal) persisted over the years far more for males than females. These tendencies were anger arousal, achievement drives, overt heterosexuality, and spontaneity.

These findings regarding continuity of behavioral and personality tendencies from infancy on into the adult years should be viewed with caution. As Elder (1980) points out, researchers have been so occupied in looking for trait continuity that they fail to find the discontinuity and emergence of new traits that may appear during adolescence and later.

Sexual Behaviors of Children:
Voyeurism, Exhibitionism, and Sexual Curiosity

Although there seems to be no other systematic longitudinal research on the development of sexuality from infancy through the adolescent years, it is commonly observed that infants (particularly boys) discover their genitalia early and derive pleasure from self-stimulation. The way in which parents or parent substitutes react to these early manifestations of infant sexuality are thought to have considerable effect on the child's developing self-concept as a sexual being. It is further observed that little children, through social learning, generally acquire the idea that all matters pertaining to sex have a special aura of forbidden pleasures. Seeing others nude and exposing the self (especially when the opposite sex is involved) take on exciting, erotic meanings. Most children probably engage in these activities throughout childhood—ah! the joy of playing doctor.

Sexual matters become confused with the elimination process in early childhood, because many of the same or nearby parts of the body are involved. (See also Chapter 2 concerning Freudian theory of oral and anal sexuality.) Depending on attitudes of families and other socializers, children acquire accepting or rejecting and differentiating or nondifferentiating attitudes about sexual and eliminative functions. The concept that sex is dirty can be indoctrinated by overly anxious toilet training procedures.

Young children also enjoy talking about sex, including elimination functions. Most parents find this kind of talk difficult to accept and tend to forbid it, as do other socializers of young children. As a result, most children learn early that sex is something one cannot talk about in an open, realistic way. It is likely that later difficulties males and females have in verbal communication about their sexual feelings stem from these early childhood experiences.

In general, it is difficult for parents to find appropriate ways to deal with the sexuality of young children. According to psychoanalytic thinking, this is largely because of the Oedipal situation. (See Chapter 2.) Whether or not this theory is accepted, the fact remains that parents need to help children learn to control their primitive interests in matters pertaining to both sex and elimination, just as parents need to help children learn to control other impulsive reactions, such as aggression. Ideally, children learn that these responses are natural but need to be expressed in limited, socially acceptable ways. However, many children learn to feel guilty about sex and therefore repress and deny their sex interests because of punitive and overcontrolling socialization experiences as they grow up. This often leads to later difficulty in coming to terms with their sexuality. Other children learn few or no controls of their sex impulses from their parents and tend to behave in overly impulsive ways in their adolescent and adult years.

As adolescence approaches and more specialized sexual interests are aroused, sexual activities generally increase. Sexual expression takes a variety of forms depending on the characteristics of individuals and their social groups. Sophistication at dissemblance from others, and often the self, generally increases. Those adolescents who continue to express sexual interests on a direct, childish level of overt and compulsive voyeuristic or exhibitionistic behaviors are thought, by many students of the subject, to be displaying psychological problems. Knowledge about sex is sought from parents, peers, books, movies, magazines, and the like. Children and adolescents usually gain a mass of confused information and misinformation through this process. They also acquire "healthy" or "unhealthy" attitudes and feelings about male and female sexuality. Males are less likely than females to receive sex information from their parents and teachers because girls are thought to be more in need of knowledge that can protect them. This creates particular problems for boys, because they are socialized to think they should be more expert on the topic of sex than girls. In addition, they may have greater difficulty acquiring a sense of sexual adequacy than girls do.

Learning about sex is also a difficult process for children and adolescents because of limitations in their cognitive development. As discussed in Chapter 2, it is not until the middle or later stages of adolescence that the young person is able to think in conceptual, nonegocentric, future-oriented terms. The concepts that a sexual relationship involves another person who may have different ideas about it, that pregnancy might very well occur, and that planning for contraceptive use is important are difficult for the younger teenager to grasp. (See also Chapter 6.)

This difficulty is not simply a cognitive one. As discussed earlier, young adolescents usually have not arrived at a stage of personality integration and ego and moral development that allows them to behave in realistic, responsible ways with respect to their sexuality in a partner relationship. Then, too, even more so than in childhood, few adolescents have the opportunity to discuss sexuality in a male–female situation, relatively free of anxiety and confusion. Thus, they have further difficulty in acquiring communication skills that would make it possible to talk with dating partners or future mates about their sexual values, needs, and feelings. Sex tends to become something you do but cannot discuss with the person most closely concerned. Under these conditions, sexual activity may become a substitute for interpersonal intimacy.

In brief, the many ways parents handle their own mate relationships and interact with their children in the broad area of love and sexual expressions of all kinds (including reproduction and family planning) have a deep effect on the developing sexuality of the child and later the adolescent. These learnings, combined with other, possibly inherent characteristics, are carried by the young person into the neighborhood, school, and community, where the learnings are further affected by the knowledge and attitudes of peers and influential adults. (See Chapter 2 for a discussion of the impact of family structure and size and of developmental stage and processes on the development of children and adolescents, including the development of their sexuality.)

MASTURBATION

It appears there are no satisfactory studies of masturbation that meet the criteria of adequate sampling, data collection techniques, and statistical analysis. Moreover, none of the few available studies is based on a coherent theory. Although these comments also apply to much of the other research about sexual attitudes and behaviors, they apply more cogently to this topic than to such subjects as nonmarital petting and intercourse.

Contemporary writing on the subject generally emphasizes the normality of masturbation among children and adolescents and sharply calls into question traditional beliefs that such behavior is sinful and dangerous. There still may be some validity to the concepts, especially pronounced by Freud and his followers, that compulsive masturbation and masturbation coupled with withdrawn behavior are symptoms of emotional disturbance. Compulsive withdrawn behavior of any sort can be a symptom of disturbance, especially in a culture that values flexibility and sociability. When this behavior is sexual, the problem is magnified because of social prohibitions against overt sexuality.

Though various investigators find different rates of masturbation, it appears that about 50 percent of today's teenage boys and about 33 percent of the girls masturbate by age 15. This figure probably rises to about 85 percent for males and 60 percent for females by age 20 (Abramson, 1973; Arafat & Cotton, 1974; Hunt, 1974; *Playboy,* 1976; Sorensen, 1973). There appears to be a reduction in fear and guilt about masturbation among contemporary adolescents, though considerable embarrassment about the practice remains (Hunt, 1974; Sorensen, 1973).

Although the data are conflicting, the principle seems to emerge that both males and females, on the average, start masturbating at younger ages than formerly and that a larger proportion of adolescent females are engaging in this behavior. Whether overall male rates are rising or declining is open to question. On the other hand, the weight of evidence is that the rates for females by age 20 or so are probably twice as high as they were a generation ago. This is in line with other findings, to be reported later, regarding higher rates of nonmarital petting and coitus for females and a changing culture that seems to support equal sexual freedoms for men and women.

Further interesting findings were obtained by Sorensen (1973). Like Kinsey, Hunt, and Arafat and Cotton, he found that girls masturbated less often than boys and less frequently reached orgasm. Girls were less likely to report enjoyment of masturbation; similar findings were obtained in a small study by Arafat and Cotton (1974).

Moreover, nonvirgins were more likely to masturbate than virgins; young people who engaged in necking and petting were more likely to masturbate than the totally inexperienced. Girls, but not boys, who were currently engaged in coital experience were more apt to masturbate than any other group. Among other things, these findings suggest that the development of an orgasmic response may be more difficult for girls than boys. Sorensen finds that many girls who have intercourse do not reach full orgasm. Perhaps they turn to masturbation for release of accumulated tension.

Masters and Johnson (1966) amplify Kinsey's (Kinsey et al., 1953) earlier findings that masturbation by females promotes their sexual responsiveness and orgasmic capability. Masters and Johnson have found that virtually all females they observed are orgasmic if they use appropriate masturbatory techniques and learn to accept their own sexuality. Sorensen's findings also suggest either that masturbation promotes heterosexual sex behaviors (especially coitus) or that these behaviors stimulate the need and desire to masturbate. Probably both factors are operating.

Both Kinsey (Kinsey et al., 1953) and Hunt (1974) assessed the relation of masturbatory attitudes and behaviors to socioeconomic status. It was found in both studies that blue collar males and females were less approving of masturbation than were white collars and less likely to practice it. Also, these studies showed that females, but not males, who were high in religiosity were less likely to masturbate (analogous to findings for nonmarital petting and intercourse).

These scattered research findings tell us very little about the role of masturbation in the development of human sexuality. It is rather astonishing that so much is written on the topic in the clinical and popular literature but that so little research has been done from the developmental viewpoint.*

HOMOSEXUALITY

As in the case of masturbation, only a cursory review has been made of the research related to the topic of adolescent homosexuality.† This review strongly suggests that little is known about the subject, although a great deal has been written about it, especially in recent years. Advocacy of a more liberal attitude has been the major theme of much recent writing, similar to general cultural trends toward greater permissiveness about all forms of sexual expression. For example, a 1969 report of a National Institute of Mental Health Task Force on homosexuality urges more research, training, education, and preventive and treatment strategies, as well as a more liberal social policy toward homosexuals (Sex Information and Education Council of the United States, 1970).

Before the "Freudian enlightenment," prevalent attitudes held homosexuality to be sinful and dangerous. Remnants of these beliefs are still found within the culture and the law. Freud and many of his followers attempted to take the sin out of homosexuality and substituted a sickness model, hoping to replace sympathy and treatment for condemnation and punishment. Beliefs that homosexuality is a symptom of emotional disturbance or mental illness still prevail in the minds of many.

More recently, from about the mid-1960s onward, beliefs and attitudes about homosexuality have moderated further, again in keeping with larger cultural trends that favor sexual freedom, individuality, and personal "authenticity." Numerous gay civil rights and activist groups throughout the country have promoted the concept that homosexuality is simply another form of love–sex behavior and a matter of personal choice. According to their views, the only problems associated with this orientation are those imposed by society itself in erecting barriers to employment, housing, social gathering places for homosexuals, and the right to marry and adopt children. The arguments of these groups have been

* Although a number of observational studies of many kinds of sex behavior have been carried out in anthropological research in a number of (mostly primitive) societies and another group of investigators has studied animal behaviors, we still know little about the part that masturbation plays in the development of human sexuality over the life span in a technological, complex society such as that in the United States.

† Homosexuality is to be distinguished from homosociality. The first implies specific physical–sexual contact with the same sex; the latter implies close same-sex friendships—a topic discussed in Chapter 2.

effective in removing or reducing some of these restraints in many communities.

The few studies of adolescent and youth attitudes toward homosexuality show an increasing proportion of people who are accepting of it for others, if not themselves. About one-half of blue-collar youths and three-fourths of college students in 1971 found "nothing morally wrong about homosexual behavior between consenting partners" (Yankelovich, 1974, p. 48). About one-half of adolescents in the Sorensen (1973) study had heard of homosexuality and had some understanding of it. Most of this group expressed tolerant attitudes toward the individuals involved but had difficulty accepting the specific behaviors.

Incidence

Only a few studies using large samples have attempted to assess the incidence of homosexual behavior (Hunt, 1974; Kinsey et al., 1948, 1953; *Playboy,* 1976; Sorensen, 1973). It appears that homosexual contacts are most common before age 15 and that the incidence is higher for boys than girls. Sex play, consisting of exhibitionism, voyeurism, and mutual masturbation occurs fairly frequently in groups of boys between the ages of 8 and 13. About 10 percent of boys and 5 percent of girls may engage in sex relations with the same sex at least once during early adolescence. Among college students in 1976, 12 percent of males and 4 percent of females in a national sample said they had had at least one homosexual experience (*Playboy,* 1976). Only about 3 percent of males and half that many females are thought to engage in long-term, serious homosexual relationships. Although the Kinsey data suggest considerably higher rates of homosexuality than those cited above, a recent reanalysis of his data shows them to be in line with these figures. Despite the higher visibility of homosexuals in today's society, the prevalence of this behavior appears not to have increased. If anything, it may have decreased (Freedman, 1971; Hunt, 1974; Karlen, 1971; Komarovsky, 1976).

In actuality, we have very incomplete knowledge about the homosexual feelings, interests, and behaviors of children and adolescents and the meaning this may have in relation to their overall development. Like masturbation, this topic has been so loaded with prohibitions and repressions from early childhood onward that ordinary survey and interview techniques are unlikely to obtain an in-depth understanding of this topic.

Causes

Only a few studies of the causes of homosexuality appear to be available that even approach the requirements of careful scientific methods. Some insights are offered from studies with animals, but these contain the well-known problems of generalizing from animal to human behavior.

Bieber and his coauthors (1962) report on a well-known study of 106 male psychiatric patients who were self-acknowledged homosexuals compared with a matched group of psychiatric patients who claimed no homosexual experiences. In-depth psychiatric interviews revealed significant differences between the groups with respect to parent–child relationships. The mothers of the homosexuals were more likely to be described by their sons as domineering, overprotective, seductive, puritanical, frigid, preferring the son to the father, encouraging "feminine" interests in their sons and discouraging "masculine" ones, interfering with the son's social contacts with girls, and maintaining a close confidential relationship with the son. Sons tended to respond to these maternal behaviors dependently rather than rebelliously. Homosexual men were also more likely to have poor relationships with their fathers, with the sons failing to rebel against paternal rejection and control.

Another study of male cardiovascular, rather than psychiatric, patients yielded fairly similar findings (R. Evans, 1971). Evans also found that homosexuals more often described themselves as children as frail or clumsy, nonathletic, avoiding fights, playing with girls, and loners.

It should be borne in mind that the above findings do not apply to all male homosexuals studied. Moreover, some of the nonhomosexuals had similar family background characteristics.

A study of homosexuals drawn from the community compared with a matched group found that homosexuals were more apt to identify with their mothers though they were not different on measures of self-esteem and the ego ideal to which they aspired.

From the viewpoint of classical analytic theory, boys with close relationships with mothers of the kind described and distant relationships with rejecting fathers would have an exceptionally difficult time resolving the Oedipal conflict and would feel guilty about having sex relationships with women, whom they would see as their mothers. They might, therefore, turn to men for sexual fulfillment but would have difficulty establishing close relationships because of a primary attachment to their mothers and resentful feelings toward their fathers and other men.

A less involved explanation could be offered from findings of these kinds: Boys and men from such families would tend to be identified with females rather than males and would have failed to learn appropriate male family roles. (See also Chapter 2.)

Female homosexuals have been studied less extensively than males. Largely theoretical formulations hold that these females had particularly close attachments to their fathers or, conversely, strongly identified with their mothers in opposition to fathers who were brutal or alcoholic or in other ways failed to perform positive husband–father functions. In such cases, some girls adopted distrustful, antagonistic attitudes toward males and related closely only to females.

Experiments with such animals as guinea pigs, rats, and rhesus monkeys show that injection of male hormones prenatally promotes male play, courting, and copulating behavior among all animals born in the litter. Conversely, female sex behavior is exhibited when cyproterone acetate (androgen inhibiting) is injected prenatally.

Money and his associates have carried out extensive studies of humans born with gender anomalies. They, too, find the importance of hormonal functioning in human development and gender behavior. However, in most cases, they find that social and psychological variables, including gender assignment to the young child, are usually far more important than biological ones in determining attitudinal and behavioral outcomes (Money, 1968).

Some theorists in the field hold that homosexuality is simply a learned behavior that has been positively reinforced by a series of gratifying homosexual experiences and few negative ones. This behavior may have had more rewards than heterosexual behavior, which may have met with few positive experiences and many negative ones. Early-maturing boys, in line with this behavioral theory, may be more likely to become homosexual than late-maturing ones because they are physically ready for heterosexual experiences at an earlier date than is generally accepted by society and thus move to homosexual relationships.

Although it is commonly recognized in the literature that adolescents (especially boys) are often inducted into homosexual behavior through the advances of homosexual adults, this fact appears to be inadequately considered in the research.

Insufficient attention also is given in most of the research to the effects of a single-sex living situation on the sexual interests and behaviors of children and adolescents. For example, as a past consultant to a number of all-girl camps, it has been the writer's personal observation that pre-adolescent and early adolescent girls often form strong affectional attachments to older campers and counselors; these attachments have strong homosexual overtones, though they infrequently result in overt homosexual behaviors. It is probable that these attachments come about largely because of homesickness for parents and siblings, a different set of cultural norms, plus rising sexual interests. The psychological milieu of the situation has been observed to be heavily affected by the sexual orientation of camp leaders. If some of the stronger ones appear to be committed homosexuals, a group contagion effect can be noted, with a large number of campers pairing off into "loving couples." Considerable anxiety may result, with even younger children becoming overtly aware of a homosexual life-style in the camp. It further has been observed that the great majority of these girls return to their heterosexual orientation soon after they reach home.

Situations of these kinds have been celebrated far more in literature than in scholarly studies. On balance, it seems rather surprising that so little scientific attention has been paid to the effects of varying life situations outside the home on the social and psychological sexual development of children and adolescents.

Some Critical Issues

In the sexually stimulating climate of the present day, teenagers are forced to think more about sexual aspects of their lives than was formerly the case. They more or less must make a public statement about their sexual identity but have more difficulty in doing so because there are fewer guidelines than there used to be about any aspect of sexual behavior. The greater freedom that they experience is likely also to bring with it greater anxiety because of the choices that are open to them and are required of them.

Gagnon and Simon (1973) point out that adolescents who are homosexuals live in a particularly uncomfortable world with almost no guidelines. Coming to terms with their own sexuality in deciding to "come out of the closet" tends to bring an end to a chaotic period they have experienced partly because of the lack of public markers regarding what they are feeling or thinking. The sexual information blackout during adolescence, the stigmatized status of the homosexual, and the fears of being different contribute to great pain. Figuring out a sexual identity takes much more careful thought for the homosexual than for the heterosexual.

Trying to find a social life in a circle of acceptable friends is particularly difficult for the homosexual adolescent. There appear to be a wide variety of gay bars that cater to people with differing tastes. Some of these bars are almost exlusively sexual in purpose, whereas others incorporate a number of more sublimated and socially acceptable interests. Apparently, lesbian bars are less apt than bars for gay men to be specifically sexual.

According to Gagnon and Simon, when gays first come out they tend to be widely promiscuous for a while. This period of excited experimentation is usually followed by a more stable one. Deciding to come out is usually an enormous problem for adolescent homosexuals. It is often laden with feelings of guilt, shame, fear and worry regarding what parents will think, and disturbed anxiety about one's educational and occupational future. Many adult as well as adolescent gays move back and forth between being secret about their orientation and being open to some people. Some use casual, impersonal, hidden, and occasional sex because of these fears and fail to form lasting, affectionate relationships.

Since some communities have laws against homosexual activities, especially for youths, young homosexuals are especially vulnerable to being arrested when they go to gay meeting places. They are vulnerable on two counts: their youth and their homosexual orientation. It is often especially dangerous for both an adolescent and an older man if they enter into a relationship together because of the legal proscriptions against homosexuality itself and particularly for young people.

In Summary

It appears that homosexual play is fairly common in preadolescence, especially among boys. A small proportion of adolescents seems to experience active homosexual episodes. These are more apt to occur in early adolescence. An even smaller proportion (about 3 percent of boys and fewer girls) appears to engage in committed homosexual relationships. In general, the incidence of these behaviors apparently has not risen over the past 30 years, although expressed attitudes have become much more permissive, especially among people with a college education.

The causes of a homosexual orientation are not clearly known. Some evidence suggests origins in disturbed family relationships, in social learning, in prenatal endocrine factors, and in one-sex living situations at critical periods of development.

CHAPTER 5

Adolescent Nonmarital Heterosexual Behaviors and Attitudes

INTRODUCTION

Heterosexual behaviors and attitudes during adolescence usually have been researched and discussed in specific sexual terms. Research generally has referred to such sex activities as kissing and hugging, light and heavy petting, and intercourse. The general view is that these are step-by-step behaviors toward ever-increasing physical intimacy. Although this is likely to be true, it is a limited approach to the young person's overall development as a masculine or feminine human being during the adolescent years. It would be more appropriate to think of nonmarital* sexual attitudes and behaviors as those that encompass the development of adolescents in their interests and abilities to form intimate interpersonal social, psychological, and physical relationships, as they move from their families of origin to families they may form in the future. However, the nature of the available research requires an overemphasis on specific sexual subjects.

ATTITUDES

Overview

There are a number of studies of adolescent and youth attitudes toward nonmarital sex behaviors. The relationship between attitudes and behaviors is a perpetual, unresolved problem. It is probable that they interact in complex ways, with each affecting the other.

Although attitudes toward nonmarital sexual behaviors have fluctuated considerably over the years, it is beyond the scope of this chapter to dis-

---

* The term *nonmarital* intercourse and other forms of sex behaviors rather than *premarital* is used throughout this book, since the latter term assumes eventual marriage—an unwarranted assumption in this day of lower marriage rates.

cuss these shifts in any depth. Sharp changes in the United States toward greater sexual liberalism occurred in the early 1900s and were reflected in the more emancipated behaviors of a sizable proportion of middle- and upper-class women in the 1920s. These changes have been documented by the research of Kinsey and his associates (1948, 1953) and by numerous novelists and essayists of the period.

Increasing urbanization and industrialization in the United States, rising employment for women, an increase in women's rights, and greater contact with other cultures (especially in World War I) were largely responsible for these trends. As women became more emancipated from earlier puritanical prescriptions, men became more emancipated, too, especially in terms of greater freedom to have nonmarital relations on a more equalitarian, companionship basis with women in their own reference groups (Reiss, 1960).

This trend toward increased sexual liberalization has strengthened recently, especially since the mid-1960s, as shown in Chapter 3. However, it is probable, though formal research is scanty, that greater liberalization of attitudes, if not of behaviors, had taken place between the 1920s and the 1960s than is generally acknowledged, especially as a result of upheavals caused by World War II. Reiss (1976) postulates that, while such changes may have occurred, the 50-year period between 1915 and 1965 mostly represented a time in which value shifts were being consolidated. By 1965 the United States was changing from an industrial to a postindustrial society, and this brought forth a period of extensive social upheaval, including a push for more sexual freedom and youth autonomy.

There is considerable evidence that, by the mid-1960s, high school and college males had become more accepting than they were earlier of the concept of sexual expression primarily within an affectional, if not committed, relationship (DeLameter & MacCorquodale, 1979; Komarovsky, 1976; Sorensen, 1973). By the early 1970s, love and affection were highly esteemed by both sexes, with serial, if not permanent, monogamous intimate relationships being favored by the majority.

Strong double-standard attitudes toward nonmarital sex behavior were found in various studies from the 1930s through the early 1960s (Burgess & Wallin, 1953; Ehrmann, 1959; Kinsey et al., 1953; Reiss, 1967; Terman, 1938). In general, young women tended to equate sex with love and feel that petting or coitus were unacceptable outside of a love relationship. However, young men were more likely to think that sexual permissiveness was acceptable in both love and casual relationships. These attitude differences had declined by the mid-1960s and continued to do so through the 1970s (Croake & James, 1973; DeLameter & MacCorquodale, 1979; Hunt, 1974; Packard, 1968; Reiss, 1976; Sorensen, 1973;

Yankelovich, 1974). Although young men have more recently espoused an equal sex standard for males and females, several studies show that many still tend to feel that they want their wives virginal at marriage or to have had a sex relationship only with them (Chilman, 1974; Packard, 1968; Sorensen, 1973; Yankelovich, 1981).

As might be expected, college men tend to receive social support from their peers for nonmarital sex activity, whereas women generally do not (Carns, 1973). The evidence is suggestive, but not consistent in all studies, that females are more likely than males to behave in accordance with their own sex standards and males to behave opportunistically. This may be related to the now less prevalent concept that females in a relationship set the limits for sex behavior and that males "have a right to get what they can." It may also be related to the now debatable Kinsey finding that inexperienced females have a weak sex drive. In writing on this topic, Reiss (1976) hypothesizes that women's roles are closer to the family than are men's and that their more firm and clear sex standards are tied to the marriage goals of most of them. (See Chapter 2 for a more extensive discussion of differences between the sexes.)

In general, attitudes toward nonmarital petting and intercourse became more liberal among high school and college students from the mid-1960s through at least 1974, with the greatest changes occurring for women (Bell & Chaskes, 1970; Christensen & Gregg, 1970; Ferrell et al., 1977; Glenn & Weaver, 1979; Robinson et al., 1972; Yankelovich, 1974; Zelnik & Kanter, 1977). By the early 1970s, the great majority of college men and about 66 percent of college women in at least one university said they favored nonmarital coitus. By 1976, a national survey of colleges showed that about 85 percent of college males and females approved of nonmarital intercourse (*Playboy,* 1976). There was also a growing tendency for adolescents and youths to hold that sexual behavior is more a matter of personal choice than of morality (Robinson et al., 1972; Sorensen, 1973; Yankelovich, 1974).

Mahoney (1979) measured changes in attitudes toward sex in two nationally representative surveys of 1972 and 1975. He found marked shifts in attitudes over these three years for two groups of people: Lower-class women became much less restrictive in attitude, and middle-class women moved toward even greater permissiveness. This is fairly similar to findings obtained by Yankelovich (1974), as reported in Chapter 3. Moreover, Yankelovich reported in 1981 that a large majority of parents of college-age students favored premarital affairs for their youngsters who were "in love" as contrasted to their position in 1967, when over 80 percent of parents condemned such behaviors.

A 1973 Gallup poll showed that fewer than 50 percent of all adult

Americans said that nonmarital intercourse was wrong—a 20 percent decline from 1969. A somewhat larger proportion of women than men thought this: 53 percent compared with 42 percent. Expectedly, older people were more conservative in their attitudes than younger ones. In 1973 only 29 percent of people between the ages of 30 and 45 expressed disapproval of nonmarital intercourse. Many of these people would have had adolescent children and appeared to be far less conservative in their sexual attitudes than might be supposed.

The largest shift toward liberality occurred among high school, compared to college, graduates. Regional differences were also found, with Southerners being the most conservative and Easterners the most liberal. As might be anticipated, single people were more liberal than married people. Black males were found to be more permissive in their attitudes than any other young group studied in both 1964 and 1973. Moreover, black females were more permissive than white females (Reiss, 1967; Yankelovich, 1974). And shifts toward more permissive attitudes were far more marked for white women than for white men. By the late 1970s, the measured attitudes of the two sexes had become quite similar (Reiss & Miller, 1979).

Factors Associated with Attitudes

We have already seen that attitudes about sexual behavior tend to vary by time periods, region of the United States, educational level, race, age, and sex. Other factors also affect these attitudes. For instance, Cvetkovich and Grote (1976), in a report of an American Public Health Association study in three locations, showed that sexually liberal attitudes are associated with experience in nonmarital intercourse, especially for white girls but somewhat less so for black girls. This is true to a considerable extent for white boys but to a lesser extent for black ones. This is not to imply that all these respondents approved of nonmarital intercourse. Many were only somewhat rather than fully approving. Generally similar results were obtained by Bell and Chaskes (1970), Lewis and Burr (1975), and De-Lameter and MacCorquodale (1979). As Cvetkovich and Grote comment, one cannot tell whether these permissive attitudes followed or preceded coital behavior. For instance, many of the white girls said they gave in because their boyfriends expected it of them, rather than because they approved of nonmarital coitus for themselves (Cvetkovich & Grote, 1976).

The Jurichs (Jurich & Jurich, 1974), following Kohlberg's (1964) formulations, hypothesize that levels of cognitive moral development are associated with traditional or permissive sex behavior attitudes. In a study of a small group of college women, they found that subjects who were rated at low levels of cognitive moral development were significantly more likely to espouse traditional, double-standard, or permissiveness-without-affection values. Those at moderate levels advocated permissiveness with affection, and those at the highest levels thought that any kind of nonexploitative sex relationship was acceptable. This research tends to assess particularly the ability to arrive at independent, abstract principles. Intellectually, the concept that any sex relationship is acceptable as long as it is nonexploitative has a highly rational appeal in this age of readily available contraceptives and abortion. Definitions of exploitation, however, may be a bit difficult to arrive at, especially from the more subtle emotional points of view of the various people involved.

Christensen and Gregg (1970), in their 1958 and 1968 studies with comparable samples in three universities (Intermountain, Midwestern, and Danish) obtained the findings shown in Table 5.1. These data show increased liberalization of attitudes and behaviors of men and women in three different settings between 1958 and 1968. The data also indicate culturally related variations. They further show, as do other studies, various kinds of gaps between attitudes and behaviors in the different locations at different time periods.

Reiss (1967), Heltsey and Broderick (1969), and Staples (1973) found that conservative sex attitudes were associated with religiosity for whites but not for blacks. Reiss and others have speculated that the lack of association for blacks is related to the different beliefs and functions of white and black churches. Although the former generally hold that sex outside of marriage is wrong, the latter put little emphasis on this point.

TABLE 5.1.   Percentages Expressing Approval of Nonmarital Coitus
and Percentages with Nonmarital Experience

	Intermountain		Midwestern		Danish	
	Males	Females	Males	Females	Males	Females
Approval of nonmarital coitus						
1968	38.4	23.5	55.4	37.4	100.0	100.0
1958	23.3	2.9	46.7	17.4	94.0	80.7
Have nonmarital experience						
1968	36.5	32.4	50.2	34.3	94.7	96.6
1958	39.4	9.5	50.7	20.7	63.7	59.8

It is theorized that the black church more likely serves as a place for comfort and release of pent-up tensions than as an institution for moral guidance. However, it seems that this theory is too general; black churches vary by denomination, region, and social class. Moreover, in the past 15 years or so, churches are more apt to be racially integrated than formerly (e.g., at the time of the Reiss study).

The growth of new forms of religion and of religiosity among a fairly large group of young (and older) people since the late 1960s is probably creating more conservative sexual attitudes among a portion of the population. For instance, such popular movements as the Charismatic Christian, Pentecostal, and Evangelical religions are strongly puritanical in character and hold sexual freedoms in deep disfavor.

Reiss (1967) has hypothesized that liberal attitudes toward sexual behavior are one aspect of a generally liberal viewpoint. However, his research showed that this held true only for middle- and upper-class people. Later studies to test his theory obtained somewhat similar results (Cannon & Long, 1971). Research directed toward further testing of the Reiss theories during the 1970s largely showed that the question was extremely complicated and difficult to prove or disprove (Clayton & Bokemeier, 1980).

LEVELS OF SEXUAL INTIMACY PRIOR TO INTERCOURSE

Overview

At least until recently, studies showed that most adolescents, especially young women, moved gradually toward advanced levels of sexual intimacies, such as heavy petting and intercourse, through a series of dating and going-steady experiences. A learning period was generally involved during which young people came to know each other better, to develop an affectional relationship, and to respond to each other physically. Kinsey and his associates (1953) found that young women seemed to develop their sexual interests through experiencing sexual stimulation in a relational context, whereas young men generally acquired sexual experience earlier, primarily through nocturnal emissions and masturbation. Higher rates of early masturbation among today's females, along with cultural changes and more opportunities for privacy, may mean that today's young people are more likely to move quickly into physical intimacies than they did before 1965.

Kinsey and other researchers found that the sexual revolution of the 1920s brought with it permissive petting behaviors for the more liberated adolescents. Before that time, most middle-class females in the United States probably did not experience nonmarital intimacies. They were supposed to be completely virginal at marriage—untouched except, perhaps, for a chaste kiss.* Females were to be chaperoned on dates so that all temptations could be held at bay. This was the predominant theme in many "civilized" societies, although there were variations by social class, race, and nationality (Reiss, 1960). This theme was not nearly so strong for the majority of black people, who suffered from the situations and customs of slavery, the Reconstruction period, and continuing discrimination (Bernard, 1966).

Liberalization of the sexual code following World War I included unchaperoned dating for adolescent males and females. The dating game grew in popularity and prevalence for the next 20 years. It spread to younger teenagers and became a social popularity contest: the more dates with the more partners, the better. About the time of World War II, however, dating patterns changed to the custom of going steady in high school and even junior high, a practice formerly reserved for college-age youth. The prevalent practice of steady dating very likely increased the incidence of petting, especially heavy petting, because this was widely viewed by many youths as acceptable in the context of such a relationship (Reiss, 1960).

It appears that rates of nonmarital petting, particularly heavy petting, increased somewhat between the early 1920s and the early 1970s, especially for females and younger adolescents (Chilman, 1963; Ehrmann, 1959; Kinsey et al., 1948; Luckey & Nass, 1969; Robinson et al., 1972; Sorensen, 1973; Vener & Stewart, 1974). However, data on this subject are sketchy and unsatisfactory. Apparently, petting to orgasm has occurred for over half of both the male and female adolescent participants for at least the last half century. Males have been more likely than females to engage in heavy petting and at younger ages. They also have been more likely to move rapidly from petting to intercourse.

Over the years, there has been a large numerical gap for females between those who participated in petting and those who had intercourse. For instance, Kinsey and his associates (1953) found that about 84 percent of the females in their study were petting by age 18 but only 10 percent were having intercourse. Similar findings were obtained by Chilman in 1961. By 1968, however, Luckey and Nass (1969) found this "erotic gap" to have narrowed, with 68 percent of the females experiencing petting by age 19 and 43 percent experiencing intercourse.

* This generalization may be more celebrated in stated attitudes than practice. Recent historical research is beginning to reveal more liberated nonmarital sexual behaviors among American women in the past than has been usually supposed.

TABLE 5.2. **Heterosexual Activity for Boys in Community B by Age, 1970–1973**

	Percentage of boys who have participated in an activity at least once									
	13 and younger		14		15		16		17 and older	
Level of sexuality activity	1970	1973	1970	1973	1970	1973	1970	1973	1970	1973
Held hands	79	80	83	87	92	93	90	90	93	92
Held arm around or been held	60	67	79	78	83	87	90	87	90	90
Kissed or been kissed	63	65	72	78	76	84	86	85	86	87
Necked (prolonged hugging and kissing)	46	48	54	56	64	70	76	69	77	78
Light petting (feeling above the waist)	37	40	49	55	59	66	70	65	71	71
Heavy petting (feeling below the waist)	32	34	36	42	44	56	53	55	62	62
Gone all the way (coitus)	24	28	21	32	26	38	31	38	38	34
Coitus with two or more partners	14	17	14	15	11	21	16	23	17	23
Number in sample	192	180	208	220	193	191	217	176	179	173

TABLE 5.3. Heterosexual Activity for Girls in Community B by Age, 1970–1973

	13 and younger		14		15		16		17 and older	
Level of sexual activity	1970	1973	1970	1973	1970	1973	1970	1973	1970	1973
Held hands	78	84	91	87	92	89	95	91	95	97
Held arm around or been held	68	72	85	81	88	87	94	90	92	96
Kissed or been kissed	66	68	80	75	82	82	92	89	90	96
Necked (prolonged hugging and kissing)	46	43	64	56	69	65	81	77	82	84
Light petting (feeling above the waist)	27	31	41	40	49	55	66	65	71	71
Heavy petting (feeling below the waist)	21	17	20	28	28	40	47	49	57	59
Gone all the way (coitus)	10	10	10	17	13	24	23	31	27	35
Coitus with two or more partners	7	4	4	5	4	10	8	13	8	14
Number in sample	191	222	197	218	195	220	200	190	142	185

Percentage of girls who have participated in an activity at least once

Males, too, have experienced a gap, though a smaller one, between petting and intercourse. This gap has not narrowed so much over the years, primarily because male rates of intercourse have been consistently higher than female rates until at least the early 1970s.

It is frequently observed that nonmarital petting, especially heavy petting to orgasm, has been a device used to maintain the technical virginity of females. Although this is undoubtedly true, the gradual growth of sexual intimacies may also aid young people in their evolution into sexually mature adults. This may be truer for females than for males, unless the nature of their sexual interests and responses changes in reaction to present socio-cultural trends toward a more sexually permissive society for females as well as males.

Male writers on the subject are frequently puzzled by the apparent contentment of young women to restrict themselves to heavy petting without moving on to intercourse. There are a number of practical reasons for this behavior: It greatly reduces the chance of becoming pregnant; females may be more readily orgasmic through direct clitoral stimulation brought about by petting; and withholding full intercourse from the male until marriage is likely to increase his desire for this commitment. Freud's idea that sexual expression short of intercourse denotes infantile sexuality has been enthusiastically endorsed by other males, who find intercourse far more physically satisfying than petting.

There is scanty evidence concerning the petting behavior of black adolescents. The little that we have suggests that far fewer have substituted petting for intercourse over the years. Because female virginity and births only within marriage appear to have been less emphasized by blacks than whites (except for the relatively small group of middle-class blacks), it seems likely that petting without subsequent intercourse is not widely practiced among the majority of black adolescents (Rainwater, 1970).

Vener and Stewart provide particularly valuable data from replication studies about progressive stages of sexual intimacy among high school students in both 1970 and 1973 in a largely white, middle- and upper-working-class school in a nonmetropolitan Michigan community. These researchers found that about 59 percent of high school girls, age 17 or over, engaged in heavy petting in both 1970 and 1973. The percentages were slightly higher for boys of this age (Vener & Stewart, 1974, p. 732). (See Tables 5.2 and 5.3.)

The incidence of this behavior increased at every age from 13 or less to 17 and older for both boys and girls, with the greatest increase occurring at ages 15–16 for both sexes. A statistically significant increase in petting behavior for the years 1970 and 1973 occurred for both boys and girls at ages 14–15 and 15–16. This further supports other findings that a recent major change in adolescent sex behavior is the earlier incidence of sexual intimacies.

Factors Associated with Petting Experience

Expectedly, rates of petting increase with age, largely as a part of normal adolescent development and experience. These changes are shown by the Vener and Stewart data and a number of other studies, including a large Wisconsin study by DeLameter and MacCorquodale (1979).

Sorensen (1973), like others, found that there was a strong tendency for young people to move into early physical intimacies by age 14 or 15 and progress further by age 16. His findings about the young people with no petting experience (mostly those under age 15 or 16) suggest that most had not yet fully entered the adolescent stage, with its push for independence from parents and for intimate love–sex relationships with peers. However, some of them may have been timid and withdrawn in personality structure, some may have been late in physical maturation, and a few may have had a homosexual orientation. In addition, a number of studies show that little or no experience in petting is often related to religiosity, defined as frequent attendance at religious services (Kinsey et al., 1948, 1953; Reiss, 1967; Robinson et al., 1972; Sorensen, 1973).

Sorensen further found that young people who had engaged in petting but not in intercourse were a midgroup: more conservative in attitude and younger than the nonvirgins, but less conservative and older than the beginners. Members of the midgroup were more restless and dissatisfied with their sex lives than either of the other two groups and also reported poorer grades in school. This suggests that many were in a transition stage of middle adolescence and that a number might move toward full intercourse experience in the next few years.

NONMARITAL COITUS

Rates of adolescent nonmarital intercourse appear to have increased even more sharply than those of petting in recent years, with a clear and continuing rise since about 1967. This is particularly true for white females. (Findings of major studies concerning rates of nonmarital intercourse for adolescents aged 12–19 are found in Table 5.4.)

By 1973, studies in various localities showed that about 35 percent or more of high school seniors, both male and female, were nonvirgins. In the same year, figures for college students rose to about 85 percent for males

TABLE 5.4. Percentages of Adolescent Females and Males Reporting Nonmarital Intercourse, as Shown in Various Studies

Investigations, dates of studies, and description of samples

Kinsey, Pomeroy, Martin, and Gebhard, 1938–50—Nonrandom sample, mainly northeast and north-central urban white females and males

Age at first intercourse by years of education

	Females					Males			
Age	0–8	9–12	13–16	17	Total	0–8	9–12	13	Total
13	9	1	—	—	1	14.5	16.2	3.1	14.8
14						28.0	33.4	6.0	27.8
15	18	5	2	1	3	42.2	44.7	9.5	38.8
16						56.9	58.1	15.5	51.6
17						66.8	68.3	23.1	61.3
18						76.1	73.7	30.8	68.2
19						80.0	75.6	38.0	71.5
20	25	26	20	15	20	82.9	75.1	44.4	73.1

Gebhard, Pomeroy, Martin, and Christensen, 1938–55—Nonrandom sample, northern urban black

Age at first intercourse by education

	Females			Males
Age	8th grade	High school	College	
15	62	48	8	No males included in study
20	82	82	49	

Lake, 1966–1967—Nonrandom national sample of 1500 females, ages 15–19 (only 15% in college)

Age at first intercourse

Age	College	Males
15	6	No males included in study
16–17	13	
18–19	25	

76

Age at first intercourse by education

Age	College bound	Not College bound	Total	Education	
15	4	11	10	College bound	16
17	12	40	27	Not college bound	31
18	23	40	38	Total	21

Simon, Berger, and Gagnon, 1972– Random sample, males in Illinois

First intercourse by age 17 and occupational status of head of household

Year of birth	Low occupational status		High occupational status		
	Black	White	Black	White	
1920–1929	41.6	2.5	34.6	3.6	No males included in study
1930–1939	47.6	13.1	40.7	7.8	
1940–1949	51.9	13.3	52.2	13.6	
1950–1959	65.5	33.3	65.5	26.2	

Udry, Bauman, and Morris, 1969–1970— Low-income-area probability sample of 16 cities. Retrospective interviews with black and white females in birth cohorts by decades and by occupational status of man who was head of household when subjects were ages 10–14

First intercourse by grade

Grade	Females	Males
10	26	21
11	40	28
12	55	33

Jessor and Jessor, 1972—Random sample of high school students in a small Rocky Mountain city (52% original sample responded)

TABLE 5.4 (Continued)

Investigations, dates of studies, and description of samples	Females	Males

Miller, 1972—Junior and senior students in two San Francisco high schools, by socioeconomic status (SES), ages about 16–18

First intercourse by SES

SES	Females	Males
Middle	58 (mostly white)	No males included in study
Lower	48 (races mixed)	

Hunt, 1972—Retrospective data, national probability sample, with considerable sample loss

Age at first intercourse

Age	Females	Males
17	25	50

Sorenson, 1972—Partial national sample, with many unknown biases of females and males of both races (white majority)

Age at first intercourse

Age	Females	Males
12	3.2	9.7
13	8.5	20
14	14.5	30
15	26	40
16	35	49
17	37	55
18–19	45	57

Percentage of never-married women by age at first intercourse

Age	1979 Total	1979 White	1979 Black	1976 Total	1976 White	1976 Black	1971 Total	1971 White	1971 Black
15	22.5	18.3	41.4	18.6	13.8	38.9	14.4	11.3	31.2
16	37.8	35.4	50.4	28.9	23.7	55.1	20.9	17.0	44.4
17	48.5	44.1	73.3	42.9	36.1	71.0	26.1	20.2	58.9
18	56.9	52.6	76.3	51.4	46.0	76.2	39.7	35.6	60.2
19	69.0	64.9	88.5	59.5	43.6	83.9	46.4	40.7	78.3
15–19	46.0	42.3	64.8	39.2	33.6	64.3	27.6	23.2	52.4

Zelnik and Kantner, studies in 1971, 1976, 1979—National probability samples of white and black females, ages 14–19

Percentage of never-married men by age at first intercourse

Age	White	Black
17	54	60
18	64	80
19	77	80
20	81	86
21	68	89

Zelnik and Kantner—National sample of men studied in 1979 with self-administered questionnaires, considerable sample loss

Age at first intercourse

	1979 Total	1979 White	1979 Black	1976 Total	1976 White	1976 Black	1971 Total	1971 White	1971 Black
Mean	16.2	16.4	15.5	16.1	16.3	15.6	16.4	16.6	15.9
(N)	(933)	(478)	(455)	(726)	(350)	(376)	(936)	(435)	(501)

TABLE 5.4 *(Continued)*

Investigations, dates of studies, and description of samples	Females	Males			

Age at first intercourse by race

Investigations, dates of studies, and description of samples	Females	Age	White	Black	Hispanic
Finkel and Finkel, 1974—Sample of males in three high schools in large northeastern city	No females included in study	12	6.	45.9	23.3
		13	12.4	60.7	32.8
		14	23.7	74.0	49.8
		15	35.7	78.7	68.7
		16–17	48	84.0	75

First intercourse by race

Investigations, dates of studies, and description of samples		Females	Males
Cvetkovich and Grote, 1974–1975—Nonrandom sample of black and white females and males, ages 16–17, in two cities and one town	Black	63	92
	White	36	51

Age at first intercourse by type of school

Investigations, dates of studies, and description of samples	Age	Females			Males			
		School A	School B	School C	School A	School B	School C	School B
Vener, Stewart, and Hager, 1972—Replication studies with large, similar populations and same instruments, 1970 and 1973. Large sample, nonmetropolitan Michigan area: three high schools in 1970; one in 1973. Probably white majority. School A—Professional–managerial community; B—lower middle- and upper-working class community; C—semirural, working-class community.	13 or less	7	10	7	8	10	24	28
	14	7	10	8	7	17	23	32
	15	12	13	13	19	24	15	38
	16	18	23	21	21	31	31	38
	17 or more	26	27	40	31	35	38	34

TABLE 5.5. College-Level Females and Males Reporting Nonmarital Intercourse, as Shown in Various Studies

Date of study	Sample	Percentage of group	
		Females	Males
K. Davis, 1929	1200 college level women, single, mean age 37 at time of study	11	NA
Hamilton, 1929	100 college students married at time of study (retrospective study)	35	54
Bromley and Britten, 1938	618 single females and 470 males with college or high school education, ages 16–23 at time of study	25	51
R. Peterson, 1938	419 male college students	NA	55
Porterfield and Ellison, 1946	328 single female and 285 single male college students	9	32
Kinsey et al., 1940s and 1950s	5000(+) college-level females and 3000(+) males (retrospective study)	20–27	49
R. Ross, 1950	95 single male college students, age 21	NA	51
Gilbert Youth Research, 1951	National sample of college students, single, ages 17–22 at time of study	25	56
Landis and Landis, 1953	1000 female college students and 610 male college students, single and married	9	41
			Age 18–21
Ehrmann, 1953	315 single females, ages 18–21 (interviews and question-naires); 274 single males, ages 18–21 (questionnaires); 50 single males, ages 19–24 (interviews); in a southern university	14	57
			Age 19–24
		NA	68

81

TABLE 5.5 (*Continued*)

Date of study	Sample	Percentage of group			
		Females		Males	
		Single	Married	Single	Married
Chilman, 1961	Random sample of 50 single females and males and 40 married females and males, ages 18–21 in a northeastern university	9	46	46	72
Mirande, 1966	Single undergraduate sociology students in a midwestern university	23	NA	63	NA
Freedman, 1965	Random sample of Stanford University senior female students, white, mostly upper-middle class	22	NA	NA	NA
		1965	1970	1965	1970
Robinson, King, and Balswick 1965 and 1970	Representative samples from undergraduate social science class in a large southern university: 115 females and 129 males in 1965; 158 females and 137 males in 1970	29	37	65	65
Kaats and Davis, 1967	Survey in two introductory psychology courses	41–44	NA	60	NA
Carns, 1967	Probability sample of 1177 students in nation's nonreligiously based colleges and universities; interview study; adequate reliability stated	32.2		57.4	
		1958	1968	1958	1968
Bell and Chaskes, 1958 and 1968	Matched samples at an urban Pennsylvania university: Dating Steady	 10 15	 23 28	 NA	 NA

	Single	Married	Single	Married
	1958	1968	1958	1968
Luckey and Naas, 1967 Survey of 21 nationally representative colleges and universities	43.2		58.2	
Schultz et al., 1977 Survey of 2000 University of Wisconsin undergraduates in 1964 and 1968				
Females				56
Males				65
Christensen and Gregg, 1970 Studies in 1958 and 1968 (same instrument and similar samples); three samples of college students—Mormon (Utah), Midwest, and Danish (omitted here); mostly white				
Mormon	10	32	39	37
Midwest	21	34	51	50
Playboy magazine, 1970 Survey of 7300 students from 200 colleges		51		81
Playboy magazine, 1971 Survey Number 2 Random sample of nationally representative colleges		56		77
Bauman and Wilson, 1968–1972 Random sample of University of North Carolina undergraduates, single, white, native born	46	73	56	73
Jackson and Potkay, 1972 Random sample of females in college dorms	43		NA	

TABLE 5.5 (*Continued*)

Date of study	Sample	Percentage of group Females		Males	
		1958	1968	1958	1968
Simon, Berger, and Gagnon, 1972	1967 national sample of 584 female and 593 male college students				
	Freshman		19		36
	Sophomores		30		63
	Juniors		37		60
	Seniors		44		68
	Total		32		56
Jessor and Jessor, 1973	Random sample of college seniors in a Rocky Mountain community; over 50 percent sample loss[a]		85		82
Sarrel and Sarrel, 1974	Study of 1200 entering freshmen, sophomores, juniors, and seniors at Yale University, in 1968 and 1972	29	75	33	62
Chilman, 1974	Random sample of white freshmen in a large, urban mid-western university (majority age 18)		39		50
Playboy magazine, 1976	Random sample of 3700 students from 20 colleges and universities across the country		76		76

	1976	1976
DeLameter and MacCorquodale, 1979		
Representative sample of		
(a) 985 single and female undergraduate University of Wisconsin students	65 (by age 18)	82 (by age 18)
	90+	95
(b) 663 single male and female Madison, Wis., residents, ages 18–23	(by age 20)	(by age 20)
Eighty-eight percent of student sample and 62 percent of community sample reached.		
Total sample largely white, middle class		

[a] When these students were freshmen in 1970, 51 percent of the females and 46 percent of the males were self-reported nonvirgins. By their sophomore year, this was true for 70 percent of the females and 65 percent of the males; by their junior year (1972), these figures were 80 percent and 74 percent, respectively. Thus, rates increased by 50 percent from the freshman year to the senior year. These data, interesting in themselves as descriptive of change for groups of college students over time, also indicate the importance in such studies of delineating the age and college years of the group under consideration and the difficulty of comparing one study to another when these facts are unknown.

and 60–70 percent for females.* By contrast, between 1925 and 1965, available research indicated rates of about 10 percent for white high school senior women and about 25 percent for white college senior women. Comparable figures for white males were about 25 and 55 percent. Thus, it appears that between about 1967 and 1974, nonmarital intercourse rates rose for white females by about 300 percent and for white males by about 50 percent. Somewhat similar trends have been observed in many parts of the world, most notably the industrialized countries and those developing nations in stages of rapid industrialization (George Washington University Medical Center, 1976). Findings of major studies concerning rates of nonmarital intercourse for college-level males and females are found in Table 5.5. We cannot be confident that the rates for noncollege youths between the ages of 18 and 21 have risen in similar fashion, because adequate data are not available for this group.

By 1973 nonmarital intercourse was occurring at younger ages than in the past, with about 25 percent of white males and females, 80 or 90 percent of black males, and 50 percent of black females apparently being sexually experienced by age 15 or 16 (Finkel & Finkel, 1975; S. Jessor & Jessor, 1975; Kantner & Zelnik, 1972; Sorensen, 1973; Vener & Stewart, 1974; Vener et al., 1972).

Rates for nonmarital intercourse have risen more sharply than those for nonmarital petting, with the probability that by 1973 heavy petting was far less of a substitute for intercourse than it once was. Inspection of data regarding heavy petting and intercourse suggest that, especially for young people over age 18, rates of nonmarital physical intimacy per se have not risen as markedly as it would appear, especially for females. It looks as if, compared with the early 1960s, fewer young women stopped with heavy petting to orgasm. Rather, they tended to move on to intercourse. More liberal sex attitudes, plus the greater availability of effective contraceptives, may account for some of this change.

Inspection of the Zelnik and Kantner data from three national surveys of women 15–19 years old in 1971, 1976, and 1979 reveals an increase in the rates of nonmarital intercourse at each time period (see Table 5.4; Zelnik & Kantner, 1980b). For the total age group, the rates rose from 27.6 percent in 1971 to 39.2 percent in 1976 and 46 percent in 1979. The proportion of young women who experienced coitus increased for each age group studied. For example, 14.4 percent of 15 year olds reported intercourse experience in 1971 compared to 22.5 percent in 1979.

Zelnik and Kantner (1980) included a national probability sample of

---

* Interestingly, by 1976, a national survey of colleges sponsored by *Playboy* magazine showed that rates of nonmarital coitus were 74 percent for both sexes and that the rates for males had decreased by about 8 percent, whereas the rates for females had increased by about 10 percent in the past few years.

young men in their 1979 survey. As shown in Table 5.4, they found some-what higher rates of participation in coitus among the young white men than among the young white women but this was not true for the black youths. Data regarding the males in the Zelnik and Kantner study should be considered with caution, however. According to Zelnik,* it was extremely difficult to reach the male sample and many cases were lost.

As of 1976, the great majority of young people (perhaps especially those of higher socioeconomic levels) appeared not to be promiscuous. Most lim-ited their sex activity to one partner within a steady, committed relationship. However, there might be a series of partners over time. Although the con-cept of casual sex was being increasingly accepted by youths, this appeared not to be the norm. By 1976, the number of partners reported by sexually active young women had increased slightly, with 31 percent of the group saying that they had had two to three sex partners in that year, compared to 25 percent reporting this in 1971. However, this slight increase probably does not reflect a growing tendency toward promiscuity.

Later average age at first marriage is probably one of the causes for higher rates of nonmarital intercourse in recent years. It may well be that coitus among adolescents and youths has not actually risen so greatly, but that much more of it occurs before marriage, especially for females.

Although double-standard behaviors and attitudes decreased between 1965 and 1974, there still seemed to be a tendency in the mid-1970s for males to start sex activity at younger ages, to be more aggressive in their pur-suits, and to be more likely to have multiple partners (S. Jessor & Jessor, 1975; *Playboy,* 1976; Sorensen, 1973; Vener & Stewart, 1974; Vener et al., 1972; Zelnik & Kantner, 1980).

Factors Associated with Nonmarital Coitus

Age, Dating Frequency, and Being in Love

A number of studies examine the association between adolescent nonmarital intercourse and other variables. As in the case of petting, the likelihood of nonmarital coitus increases with age. It also is more apt to occur (as one might expect) for those who date frequently, who go steady, or who con-sider themselves in love (DeLameter & MacCorquodale, 1979; Reiss, 1976; Sorensen, 1973; Spanier, 1975).

Social Reference Groups

Some studies that find a positive correlation between having sexually per-missive friends and being sexually active conclude that peers strongly influ-ence sexual behavior (Carns, 1973; Jackson & Potkay, 1973; Mirande,

* Personal communication, 1980.

1968; Spanier, 1975). On the other hand, sexually active young people may discover friends who have similar attitudes and behaviors. A number of studies (but not all) find evidence that males are more heavily influenced by peers in their sex behavior than are females, with strong pressures frequently being experienced by males to have intercourse.

Education and Its Effects

Positive attitudes toward education, higher levels of educational achievement, and clear educational goals appear to make nonmarital intercourse less likely for both white and black females (Gebhard et al., 1958; S. Jessor & Jessor, 1975; Udry et al., 1975; Zelnik, 1981). The association between educational achievement and lower likelihood of nonmarital coitus is doubtlessly tied to interacting socioeconomic, social-psychological, and situational variables. For example, the student who does well in school is apt to come from a family background of higher socioeconomic status; to value achievement; to be more rational, controlled, and conforming in orientation; to be oriented to work rather than play; to operate on a higher level of cognitive development; and to be able to foresee and plan for the future (Conger, 1973). These same characteristics may make the student less likely to engage in nonmarital intercourse during the high school years. In some ways, these characteristics are similar to those Jessor and Jessor (1975) found to discriminate between virgins and nonvirgins of high school age, as shown in a later section.

Especially for females, involvement in a sexual relationship may frequently mean lesser involvement in educational achievement. Conversely, involvement in educational achievement (and thereby pleasing her parents and teachers) may make the girl less interested in involvement with a male or may make her less interesting to males. For example, strong educational drives and intellectualism can serve as a defense mechanism against openness of the personality to feelings and maturing sexuality.

Lack of educational success in high school may be more ego deflating for girls than for boys. This finding was obtained in a recent inner-city study by Douvan and associates.* Boys have an alternate route to high school success through athletics and, if they achieve in this realm, are less threatened by high school failure than are girls. Low self-esteem generally leads to anxiety about the self. One way to assuage this anxiety is to seek self-confirmation through a love–sex relationship, as Miller (1973b) found in his study of sexually active girls.

Psychological Characteristics

Several studies have closely examined psychological characteristics significantly associated with nonmarital coitus during the high school years. One

* Elizabeth Douvan, personal communication, 1976.

investigation (Cvetkovich & Grote, 1975) found that male and female non-virgins tended to have a more permissive, risk-taking attitude toward sex relations and fewer reported themselves as religious—a frequent finding. Sexually active females, furthermore, seemed more likely to espouse a traditional female sex role, saying they participated in intercourse because the male expected it. Unlike the nonvirgins, the virgin females were likely to associate sex relations with the intimacy and interpersonal relations involved. The authors speculate that these findings suggest that nonvirgin females were lower than the virgins in ego strength.

Another highly adequate study (S. Jessor & Jessor, 1975) finds that non-virgins of high school age, compared to virgins, are more apt to have attitudes similar to those of other "deviant" youngsters:—those who use drugs or alcohol, have a delinquent orientation, or are involved in student radicalism.* In general (according to Jessor and Jessor), nonvirgin adolescents had significantly higher scores for independence-achievement disjunction, valuation of independence and deviance, positive attitudes toward sex, parental acceptance of deviance, and peer acceptance and modeling of deviance. They had lower grade point averages in school, lower acceptance of parental controls, and lower expectations of achievement. Nonvirgin boys, but not girls, had higher measures of self-esteem. On the other hand, nonvirgin girls, but not boys, were more likely to place a high value on affection and to feel they received little parental support. They saw their parents and friends as being in conflict with each other. The nonvirgin girls also were higher in social criticism and alienation and lower in religiosity than virgin girls.

These findings are extremely provocative, especially in terms of differences between the sexes. Although it appears that high self-esteem is associated with nonvirginity for boys, this is not the case for girls.† It is noteworthy that high school girls who participate in nonmarital coitus appear to be especially lacking in affection and support from their parents and seek

* It seems to the writer that it may be an error on the part of the Jessors to label nonvirginity, drug and alcohol use, and radical political activity as deviant for high school youth if by deviant one implies delinquent. None of these behaviors, in moderation, seems to be deviant, in the perjorative sense, in today's society, at least in its more liberal components. However, if deviant is interpreted as normal adolescent rebellion against adult norms, the concept seems appropriate. All the above behaviors (in moderation) can represent a potentially healthy adolescent push toward independence and adulthood. On the other hand, these behaviors could be termed conforming for those adolescents who come from families who hold so-called deviant values and belong to social groups who also espouse them. (For an elaboration of these points, see Reiss, 1970.)

† This may in part reflect the psychological effects of the double standard that condemns nonmarital sex activity for girls but not for boys.

it through an affair with a boy. This lends further credence to the speculations concerning lower ego strength of nonvirgin girls as proposed by Cvetkovich and Grote (1975) and as cited above. The results of the Jessor study further suggest that nonvirgin high school girls are actively rebelling against social traditions, although Cvetkovich and Grote found that their nonvirgin female respondents tended to be traditional, at least in terms of the female sex role. It cannot be said with confidence, however, that the studies actually obtained different results, because the questions they asked about traditionl attitudes were not the same.

The growth of independence from parents as a significant factor in participating in nonmarital coitus is a major finding in the DeLameter and MacCorquodale (1979) study of college students and noncollege youths. These investigators stress the importance of moving from dependency on parents, to peer attraction, to involvement with a lover as three basic steps toward nonmarital intercourse.

A number of studies show that nonvirgins are more likely than virgins to use drugs and alcohol. However, aside from the research by Jessor and Jessor, several studies show that promiscuity is associated only with heavy drug use and use of hard drugs (Arafat & Yorburg, 1973; Vener & Stewart, 1974).

It is probable that there are a number of subgroups within the larger virgin and nonvirgin groups and that differing psychological needs and attitudes characterize these smaller clusters. For example, Sorensen (1973) made a useful discrimination between sexual "adventurers" (those with multiple partners) and sexual "monogamists" among his sexually active high school youths. Adventurers (most of whom were males) were especially apt to be in poor communication with their parents and to have difficulty in making close interpersonal relationships.

A group of highly aggressive college men were studied in another project (Kanin, 1967). They appeared to be manipulative, exploitative, and dishonest in their approach to females—somewhat like the adventurers mentioned above. They were more apt than other males to be nonvirgins, especially sensitive to peer group pressure, and likely to feel that low sex activity would occasion a loss of status with their friends. They also reported that their sex experiences were rarely satisfying. These findings suggest that this is a group of males who are low in self-esteem, unsure of themselves as men, and hostile in their attitudes toward women, and who engage in coitus primarily to counteract their own sense of inadequacy.

Family Relationships

A number of studies found that parent–youth relations made a difference in adolescent sex behavior (Bowerman et al., 1966; DeLameter & MacCorquodale, 1979; Fox, 1980; S. Jessor & Jessor, 1975; Kantner & Zelnik, 1972; Ladner, 1971; Reiss, 1967; Simon et al., 1972; Sorensen, 1973). Adolescents were more likely to have nonmarital intercourse if their mothers held nontraditional attitudes, especially if their mothers failed to combine affection with firm, mild discipline. (Large bodies of child development research report the central importance and generally beneficial effects of these two dimensions of parent behavior.) They were also more likely to have nonmarital intercourse if they perceived themselves to be in poor communication with their parents and unhappy at home.

These findings do not necessarily mean that good parent–youth communication or lack of parent–youth conflict will prevent nonmarital sex activity among adolescents. It may also be that in many cases when young people become sexually active, they become less attached to their parents, perhaps unable to talk to them about their sexual behavior or perhaps more rebellious toward parental norms and controls.

A number of studies show that at least one-third of the adolescents who are sexually active report anxiety and guilt about their behavior. This is especially true of females (Bardwick, 1973; Hunt, 1974; Miller, 1974; Reiss, 1973; Sorensen, 1973). The degree of guilt is associated in part with the attitudes of the peer groups to which the young person belongs (Perlman, 1974). It seems likely that in a time of change from traditional to nontraditional values, people who engage in the new freedoms would find the transition process disturbing to their belief systems and their sense of self-respect, as well as to their relationships with other significant people in their lives, such as parents. Of course, feelings of guilt and anxiety will vary enormously from person to person depending on his or her early socialization and the attitudes of the person's partner as well as those of influential close friends.

There are a number of suggestions in the research that adolescents who engage in sex relations at a very young age (12 or 13) may have special problems. Vener and Stewart (1974) speculate that they have less internalized guilt about sex relations. Sorensen's group of disturbed youngsters who were promiscuous sex adventurers also tended to have their first coitus at age 13 or so. Steinhoff (1976) found that young, sexually active adolescent girls were more likely to engage in sex behavior largely to please their boyfriends and did not enjoy it themselves.

As shown earlier in this chapter, nonmarital intercourse in early adolescence particularly may create problems for teenagers. Conversely, young adolescents with problems or values different from those of the mainstream culture may be especially likely to engage in nonmarital coitus. Psychological problems conducive to this behavior might be low self-regard, poor impulse control, and low levels of cognitive development.

Situational problems also may be conducive to this behavior. For instance, many of today's teenagers lack adequate parental supervision. Both parents work outside the home, in many instances, with no substitute child care being provided for older children and teenagers. Although it is frequently assumed that children over age 10 or so are able to care for themselves, this seems to be a risky supposition, especially in today's society with its many sexual stimuli, confused values, and lack of cohesive communities. When the vulnerable psychological characteristics of many young teenagers are considered, it seems unwise to expose them to the extreme temptations that a home lacking a continuous, responsible adult presence offers.

Conflicts between parents, as well as parental separation or divorce, are also associated with higher rates of nonmarital coitus among adolescent girls (Fox, 1980; Zelnik, 1981). (Data are not available at this writing for the effects on boys.)

Social Factors

The rapid increase in nonmarital intercourse, which started in the mid-1960s and was still on the rise in 1976, is one symptom of massive changes in the rest of society. Chapter 3 shows that many aspects of the social revolution of the 1960s reached extreme forms of expression by 1967–1968. As previously noted, this revolution shifted from an earlier idealistic push for orderly, intellectually enlightened social change to desperate and frequently violent eruptions. By 1967 the whole society seemed to have fallen apart, and this was the time that rates of nonmarital intercourse among adolescents (especially young women) began their sharp increase. People who had pushed for social reform in the early 1960s had become disillusioned by the late 1960s. They turned, for the most part, from urging large social changes to seeking personal freedoms, especially freedoms that involved interpersonal intimacies.

By the late 1960s and into the 1970s, a "better world" was being sought psychologically rather than sociologically. Old moralities were being discarded by many (especially the young), and new faiths were being sought in various ways, including those of "open and honest," untrammeled relationships. It appears that society had reached a turning point in 1967 (Bernard, 1975) with respect to a number of aspects of sexual behavior. Those aspects that had been deviant were becoming normative in such areas as nonmarital intercourse for young women as well as young men, equal sex roles, employment of women (including mothers of young children) outside the home, and postponement of early marriage.

By the early 1980s, a growing tide of conservatism seemed to be sweeping the country. This included a push by evangelical, religious, and other traditional groups for a return to old-time sex morality. It is too early to know how successful these pressures to turn back the clock will be. However, Yankelovich (1981), in an analysis of a number of recent national surveys, concludes that only 20 percent of the adults in the United States hold such conservative views. This small group, which tends to be older and from rural and, in some instances, low educational and occupational background, constitutes what has been called by its leaders the Moral Majority. Its members are unlikely to actually influence sex role and sex behavior mores, Yankelovich suggests, because 80 percent of the population surveyed hold views strongly in favor of freedom of choice in respect to the sexual (including the sex role) aspects of their lives. Although there is a certain amount of yearning for the "good old days" of family warmth and security, the great majority of people do not want to give up their present freedoms in order to achieve stronger family ties (Yankelovich, 1981).

Geography

Place of residence seems to have no effect on adolescent sex activity. Moreover, high rates of nonmarital intercourse are found for those adolescent girls whose parents have moved a large number of times.

Socioeconomic Status

It is becoming increasingly clear that low socioeconomic status of parents is strongly associated with early age of nonmarital intercourse for adolescent girls (Zelnik et al., 1982). This is especially true for blacks. For instance, Zelnik and Kantner (1977) found that black females whose fathers were college graduates had nonmarital coitus rates similar to white girls of the same status. Vener, Stewart, and Hager (1972) provide the best available evidence regarding the effects of socioeconomic status on white adolescents. Their 1970 study of high school students was carried out in three different kinds of communities: one in which the predominant socioeconomic status was professional–managerial; one that was mainly middle and upper-working class; and one that was semirural working class. Rates of nonmarital intercourse were quite different for both boys and girls in these three schools. There were considerably lower rates for boys in the professional–managerial community, especially at ages 13 and 14. The differences among girls were even greater. This was true at all ages, with 12 percent in the professional–managerial community being nonvirgins by age 17, compared with 27 percent in the upper-working class community and 40 percent in the semirural blue-collar community.

A recently completed 9-year follow-up study of young women and men who were in junior high school in 1970 provides interesting information regarding psychosocial influences on sexual behaviors (R. Jessor et al., 1983). The authors recognize some problems with their research: small sample of white, middle-class students from a Rocky Mountain university town; sample bias through volunteer nature of participation and thus sample loss in original 4-year study and to some extent in follow-up. Despite these problems, the findings are important for many reasons: It is the only longitudinal study of this kind; it is tied to crucial theoretical issues; and it has been carried out with consummate skill.

Analyses of their 1970–1972 data revealed that personality, perceived (social) environment, and behavioral factors were all significantly associated with virginity or nonvirginity status and timing of first intercourse (S. Jessor & Jessor, 1975). When the same groups of young people were studied in 1979, it was found that, over the 9-year period, psychological factors continued to play a large and statistically significant part in virginity–nonvirginity status and timing of first intercourse. Factors that were identified in 1970 continued to be of central importance in 1979, indicating a continuity of personality tendencies, over time, in affecting sexual (as well as other) behaviors and the effect of a wide range of psychosocial variables (far beyond specifically sexual ones) on sex behaviors, as maintained throughout this book.

Specifically, the factors revealed by the 1979 longitudinal data to be most significantly associated with early intercourse (age less than 18) are much the same as those identified in 1975. They are:

Personality
  Higher value on independence and lower value on academic achievement
  Lower expectation of academic achievement
  Greater social criticism and alienation
  More tolerant attitudes toward deviance
  Less religiosity
  Greater positive than negative reasons for engaging in problem behavior (or transition to nonvirginity)
Perceived Environment
  Less parental and greater friends' controls
  Less compatibility between friends' and parents' expectations
  Greater perceived parental approval for the problem behavior
  Greater perceived prevalence of social models who engage in problem behavior (early coitus)
Behavior System
  Greater involvement in other problem behavior
  Less involvement in such conventional behavior as going to church and doing well in school

Some members of the study population were still virgins at ages 23–25. Interesting findings were obtained concerning significantly differentiating characteristics of the virgin group. This small group of women and men tend to be highly conventional, especially in terms of personal and social controls and experiences with drugs and alcohol. They tend to be marriage oriented, religious, committed to education, and conservative in sociopolitical outlook. They see themselves as having less capability in cross-sex relationships and being less attractive physically. These same characteristics could be noted in this virgin group when they were first studied in 1970.

Another important finding was that the relative earliness versus lateness of initial intercourse in a population of the kind studied is unrelated to a wide range of later sexual attitudes, satisfactions, stresses, or behaviors in young adulthood. However, the authors of the research fail to provide analyses of what marital and parental effects, if any, can be identified with early or late transition from virginity to nonvirginity. (See Chapter 16 for independent case illustrations of many findings similar to those reported in the above study.)

Poverty and Racism

Black women between the ages of 15 and 19 are more likely than white ones to have nonmarital coitus. As shown in Table 5.4, Zelnik and Kantner found these higher rates in their nationwide surveys of 1971, 1976, and 1979. Thus, in 1979, around 65 percent of young black women in this age group reported having had sexual intercourse, whereas this was true for only 42 percent of the white respondents.

Particularly large racial differences were found for 15 year olds, with the rates being 41 percent for black girls and 18 percent for white girls. However, the rate of increase in coitus between 1971 and 1976 was considerably higher for the white study population than for the black. Whereas blacks in 1971 were more than twice as likely as whites to have had nonmarital intercourse, in 1979 they were 1.3 times as likely to have done so (Zelnik et al., 1982).

The combination of poverty and racism plays an important part in the higher rates of nonmarital intercourse among black teenagers (Udry et al., 1975). These two factors tend to breed attitudes that make it more possible to cope with the harsh situation of being poor and a victim of discrimination. Although black teenagers in low-income families, like most other adolescents, generally aspire to good jobs, adequate incomes, social respectability, pleasant homes, and a happy family life, their life experiences tend to force them to reshape their attitudes and expectancies. Many are apt to take on the life-styles that others around them have been forced to adopt. Attitudes of distrust, fatalism, hostility, anti-intellectualism, apathy, hopelessness, and alienation may develop. These attitudes are apt to have adverse effects on relations between the sexes, making them somewhat shallow and impermanent because the future is so dubious (Chilman, 1966; Ladner, 1971; Rainwater, 1970). Combined with extremely high unemployment for black males, these attitudes lead to lower marriage rates and a greater incidence of marriage breakdown. About half of low-income black teenagers have grown up in one-parent families, and marriage seems to them to be neither particularly viable nor desirable.

The inner-city environment is usually characterized by serious social disorganization, poverty, poor and crowded housing, and inadequate human services of all kinds. Nonmarital sex is prevalent, as are other forms of "deviant" behavior, on the part of both the residents and nonresidents who visit the area for illicit activities, including prostitution (Rainwater, 1970). Under these conditions, young people are exposed to sex in all its forms at a very young age, and parents have a near impossible task in attempting to control their children's behavior. This is especially true for boys, who so often lack a father in the home and who model themselves after a street culture that holds that males prove their virility by sexual exploits with a large number of women (Hammond & Ladner, 1968; Liebow, 1967; D. Schulz, 1969; Staples, 1973).

Although daughters and mothers value virginity until marriage and hope for "good steady husbands," most adolescent girls become involved in sex activity by the time they are 16 or 17, many at younger ages. If they are to go out with boys at all, such an involvement becomes virtually essential. Those girls who are educationally ambitious tend to seclude themselves socially and repress and deny their sexuality. They are backed in this by strong, controlling, achievement-oriented mothers (Ladner, 1971; D. Schulz, 1969).

Sex is viewed as a natural human behavior in the urban ghetto, and the double standard of sexual morality is far less prevalent. Therefore, sexually active females tend not to feel guilt about their behavior, as if they had done something wrong, but rather feel shame for their mistakes, particularly if they get pregnant (Rainwater, 1970).

The great majority of urban black adolescents from low-income families eventually become sexually active before marriage (Furstenberg, 1976; Zelnik & Kanter, 1980b). The life situation, needs for self-expression, the desire to be a real man or woman, and the forces of "fate" lead them to these behaviors. There are so few other ways for them to gain a sense of self-expression and status. Jobs are in short supply and low in status. (In 1982, it was estimated that youth unemployment was about 50 percent in the urban ghettos (Milwaukee Journal, 1982).) Schools are apt to be of poor quality, and education has little demonstrable payoff in terms of future employment.

The foregoing should not imply that low-income, black females are promiscuous. They are less likely than white teenagers to have had a number of sex partners, and they tend to have intercourse less frequently (Kantner & Zelnik, 1972). The fact that black females, on the average, start their sex activity when they are younger and that over twice as many have nonmarital intercourse by age 15 is probably owing in large part to the findings discussed above; most of these findings are derived from a number of small, anthropological studies of urban ghettos in a number of large American cities.

Although research is limited, it appears that poverty among white people breeds many of the same attitudes and behaviors sketched above. However, the effects of poverty on whites are not as severe, because they are not combined with the effects of racism. Kantner and Zelnik's surveys failed to reveal clear behavioral differences by income levels among whites, but it is probable that their income data were not highly reliable. Moreover, they failed to make sufficiently fine discriminations between various income, educational, and occupational levels of parents of adolescents.

A recent study (Rubin, 1976) of white, blue-collar families confirms earlier research and shows that many of these families also feel locked into a life of continuing deprivation, with little to look forward to in terms of higher education, rewarding jobs, happy marriages, and adequate income. To these families, too, there seems to be little use in deferring gratification and planning for the future. The findings of this study imply that nonmarital intercourse during adolescence is common. It is followed by early marriage, often to legitimate a pregnancy.

Religiosity

As shown in our discussion of attitudes toward sexual behavior, many studies, including those in the late 1970s, show that white adolescents who are committed to conservative religious beliefs are less likely to have early nonmarital coitus.

Biological Factors

Almost none of the social and psychological studies of nonmarital intercourse have inquired about the age at maturation of the respondents. This is an unfortunate oversight. In general, we know that the average age at puberty has declined in the past 30 years. This could surely be a factor in the higher rates of intercourse among young teenagers today, though it probably would not affect the sharp rise since the mid-1960s.

Differences in age at maturation seem to have an effect on when individuals become sexually active. For instance, Kinsey and his associates (1948) and Chilman (1963) found that early-maturing boys became sexually involved earlier than late-maturing ones. Similar, but less strong, tendencies were found for girls. Differences in age at maturation may also explain, to some extent, the higher rates of coitus among young black females, because more black than white females have been found to reach menarche at age 10 or 11. Presser (1978) found that age at first intercourse appeared to be related to age at puberty for black but not for white girls. The meaning of this finding is unclear and calls for more careful research on this topic. Data about the age at puberty of black compared with white males, seem to be missing, and this too calls for further study.

Individuals may have inherent differences in their responses to sexual stimulation. For instance, Kinsey and his associates (1948) found wide differences in self-perceived sex drive among their male respondents. Recall, too, the findings of Money and Tucker (1975) about the effects of different endocrine levels on sex development and behavior, as well as the results of Kagan and Moss (1962) regarding the lower levels of sex activity among males whose tendencies toward passivity persisted from early childhood on. (See Chapter 2.)

Table 5.6 summarizes the research findings discussed in the foregoing pages concerning factors apparently related to premarital intercourse among adolescent males and females. It will be helpful to compare these findings with the individual case studies in Chapter 16.

Adolescent Health and Nonmarital Intercourse

The rate of gonorrhea among teenagers tripled between 1956 and 1975. The Center for Disease Control estimated in 1975 that there are upwards of 2.6 million cases of gonorrhea annually. The rate for women has been rising faster than that for men. The highest rates are found among 20–24 year olds, followed closely by rates for 15–19 year olds. The teenage rate of gonorrhea was about 12.16 per 1000 for 15–19 year olds in 1975.

Other medical problems that are sexually transmitted are infections in the genitals. These infections are thought to be on the increase. Some evidence also exists that the development of cervical cancer is more likely to occur among females who have had coitus during early adolescence. The use of either the condom or the diaphragm may help to prevent the eventual development of cervical cancer (Baldwin, 1976).

Male–Female Differences with Respect to
Adolescent Nonmarital Coitus

Some comments are in order regarding male and female sexuality because we have shown considerable differences between the sexes with respect to their sexual behavior and attitudes during their teen years. (See also earlier

TABLE 5.6. Summary of Major Factors Apparently Associated with Nonmarital Intercourse among Adolescents

Factors	Males	Females
Social Situation		
Father having less than a college education	unknown	yes, especially for blacks
Low level of religiousness	yes	yes
Norms favoring equality between the sexes	probably	yes
Permissive sexual norms of the larger society	yes	yes
Racism and poverty	yes	yes
Migration from rural to urban areas	unknown	yes
Peer-group pressure	yes	not clear
Lower social class	yes (probably)	yes (probably)
Sexually active friends	yes	yes
Single-parent (probably low-income) family	unknown	yes
Residence in western states	unknown	yes (for whites)
Psychological		
Use of drugs and alcohol	yes	no
Low self-esteem	no[a]	yes[a]
Desire for affection	no[a]	yes[a]
Low education goals and poor educational achievement	yes	yes
Alienation	no[a]	yes[a]
Deviant attitudes	yes	yes
High social criticism	no[a]	yes[a]
Permissive attitudes of parents	yes[a]	yes[a]
Strained parent–child relationships and little parent–child communication	yes	yes
Going steady; being in love	yes[a]	yes[a]
Steady love partner with permissive attitudes	—	—
Risk-taking attitudes	yes[a]	yes[a]
Passivity and dependence	no[a]	yes[a]
Aggression; high levels of activity	yes	no[a]
High degree of interpersonal skills with opposite sex	yes[a]	no[a]
Lack of self-assessment of psychological readiness	no[a]	yes[a]
Biological		
Older than 16	yes	yes
Early puberty	yes	yes

[a] Variables supported by only one or two small studies. Other variables are supported by a number of investigations. The major studies on which this table is based are: Cvetkovich & Grote (1975); DeLameter & MacCorquodale (1979); Fox (1980); Furstenberg (1976); S. Jessor & Jessor (1975); Kantner & Zelnik (1972); Presser (1978); B. Schulz, 1977; Simon et al. (1972); Sorenson (1973); Udry et al. (1975); Zelnik (1980); Zelnik & Kantner (1977); Zelnik et al. (1982).

discussions of this subject in Chapters 1 and 2.) Douvan and Adelson (1966) found in their survey in the late 1950s that adolescent girls became deeply involved in their love–sex relationships. Their studies have shown that girls, more than boys, are bound up as whole personalities with sex. Sexual stimulation is often seen by girls as threatening, producing conflicts with their value systems, and not related to them as total persons.

Bardwick (1971) reports that a study of sexually active University of Michigan women students revealed that most were dependent on their male partners, found their sense of identity bound up in them, and saw their sexual liaison as mostly being a way of gaining intimacy and holding their men. Numerous other investigations revealed that adolescent girls particularly value sex as a way of feeling close to their partners; they tend to prize the relationship far more than the physical aspects of sex.

Then, too, Lowenthal, Thurnher, and Chiriboga (1974) found in their study of four life stages that adolescent girls tended to be virtually planless, their lives dependent on the males whom they attracted. Much has been written about the faulty socialization of girls for this kind of dependency. Faulty as the socialization may be, the fact remains that many females put aside their own independent life goals when they become sexually and affectionately involved with a male.

Masters and Johnson (1966, 1969) found that adolescent girls are less orgasmic than older women. There is a wider variety both within individual females and among females, in terms of orgasmic response, than among males. Anxiety, value conflicts, and inappropriate stimulation techniques are particularly apt to inhibit the female sex response. Of course, Kinsey and his associates (1953) long ago found that females were slow in being awakened to their full sex response potential and accomplished this mainly in a close love–sex partnership. Sorensen (1973) and Konopka (1967) also report that many of the girls they studied failed to reach orgasm in their sex relationships.*

Males, on the other hand, are genitally oriented toward sex from early childhood on and reach the height of their self-perceived sex drive at ages 15 or 16 (Kinsey et al., 1948). Douvan and Adelson (1966) also found in their study that there is a rapid increase in the sex drive for male adolescents, a drive that is biologically specific and difficult, if not impossible, to deny.

---

* In discussions with counseling personnel in the adolescent unit of the Milwaukee Planned Parenthood Clinic, it was learned that adolescent girls frequently complain that they do not enjoy sex and fail to reach orgasm. Their partners, boys of their own age, reportedly are so quick in their arousal and orgasmic response that the experience is often seen as being exploitative and frustrating by the girls. This clinic is helping girls reach a better understanding of their own response potential and communicate their needs to their partners.

Currently changing social norms, growing out of vast changes in society itself, are advocating different attitudes and values about female sexuality. The female body is being reeroticized as a result of the widespread availability of contraceptives and abortion. Liberated women are taking the lead in asking for equal sexual, as well as other, rights. These new attitudes and norms are creating new socialization experiences for both males and females. It is too early to know how they will affect male and female sex behavior in the future, although present trends seem to be toward increasing permissiveness for both sexes. Far more difficult but more important to learn is the effect that these behaviors will have on the mental and physical health of both males and females, on their interpersonal relationships, and on their future functioning as marital partners and as parents.

Comment

A personal comment may be appropriate here. It seems important to examine the values that appear to underlie at least some aspects of the sexual revolution. Of particular concern is an apparently growing attitude that casual sex is perfectly acceptable, that one can engage in both recreational and relational sex, and that any kind of sex between consenting partners is acceptable as long as no one gets hurt. But how can one assess in advance the hurts that may come from intimate involvements treated in a superficial way and from involvements that may become wearisome for one partner but not the other?

It is difficult for the writer to believe that one can engage equally in casual recreational and committed relational sex, as some writers in the field prescribe. Advocacy of sex as play in a consumer, leisure society seems to be a childish approach to a basically serious subject, although playful sex with one's committed partner is a different matter. As discussed in Chapters 1 and 2, sex relations between two people offer the ultimate opportunity for deeply intimate interpersonal relationships. Real intimacy becomes impossible unless responsible commitment, mutual trust, and shared identities are involved.

Both males and females have their special strengths and their special vulnerabilities. The strengths can be uniquely supported and the vulnerabilities uniquely assuaged in an enduring, intimate love–sex relationship. In an age of insecurity and depersonalization, these relationships become particularly important as a way of validating one's basic humanity.

The acceptance of casual sex seems to be linked to an easy acceptance of sex relationships for young adolescents. Do such relationships inhibit further growth of adolescents as independent, competent young people who have worked out their own sense of selfhood? Do early sex involvements, which are necessarily egocentric and immature, prevent later partnerships of greater depth and maturity? Or do such relationships perhaps help in the gradual development of a more mature sexuality?

These are puzzling questions. We cannot presume to know the answers. (Although clues from at least one study now in progress suggest that early nonmarital intercourse may have negative effects on the maturation of certain cognitive, emotional, and interpersonal skills.*) Perhaps we can find some of the answers by working with young people in sensitive ways to help them assess their own experiences and clarify their own values. This search for values has particular predicaments in the present day, when marriage has far less rationale than it once did; when births can be, and need to be, controlled; when females are moving toward more equal rights and self-support opportunities; and when all traditions are being questioned.

As we ponder the possible effects of greater sexual freedom for adolescents, it is important to consider also the apparent impact of social prescriptions that seek to prevent the participation of young people in coitus until their marriage. Although highly permissive attitudes may lead to widespread nonmarital coitus among adolescents and youths, restrictive attitudes can lead to such behaviors as early, ill-considered marriage, sexual guilt and anxiety, and a return to the double standard of sex morality and to secretive sex.

Perhaps the observations expressed here are particularly feminine, but this may lend balance to a field in which men have published much more than women. It seems as if there is a trend toward "masculinizing" female sexual attitudes and behaviors, and there may be a danger in this. Traditionally, women have brought their interpersonal values and skills to the mate relationship and have thereby helped their partners achieve fuller expression of their feelings. Denial of these feminine values and skills may endanger the quality of partnerships between the sexes.

Viewpoints given here also reflect a humanistic and romantic philosophy. This philosophy may not be appropriate for an increasingly collectivist, rational, and mechanized society. It may not apply well to popular concepts of self-expression and freedom. On the other hand, this philosophy may enrich these concepts, since putting a high valuation on human intimacy can infinitely enhance the rewards of self-expression and shared freedoms between partners who explore together their human sexuality in all its aspects.

The 1970s were known as a period of extreme narcissism. "Look out for number one" was a popular catchword of the time. By the end of this decade, there was growing awareness that such a philosophy could lead to devastating loss of psychological intimacy and trust in human relationships—a corrosive, terrifying loneliness. There was a movement away from

* George Cvetkovich, personal communication, 1977.

earlier therapeutic "wisdom"—take responsibility only for yourself—to a rediscovery of the ancient dictum of acting responsibly toward others as well as the self, being "thy brother's (and sister's) keeper," "doing unto others as you would have others do unto you." The rediscovery of the psychological wisdom of these ancient sayings is also stressed by Yankelovich (1981) in his recent writings. He points out further that the constriction of employment opportunities and the rising cost of living puts severe constraints on the economic base that served as a foundation for devotion to self-fulfillment without regard to environmental realities.

COHABITATION

Introduction

There has been a striking increase in cohabitation* among young people, as well as older men and women, since the mid-1960s. Much more is known about the prevalence and apparent causes, as well as consequences, of this life-style among college students than for any other group, including non-college youths and younger adolescents. Research to date has centered on college populations, largely as a matter of convenience to the researchers. A highly competent review of this research is presented by Eleanor Macklin (1978), who has taken leadership in stimulating studies in this field. The highlights of her review are presented here.

Trends

Macklin reminds us that in 1926 Judge Ben B. Lindsay promoted the idea of "companionate marriage," a legalized relationship involving no children, with the option of divorce by mutual consent. In 1929, Bertrand Russell carried this idea a step further in arguing that such a relationship required no legal structure if a man and a woman chose to live together without children. These concepts, part of the sex revolution of the 1920s, were strongly opposed by the majority of people, and little was heard of these proposals until the mid-1960s, a time that we have already identified as a period of enormous social change. (See especially Chapter 3.)

In 1966 Margaret Mead (Mead, 1966) proposed a two-stage arrangement of marriage. Couples should first enter into an "individual marriage"—a licensed union in which two individuals would be committed to each other as long as they wished to stay together, but without children. The second

---

* Cohabitation is variously defined. In general, it means that two unrelated persons are living together in an intimate relationship, without a legal contract.

stage, parental marriage, would be explicitly directed to forming a family and could not be entered into without a prior satisfactory individual first-stage marriage; divorce would be more difficult. This proposal created a storm of conflicting opinions, with many expressing the belief that first-stage marriages were immoral, unworkable, and exploitative (especially on the part of the male).

The apparent causes of increased cohabitation are seen as residing in overall social and economic changes, structural changes (such as changes in social and housing regulations on campuses), and the psychological characteristics of the individuals involved. It is striking that so many colleges and universities had adopted permissive attitudes toward the cohabitation of undergraduates by the late 1960s when one considers that undergraduate marriage was seen by academic administrators as a dubious arrangement in the late 1950s and early 1960s.

It is estimated from the research that as of 1975 about one-fourth of undergraduate students across the country were living or had lived in a cohabitation relationship. No data seem to be available for noncollege adolescents, ages 15–19. Glick reported in 1975 that 1960 and 1970 census figures showed a "spectacular" eightfold increase occurred during the 1960s in the number of household heads who were reported as living apart from relatives while sharing their living quarters with an unrelated adult partner (roommate or friend) of the opposite sex (Glick, 1975). These figures had shown another marked increase by 1976.

The 1976 special census survey on the marital status and living arrangements of the population showed that "1.3 million persons lived in two-person households in which the household head shared the living quarters with an unrelated adult of the opposite sex" (U.S. Department of Commerce, 1977, p. 5). Over two-thirds of the females and about one-fifth of the males in this situation were under age 25. However, the great majority of people who lived outside of a family structure reported that they were living alone.

Attitudes toward Cohabitation

A number of recent studies have assessed college student attitudes toward cohabitation. These show that only about one-fourth of college students oppose this arrangement. As in the case of attitudes toward nonmarital intercourse, most college students accept the principle of cohabitation in the context of a strong, affectionate, preferably monogamous relationship. There is some evidence, again as in the case of nonmarital coitus, that males as a group may be more accepting of cohabitation than are females and may not feel the need for as strong an emotional involvement before cohabiting.

Religiosity is associated with negative attitudes toward cohabitation. Moreover, somewhat as Jessor and Jessor (1975) found in their study of virgin and nonvirgin high school and college students, these studies have shown that females who approved of cohabitation were more likely to see their mothers as being rejecting and as holding nontraditional sex role attitudes. Young women who approved of cohabitation were also more likely to characterize themselves as independent, outgoing, or aggressive.

A number of earlier studies showed that parents are far less likely than their children to approve of cohabitation and that these differences in attitudes are often a source of intergenerational conflict and poor communication. However, by the late 1970s, the majority of parents surveyed expressed approval of cohabitation among college students who were "in love" (Yankelovich, 1981).

Nature of the Cohabitation Relationship

Macklin concludes in her research review that there is no such thing as a typical cohabitation relationship. These relationships may range from casual (a small proportion of them), to committed but not directed toward marriage, to committed and anticipatory of marriage. At least four researchers have concluded that cohabitation on the college campus is merely an added step in the courtship process—a kind of living out of going steady. Most of the cohabiting young people studied favored eventual marriage to someone but felt they were not yet personally ready for marriage or not ready to commit themselves to the person they were living with.

Cohabitants Compared to Noncohabitants

Cohabiting persons were more likely than others to be liberal in attitudes toward sexuality, politics, and drugs, and to have friends who were nonvirgins. They were also more likely to have had a number of previous sex partners. They tended to be majoring in such fields as the arts and social sciences.

Cohabiting students have been found not to differ from others in perceived success of parental marriage, parental education or income, academic performance, and attitudes toward marriage. In general, it appears that campus norms are more influential in student cohabitation than are the particular characteristics of the students themselves. (However, students tend to choose a particular college partly because of their own or their parents' personal values.)

On the other hand, Macklin writes that research to date strongly suggests that, as cohabitation becomes a more common part of the culture, the majority of college students who experience a love relationship will probably experience a cohabitation relationship at some point in their lives.

Couples who cohabit generally place a high value on interpersonal commitment and the quality of their relationships. This may be especially true of females, although the research findings are somewhat conflicting on this latter point. Although cohabitation has been advocated by some as providing an opportunity for more equalitarian sex roles, studies of married compared with cohabiting couples reveal that in both kinds of relationships sex roles tend to follow fairly traditional lines; in other words, the females generally do most of the housework.

Although the majority of cohabiting couples who have been studied maintain a sexually exclusive, monogamous relationship, a small group subscribes to the concept of "open monogamy." Following other advocates of open marriage, this group holds that heterosexual relationships should be deromanticized, that they should be honest and realistic and dedicated to the growth potential of each individual, who may need a number of relationships for his or her fulfillment. One study found that, although the majority of couples subscribed to this attitude, only about 8 percent actually engaged in nonexclusive relationships.

Research concerning self-perceived satisfactions among young married and cohabiting couples reveals that their perceptions of relationship satisfactions are very much the same. Studies also show that married couples who have lived together before marriage and those who have not appear to be similar in their marital adjustments. The degree to which both married and cohabiting couples find their relationships highly satisfying appears to depend more on their capacity for forming close, loving, interpersonal relationships than on the legal status of their partnerships. (For similar findings of large bodies of research concerning marital satisfactions, see Chapter 10.)

One study dealt with the dissolution of the cohabitation relationship. This research revealed that women, far more than men, were likely to say that it ended because of interpersonal incompatibilities, especially in terms of feeling dominated, losing personal identity, being bored with the partner, fearing own dependency on partner, and having incompatible sex needs. Although this is a small study, the female complaints are familiar and have been shown as female-perceived difficulties in partnerships with males in other studies of the male–female relationship during the college years and at other life stages (see, for example, Bardwick, 1971; Lowenthal et al., 1974; Sheehy, 1976).

Most students who have been involved in cohabitation relationships report that they have found them valuable in promoting their own personal growth and maturity. It appears that there are no more negative effects from cohabitation than from any other intense interpersonal relationship. Such a relationship is bound to have its conflicts and griefs as well as its harmonies and joys.

Interestingly, none of the research about cohabitation among college students seems to have included such subjects as contraceptive use, premarital pregnancies, abortion, or the birth of children. This strikes the writer as a rather startling oversight.

CHAPTER 6

Contraceptive Use

INTRODUCTION

In the last chapter, we saw that about 50 percent or more of young people have engaged in nonmarital intercourse before age 18 and that this rate probably rises to about 75 percent or more by age 20 or 21. Many of these sexually active young people fail to use any kind of contraceptive; even more of them fail to use effective contraceptives and to use them consistently. This chapter reviews social and psychological research related to the topic of adolescent contraceptive behaviors and the possible reasons for these behaviors.

Prevalence of Contraceptive Use

Only about 45 percent of sexually active adolescent females studied in 1976 and 1979 said they used any form of contraceptive at their first intercourse. About 33 percent had never used any form of birth control, and another 33 percent said they always used a method of birth control when they had coitus (Zelnik & Kantner, 1980b).

Only a few local studies of contraceptive use by males have been made. Cvetkovich and Grote (1976) found that 89 percent of the black males and 69 percent of the white males in their high school study population said they had had unprotected intercourse at least once. Similar findings were obtained by Finkel and Finkel (1975).

CONTRACEPTIVE METHODS

National surveys in 1976 and 1979 of a probability sample of young women between the ages of 15 and 19 showed that, although the proportion of contraceptive users among the sexually active increased somewhat between 1976 and 1979 (always used a contraceptive was 29 percent in 1976 and 34 percent in 1979), use of effective contraceptives (such as the pill) declined from 48 percent of contraceptors in 1976 to 41 percent in 1979. The use of condoms remained about the same (23 percent in both years), and the use of withdrawal increased, primarily for whites (19 percent of the methods used). Such methods as the IUD, the diaphragm, douche, and rhythm represented 6 percent or fewer of the methods used. Hence, the main method shift was from the pill, with its superior contraceptive effectiveness, to withdrawal, which has a lower effectiveness rating (Zelnik & Kantner, 1980b). As we shall discuss in more detail in later chapters, a rising proportion of adolescent girls became nonmaritally pregnant in the comparison years of 1971, 1976, and 1977 (8.5 percent of 15–19 year olds in 1971; 16.2 in 1979). Fewer than 20 percent of the 1979 study population said they had intended to become pregnant, and over 33 percent terminated their pregnancies with abortions (Zelnik & Kantner, 1980b).

These findings give rise to numerous concerns and questions. The central question is, of course, why do so many sexually active teenagers fail to use any contraceptive or fail to use the most effective contraceptives when the vast majority of them say they do not want to become pregnant?

Other important findings about contraceptive methods are reported by Zelnik and Kantner (1980b), who found that about 40 percent of sexually active females of both races depended on male methods of contraception in 1979. Because the majority of adolescent males seemed to be markedly inconsistent and perhaps unconcerned about contraceptive use, there seems to be a central problem with respect to their attitudes and behaviors and the reliance of so many adolescent girls on the contraceptive vigilance of boys (Brown et al., 1975; Finkel & Finkel, 1975; Kantner & Zelnik, 1972; Zelnik & Kantner, 1980b; Sorensen, 1973). If the few available studies are correct in their findings and can be generalized, a particular problem seems to reside with the contraceptive behavior of black males (Finkel & Finkel, 1975; Cvetkovich & Grote, 1976), especially because 80–90 percent of these males are sexually active by age 16, as reported in Chapter 5.

Variables associated with the failure of adolescents to use contraceptives at all or to use effective contraceptives consistently are revealed in a number of studies made during the 1970s (Cvetkovich & Grote, 1975; DeLameter & MacCorquodale, 1979; Finkel & Finkel, 1975; Fox & Inazu, 1980; Furstenberg, 1976, 1980; Goldsmith et al., 1972; Hornick et al., 1979; Jorgenson, et al., 1980; Ladner, 1971; Lindemann, 1974; Luker, 1975; Miller, 1976; Presser, 1977; Rosen, Hudson & Martindale, 1976; Shah et al., 1975; Zelnik & Kantner, 1974, 1980a; Zelnik, Kantner & Ford, 1983).

FACTORS ASSOCIATED WITH FAILURE TO USE EFFECTIVE CONTRACEPTIVES

Summary of Factors

The demographic variables associated with the failure to use effective contraceptives include age lower than 18, single status, low socioeconomic status, minority group membership, nonattendance at college, and fundamentalist Protestant affiliation. Among the situational variables are not being in a steady, committed relationship; not having experienced a pregnancy; having intercourse sporadically and without prior planning; contraceptives not available at the moment of need; being in a high-stress situation; not having ready access to a free, confidential family planning service that does not require parental consent; lack of communication with parents regarding contraceptives; and poor mother–daughter relationship. The psychological variables include desiring a pregnancy and high fertility values; ignorance of pregnancy risks and of family planning services; attitudes of fatalism, powerlessness, alienation, incompetence, and trusting to luck; passive, dependent, traditional female role attitudes; high levels of anxiety and low ego strength; lack of acceptance of the reality of one's own sex behavior (e.g., thinking coitus will not occur); poor communication skills about sex and contraceptives; risk-taking, pleasure-oriented attitudes; fear of contraceptive side effects and possible infertility; and wrong assumptions about the safe time of the menstrual cycle.

Demographic Factors

The part played by demographic variables, including socioeconomic status, race, and ethnicity, are not shown with sufficient clarity in the above summary. However, research reveals that poverty status often breeds attitudes of fatalism, powerlessness, alienation, and a sense of personal incompetence and hopelessness in respect to striving for high educational and occupational goals. This is especially apt to be true when racism combined with poverty reduces one's life chances (Billingsley, 1970; Ladner, 1971; Rainwater, 1970; Stack, 1974; Staples, 1973). As shown above, these attitudes are also associated with failure to use effective contraceptives. Actually, data are incomplete on these points, especially for the various Spanish-speaking and Native American groups. Recent data show that 36 percent of sexually active black adolescent girls use no contraceptives compared to 24 percent of the whites (Zelnik & Kantner 1980b).

Psychological Factors

The most frequent reason given by sexually active adolescents for not using contraceptives is: "I thought I would be lucky and not get pregnant"

(Kantner & Zelnik, 1972; Luker, 1975; Miller, 1976; Shah et al., 1975; Sorensen, 1973). There is a certain amount of validity to this viewpoint, especially among young adolescents. As remarked earlier, many are not fertile until they are a year or so past menarche. However, having coitus without contraception cannot be assumed to be safe.

Adolescents who do not use contraceptives, or fail to use them consistently, have been found in several studies to hold fatalistic attitudes: to have strong feelings of powerlessness or alienation and to feel that life is controlled by external events (Rotter's test of locus of control) (Fox, 1975; MacDonald, 1970). Similar results have been obtained in research with adults in many parts of the world, as well as in the United States (Bauman & Udry, 1972; Chilman, 1968).

A low sense of personal competence and a passive orientation toward life are also associated with fatalistic attitudes. A number of studies show that these attitudes are linked to poor contraceptive use (Cvetovich & Grote, 1976; Rosen, Martindale & Grisdela, 1976; Steinhoff, 1976). Similar findings have been obtained in small studies with adults (Keller et al., 1970; Rodgers & Ziegler, 1968).

Traditional attitudes toward the female role include a passive, dependent approach to male–female relationships. Fox (1975) found that college women who failed to use effective contraceptives consistently were more apt to hold traditional sex role attitudes. Rosen, Martindale, and Grisdela (1976) obtained similar findings for women who failed to use contraceptives at all. Risk-taking attitudes are also associated with poor contraceptive use as found by Cvetkovich and Grote (1976) and by Shah, Zelnik, and Kantner (1975).

The foregoing attitudes—fatalism, passivity, a sense of powerlessness, feelings of incompetence, and risk taking—all seem to be conceptually related to low levels of ego development and to lack of ego strength. (See Chapter 2.) These traits are similar to those observed by Miller (1976) who conducted in-depth interviews with two predominantly white, matched groups of sexually active young women (ages 17–30). One group used contraceptives and had never been pregnant; another group was seeking abortions. He observed a circular effect of the subjects' assessments of pregnancy probability. When they saw pregnancy probability as high, they became anxious and tended to use contraceptives. When anxiety about pregnancy was low, many did not use them. Pregnancy anxiety was complicated by anxiety about their own sexuality and about contraceptives. As others have found in studies of anxiety, when it was moderate, most of the subjects took action and behaved realistically (in this case, used effective contraceptives); when it became high, they tended to be immobilized. Combined anxieties about pregnancy, sexuality, and contraceptives tended to overwhelm the subjects and block effective action.

Miller saw a typical sequence of contraceptive use. In the first 1–6 months of an affair, the women did not use contraceptives. They were anxious about their relationships with their boyfriends, the chances of pregnancy, their own sexual behaviors, and general issues of family and independence. They tended to suppress a number of their worries. A missed period, often as a result of anxiety, mobilized some to start using contraceptives. Others, finding the missed period was a false scare, became desensitized to the possibility of pregnancy, which left them feeling that they were safe and did not need contraceptives.

Miller (1976) noted personality differences among his subjects in the way they handled anxiety. Some coped with it realistically, and others denied possible dangers. He observed the great importance to contraceptive use of self-esteem, future orientation, and ability to control impulses.

In a 1973a article, Miller writes in more detail about his concept of ego stress and resulting lower ego capacities as an inhibiting factor in contraceptive use. He observes that stressful events, such as the breakup with a partner, approaching marriage, and abortion with its resulting guilt and ambivalence, frequently undermine realistic contraceptive use.

Cvetkovich and Grote (1975) stress the role of cognitive development in the failure of many sexually active adolescents to use contraceptives. As shown in Chapter 2, cognitive development in early adolescence tends to be egocentric. Adolescents fantasize an imaginary audience. In performing for this audience, they have fears about their own sexuality; they find it hard to admit to themselves and others that they are becoming sexually adult. They also have their personal fable and tend to think of themselves as immune to danger. The fable may include imagined sterility or the thought that no particular incident of intercourse will result in pregnancy. Other aspects of this stage of cognitive development include poor ability to understand a situation conceptually and to foresee possible future effects of present actions.

Egocentric attitudes in early adolescence are also noted by the theorists who wrote of both personality and moral development. (See Chapter 2.) This egocentrism may be observed among those adolescent boys who feel that they have no contraceptive responsibility, rather that it should be left up to the girl (Cvetkovich & Grote, 1975; Sorensen, 1973).

Also, as shown in Chapter 2, theorists in the psychoanalytic tradition see early adolescence as a time of such severe personality disorganization that the young person would lack the ego strength to deal realistically with his or her own sexual behavior and rationally plan for contraceptive protection.

Early adolescence also is a time when impulse control is low and pleasure seeking is highly valued. A number of studies show that nonuse of contraceptives is associated with a pleasure orientation toward sex and the desire not to let planning interfere with spontaneity in sex relationships (Cvetko-vich & Grote, 1976; Luker, 1975; Reichelt, 1976; Shah et al., 1975). The feeling that planning will spoil the sex relationship is frequently expressed by females. Some commentators on this finding (most of whom are male) theorize that this attitude means that females who feel this way lack a com-mitment to their own sexuality (Miller, 1976; Gagnon and Simon, 1973). This seems to be an overly masculine and sexist interpretation of the issue. The concept of commitment to sexuality seems to be far more masculine than feminine. It is quite possible that males, for whom sex tends to be more impersonal and exclusively physical than for females, promote this theory partly because it makes eminent sense from their own perspective and partly because it would provide them more opportunities for nonrelational coitus (see Chapters 1 and 2).

The findings of Goldsmith, Gabrielson, and Gabrielson (1972) to the effect that girls who use contraceptives are more likely than others to say they find intercourse extremely enjoyable, are often quoted as proof that commitment to sexuality promotes contraceptive use. However, this study has many serious weaknesses in its design, analysis, and interpretation. It clearly fails to prove a causal connection between contraceptive use and commitment to sexuality.

There are numerous reasons that females are less likely than males to be-come committed to sexuality for its own sake, as shown in Chapter 2. Rather, they are likely to become committed to a particular person with whom they have intercourse in the context of a love relationship.

Failure to accept one's own sexuality seems to be a better concept than lack of commitment to sexuality, with respect to the difficulties that many females have in coming to terms with their own sex behavior. Because most have been socialized to protect themselves against the sexuality of males, to preserve their own virginity until marriage, and to fear a nonmarital preg-nancy, they may have problems in facing the fact that they are violating internalized norms and taking pregnancy risks.

Through having sexual relations, their sexual response potential tends to be stimulated. Sexual "needs," of which many young women were previ-ously unaware, become activated. These needs, plus the intimacy of the relationship, increase the female's dependency on her partner and her active fears that he may leave her, especially because she has become a "bad" woman and unworthy of love. She is fearful, now that she is sexually and emotionally aroused and is dependent on a love–sex relationship, that she may become promiscuous if her partner should leave her. His leaving would further reduce her chances of being loved and respected.

She is apt to be right in her belief that her male partner still holds double-standard values, even though he may say he believes in sexual freedom for women as well as men. He may have reservations about feeling love toward her after she becomes a nonvirgin. He is also likely to have problems in accepting his own sexual behavior with respect to her. Feeling guilty, he may blame her for taking part in the relationship. (Though males may not have difficulty in accepting their sexuality, they well may have difficulty in accepting some forms of their sex behavior.) If the girl feels that the boy has reservations about accepting her as both sexually active and lovable, then her conflicts about accepting her own sexuality are apt to be increased.

Because adolescents of both sexes have not yet achieved their own identity and have not yet freed themselves of strong dependency needs, a sexual relationship that involves responsibilities for one's own behavior and a responsible commitment to another person is hard to achieve. The aroused dependencies of the girl probably make her feel that the boy should take care of her in every way, including taking responsibility for contraceptive protection. The boy is apt to feel overwhelmed by the girl's dependence and to resent her expectations for protection, including contraceptive protection.

The inability of young adolescents to meet each other's dependency needs in a relationship presents further problems to both of them. Most who engage in such a relationship are likely to feel they cannot discuss it with their parents. Because of their behavior, they can no longer be so dependent on parents as they once were. The "falling in love" process always requires a loosening of ties between parents and children; this process is seen by psychoanalytic theorists as being particularly complex, as shown in Chapter 2. Although adolescents want to achieve independence from parents, the winning of independence is painful. It requires a period of trial and error and cannot be done abruptly without causing deep hurt.

It is probable that relatively few parents can calmly accept nonmarital intercourse without a marriage commitment on the part of their children, especially their young daughters. Therefore, it seems likely that many sexually active young adolescents feel they must keep their sex behaviors secret from their parents. They may well think that they cannot depend on them for help in this relationship, including help with contraceptives. The inability of many sexually active adolescents to depend on parents increases their dependency problems in their partner relationships.

In recent years, however, parents may have become more open and communicative with their youngsters about sexual behavior and contraception. The enormous publicity by the mass media on the topic of the "epidemic of teenage pregnancy" surely alerted many parents to the problem and probably increased the recognition of many that they should discuss contraceptives with their teenagers, at least with their daughters.

A 1978 mother–daughter communication study of a random sample of young women in selected Detroit high schools showed that about 70 percent of both mothers and daughters said that they had communicated at least a few times about both intercourse and contraception. Fox and Inazu (1980) found that white mothers who were high in religiosity were most likely to discuss sex and sex morality with their daughters. A long-standing good mother–daughter relationship and open communication about many topics was predictive of frequent discussions of sexual subjects during the daughter's teen years. Rather surprisingly, the daughters, more so than the mothers, said they found it difficult to talk about sexually sensitive subjects.

Mother–daughter communication about birth control rose from about 18 percent of the cases when the daughter was age 12.5 years to 66 percent by the time she was 16. Daughters who had discussed birth control with their mothers had more responsible and knowledgeable attitudes on the subject and were more likely to use contraceptives; a finding also obtained by Furstenberg (1976).

The foregoing discussion of adolescent sexuality largely applies to white and to middle-class black teenagers. Cultural patterns tend to be different for some low-income blacks. (See Chapter 5.)

Some of the comments about problems that young females may have in accepting their own sexuality are illustrated by Luker (1975), who conducted an in-depth interview study of over 500 young women who were applicants for abortions and had been contraceptive risk takers. This research provides important insights into the female point of view. Luker's major thesis is that the risk-taking behavior of these women was essentially rational and that they had reasons for their decision not to use a contraceptive or to use ineffective ones at last intercourse. Essentially, according to Luker, these women used a costs–benefits decision-making approach weighing the costs and benefits of effective contraceptive use against the costs and benefits of a possible pregnancy. Much of this reasoning was not rational in the ordinary intellectual sense, but it was rational in the personal and emotional sense. The women identified their goals and major desires and operated in such a way as to enhance the probability of achieving them. Luker details costs, as summarized below.

1.   *Acknowledgment costs.* The psychic costs are those of acknowledging that one is actually having intercourse.

2.   *Planning costs.* The psychic costs of planning ahead to have coitus are particularly disturbing to those who are not in a continuing, committed relationship in which intercourse is naturally expected by both partners. Despite changes in attitudes toward equality between the sexes, there are still feelings that the male should take the initiative in sex relations. In a

sense, girls and women seriously hazard their self-esteem as attractive, desirable females when they take the initiative in planning for intercourse, especially in tenuous relationships.

3. *Costs of continuing contraceptive use.* It is psychologically difficult to continue to take the pill if a female's sex life is irregular and if she has separated from a lover or husband. Continuation reminds her of the loss and implies that she is searching for another partner. Does such continuation, without a steady partner, imply that she might be promiscuous? And what will a man think of her if she is on the pill but not in a steady liaison? Again, although attitudes have become much more permissive concerning sexual behavior, with casual sex becoming more acceptable for both men and women, inhibition remains for many females about being considered an "easy lay."

4. *Problems in getting a contraceptive at the time it is needed.* This poses a problem especially for the female who is not in a steady relationship. Does she anticipate she might have intercourse long before the event so that she can get prepared with medically approved methods? Does she try to get a drugstore method? Supposing the drugstore is closed? And what are her feelings about being exposed as a sexually active female to the druggist and the people in the store? Then, too, there are times when one is simply carried away by passion, by love (or drugs or alcohol), and no contraceptives are available to either partner.

5. *Male atttiudes.* Many women see men as expecting or demanding intercourse. Their passive, feminine reaction persuades them to go along, even without protection.

6. *Actual or feared side effects.* A number of the respondents said they experienced pain or excessive bleeding with the pill or IUD. Weight gain was a problem for some who used the orals. There were also fears of other possible physical side effects from the pill.

7. *Fear of infertility.* A number of respondents said they feared they might not be fertile and wanted to find out. In numerous cases, they had acquired this fear from the remarks of physicians, such as "You might have trouble getting pregnant" or "We ought to know whether or not you can ovulate."

Benefits of pregnancy were cited as follows:

1. It fulfills woman's traditional role.
2. It provides a child to love.
3. It is a proof of fertility.
4. It tests a man's commitment; it may encourage his desire for marriage or bolster a failing marriage.

5. It may please a husband or lover.
6. It is a device for getting attention from parents or others.
7. Pregnancy can be a cry for help or a risk-taking thrill. (Ideas of these kinds were relatively rare.)

The majority of women saw the benefits of pregnancy largely as a way to make a closer relationship with the men they cared about.

In general, contraceptive risk taking was seen as: "I actually have a high chance of not getting pregnant at any one intercourse. Pregnancy might not be so bad, and I probably won't get pregnant anyhow." The possibility of a legalized backup abortion was seen by some women as an encouragement to take such risks.

A number of respondents took many risks without getting pregnant. Then they tended to think this was something intrinsic about themselves. This led to difficulties, especially if they established a close liaison and had intercourse more often, thus increasing pregnancy risk. They needed to see that these risks usually resided in the situation rather than in themselves.

A variety of life stresses seemed to enhance the likelihood of risk taking. These included the death of a parent, the pregnancy of a sibling, a transition point such as graduation from high school or college, vague dissatisfaction with a job, and the breaking up of an affair. (Also see Miller's (1976) comments on these points.)

Luker writes that with the availability of new contraceptive techniques and abortion, it has become increasingly difficult to get males to take responsibility for pregnancies. Pregnancy is regarded as the fault of the woman, who is made to feel guilty for being careless. (Not long ago, she was made to feel guilty for her moral weakness; now it is for her technological failure.) Luker further remarks that coitus-independent contraceptive methods, such as the pill or the IUD, remove males from a contraceptive partnership; this proved disturbing to some of the few men she was able to interview.

Cvetkovich and Grote (1976) found that in intimate, committed relationships, the young woman was more apt to be contraceptively protected, partly because her boyfriend took more responsibility for this protection. Similar findings were obtained by Foreit and Foreit (1978) and by Fisher, Byrne, Edmonds, Miller, Kelley, and White (1979). Cvetkovich and Grote also learned that adolescent males who took responsibility for contraception were likely to be older, more responsible in general, skilled in interpersonal relationships, concerned about their partner's pleasure as well as their own, secure in their self-concepts, and opposed to risk taking.

Lindemann (1974) reaches the apparently sensible conclusion from her studies that sexually active adolescents gradually move toward effective contraceptive use as they become more realistically aware of their own behavior, its possible results, and the family planning services available to them. She proposes that there are three stages of contraceptive use: (1) "natural," (2) "peer prescription," and (3) "expert." Characteristics of the natural stage are unpredictability of coitus, a belief in the spontaneity and naturalness of sex, infrequency of coitus, and movement toward clear heterosexual interests. The peer prescription stage is characterized by attempts to learn about contraceptives from friends. The most commonly used contraceptive methods are rhythm, withdrawal, foam, condoms, and douche. Use may be planned or spontaneous and is dependent, in part, on the type of relationship. Misinformation is a major problem.

The expert stage is the third and last. Lindemann comments that passage to this stage is dependent on an overall maturing process as well as increased commitment to sex behavior *and* a steady relationship with a partner. Steinhoff (1976) obtained findings fairly similar to those of Lindemann, but she expresses it as learning to *accept* one's sexuality rather than becoming committed to sex behavior. (See the earlier discussion on this point.) Regression to earlier stages of contraceptive behavior can occur as a result of changes in the life situation, most notably breaking up with a partner (also noted by Luker and Miller).

Apparently only one study seeks to learn whether adolescents find their sex relationships enjoyable and whether this factor makes a difference in contraceptive use. As shown in Chapter 5, many adolescent girls say that sex is often not satisfying and, in fact, is sometimes painful (a complaint often heard by staff in family planning clinics). Bardwick (1973) learned in her intensive clinical research that the young college women often did not enjoy the sexual aspects of their relationships and resented their responsibility for using oral contraceptives.

She further writes (as others have) that both the orals and the IUD sometimes cause cramping and excessive bleeding. Bardwick emphasizes, too, that there is some evidence that the orals can cause depression, loss or increase of libido, tension, and low energy levels in some women. It also is well known that contraceptive pills may present physical risks and that these risks may be especially great for young girls. However, this subject is beyond the scope of this discussion.

It is said frequently (especially by men) that these "minor" risks and discomforts are a small price to pay for the prevention of unwanted pregnancies (which carry a greater risk). This line of argument may fail to impress the young woman, especially if the relationship with her partner provides few satisfactions and many anxieties.

Cvetkovich and Grote (1980) stress the importance of considering variations in psychological factors associated with the use of different kinds of contraceptives. Their research reveals that young women are most apt to use a method such as the pill when they feel that they are at high pregnancy risk and are in a rewarding, committed relationship that makes the possible psychic and physical costs of this method seem worthwhile. Condom use is associated with high contraceptive communication skills on the part of young women plus a low assessment of pregnancy risks (since condoms are somewhat less effective than the pill).

Knowledge and Attitudes as Factors

At least 12 studies have sought to assess the levels of knowledge of adolescents regarding the physiology of reproduction and contraception. Most of them show that there is little, if any, relationship between levels of measured knowledge and contraceptive behavior (Cvetovich & Grote, 1975; Goldsmith et al., 1972; Grinder & Schmitt, 1966; Miller, 1976; Monsour & Stewart, 1973).

For instance, Miller (1976) found contraceptive knowledge had little effect on sexually active young women if they were in a sexually stimulating situation. They tended to have coitus whether or not they were contraceptively prepared. Then, too, although three-fourths of his study population understood the principles and timing of ovulation, relatively few could apply this knowledge to calculating their own periods of probable fertility. Apparently this knowledge remained only on a general, intellectual level and was not incorporated into behavior. (See case illustrations in Chapter 16.)

Fairly similar results were obtained by Monsour and Stewart (1973) in their study of a group of abortion-seeking college women. These researchers write, "Factual data and knowledge seem useless in the face of their lack of psychological knowing. Factual information from sex education courses, contraceptive publicity, and awareness of available services do not penetrate their sense of personal awareness and acceptance of their own sexuality" (p. 813). The apparent lack of significant effects of sex education at school was revealed in a small study of boys by Finkel and Finkel (1975). Although a slight increase in knowledge occurred following a sex education course, self-reported contraceptive behaviors did not change.

About 60 percent of the Kantner and Zelnik (1972) sample thought that pregnancy can occur immediately after menarche. Black girls were more apt than white girls to think pregnancy could only happen "some time later." As the authors comment, this group of teenagers was technically correct in their perceptions, but such a concept could easily lead to unplanned pregnancies.

Over twice as many whites (42 percent) as blacks (18 percent) could correctly identify the period of ovulation. Nearly all the blacks thought that the time of greatest pregnancy risk was right before, during, or right after menstruation. Over 33 percent of the black subjects thought the risk was the same throughout the month.

Knowledge of pregnancy risk was highest for whites whose families were in higher income groups and for older girls and college students. It was also high for both races when their parents were college graduates. The most poorly informed subjects of both races lived in inner cities or the metropolitan fringes and had migrated from farms to urban areas. In terms of religious affiliation, the Jewish girls were the best informed and the fundamentalist Protestants, the worst.

To a considerable extent, the subjects in the Kantner and Zelnik study who knew the least about pregnancy risks were also those who were most likely to have unprotected early nonmarital intercourse.

These findings could easily lead to the conclusion that lack of adequate knowledge is a key factor in the problem and that specially targeted sex and contraceptive programs are particularly indicated for these vulnerable groups. However, the total life situation, stage of development, and related life-styles of young people are probably the more basic factors associated with both low-tested information and contraceptive risk taking, as shown in the foregoing discussion of social, psychological, and knowledge factors in contraceptive behavior. Traditional sex and contraceptive education would probably have little impact on related behaviors. This does not imply that sex and contraceptive education is useless, but it does suggest that such education by itself is unlikely to make much of an impact on the contraceptive behaviors of teenagers. (See later chapters that deal with sexuality education, counseling, and family planning services.)

Relationships with Parents

Only a few adequate studies have sought to assess the effects of parent–youth relationships on contraceptive use. Presser (1975) hypothesized that feminine role socialization, as indicated in part by maternal attitudes and behaviors and the mother–daughter relationship, would have a strong effect on family formation behaviors of adolescent girls, but she found little systematic support for her theory.

For the most part, Kantner and Zelnik (1972) found little association between family structures and the use of contraceptives. Furstenberg (1976) learned that discussion of birth control by mothers prompted its use, especially if mothers were specific in instructions about female-oriented techniques. As will be shown in a later section, Ladner (1971) observed the important negative effects of anticontraceptive attitudes of mothers and daughters on adolescent girls in a black ghetto.

As mentioned earlier, in a more recent study of an urban, racially mixed population, Fox and Inazu (1980) found that frequency of discussion of both intercourse and birth control by mothers and communication with their adolescent daughters had a number of positive effects. The more frequent the discussion, the more likely the daughters were to believe that they, rather than their male partners, should take responsibility for discussing contraception and that they would know what to say about the topic. Also, frequent discussion was associated with higher levels of birth control knowledge and, for sexually active daughters, use of effective contraceptives. Fox and Inazu speculate that these positive outcomes were at least partially a result of a kind of anticipatory rehearsal in communication between couples, along with desensitization of the topic.

Personnel at family planning clinics often observe that adolescent girls say they could not possibly talk to their parents about contraceptives; this is a source of great concern to these young women. Conversely, a number of parent educators report that parents say they could not talk to their teenagers about contraceptives because this would seem to condone nonmarital intercourse. There seems to be no basis for this belief, but it is a topic that requires further research.

One small study (Burger, 1974) found that a group of black adolescent girls said that their mothers would not let them have contraceptives until *after* they had become pregnant. (This was also a policy in many of the welfare agencies until the late 1960s and early 1970s.)

Somewhat more complex findings were obtained by Furstenberg and Crawford (1978) in an intensive clinical study of a small urban sample. They found that adolescent mothers often remained with their parents following the baby's birth and that the presence of the young mother and child in the family often strengthened family cohesion. In some cases, it might be hypothesized that the daughter lets herself get pregnant as her contribution to family purpose and unity.

Effects of Pregnancy and Marriage

Research findings are conflicting and limited concerning the effects of marriage plans on contraceptive use. Shah, Zelnik, and Kantner (1975) found few effects, but Steinhoff (1976) learned in her Hawaiian study that couples who planned a marriage in the near future tended to relax in contraceptive vigilance. Luker (1975) found that some young people (both male and female) did not use contraceptives because they hoped a pregnancy would precipitate marriage.

As one might expect, married adolescents are more likely than single ones to use effective contraceptives consistently. Contraceptives are obtained with less embarrassment, and the fact of marriage condones coitus (Presser, 1975; Kantner & Zelnik, 1972).

Although the majority of teenagers say that they do not want a nonmarital pregnancy (Furstenberg, 1976; Presser, 1975; Shah et al., 1975), studies also show that many are ambivalent on this subject (Goldsmith et al., 1972; Luker, 1975; Sorensen, 1973).

Reportedly (with no formal research), a small group of middle- and upper-middle-class avant-garde teenagers value pregnancy as a way of being "natural" and free of hypocritical hangups. Having an out-of-marriage baby while you are still in high school somehow proclaims that you are an authentic, unfettered child of the universe. Although this attitude seemed fairly prevalent during the early and mid-1970s, its popularity seemed to have waned by 1980.

Teenagers who have been pregnant have a greater tendency to use contraceptives than those who have not, although many adolescents have several pregnancies while they are still in their teens. Kantner and Zelnik (1973), as well as Presser (1975), found that the previously pregnant are more likely to use pills or IUDs; this was especially true for black females in the Kantner and Zelnik study. However, as Furstenberg (1976) learned in his longitudinal research, contraceptive vigilance tended to decline among young mothers after a few months of use, even though most of them said they did not want another pregnancy.

Influence of Racism and Poverty

As shown in the foregoing section, a few studies reveal that black adolescents are less likely than white teenagers to use effective contraceptives con-

TABLE 6.1.   Reasons Given by Never-Married, Sexually Active Females, Ages 15–19, for Not Using Contraceptives, 1971 [a]

Reason	Percentages	
	White [b]	Black [c]
Time of month	45.2	24.3
Low risk	26.4	43.0
Not available	32.1	26.3
Hedonistic objection	23.9	23.2
Want pregnancy	12.5	24.7
Moral–medical objection	10.8	17.2

[a] Table adapted from Shah, Zelnik, and Kantner, 1975.
[b] Number in sample = 454.
[c] Number in sample = 522.

sistently. However, the research on this point is inadequate, especially in the case of males. The reasons that adolescent females give for not using contraceptives were studied, by race, in the Kantner and Zelnik investigation. They are reported by Shah, Zelnik, and Kantner (1975), as shown in Table 6.1.

Data in this table show that about 70 percent of girls of both races did not use contraceptives because they thought they were at low risk of pregnancy. The whites were more likely to reason that they were at the safe period in the menstrual cycle; the blacks were more apt to think that they were too young or had coitus too seldom, or to have a general belief they could not get pregnant. Although these reasons might indicate a lack of knowledge, it seems likely that they were also rationalizations, at least in some instances. However, if the subjects were correct in their estimation of their ovulatory phase, white girls as a group were more likely to be protected from pregnancy than black girls.

Nonavailability of contraception was defined as not knowing where to get contraceptives or thinking they were too expensive, not having them at the time, or not knowing they existed (5 percent for the last category). A slightly smaller percentage of the black females cited nonavailability as the reason for their failure to use birth control.

Hedonistic reasons, given by about 23 percent of each race, centered around the thought that contraceptives reduced the pleasure, convenience, or spontaneity of sex. The similarities of the two races in this respect counteract a folk myth that black girls are more heedlessly "sexy" than white girls. Findings generally similar to those presented in Table 6.1 were obtained in two studies of small samples of low-income black adolescents (Burger, 1974; Furstenberg, 1976).

Ladner (1971), in her anthropological study of adolescent females in a St. Louis ghetto, advances some probable reasons for use and nonuse of contraceptives in this population. As both Burger (1974) and Furstenberg (1976) found, fear of contraceptives was widespread in the community. Although this was truer of older women, many teenage girls also expressed fear. There were worries that contraceptive use would cause death of the infant or mother, deformity in the baby, and infertility. Contraceptives were often viewed as a form of murder and "against nature."

Ladner reports that her respondents expressed strong feelings about the great value of life per se. Children were held in high esteem, as was fertility. In the traditional view, according to Ladner, a girl becomes a woman through having a baby; she performs her basic function and joins the community of experienced mothers. Through motherhood she can gain maturity, strength, autonomy, and respect. Adolescence is not seen as a life stage and as a period of preparation for maturity; rather, children move into adulthood when they become parents (a view held by most rural, traditional societies).

E. Davis (1974) provides rich insights from her overview of theory and research concerning the difficulties of rational, trusting, realistic, future-oriented behavior on the part of people who live in urban black ghettos. Although she does not discuss family planning per se, she addresses many of her remarks to the use of health services in general. Her main point is that life conditions in the black slums are such that they severely strain ego functioning and cognitive development—factors important to the consistent use of effective contraceptives, as we have seen

Davis writes that this population is generally hesitant to seek health services of a nonemergency kind or at the early stages of a physical or emotional problem. Distrust of authority, tendencies toward depression and denial, and learned passivity all play into this behavior.

Because many of the mothers and grandmothers in urban black ghettos have had little experience with contraceptives and traditionally are opposed to them, adolescents in these families probably would have little socialization for contraceptive use.

As remarked in Chapter 5, the life conditions for inner-city adolescent black males are threatening, especially to their sense of masculine adequacy. This probably is one reason that they seem to take so little responsibility for contraceptive use. Impregnating a female affords them proof of virility.

Inner-city black males also tend to be attracted to antiestablishment Black Power movements. A 1975 publication on family size and the black American (Population Reference Bureau, 1975) traces the origins and expressions of the anticontraceptive position of some black organizations. Although such "establishment groups" as the National Association for the Advancement of Colored People and the Urban League have taken positions favoring family planning, other groups, such as the Student Nonviolent Coordinating Committee, the Black Panthers, and the Black Muslims have been opposed to contraceptives and limitation of family size. Some proclaim that such limitation is a genocidal plot by the white establishment and that the main hope for strength among black people lies in their numbers. Others (especially the Black Muslims) hold that self-control (as in the use of rhythm and withdrawal) is much more natural and moral than artificial control.

As the authors of this publication remark, black people have many past and present reasons for suspecting that white people are attempting to exploit and control them. However, females tend to be less suspicious than males of the family planning movement.

Black people are not the only ones to suffer from poverty and feelings of being trapped in a low socioeconomic position. As shown in the preceding chapter, many members of blue-collar families also feel depressed and hopeless about themselves and their futures and believe that planning for better lives will avail them little (Rubin, 1976). The life situation and resultant attitudes of this group and of whites at an even lower socioeconomic status probably go a long way toward explaining the finding that adolescents from these families tend not to be consistent users of effective contraceptives.

STRUCTURAL BARRIERS TO CONTRACEPTIVE USE

As we have seen, a combination of demographic, social, psychological, familial, and situational variables interact to affect contraceptive behaviors. Impediments to contraceptive use do not reside only within the young people themselves. As discussed in detail in a later chapter, it is important that high-quality, confidential services be readily available to adolescent women and men.

Many people fear that the provision of contraceptive services for adolescents will increase the numbers who engage in intercourse. However, as the foregoing research review shows (see especially Chapter 5), teenagers participate in sex relations for a number of physical, social, and psychological reasons that have little, if anything, to do with the availability of contraceptive services. Also, as shown in this chapter, the great majority of sexually active teenagers do not use a medically prescribed contraceptive method when they first start having intercourse. In fact, a number of studies show that about 75 percent of adolescent girls do not come to a contraceptive clinic for help until they have been sexually active for more than a year. Almost all of them have had intercourse before they apply to clinics for contraceptive assistance, thinking (perhaps rightly) that contraceptive services may not be available to them *before* they become sexually active.

In general, most of the research about contraceptive use tends to be sexist. Most of the studies involve only female subjects. This seems to imply that, inevitably, females should be the ones to assume contraceptive responsibility. However, the research shows that a large proportion of adolescent females depend on their partners to use condoms or withdrawal, and few studies have investigated the attitudes or behaviors of males in this respect.

Thus, there is a particular need to learn much more than we now know about the attitudes and behaviors of young men in respect to their sexuality and contraceptive use. Also, there is a need to devise creative programs and sexuality education, as well as counseling and contraceptive services that particularly attract and hold young males.

CHAPTER 7

Social and Psychological Aspects of Abortion: Research Evidence

There is very little social and psychological research concerning the use and effects of abortion among adolescents. Thus, there is little systematic information available on this topic. An intensive study of women who were seeking abortions in the Balitmore–Washington area showed that most of the respondents approved of abortion as a supplement to contraceptive failure but not as a substitute for contraceptives (McCormick, 1975). Although all the women in the McCormick study were seeking an abortion, some of them saw it as sinful and unacceptable. Another group saw it as acceptable only under limited conditions. Others, who accepted abortion in general, were not sure they could really accept it for themselves. Despite the negative and conflicting attitudes reported, the one overriding and recurrent theme throughout the interviews was the conviction expressed by many of the women that abortion was the only way out of their dilemma.

Only a very few studies have been conducted in the United States concerning the reactions of adolescents to abortion. None of them assess the reaction of putative fathers. Understandably, many of these studies are carried out in abortion hospitals and clinics, and the effects of abortion are studied soon after the event. This timing of the study may produce both positive and negative biases. Patients may be more upset immediately after the event than they would be later. However, some patients may have immediate reactions of relief but over time might develop quite different feelings. There seem to be no adequate long-term studies of young people that carefully assess the physical, psychological, and social effects of having had an abortion. Of course, any study of this kind should simultaneously assess the effects of *not* resolving a pregnancy through an abortion. Such a study also should assess the effects of contraceptive use on a comparable group of adolescents.

It is frequently hypothesized that abortions inevitably must create feelings of guilt and anxiety in the young woman who undergoes this procedure. To test this theory, Fingerer (1973) gave tests of anxiety and depression to various groups of subjects: graduate students who role played the decision to seek an abortion, people who accompanied abortion patients to a clinic, and patients on the day after their abortions. The patients had the most favorable scores. According to the author, this indicates that the possibly negative effects of abortion reside more in psychoanalytic theory and cultural myths than in the actual event. On the other hand, it seems possible that the people who actually had an abortion had a psychological stake in denying any feelings of anxiety and depression that they might have had.

The few available studies of the psychological effects of abortion rarely focus on adolescent patients alone. In general, patient reactions soon after the abortion have been observed to be largely positive, and the majority of patients express a predominant feeling of relief (Osofsky & Osofsky, 1972).

Studies of adolescent girls who had abortions show that only 15–20 percent seemed to have negative feelings about them in later follow-up interviews (J. Evans et al., 1976; Monsour & Stewart, 1973; Perez-Reyes & Falk, 1973). Perez-Reyes and Falk concluded, on the basis of psychiatric interviews and psychological testing, that the physical and mental health of young abortion patients (under age 16) was considerably better following abortion than it had been immediately preceding it.

Evans, Selstad, and Welcher (1976), who followed up a group of adolescent girls 6 months after their abortions, found that the 20 percent who said they regretted having an abortion were more likely to be Catholic, Chicano, and very young; to hold conservative attitudes toward abortion; to come from single-parent and low-income homes; and to have done poor work in school.

Osofsky and Osofsky (1972) suggest that the small group of patients who have negative reactions to abortion are more likely than others to have had a history of personal problems before they had the procedure. This point is also supported in a study by Martin (1973). Further insights about factors associated with adverse reactions show that these reactions are more likely to occur when the young woman receives no emotional support from her parents or partner (Bracken et al., 1974). Also, feelings were more likely to be negative when the girl felt she was forced into her decision by her parents or sex partner (Barglow & Weinstein, 1973; J. Evans et al., 1976).

Cobliner, Schulman, and Romney (1973) report on a clinical study of adolescent patients in a New York City hospital. Their somewhat impressionistic observations, though lacking in scientific rigor, offer clues for further research and for services to abortion patients. They found many of the adolescent patients were constricted in their self-awareness, rather mechanical in their attitudes toward the expression of sex, basically lonely and isolated although members of peer groups, frequently hurt by their parents' disinterest in the pregnancy and lack of commitment to the relationship,

TABLE 7.1. Major Studies on Psychological Effects of Abortion on Adolescents

Study and date	Sample	Methods	Findings
Bracken and Suigar, 1972	Sample of 489 successive abortion patients in a New York City hospital	Two self-administered questionnaires; data on reactions taken in recovery room	Self-reported negative reactions were associated with being single, young, lacking support from partner or parents.
Osofsky and Osofsky, 1972	Sample of 380 abortion patients in a Syracuse hospital; many between ages 16 and 20	Interviews shortly after abortion performed	Majority of patients expressed happiness and relief. About 16 percent of patients were judged unhappy and 25 percent expressed guilt. Catholics were the most apt to express guilt.
Barglow and Weinstein, 1973	Sample of 25 adolescent girls undergoing abortion in first trimester	Interviews soon after abortion	Impression was that many had a mourning experience after abortion. Difficulties arose when the decision to abort was heavily influenced by parents, peers, partners.
Martin, 1973	Nonrandom sample of adolescents who had had an abortion and volunteered to be interviewed	Taped interviews and judgments of psychological traits by three judges (methods questionable); unspecified correlation techniques to assess relationship of many traits to self-reported, postabortion adjustment	Findings need to be viewed with caution. Girls who had difficult postabortion adjustments appeared to be emotionally involved with their pregnancies, lack close friends, have poor relations with their parents, be unhappy about choosing an abortion, have received no support from sex partner. The situations of the girls who had favorable postabortion adjustments tended to be opposite.
Monsour and Stewart, 1973	Sample of 20 young, single college students who had had an abortion	Interviews 6 months after abortion	All continued in college; only one reported postabortion adjustment problems.

| Perez-Reyes and Falk, 1973 | Sample of 41 girls under age 16 who had hospital abortions | Interviews and testing before and soon after procedure | About 66 percent said they were happy that they had had abortion; about 15 percent had adverse feelings of depression, guilt, anger and anxiety. The physical and mental health of the patients appeared to be better after abortion than immediately before. |
| Evans, Selstad, and Welcher, 1976 | Sample of 333 Anglo- and Mexican-American, single, adolescent girls known to pregnancy health services in Ventura County, Calif. | Interviews and reinterviews following abortion (6 months later) | About 20 percent regretted the abortion. They were more likely to be Catholic, Chicano, young; of low socioeconomic status origins; poor students; to have conservative abortion attitudes; and to feel abortion was forced upon them. |

often in poor communication with their parents, and lacking in reality appraisal of what it means to care for a baby.

When the patients consented, interviews also were held with their mothers. These interviews often were helpful in establishing much better parent–daughter communication and in working out appropriate varieties of plans for handling the pregnancy. Opportunities for discussion of feelings about the abortion after the event were welcomed by many patients, but others did not want to explore their reactions further. Close friends in whom they could confide were helpful to many. A summary of the major studies regarding the effects of abortion on adolescents is found in Table 7.1.

There have been several recent studies of repeat abortions. Accurate information about the exact proportion of women who have more than one abortion is rare. One study found the rate to be 33 percent in one New York State clinic (Robbins & Lynn, 1973). The main reasons for the second abortion were the patient's misinformation about pregnancy risk and contraceptive use as well as fear of side effects and method failures. Women who have repeat abortions are not significantly different from other abortion patients in terms of age, race, marital status, or education.

For a further discussion of abortion, see Chapter 14.

CHAPTER 8

Adolescent Childbearing in General

This chapter covers the subject of adolescent childbearing, in general. After a discussion of childbearing trends, we will examine the apparent causes and consequences of adolescent parenthood. Later chapters are devoted to childbearing outside of marriage (Chapter 9) and early marriage and childbearing (Chapter 10).

Contrary to popular impressions, the rates of adolescent childbearing in the United States have declined steadily from a high in 1957 to close to an all-time low in 1978 (see Figure 8.1 and Table 8.1). During this entire period, birthrates for women between the ages of 20 and 29 were considerably higher than those for teenagers. Until recently there has been concern over a slight rise in the birthrate for teenagers under age 17. However, this rate declined steadily from 1975 through 1978—the last date for which figures are available (U.S. Department of Health and Human Services, 1980).

The birthrates for both white and black adolescents fell from 1957 on. The rate for black teenagers was higher than that for whites at all time periods, but the differences between the two racial groups have become less in recent years. Note that rates presented in both Figure 8.1 and Table 8.1 are per 1000 women in specified age groups. Thus, in percentage terms, it can be seen that about 5 percent of young women ages 15–19 gave birth to infants in 1978.

Although the teenage birthrate fell between 1957 and 1978, the *numbers* of babies born to adolescents increased during the early 1970s because there were so many adolescents in the population—products of the 1948–1958 baby boom. By the early 1980s, the numbers of adolescents in the population were declining, and this drop will continue until at least the 1990s—a result of the falling birthrate throughout the 1960s and 1970s (Baldwin, 1980).

What, then, has been the basis for the widespread claims of the past 10 years to the effect that the United States has been experiencing an "epidemic of teenage pregnancy" (Alan Guttmacher Institute, 1976)? One of the reasons for this claim has been a public relations effort by the Alan Guttmacher

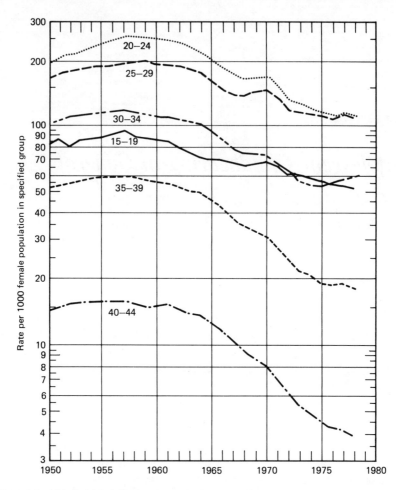

Figure 8.1. Birth rates by age of mother: United States, 1950–1978. Beginning 1959 trend lines are based on registered live births; trend lines for 1950–1959 are based on live births adjusted for under-registration. (From U.S. Department of Health and Human Services, *29*, 1, Supplement. April 28, 1980.)

TABLE 8.1.   Births per 1000 Women Aged 14–19, by Single Years of Age, for All Women: United States, 1920–1978 (Baldwin, 1981)

Period	14	15	16	17	18	19
1920–1924	3.6	11.9	28.6	57.9	93.1	125.4
1925–1929	3.9	12.3	28.5	55.6	86.9	114.0
1930–1934	3.4	10.9	25.2	48.6	75.3	99.0
1935–1939	3.7	11.5	26.0	49.0	75.0	97.0
1940–1944	4.0	12.7	27.8	52.2	81.7	109.2
1945–1949	4.9	15.5	34.1	63.7	99.4	133.0
1950–1954	5.9	19.3	43.1	79.7	123.1	162.6
1955–1959	6.0	20.1	45.7	85.8	136.2	184.0
1960–1964	5.4	17.8	40.2	75.8	122.7	169.2
1965	5.2	16.5	36.0	66.4	105.4	142.4
1966	5.3	16.4	35.5	64.8	101.8	136.1
1967	5.3	16.5	35.3	63.2	97.5	129.5
1968	5.7	16.7	35.2	62.6	95.7	125.2
1969	6.0	17.4	35.8	63.1	95.7	124.5
1970	6.6	19.2	38.8	66.6	98.3	126.0
1971	6.7	19.2	38.3	64.2	92.4	116.1
1972	7.1	20.1	39.3	63.5	87.1	105.0
1973	7.4	20.2	38.8	61.5	83.1	98.5
1974	7.2	19.7	37.7	59.7	80.5	96.2
1975	7.1	19.4	36.4	57.3	77.5	92.7
1976	6.8	18.6	34.6	54.2	73.3	88.7
1977	6.7	18.2	34.5	54.2	73.8	89.5
1978	6.3	17.2	32.7	52.4	72.2	88.0
Percent declined from highest rate to 1978						
	15	15	28	39	47	52

From: 1920–1973: National Center for Health Statistics, *Fertility Tables for Birth Cohorts by Color: United States, 1917–73,* DHEW Publication No. (HRA) 76–1152, U.S. Government Printing Office, 1976, p. 37.
1974: National Center for Health Statistics, *Vital Statistics of the United States:* 1974, "Volume 1-Natality," DHEW Publication No. (PHS) 78-1100, U.S. Government Printing Office, 1978, p. 32.
1975: National Center for Health Statistics, *Vital Statistics of the United States:* 1974, "Volume 1-Natality," DHEW Publication No. (PHS) 78-1100, U.S. Government Printing Office, 1978, p. 32.
1976–1978: National Center for Health Statistics, Unpublished tabulations.

Institute and its close associate, the Planned Parenthood Federation of America. The campaign was launched to persuade citizens that federal funding of family planning services for adolescents was a crucial government activity that deserved strong public support. Since there has been massive resistance to such programs in the past, it may well be important to carry out such a campaign in order to win citizen support for programs that meet the contraceptive needs of the growing proportion of sexually active teenagers. (See also Chapters 5, 6, and 14.)

Major concerns about adolescent pregnancy and childbearing have centered on the following factors:

1. There has been a rise in teenage pregnancies but not births, because about one-half of these pregnancies were terminated by legalized abortion in the years 1973–1977.

2. The proportion of illegitimate to legitimate births rose markedly from 1955 through 1978 for both white and black teenagers. The proportion of illegitimate to legitimate births to white adolescents was about 5 percent of all babies born to them in 1955 and over 20 percent in 1978; for blacks, the figures were about 42 percent in 1955 and over 80 percent in 1978. The percentage of illegitimate births has been higher in recent years for adolescents of both races than for women in older age groups (O'Connell & Moore, 1980).

3. Rates of adolescent premarital pregnancies with births occurring after marriage also rose between 1959 and 1978. About 50 percent of first births to married white teenagers were premaritally conceived in 1975–1978 compared to about 25 percent in the mid-1950s. The rates for black teenagers were lower because so few married to legitimate an out-of-wedlock pregnancy (O'Connell & Moore, 1980).

APPARENT CAUSES OF ADOLESCENT CHILDBEARING

On the face of it, the causes of adolescent childbearing are deceptively simple. They are the same as the causes at any age, except in this case, the actors are adolescents who engage in intercourse, fail to use effective contraceptives or experience a contraceptive failure, are fertile, do not halt a pregnancy through abortion, and experience a live birth. These seemingly simple causes become far more complex when each set of behaviors is studied in depth, as shown in preceding chapters. A review of Chapter 5 shows that over 80 percent of contemporary adolescent men and women over age 18 or 19 have experienced intercourse outside of marriage. Such behavior has become normative since the early 1970s. Rates are considerably lower for younger adolescents.

As shown in Table 5.6, a number of interacting biological, social, and psychological factors have been revealed by a variety of studies to be associated with participation in coitus in the early or middle teen years.

Much higher rates of teenage parenthood would surely have occurred during the 1970s had it not been for the availability of contraceptive and abortion services. Baldwin (1980) uses data from a number of sources to present an estimate of the important roles played by these programs (especially abortion services) in lowering the rate of births to teenagers (see Table 8.2). Basically, the rate of conceptions among teenagers rose during the 1970s because of increased sex activity and inadequate use of effective contraceptives. The rate of conceptions would have been higher without the availability of low-cost family planning services; the rate of births would have been higher without the availability of low-cost, confidential, legalized abortion.

As in the case of early nonmarital intercourse, no use or poor use of contraceptives is associated with a large number of interacting social, psychological, situational, and biological factors. (See Chapter 6, particularly Table 6.1.) Especially when we consider the findings of both Tables 5.6 and 6.1, we see that sexually active teenage women who fail to use effective contraceptives consistently are apt to be a highly vulnerable group whether or not they become adolescent parents. Adolescent parenthood is apt to increase already present multifaceted vulnerabilities, but it is rarely the single cause of problems.

TABLE 8.2.   Trends in Conceptions: U.S. Women Aged 15–19, 1974 and 1977 [a]
(Numbers in Thousands)

Characteristics of Women 15–19	1974	1977	Percentage Change
A. Number of women	10,253	10,420	+ 1.6
B. Birth rate per (1000)	58.7	54.0	− 8.0
C. Sexual activity			
Percentage ever-married	12.5	9.4	−24.8
Percentage of never-married who are			
sexually active	32.4	38.6	+19.1
Percentage of all women who are			
sexually active	40.8	44.4	+ 8.8
D. Number at risk of pregnancy			
(Ever-married and sexually active			
never-married	4183	4647	+11.1
E. Number of births	595.4	559.1	− 6.1
F. Births per 1000 sexually active	142.3	120.3	−15.5
G. Number of induced abortions	279.8	397.7	+42.1
H. Estimated conceptions			
(Births and induced abortions)	875.2	956.8	+ 9.3
I. Conceptions per 1000 women	85.4	91.9	+ 7.6
J. Conceptions per 1000 sexually active women	209.3	205.9	− 1.6
K. Abortions per 1000 sexually active	6.7	8.5	+26.9

[a] Adapted Baldwin, (1980).

Few studies have been carried out to learn what traits characterize teenage abortion users. A few investigations in the early 1970s showed that adolescent abortion users, compared to nonusers, tended to be white, middle class, and oriented toward high educational–occupational goals. However, as legalized, low-cost abortion became more readily available, it was elected by a large number of teenagers of all races and socioeconomic levels.

APPARENT CONSEQUENCES OF EARLY CHILDBEARING*

At least eight major studies concerning the consequences of early childbearing for parents appeared between 1976 and 1980 (Furstenberg, 1976; Kellam, 1979; Maracek, 1979; McCarthy & Menken, 1979; Moore & Hofferth, 1978; Morrison, 1978; Russ-Eft et al., 1979; Sandler, 1979). Most of these studies reanalyzed large bodies of previously gathered data. Most were stimulated and supported by the Center for Population Research, National Institute of Child Health and Development.

Card (1978) analyzed data obtained from the 1960 Project Talent national survey of a random sample of high school youth. This survey had been repeated with smaller samples from the original population in both 1965 and 1971. It thus afforded follow-up data for a group of young people who could be compared on a number of educational, occupational, and other demographic variables in terms of such factors as timing of first births and marriages. Two major problems are attached to the findings:

1. There was a severe sample loss of almost 80 percent at the 11-year follow-up of the 1960 ninth grade cohort that was used for analysis. This loss introduced an unknown, perhaps severe, bias in the findings.
2. The findings pertain to a cohort of young men and women who attended high school in the early 1960s, which is a very different period from the present. Among other differences, there was a lack of availability of contraceptives and legal abortions for teenagers at that time and schools tended to exclude married teenagers and pregnant girls.

Other consequence studies that share the time-bound sample problem of the Card analysis are described later and particularly include the Kellam, Maracek, Sandler, and Russ-Eft analyses.

* Much of the material that appears in the following section was originally written for an article that was first published in the *Journal of Marriage and the Family* (Chilman, 1980a).

The results of the Project Talent study show that a number of factors are significantly associated with becoming a young teenage parent—factors that might be considered causative. These include being black and of lower socioeconomic status, and having low cognitive development scores, few intellectual interests, unclear educational goals, and measured personality characteristics that indicate high levels of impulsivity and lower scores on items having to do with being "mature, calm, cultured, vigorous and leadership-oriented" (Card, 1978, p. 30). The foregoing results are similar to those that other studies have found to be associated with early participation in coitus and poor use of contraceptives. (See Chapters 5 and 6.)

Recognizing the possible effects of these characteristics on later apparent outcomes of early childbearing, Card, in her analysis, statistically controlled for the influences of race, socioeconomic status, and academic aptitudes. However, she seems not to have controlled for the possibly strong effects of educational goals, interests, and personality traits—all factors that have been shown to be closely associated with later educational and occupational success. Thus, her findings along with those of such investigators as Kellam (1979), Menken (1981), and Trussel (1981) need to be viewed with caution in respect to the intricate, inadequately resolved cause–consequence puzzle.

Moore and Hofferth (1978) based their work on data drawn from two sources. First was the National Study of the Labor Market Experience of Young Women, a national random sample of 5000 young women aged 14–24 in 1968, with three waves of interviews from 1968 to 1973; and second was the National Panel Study of Income Dynamics, a national sample of 5000 families, with five interviews from 1968 to 1973. Causal models were used, including path analysis. The dependent variable was age at birth of first child. The independent variables were completed education, later childbearing, marital disruption, labor force participation, and welfare dependency.

The source of data for McCarthy and Menken (1979) and Trussel and Menken (1978) was the National Survey of Family Growth, a 1973 national probability sample. Multiple regression techniques were used; correlates of early childbearing were sought in respect to marriage, remarriage, marital disruption, and later childbearing.

Only a preliminary report is currently available for Morrison (1978), who worked from the National Longitudinal Study of High School Seniors, a national sample of 20,000 young men and women, with data gathered in 1972 and 1976. Path analysis was among the methods used to assess the impact of childbearing and marital status on expected educational attainment, feelings of self-esteem, attitudes toward locus of control, work orientation, family orientation, career satisfactions, expected numbers of children, homemaker aspirations, and welfare dependency.

Furstenberg's (1976) 5-year longitudinal study of adolescent mothers, both married and single, compares a wide range of outcomes for them and their children to outcomes for the school classmates of those teenagers who deferred childbearing until they were somewhat older. His data are the best by far that are available, but they are limited by these factors: The sample is predominantly made up of black, low-income teenage women in Baltimore during the late 1960s and early 1970s, and outcome measurements are limited to the study's 5-year period. Thus, interpretations of his findings beyond these sample constraints should be made with caution. Note that the other major studies on this topic also have samples that are chiefly black, female, and low income (Bowerman et al., 1966; Presser, 1975).

Kellam (1979) studied data, originally gathered for other investigations, concerning a population of 1000 low-income black women and their children in a Chicago neighborhood; the interviews were repeated 10 years later. The study observed effects of early pregnancy on the life satisfactions and psychosocial adjustments of adolescent mothers, compared to older mothers, and the effects on development and behaviors of the children of adolescent mothers.

Presser (1976a, 1980) worked with a random sample of 408 young New York City mothers of first-born children; there were three waves of interviews from 1972 through 1975. Multiple regression was among the techniques used to investigate the impact of maternal age at first birth on later education and welfare dependency.

Maracek (1979) reanalyzed data from the Philadelphia Collaborative Perinatal Project, 1959–1962. The sample included more than 500 low-income women, the majority of whom were black. Because black women constituted a more representative sample than did white women, the available data were superior for the black segment of the study. Tests of significant differences between groups were made in order to ascertain apparent effects of age at first birth on the mothers' later marital stability, income, further childbearing, and education; on the occupational status of the male partner; and on the mothers' children, who had also been observed and tested.

Sandler (1979) worked with data originally gathered in a Tennessee collaborative perinatal research project of 1965–1969 from a sample of 316 low-income mothers of first-born children. Tests were made of significant differences between adolescent and older mothers with respect to childrearing attitudes, mother–infant behavioral interactions, and maternal perceptions of the temperaments of their infants. Findings concerning the effects on infants are discussed below.

Russ-Eft and associates (1979) used data obtained from follow-up, indepth interviews with a small sample of respondents who had been part of the 1960 Project Talent study population. Their work produced detailed case studies of the correlates of early childbearing with respect to later completed education, job satisfaction, marital and parent satisfaction, and income satisfaction. They used careful controls for the effects of exact socioeconomic status; this procedure is unfortunately relatively rare in most of the studies.

Later correlates of early childbearing for parents, as found from the studies outlined above as well as from other investigations, are summarized as follows:

1. *Educational.* Adolescent pregnancy and/or parenthood was *one* factor in dropping out of high school.

An early marriage was closely associated with dropping out of school; the critical factor was early marriage rather than pregnancy or parenthood.

Adolescent mothers tended to have done poorly in school and to have had low school interests and goals *before* pregnancy occured.

Adverse educational effects, especially for middle- and upper-class white, but less so for lower-class black, teenagers were found, especially if they became adolescent mothers when they were younger than 17.

Half or more of early school dropouts returned to school in later life, often in early middle age.

Availability of child care, especially by family members, was an important aid in school return of young mothers.

2. *Later family size.* Larger family size was likely, especially if the first birth occurred before the mother was age 15 or 17, particularly if she was black and especially if she married. However, recent data analyses show that this finding is less true than formerly believed, partly because young women of today of both races have better control of their fertility than was once the case (Millman & Hendershot, 1980).

3. *Marriage and marriage disruption.* The majority of unmarried adolescent parents married within a few years of the first child's birth. Early first marriages with or without adolescent pregnancy were more likely than later first marriages to dissolve in a few years. Early marriage rather than the timing of the birth appeared to be a key variable in later marital disruption, according to some studies. Adequate wages for male employment were also a key factor in marital stability. In general, higher rates of separation and divorce have been experienced by people of lower socioeconomic status. This status is also associated with early pregnancy and early marriage. Thus, higher rates of marital breakdown for adolescent parents may be largely a result of lower socioeconomic status in the family of origin rather than of early childbearing per se.

Marriage did not necessarily improve the situation of teenage mothers, because those who married were less likely to return to school than those who remained single, according to one study of urban, low-income black mothers.

4. *Labor force participation.* Later occupational status, hours worked, and wages earned were not directly associated with maternal age at first birth when appropriate controls were used for the effects of race and original socioeconomic status. Analyses were carried out for long-term, rather than short-term, employment effects.

Timing of first pregnancy appeared to have no effect on occupational status of male partners.

Young married men and women expressed somewhat more job satisfaction than did singles.

Young married women with children were slightly less satisfied with their career prospects than were young married women without children. No differences were found between single parents and single nonparents. Adolescent parents, by age 30, were somewhat more dissatisfied with jobs (30 percent dissatisfied) than were young people who postponed parenthood.

5. *Effects on welfare assistance.* Adolescent single mothers were slightly more apt than adolescent marrieds or nonmothers of similar backgrounds to be dependent on Aid to Families with Dependent Children when the children were very young, but this higher dependency rate was short lived.

In later years, women who had been adolescent mothers were especially apt to be welfare dependent when they were compared to the general population. However, it would have been more appropriate to compare these women to a demographically similar population of mothers, different only in having their first child after they reached age 20.

Availability of welfare assistance made it possible for a sizable proportion of adolescent mothers to return to school.

Black adolescent mothers were more apt than those who were older at first birth to have grown up in a family that received public assistance. Dependence on public assistance after a child's birth was most apt to occur for very young adolescent mothers.

6. *Maternal behavior and attitudes with first-born children.* The majority of adolescent mothers appeared to be as competent and caring as older mothers who were otherwise comparable in terms of race and socioeconomic status.

The majority of mother–infant interactions were rated as appropriate, but significantly more mothers with first births before age 18 were rated as overly protective or too inattentive at the child's 4-month-old testing; the rating improved somewhat at 8-month observations.

No significant differences were found between adolescent and postadolescent mothers in respect to accidents occurring to their children.

No significant differences were found in measured child-rearing attitudes or maternal perceptions of the temperaments of their infants. Adolescent mothers were observed to be high on maternal warmth and physical interaction; they were lower than older mothers on verbal interaction.

Inspection of the findings presented above seems to indicate that, in general, the direct social and psychological effects of early childbearing per se appeared to be fairly minimal for young people in many aspects of their later lives. Moreover, Baldwin and Cain (1980) report, in a review of pertinent research, that adverse effects of early childbearing on the health of the mother tend to disappear when free or low-cost, high-quality medical care is made readily available. Earlier observed negative health consequences seem to have been caused by the poverty of many of the young women and their resulting inability to get adequate obstetrical care, rather than by their age.

None of the preceding statements should be interpreted to mean that adolescent motherhood, either marital or nonmarital, is perfectly acceptable from the viewpoint of both society and of young parents. As indicated in earlier chapters in the discussion of coital, contraceptive, and abortion behaviors, young women who tend to become adolescent parents also tend to be burdened with a number of preexisting social, economic, psychological, and familial problems. Early parenthood would probably impose added strains on young people who are already highly vulnerable. If they defer parenthood until they are older, they may be better able to cope with its demands. However, their delay in childbearing surely would not guarantee educational, financial, and occupational improvements in their lives. These improvements depend far more on a series of social and economic reforms than they do on deferring childbirth until the young person is no longer a teenager.

It is important to think clearly and carefully about these issues. An assumption that adolescent parenthood inevitably brings a host of problems in its wake for the young mothers, fathers, and their children can become a self-fulfilling prophecy. It can also lead to unrealistic expectations on the part of citizens who are persuaded to believe that prevention of teenage childbearing will, ipso facto, reduce early school leaving, youth unemployment, severe maternal and child health problems, and welfare dependency. Would that it were so simple to eradicate these complex problems—problems that are tied more to the operation of the social and economic systems than to the specific behaviors of a (generally) oppressed group of young people.

CONSEQUENCES FOR CHILDREN OF ADOLESCENT PARENTS

We now turn to an allied, but different, consequence question. How are developmental outcomes of children correlated with maternal age at the time of the child's birth? At least six recent studies have sought answers to this question. The methods of most of these investigations are summarized above (Furstenberg, 1976; Kellam, 1979; Maracek, 1979; Sandler, 1979). Two more studies focus particularly on outcomes for children (Card, 1978; Dryfoos & Belmont, 1978).

Dryfoos and Belmont (1978) analyzed data from two national studies: the National Health Examination Survey and all the collaborative perinatal projects. Through regression analyses, the effects of adolescent parenthood were examined in the following areas: measured intelligence, socioemotional problems or characteristics as reported by parents and young people on questionnaires, and academic achievement. Two cycles of studies of the Health Examination Survey were used: Cycle 2, when the respondents were between ages 6 and 11, and Cycle 3, for respondents between ages 12 and 17.

Card (1978) analyzed data available from Project Talent. (See discussion of Card's 1978 report, above.) She compared data from the follow-up survey for a group of respondents whose parents had been under age 15, age 15–17, or age 18 or older when the respondents were born. These three groups were compared to each other on many social and psychological characteristics measured in high school and on outcome measures at the 11-year follow-up. The analyses employed statistically sophisticated methods, including appropriate controls for the probable effects of race, sex, and socioeconomic status.

Correlates of early childbearing for the children of adolescent parents, as found from the investigations described above, are summarized as follows:

1. *Physical health.* There appear to be no adverse effects associated with young maternal age if high-quality prenatal and later health care are available.

The health of the child tends to be better if two adults, rather than one, are in the home.

2. *Cognitive development.* Significantly lower scores for children of adolescent mothers tend to become minimal when appropriate controls are instituted for the adverse effects of poverty, racism, and family headship. Sons of adolescent parents may be more adversely affected than daughters in respect to cognitive development and educational achievement.

The presence of another adult in the household appears to reduce adverse cognitive development effects seemingly associated with families of single adolescent parents.

3. *Socioemotional adjustments and personal characteristics.* No significant differences were found during infancy, early childhood, or early adolesence, if appropriate controls were employed for effects of poverty, racism, and family headship.

A small, but statistically significant, number of children (especially sons) of adolescent mothers were rated as having behavior problems.

4. *Overall behavioral development.* A somewhat larger proportion of children of adolescent mothers (about 9 percent compared to about 4 percent of other children) were rated slow in overall development; a small group of boys seemed to be particularly affected.

Infant sons of adolescent black mothers, compared to those of older black mothers, had higher ratings of slow responses to their mothers.

5. *Educational achievement of children.* No significant differences were found in some studies; in others, slight differences were largely explained by somewhat lower levels of cognitive development.

At age 7, children of adolescent mothers were somewhat more apt to repeat a grade; on the average, sons had somewhat lower reading achievement scores; a larger proportion of sons of very young adolescent mothers were rated as having learning disturbances.

A slightly greater tendency for school adjustment problems in first grade was likely to increase over the years, with severe behavioral and school problems more likely to be present by adolescence for a small group, especially for those from low-income black families.

6. *Family composition and structure.* There was a greater tendency for marital disruption, single-parent households, and remarriage, so that a child of adolescent parents often had a stepfather or was cared for by a grandparent or other relative.

There was a slight tendency for children, as teenagers, to repeat the parental pattern of early childbearing and/or marriage, as well as to have larger families. This tendency remained even after the effects of racism, poverty, and family headship were statistically controlled.

IN SUMMARY

This discussion of adolescent childbearing, in general, shows that there has been a marked decline in the rate of adolescent parenthood (though not pregnancy) since its peak in 1957, that its apparent causes are multiple and complex, and that its age-related specific effects are far less clear and less inevitably devastating for both parents and children than often described in both the popular and scientific literature. Many of the seeming consequences of adolescent childbearing have their roots in the multiple developmental and situational life deficits imposed by poverty, racism, and a complex society rather than in the specific age of the young parents. In general and on the average, early childbearing would seem chiefly to add to the vulnerabilities of an already troubled population of young people. These findings have numerous implications for human service professionals at policy, planning, and direct services levels, as we shall see in Chapters 11–15.

CHAPTER 9

Unwed Adolescent Parenthood

TRENDS IN RATES AND ATTITUDES

As shown in Chapter 8, the rates of childbearing outside of marriage rose markedly for adolescents from 1955 through 1978. In 1978, about 20 percent of babies born to white teenagers and 80 percent of those born to black teenagers were illegitimate. To put this matter in a different and clearer perspective, it is important to note that 1.2 percent of white adolescents and 9.5 percent of black adolescents became unmarried mothers in 1975. However, these figures may seem artificially low because a child needs a great deal of care for at least the first 5 years of life. Thus, with illegitimacy rates this high each year for 5 years, a large proportion of the nation's young mothers probably would be involved in intensive child-care responsibilities for a number of years, either as single parents or within a marriage that involved a premaritally born child or children.

One of the reasons for increased rates of illegitimacy is that early marriage became much less popular in conjunction with the pervasive social changes of the 1960s and 1970s. As one might expect, mothers under age 18 were especially unlikely to be married—fewer than 5 percent of all young teenage women married during the 1970s. In 1960, about 25 percent of 18-year-old women were married compared to about 10 percent in 1975 (U.S. Department of Commerce, 1975). As shown in Chapter 3, unmarried parenthood became acceptable as a life-style in the opinion of over half the population by the early 1970s; marriage to legitimate an out-of-wedlock pregnancy was no longer seen by many as necessarily useful or desirable. In fact, marriage itself was no longer viewed as *the* best life pattern for either women or men.

Along with a greater public acceptance of unmarried parenthood has gone a trend for adolescent parents to keep their babies rather than place them for adoption. As of 1976, 93 percent of unmarried adolescent mothers reported that their children resided with them (Baldwin, 1980).

Despite the growing public acceptance of unwed parenthood, adolescent women appear to see society as being fairly conservative regarding this topic. Over half of those interviewed in a 1976 national study said that they thought that, in general, society strongly or very strongly condemned unwed mothers (Zelnik, 1981). This study showed further that black adolescent women were less likely than their white counterparts to believe that neighbors were strongly condemning of this status. Moreover, two-thirds of the respondents said they thought that "people look down on an illegitimate child." About two-thirds of the young black women and one-half of the young white women said they thought society should help unwed mothers regardless of the numbers of children they had. Only a few respondents said society should never help these mothers.

Similar questions had been asked in a comparable 1971 study. Comparing responses for that year and 1976, Zelnik (1981) concluded that somewhat more permissive attitudes were perceived in 1976 and that, in general, young black women saw social attitudes as being somewhat more permissive than did young white women.

Conflicting perceptions of ideal life goals may be one cause of unwed parenthood for particular groups of young women. Zelnik (1981) found in both 1971 and 1976 that groups in his national samples of adolescent women differed in their stated ideals of the best ages for marriage and childbearing. These group differences occurred in respect to the achieved educational levels of parents in the family of origin. For instance, in 1976, young women whose parents were less than high school graduates thought that age 21.1 was the ideal for first marriage and that 21.6 was the ideal for the birth of the first child. Since there is only a 6-month difference between these two ages, it appears that either the young women approved of premarital conception or were lacking knowledge concerning the usual 9-month period of gestation. Young women whose parents had higher levels of education saw the ideal times for both marriage and childbearing at somewhat older ages and thought that the birth of the first child should be deferred until 2 years after marriage. (See also Chapter 8.)

APPARENT CAUSES OF NONMARITAL ADOLESCENT CHILDBEARING

On the face of it, the causes of nonmarital adolescent childbearing are deceptively simple. They are the same as those for marital adolescent childbearing except that the young person does not marry either before pregnancy or following pregnancy and before the child's birth. Despite this rather obvious statement, it is interesting to note that a huge number of studies have been undertaken attempting to find out the causes of illegitimacy in general and illegitimacy among adolescents, in particular. The major studies are briefly reviewed in the following pages.

Complicated questions arise in a search for the causes of unmarried adolescent parenthood. Why do some teenagers have nonmarital intercourse while others do not? Why do sexually active adolescents fail to use effective contraceptives consistently? Why do large numbers fail to marry if they are pregnant? In general, it is more appropriate to look for causes of illegitimacy by examining the causes of the above behaviors, rather than to look at illegitimacy as a separate entity. (See Chapters 5, 6, and 7.) However, because some studies consider the social and psychological causes of illegitimacy among adolescents as a separate topic, these investigations are reviewed here.

Possible Social Causes

Historically, illegitimacy has been seen as a severe problem in most countries. A woman who had a child out of wedlock was considered beyond the pale of "decent" society. Her chances of a "respectable" marriage were usually ruined. Most employment was barred to her. She and her child were often disowned by her family. Children of unmarried mothers generally were termed bastards and had little future within the bounds of "normal" society. Frequently deprived of financial support and an education, these children had little chance of rising from the underclass to which they and their mothers usually were relegated. Such children frequently were seen as having genetic defects inherited from their sinful mothers. It was anticipated that they would turn out badly. With such forecasts for their futures and with so few life chances from infancy onward, it is little wonder that so many illegitimate children fulfilled the gloomy forecasts made for them.

Conventional wisdom dictated that girls from "respectable" (i.e., skilled blue-collar, upper- or middle-class) families could not possibly give birth to a child outside of marriage. Placing the child for adoption or marrying the putative father were seen as her only options. Abortion was rarely available except for those who had ample funds; even so, it was viewed as a highly questionable procedure. The whole affair of the young woman's pregnancy and the birth of the child was considered a matter of utmost secrecy. Otherwise, the future of both mother and child would be irreparably damaged.

In a cultural climate of this sort, most girls who came from other than poverty backgrounds seemed to be asking for trouble if they let themselves become nonmaritally pregnant. Many of the formulations that such girls had special psychological problems and needed specialized guidance arose in this cultural context.

Considerable changes have occurred since the late 1960s, as detailed in Chapter 3, but this is not to say that the resolution of a teenage girl's pregnancy has become a simple matter. Although the cultural climate has become more sexually permissive, norms and values of earlier times still have a strong influence on social attitudes toward unwed pregnant teenagers. The conviction of most people that the unwed mother's future and that of her child will be seriously jeopardized in numerous ways is still fairly prevalent, although it has far less rationale in the current climate than it once had.

The acceptability of unmarried motherhood varies for people of different ethnic and racial origins. For example, traditional Hispanic-American family norms hold that a girl who becomes nonmaritally pregnant is "ruined" and can never make a respectable marriage. Such beliefs were prevalent in many similar subcultures at least through the mid-1960s. Special protective services had been set up for unmarried mothers and their children during the 1800s. These services continued to operate, often under religious auspices, until the very recent past, and some of them continue at the present time.

For many groups in this country, cultural attitudes toward illegitimacy have moderated recently because of vastly changed social and economic conditions. Generally speaking, illegitimacy no longer presents the critical problem it once did. This is because of such factors as less emphasis on inheritance of land and capital by family members, more jobs for women, the push for equal rights of women, welfare programs for mothers and children, and more permissive attitudes toward sexual behavior.

To a large extent, marriage is no longer seen as the life goal for women, and rising divorce rates make the young leery of the advantages of marriage for themselves and any children they might have. Moreover, there tends to be less pressure than formerly to legitimize a child through marriage.

Urbanization is clearly one of the social causes of higher rates of illegitimacy in general. Gendell (1974) argues that the higher illegitimacy rates in cities are due largely to the presence of such a huge proportion of poor and minority group people. Many sociologists would argue that urbanization itself generally causes an increase in many kinds of deviant behaviors. Especially for those who are making the transition from rural to urban life, urbanization tends to bring about personal and familial disorganization, because old norms and values no longer readily apply, social controls are harder to enforce, life is more anonymous, and temptations increase. The impersonal, complex, competitive life of the city is apt to heighten feelings of anomie, personal insignificance, and powerlessness. The adverse effects of urbanization can be seen in many of today's rural–urban migrants. This may be particularly true for the teenage children of these migrants, who are caught in the classic second-generation conflict between traditions of their parents and the only partially assimilated values and norms of the long-time residents they seek to emulate. These negative effects of rural–urban migration are particularly visible among black people, partly because they themselves are so visible.

Industrialization also plays a part in promoting higher rates of births out-side of marriage. Its effects include the decreased salience of the family as an economic unit and greater financial independence for women through their increased employment opportunities outside of the home (H. Ross & Sawhill, 1975).

Moreover, as societies become more highly organized and as concern grows for the social and economic well-being of all people, more programs are launched to promote the general welfare, and more official attention is then paid to behavior that may be a threat to the well-being of the larger society as well as to individuals. For instance, when few federal assistance programs were operating in the United States (before the mid-1930s), little attention was paid to the health, education, and welfare of poor people, espe-cially those in isolated rural areas. With the launching of such social security programs as unemployment compensation, old age insurance, and maternal and child health and child welfare services, illegitimacy acquired a newly important status.

Illegitimate children were not eligible for social insurance benefits. Public health and child welfare professionals, deeply concerned about the impact of illegitimacy on the physical, social, psychological, and economic well-being of mothers and children, emphasized the importance of the child's legitimacy. More careful records were kept about this matter. Earlier cus-toms, especially prevalent among the poor, sanctioned entering into a common-law marriage (formalized largely by a couple's living together for a period of time). Such a marriage was no longer considered adequate for the legitimation of children.* The more careful accounting of illegitimate births following the passage of the Social Security Act in 1935 probably played a part in the observed rise in rates of illegitimacy from 1940 on.

In an article on possible causes of illegitimacy, Cutright (1971) discusses theories of the effect of social norms on birth outside of marriage. These theories hold that, when norms are restrictive of illegitimacy, rates will be low; when they are permissive, rates will be high. Through a complex analy-sis of rates of illegitimacy in many countries, he concludes that these rates have not consistently supported this formulation. The matter is far more complex than a simple ordering of norms for or against unwed parenthood.

Presser (1975) hypothesizes that socialization for female roles through

---

* The writer was a child welfare worker in rural Virginia in the early 1940s. In her own experience, much effort was expended in attempting to persuade common-law partners with children to legalize their marriages through a formal ceremony. In more than a few cases, couples who followed this advice later complained that feeling legally tied to each other took all the romance out of their relationships. Some were subsequently divorced. This seems to have been a preview of trends observed in the 1970s toward couple cohabitation rather than marriage.

the mother–daughter relationship has a strong effect on the young woman's marital status and the timing and number of her pregnancies. However, Presser fails to find much support for this theory in her study of a sample of young mothers in New York. No significant associations were made between the education and occupation of the mothers of the women studied nor between the goals they reportedly supported for their daughters and the actual behavior and stated goals (as of age 16) of the young mothers. However, daughters whose mothers had early pregnancies were more likely to become pregnant as teenagers. The fact that an association was found between early maternal childbearing and the behavior of daughters suggests that actual maternal behavior is apt to be more influential than stated maternal attitudes and goals for children. This is a common finding concerning the effects of parental developmental outcomes of children (Chilman, 1973; see also the case of three generations of premaritally pregnant women, cited in Chapter 16).

We have seen earlier that there have been profound changes in the predominant culture of the United States concerning popular views of sexual behavior. Changes toward greater permissiveness gained strong momentum in the 1920–1930 period, the time of the first sexual revolution. The period from 1930 to 1965 has been depicted as a time of gradual consolidation of these changes. Another surge toward even greater sexual freedom began in about 1966 and may still be in progress in the early 1980s. Rates of teenage illegitimate pregnancies also have risen steeply since about 1966, with a particularly sharp increase between 1966 and 1970.

It looks as if this increase is partly a result of cultural lag; that is, contraceptive service programs for teenagers have lagged behind changes in sex attitudes and behaviors on the part of many of the nation's adolescents. For instance, although changes in public policy made free or low-cost federally funded family planning services available to adults in 1966, it was politically unfeasible to make such services available to adolescents. (In actuality, because of opposition of the Catholic Church and other conservative groups, it was difficult to make federal funds available for family planning services at all, and even more difficult to get these services implemented throughout the country.)

Family planning services for single adolescents were (and are) hard for the general public to accept. Cultural leaders and the decision makers are generally over age 21. Most of them are parents. Many are concerned, perhaps rightfully, about the effects of intercourse on adolescents who are generally too young to marry and who seem to be too young to form mature, responsible relationships. Many fear that the ready provision of contraceptives and abortion services through the official recognition and institutionalization of family planning services will cause an increase in nonmarital sex behavior.

Problems that adults have in accepting sexual freedom for adolescents create conflicts, confusion, and anxieties in both parents and teenagers. Thus, even when family planning services are made available, internalized traditional social norms make it difficult for some teenagers to use these services or discuss their need for contraceptives or abortion with their parents or other adults who might be able to help them (teachers, doctors, religious leaders, social workers, and the like). Most of these potentially helpful adults also have had little in their training or experience that would prepare them to be of effective assistance to today's sexually active adolescents. This suggests important contributions that knowledgeable and skilled human service professionals can make in working with adolescents, parents, and the community to help teenagers handle their own sexual behaviors more effectively and to obtain related and needed services. (See Chapters 11–15.)

Welfare Programs as a Cause of Illegitimacy

There is widespread public concern about the rising rates of welfare dependency in the United States. The Aid to Families with Dependent Children (AFDC) program is the major source of public assistance for poor people, especially for mothers and children. The number of people on AFDC rolls increased steadily from the early 1960s through the 1970s, despite the strong economic growth during much of this period. Because almost half of the women who receive aid from this program are single mothers, it is often assumed that the availability of welfare benefits *causes* illegitimacy.

A full discussion of the reasons for the rise in the number of AFDC recipients is beyond the scope of this book. A few of the probable causes are sketched here. They include a shift in the nature of the nation's economy that drastically reduced the employment opportunities for people with little education and few skills; the costs of living in a largely urban, industrial society; the rising aspirations and political strength of the dispossessed; the 1946–1958 baby boom; and greater awareness on the part of the general public that unalleviated poverty for some creates social and health problems for the entire society (leading, for example, to the passage of the Social Security Act in 1935 and the federal government's war against poverty in the mid-1960s).

The AFDC program, one part of the Social Security Act, has been criticized for providing assistance mainly to mothers and children. It is observed frequently that the nature of this program discourages marriage among people who need welfare benefits. At present, there is no nationwide, federally aided public assistance program for families wtih husbands living in the home, especially if the husband is "employable." States may elect to include husband-present families in their AFDC programs, but many fail to do so.

A strange anomaly occurred through a Supreme Court ruling in the late 1960s that made it possible to aid a family if a man is present in the home if he is a boyfriend, but not if he is an employable husband.* In most states, general assistance to families with fathers present is either unavailable or at extremely low levels. Thus, public assistance policies present a barrier to the family with two natural parents living in the home (H. Ross & Sawhill, 1975).

Some critics of the program and its recipients claim that this situation *causes* women to have illegitimate children so they can go on welfare. It would be more accurate to suggest that defects in the AFDC and state general assistance programs make it almost impossible for husband–wife families with young children to stay together when steady employment at adequate wages its not available; these defects also provide little or no impetus for the young couple to marry.

Several studies analyze large bodies of data from many countries and fail to find that the availability of benefits from the AFDC program (or similar public assistance programs for unwed mothers and their children) causes an increase in illegitimate births in this and many other countries (Cutright, 1971; Holmes, 1970). Ross and Sawhill (1975) review numerous sources of data and find that, apparently, women do not have children in order to go on welfare. However, the availability of public assistance may influence them not to marry a poor prospect. Moore and Caldwell (1977) reach a similar conclusion in their extensive review of research. They add, however, that women may be more likely not to have an abortion or not to place their babies for adoption because welfare benefits are available. In sum, the availability of public assistance does not appear to cause out-of-marriage pregnancy, but it may affect what the young woman does about this pregnancy. Moore and Caldwell (1977) also conclude, on the basis of sophisticated data analysis as well as review of a number of studies, that the size of welfare benefits does not affect the decision of unmarried mothers to keep their babies.

Through their analysis, Ross and Sawhill conclude that welfare reform that ceases to particularly favor female-headed families probably would be of some use in reducing the proportion of families headed by women. For much too long, the majority of people in the United States have mistakenly assumed that any man who wants to can find a job. Many have opposed federally aided public assistance programs for able-bodied men. The time is

---

* The Supreme Court went further in 1970 and stated that the resources of men who assume the role of spouse (including nonadopting stepfathers) cannot be considered available to children unless there is proof of an actual contribution to those children. If a man is not the natural parent of the children, no presumption that he supports them may be made in determining their eligibility for benefits. Thus, it is to the economic interest of unmarried mothers and their children (and to fathers) for the mothers to marry someone other than the biological parent.

long overdue for citizens to realize that unemployment and underemployment are chiefly problems of the economy, rather than of individuals. Public assistance and job development programs for both males and females are needed when jobs at adequate wages are not available in the private sector.

Unemployment as a Cause of Illegitimacy

Poor employment opportunities are cited as one cause of unmarried parenthood by such researchers as Presser (1974), Ross and Sawhill (1975), Cutright (1972), and Furstenberg (1976). High unemployment rates of youths, especially black youths, frequently make marriage unfeasible for a teenage couple, even though the girl may be pregnant.

Then, too, when good job opportunities are not available for adolescent girls and young women, their motivation not to have a child may be reduced because alternative roles are not available to them. Ross and Sawhill (1975) write that many strategies are needed to promote stable, satisfying marriages. These strategies include more steady jobs at adequate wages for both sexes, as well as shifts toward marital customs that favor sex role equality and, thereby, provide greater potential psychosocial marital satisfactions for both females and males.

Note the importance of steady employment at adequate wages in the Ross and Sawhill analysis. They report that when the total benefits package available through AFDC programs (assistance grants, food stamps, Medicaid, and housing subsidies) is put together, one finds that mothers with children are frequently better off financially if they do not marry or if they separate or divorce. Many men who have low-level jobs cannot make nearly as much as welfare programs often provide. Though some would conclude that this suggests a lowering of welfare benefits, it is important to recognize that AFDC allowances are computed on the basis of a minimum subsistence budget, which is provided at a level far below the actual financial needs of most families.

Many would argue that young women should not get pregnant without being married and that marriage plus children should not occur unless the husband is earning enough to support a family. This is a rational proposition; but, as shown in earlier chapters, sexual and contraceptive behaviors do not readily lend themselves to purely rational decision making, especially for people whose total life situation has made rational planning seem useless.

Psychological Causes of Illegitimacy

Research about psychological causes of illegitimacy is highly unsatisfactory. Many of the studies of unmarried mothers involve special groups that can be reached easily for research, such as teenage girls in abortion clinics, maternity homes, or programs for the nonmaritally pregnant (Barglow et al., 1968; S. Hatcher, 1973; Rains, 1971; D. Shapiro, 1967). A few studies also have looked at the psychological characteristics of AFDC recipients (Griswold, 1967; Reeder & Reeder, 1969). Other so-called studies are chiefly clinical observations made by medical (especially psychiatric) and social work personnel who work with young unmarried mothers. Almost all these studies fail to compare unmarried mothers with young women who do not have an illegitimate child but who otherwise have similar demographic characteristics. Also, much of the research looks at young women at a time of crisis—when they are pregnant outside of marriage. Psychological measures and observations obtained during this period may not reveal characteristic personal traits of the respondents.

An extensive literature about the presumed psychological problems of unmarried mothers has been widely disseminated in such fields as psychiatry and social work. This literature has been highly influential in these professions and such others as nursing, education, gynecology, and adolescent medicine. Much of this literature propounds that unmarried mothers have deep personality disturbances. It is often said that they have an unconscious need to become pregnant; that they are trying to hurt their parents or become dependent on them again; that by having a child they are competing with their mothers; that their unresolved Oedipal conflicts lead them to become pregnant by a father substitute; that they suffer from character disorders and childishly act out their impulses; and so on. Although psychological mechanisms of these kinds probably do sometimes play a part in causing unwed motherhood, it is probably fallacious and too unidimensional to conclude that all, or even most, young unmarried mothers have unique, deep-seated personality problems that caused their situation.

Theories of family development and family systems are enriching both clinical practice and research in many areas of human behavior, including adolescent sexuality. (See Chapter 2.) In this context, recall that Furstenberg (1980) found that the arrival of a baby to an unmarried adolescent daughter is often observed to unite a faltering family lacking in a significant familial goal. It is as if some daughters, in scapegoat fashion, act out the various stresses of different family members through becoming pregnant without marriage and presenting the family with a (sometimes) unifying crisis. Such cases are sometimes observed, too, by therapists in clinical practice. Furthermore, recall the observations made by Fox (1980) regarding the pressures on women at midstage of their lives and how the resulting maternal conflicts can affect crucial mother–daughter relations.

These findings have important implications for human service professionals who work with adolescents in respect to their sexuality. Obviously, a family treatment approach is often indicated, contrary to the all-too-frequent assumptions of counselors and educators that parents (being "hopeless") must be excluded from the adolescent's personal life. The role of the adolescent's parents and siblings will vary from person to person, and no flat rules can be made as to either the part that family dynamics play in the adolescent's behavior or the wisdom of working with adolescents within or outside of the family context. (See also Chapters 11 and 13.)

A good deal of the clinical literature states that many, if not most adolescent unmarried mothers became pregnant as the result of one coital experience. From a physiological standpoint, this seems unlikely. It is more probable that this is what many unwed pregnant girls tell middle-class professionals because they fear moral disapproval. The fact that so many professionals take these statements at face value may well reflect their own inhibitions about nonmarital sex.

Popular formulations such as many of those sketched above have an important bias. It is blatantly sexist to assume, as much of the social and psychological research and clinical literature does, that nonmarital pregnancy and childbearing is a particularly female problem. Although it is the young woman who becomes pregnant, her male partner shares equally in creating this condition. In fact, he may play a larger part by inducing her to have intercourse.

This sexist bias has prevailed over thousands of years in many parts of the world. The mere physical fact that it is the woman who gives birth has been generalized to the assumption that she is the one who is responsible for the pregnancy. The generations-old,widely prevalent double standard of sex morality is linked to these sexist assumptions. (See especially Chapter 2.)

This sexist bias is further reflected in much of the research about illegitimacy (not to mention nonmarital sex, contraception, and abortion) by the fact that only a few investigators have studied unmarried fathers. There are only two studies that seek to learn the causes of unmarried fatherhood (Pannor, 1971; Robbins & Lynn, 1973). These studies are characterized by extremely small and seriously inadequate samples. They reflect a general difficulty in studying unmarried fathers. Aside from the sexist bias in much of the research, there are extreme problems in reaching a sample of unmarried fathers. Most unmarried mothers become known to human service agencies because they must at least seek medical help. Unmarried fathers, fearful of disapproval and of being held responsible for financial support, are leery of contacts with either researchers or human service personnel.*

A few studies have sought systematically to assess the psychological char-

---

* Along these lines, sexism operates in an opposite direction. There has been a far greater tendency to think that fathers rather than mothers should support illegitimate children. Of course, this is because until recently few (especially white) mothers of young children were in the work force. Custom plus lack of job opportunities usually kept young mothers at home. They were barred from many jobs, particularly if they were mothers of illegitimate children.

acteristics of a group of adolescent unmarried mothers against a generally comparable group of nonmothers (Pope, 1967; Vincent 1961). Few, if any, significant differences were found between the groups studied. Any professional who has had experience in working with adolescent unmarried mothers learns that each young woman deals with the situation differently, dependent on many factors: her cognitive level and abilities, her personality structure (most notably her stage of ego development and use of defense mechanisms), her stage of adolescence in terms of dependence–independence conflicts, her values, her relationship to her parents and their cultural norms and personalities, her relationship to her boyfriend and his reaction, her physical condition, and the kinds of material resources available to her. These observations do not reveal much about the causes of illegitimacy, but they do suggest that unmarried mothers vary a good deal and warn us not to seek pat, easy answers to the reasons for their situation.

A few studies have explored the concept of generational recidivism (repetition of a behavioral pattern from generation to generation) as a cause of illegitimacy. However, this theory failed to be substantiated in the research of Vincent, Haney, and Cochrane (1969). Only slight evidence to support this concept is provided in a small study by Robbins and Lynn (1973) and in Presser's (1976a) New York study.

A few more words about the alleged psychological causes of teenage illegitimacy are in order. It is said frequently that psychologically deprived girls sometimes have babies in order to have something to love. It seems unlikely that most of these teenagers would deliberately plan to have intercourse in order to get pregnant, but, as shown in earlier chapters, young women who yearn for affection are more likely than others to have nonmarital coitus. Also, some of these young women are less likely to use contraceptive protection when they fear that their mates might leave them. Having a baby can be a confirmation of a woman's sense of feminine adequacy, especially when other kinds of status are lacking. Then, too, babies seem to be a great source of comfort and fulfillment to many mothers, married or single.

Although easier acceptance of illegitimacy tends to be more characteristic of low-income women, a small group of avant-garde females from more affluent backgrounds has also advocated unmarried motherhood in recent years. Some say they like having children but not husbands. Some also say that having a baby outside of marriage shows they are attuned to the natural world and are free of artificial arrangements, one aspect of the counterculture philosophy.

Race and Illegitimacy

The causes of far higher rates of illegitimacy among black adolescent girls compared with white teenagers have been difficult to understand, and few systematic studies have satisfactorily addressed this issue. The best source of possible explanations is afforded by Kantner and Zelnik (1972) and Zelnik and Kanter (1980a, 1980b). They found that black adolescent girls, compared with white teenagers, were twice as likely to have nonmarital intercourse and to begin their sexual activities at a significantly younger age. Black teenagers were also half as apt to use contraceptives consistently and only one-third as likely to get an abortion. Moreover, white nonmaritally pregnant girls (50 percent of them) were five times as likely as black adolescent females to marry before the baby was born. Furthermore, the black respondents were more inclined to have a second or third illegitimate child while they were still teenagers, partly because they started having nonmarital intercourse when they were younger.

As discussed in Chapter 5, research shows that adolescent women from one-parent families are more likely than those from two-parent, "happily" married, stable families to have early nonmarital coitus. Zelnik (1981) reports that 1971 and 1976 national studies of young women revealed that the black respondents were far more likely than white respondents to come from single-parent, unstable, or stepparent families. For example, in 1976, fewer than 50 percent of the black women and over 80 percent of the white women in his sample said they came from two-parent families. Moreover, only about 33 percent of the black respondents compared with 71 percent of the white respondents, came from "ideal" families (families in which the biological mother and father were both present for the first 15 years of the young person's life) (Zelnik, 1981). About 33 percent of the black women, compared to 10 percent of the white women came from "least ideal" families (those in which there were single parents, dissolved marriages, foster homes, or various parent surrogates). The greater tendency for young black women to come from less than ideal family structures probably plays a part in the higher rates of unwed parenthood found for black adolescent women. This may be an especially cogent hypothesis when it is also recognized that census data show a very strong relationship between poverty and female-headed families (U.S. Department of Commerce, 1976). Thus, it can be assumed that many more black, than white, adolescents grew up in families burdened with the triple problems of poverty, racism, and single-parent status.

As discussed in early chapters, the life situation and resulting values and norms of low-income black adolescents probably play a part in higher rates of unwed parenthood. Marriage to legitimize a child is seen by many low-income black people as neither very practical nor moral. All too often the father of the baby is an unemployed or underemployed youth with little chance for financial improvement. Teenagers observe that marriages in poverty are apt to be fragile and conflict ridden. The community usually holds that marriages should be entered into because they have a good chance of

succeeding and because the couple wants to (and can) live together and establish their own home. Otherwise, the young mother and her child can
live with relatives (often her own mother) or friends and not be committed
to a new life pattern that may prove to be too onerous. Or failing these arrangements, if she cannot find employment and care for her child, she can
go on welfare (Moore & Caldwell, 1977; Pope, 1967; H. Ross & Sawhill,
1975; Stack, 1974).

Billingsley (1970) writes that there are many family forms in the black
community. These include the nuclear, the attenuated (father or mother and
child), and the extended multigenerational family. There are also augmented families, which include roomers, boarders, or long-term guests. He
holds that illegitimacy is considered irrelevant in the low-income black
community.

Ladner (1971), Rainwater (1970), and D. Schulz (1969), as well as
others, would not agree that illegitimacy is considered irrelevant in the black
community. It is not held to be desirable but is usually accepted as an unfortunate but often inevitable event. However, motherhood itself is seen by
many adolescent girls as having beneficial effects in helping them mature
and gain status as women (Ladner, 1971; Rains, 1971; Stack, 1974).

Furstenberg's study of an adolescent clinic population of urban, low-income black (and a few white) girls revealed that only 20 percent said they
were happy when they found they were pregnant. Another 20 percent had
mixed feelings, and the rest had negative ones. A very few said their mothers
were pleased; many were reportedly hurt and depressed or angry. This
hardly sounds as if the grandmothers easily accepted an illegitimate pregnancy for their daughters; in many cases, it meant more burdens for the
grandmothers (Furstenberg, 1976).

Low-income black males tend to hold negative attitudes toward marriage
(Broderick, 1965; Liebow, 1967). However, a number of studies have found
that many low-income black men continue an interest in their children and
the mothers of these children even if they are not married (Furstenberg,
1976; Ladner, 1971; Liebow, 1967; Sauber, 1970).

As remarked earlier, illegitimacy becomes a critical issue particularly
when children stand to inherit land and money from their families. Because
poor people have little, if any, land and money to pass on to their offspring,
legitimacy is less of an issue for this group. Because so many black people
are poor and many are at particularly low-income levels, they might be especially unlikely to concern themselves with legitimate heirs.

To the extent that one believes that traditions developed under slavery
make a difference in the values and norms of today's black families, it could
be argued that the high fertility values and prohibitions against marriage
that were held by white owners with respect to their black slaves became
incorporated into the black culture. Then, too, most of today's black fami-

lies have their roots in the southeastern United States, where fertility values in general have been high owing in large part to the predominantly rural economy of the past.

Cutright (1972) musters considerable data to bolster his contention that increases in fecundity, especially among blacks, have played a large part in the rise of teenage illegitimacy from the 1940s through the late 1960s. He holds that public health services and other reforms over the past 40 years have improved the fecundity of black people and have also reduced the infant death rate. He also argues that age at menarche has fallen since 1945. (However, the data presented by Cutright on this latter point do not explain racial differences in illegitimacy rates.)

Ventura (1969) suggests that increased fecundity and lower maternal and infant deaths among black women are partially a result of gains in controls over venereal diseases. For example, between 1974 and 1963, the rate of gonorrhea declined by half in the nonwhite population (although it has increased somewhat lately). She also points out that there is a marked increase in nonwhite babies born in hospitals, an increase from 27 percent in 1940 to 92 percent in 1965.

In general, life conditions and health care for many blacks and other low-income people improved during the 1940s and on through the 1960s owing to a number of social, political, and economic developments. These include the Social Security Act of 1935, the rural–urban migration of black and other rural families, increased employment opportunities for black people, public housing and public health programs, civil rights legislation, and general economic improvement. Although these various developments have far from reached their goal of markedly improving the life conditions of poor people (both white and black) and other problems have arisen (perhaps most notably the severe problems of the urban black ghettos), still the overall average life conditions of poor and minority group families measured by many health, housing, education, income, legal, and employment indicators are better than they were before 1940. Better, but not good: Much remains to be done to reduce racial and socioeconomic inequities.

In many societies, when changes are made in the fecundity and fertility rates of a people, the culture tends to adapt slowly to the changed conditions. Fertility values tend to remain high for a period of time, although they are no longer needed to assure a population of adequate size for the future (Chilman, 1968).

APPARENT CONSEQUENCES OF NONMARITAL ADOLESCENT CHILDBEARING

A large number of studies have also been undertaken attempting to identify the so-called consequences of nonmarital adolescent childbearing for both the young teenager and for the children of such teenagers.

Health Consequences

There appear to be no studies that compare the health of unwed adolescent parents and their babies to that of young married families. It seems likely there would be no differences between the two groups unless the pregnant unmarried adolescent girl is especially fearful of seeking medical services prenatally or is unable to obtain these services.

Social and Psychological Effects

Table 9.1 summarizes all available social and psychological research regarding the factors significantly associated with the apparent outcomes of unwed adolescent parenthood compared to adolescent parenthood within marriage. Furstenberg's (1976) 5-year longitudinal study, despite its sample limitations, furnishes the best data on this topic. Details of his findings and those of other researchers are presented in the table and therefore are discussed only in summary form here.

We find that educational outcomes for Furstenberg's sample showed that young mothers were most apt to return to school if they held high educational goals and had help with child care. Remaining single often occasioned more help from the teenager's family in many respects, including child care. Marrying a young man who was a school dropout often meant a young mother also stayed out of school. No other investigator seems to have compared adolescent single to married mothers in respect to educational outcomes.

Furstenberg also found that marriage could have an adverse effect on the adolescent mother's economic resources if the marriage were followed by separation, which tended to occur in over half the cases. Understandably, adolescent mothers were in the best economic position if they and their husbands were both employed and child-care resources were available through either informal or formal arrangements. Few young husbands were able to support their families adequately through their sole efforts. This was because of high unemployment rates and poor wages for black inner-city youths. Recall, also, the earlier discussion of the poor employment situation of minority group, inner-city youths as well as the negative effects of welfare policy that tends to discriminate against needy two-parent families.

Employment opportunities for young women under age 20 tend to be even more limited than for young men. Presser (1975) found that whether or not a young woman obtained a job following the birth of her child seemed to depend mostly on whether or not she had been previously employed, not whether or not she was married, and (for somewhat older adolescents) her age was more or less unimportant.

The effects of nonmarital adolescent childbearing on marriage appear to

TABLE 9.1. A Summary of the Apparent Consequences of Illegitimacy for Adolescents and Their Children

Factor and study	Sample	Methods	Findings
Education Furstenberg, 1976	Longitudinal study of a select sample of low-income, pre-dominantly black, adolescent females	Interviews, tests, observations	Adolescent mothers who were most apt to continue schooling were those with high educational ambition. Marriage interfered with schooling unless husband was also educationally ambitious and supported wife's goals. Young mothers were most apt to finish high school if they remained single and lived with their parents who provided child care. A second pregnancy usually prevented further education.
Employment and income Furstenberg, 1976	Longitudinal study of a select sample of low-income, pre-dominantly black, adolescent females	Interviews, tests, observations	Over a 5-year period, a number of income patterns prevailed. Most common income sources were personal earnings, public assistance, husband's earnings. Adolescents who had not had a pre-marital pregnancy were in best economic condition, but this group had a higher level of ambition. Respondents went on and off welfare in response to changes in job market. Those who married and then separated were in worse condition than those who remained single. Income was not related to age at first pregnancy. Having more than one child often caused mother to need public assistance. Employment of young mothers was dependent, in part, on child-care resources. Families of single mothers more apt to help with child care.
Presser, 1975	A large sample of New York City mothers with first-born children	Interviews and reinterviews	Employment of mothers was mostly related to whether they had held jobs before the child was born, more or less regardless of the mother's age and marital status.

160

Cutright, 1973a	Secondary data from 1967	Complex data analysis	Little economic effect found for women who had had an illegitimate birth 15–20 years earlier, especially in the case of black women.
Marriage Furstenberg, 1976	Longitudinal study of a select sample of low-income, predominantly black, adolescent females	Interviews, tests, observations	Young mothers were rarely married before birth of first child. Marriage was often deferred until father had a job; black women were very cautious about getting married; especially when age 18 or less. Girls with highest educational–vocational goals were least likely to marry. Not marrying father did not prevent marriage; marriage was more apt to occur if parents of girl were sexually conservative. Marriages most likely to last were those based on long prior acquaintances and mutually exclusive commitments, plus higher educational–occupational status of husband. Adolescent unwed mothers who married were apt to be in a worse situation than those who did not. Half of these marriages ended in separation in a few years.
Effects on later fertility Cutright, 1973a	Secondary data from 1967 National Survey of Economic Opportunity	Complex data analysis	Unwed mothers who never married had the smallest number of children. Whites who had been unwed mothers and married later had more children than white women who had not had an illegitimate child. This was not true for black women.

TABLE 9.1 (*Continued*)

Factor and study	Sample	Methods	Findings
Furstenberg, 1976	Longitudinal study of a select sample of low-income, pre-dominantly black, adolescent females	Interviews, tests, observations	Both married and unmarried mothers had more children than they wanted. Both groups rapidly increased family size. Women with high educational goals and who remained single were less likely to have more than one child. Fertility rates did not differ between employed and unemployed respondents. Even though family planning services were available, they were not used consistently.
Social consequences[a] Bowerman, Irish, and Pope, 1966	Large sample of predominantly black, low-income women in North Carolina	Interviews	Seventy percent of white unmarried mothers and 40 percent of black unmarried mothers said they had tried to keep their pregnancy secret, but few women of either race said they had lost the respect of their friends because of their pregnancy.
Ladner, 1971; Schulz, 1969	Anthropological studies in urban black ghettos	Interviews and observations	Adolescent girls tended to gain status as women as a result of having children, whether married or not. It usually allowed them a freer social life with fewer parental controls.
Rubin, 1976	A small group of white, blue-collar families in California; most families in their late twenties and thirties	Series of intensive interviews with both husbands and wives	Participants thought that it was a social requirement to marry to legitimate a premarital pregnancy. Other options were considered unacceptable.
Effects on mothering behaviors Furstenberg, 1976	Longitudinal study of a select sample of low-income, pre-dominantly black, adolescent females	Interviews, tests, observations	Only 4 percent of young mothers gave up child for adoption, and 7 percent of the children lived apart from mothers. No differences in mothering behaviors were associated with age or marital status. Most mothers were seen as responsible and competent.

| Effects on children
Furstenberg, 1976 | Longitudinal study of a select sample of low-income, predominantly black, adolescent females | Interviews, tests, observations | By age 3, no differences had been found in scores on the Preschool Inventory Test among children whose mothers were married or single. Higher scores were found for those children who were cared for by more than one adult. Children whose parents married early and stayed married had the highest scores in the group. Children of young mothers were compared with children of other parents who had their youngsters in preschool programs. The latter group had higher test scores, but investigator thinks this is partly because these children came from families of higher socioeconomic status and partly because they were all in preschool. |

[a] Although a number of investigators point with alarm to the large number of repeat pregnancies of unwed adolescent girls, they fail to compare these rates over time to (1) married teenagers and (2) older women of the same race and socioeconomic status as the single, adolescent group. If these comparisons were made, it seems possible that early childbearing outside of marriage does not differentially affect later completed fertility rates.

be numerous. Furstenberg and others conclude that the birth of an illegitimate child often hastens a marriage, even though many of the young women in the sample said they preferred not to marry for quite a period of time and a large proportion managed to delay their marriages for several years until the young father graduated from high school and/or obtained a job. These marriages of young parents were highly vulnerable to dissolution, with well over half having failed within a few years. The highest rate of success was for those in which the husband was the child's father, those based on long-term positive dating relationships prior to marriage, and those in which the husband was steadily employed and had adequate wages, with the last characteristic being the most important. Early, forced marriages that ended in separation were often viewed by the young mothers as having been severely traumatic; most of these mothers remained separated rather than obtaining a divorce, and many said they never wanted to marry again.

Rubin's (1976) in-depth study of white working-class families shows a somewhat different pattern, with marriage being seen as an absolute requirement by both men and women if a girl becomes pregnant. Moreover, young women looked forward to marriage as a (usually misplaced) hope for escape from an unhappy home life.

A number of studies of low-income, black populations show that having had an illegitimate child does not seem to stand in the way of a later marriage, although having more than one such child does decrease marital opportunities, possibly because of the larger support responsibility. Extension of these findings to other groups in the population should be done with extreme caution, however. This includes middle- and upper-class black families, who often take a severely negative view toward early unwed childbearing.

Fertility was found to be somewhat higher in the Furstenberg sample if the young mother married. This finding may be compounded by the fact that girls with high educational goals were the least likely to marry and the least likely to bear more than one child. However, both married and unmarried teenagers had unplanned pregnancies and more than they wanted.

As previously mentioned, the social consequences of unwed adolescent parenthood are probably less severe in many sectors of contemporary society than they were in the past. Again, available formal studies on this topic are mainly of low-income, largely black populations. According to the findings of Bowerman, Irish and Pope (1966), Ladner (1971), and D. Schulz (1969), there seem to be few, if any, adverse social consequences for adolescent unwed mothers in the populations studied. Of course, familial and community attitudes about this matter will vary from case to case, and human service professionals who deal with individuals will need to be sensitively alert to this fact.

A similar observation applies to the effects of unwed parenthood on the children of adolescent parents. Again, Furstenberg is the only investigator who provides adequate data on this subject. He found that almost all the children in his sample lived with their mothers. Moreover, no differences in mothering behaviors associated with age or marital status were observed. Most mothers appeared to be responsible and competent. Family members gave a great deal of help with child care, especially if the mother remained single. Children whose parents married early and stayed married had the highest cognitive development scores in the group, but they were followed closely by other children who lived in homes where two adults (rather than one) had responsibility for the children.

IN SUMMARY

Attempts to understand the *causes* of illegitimacy are best met by research that seeks the reasons for the various behaviors that are linked to births outside of marriage, rather than by studying illegitimacy per se.

In considering research results regarding illegitimacy as a separate topic, it appears that the following factors might be considered causative of unwed parenthood: changes in the nature of society that reduce the salience of the two-parent nuclear family to the economic well-being of parents and children; associated changes in cultural norms with the result that illegitimacy is no longer so stigmatized as it was earlier by the mainstream culture; and the failure of the culture to adapt rapidly enough to changing youth norms with respect to nonmarital coitus so that there is inadequate provision of family planning services for adolescents.

Studies of psychological causes of illegitimacy are markedly inadequate. There is no systematic evidence that unmarried adolescent parents are psychologically different from other adolescents of comparable demographic backgrounds. Most of the research in this area is highly sexist with its assumption that unmarried mothers have unique personality problems and with its scant attention to unwed fathers. (See also Chapters 6, 7, and 8.)

The apparent causes of higher rates of black, compared with white, adolescent illegitimacy would seem to be the effects of poverty and racism on norms regarding sexual behaviors and unmarried parenthood; higher rates of nonmarital coitus and sexual initiation at earlier ages; less tendency to use contraceptives or abortion (see Chapter 14 regarding recent trends in abortion behavior); less tendency to marry to legitimate a nonmaritally conceived child; higher rates of unemployment among black youths; higher rates of breakdown in families of origin; and slowness in adapting fertility-related cultural patterns to the changed conditions of improved fertility brought about by public health and welfare measures.

Relatively little is known about the *effects* of unwed parenthood on adolescents and their children. The only longitudinal study on this subject was carried out by Furstenberg (1976) with a relatively small sample made up predominantly of low-income black females living in Baltimore, Maryland. An analysis of his findings leads to the tentative conclusion that few severely adverse consequences as a direct result of early, unwed childbearing per se could be found for his group in terms of education, employment, marital, social, and parenthood outcomes.

Contrary to general assumptions, marriage by young unwed mothers of predominantly minority group, lower socioeconomic family backgrounds does not generally resolve their difficulties. In fact, it often compounds them. The males who are the putative fathers, in most cases, tend to have a number of psychosocial characteristics that make both high school graduation and steady, well-paid employment difficult to achieve. Then, too, unless the young couple has had a sound relationship for a considerable period of time, the marriage may be fraught with conflict and may soon end in separation.

At least for the low-income, predominantly black groups studied, being an unwed adolescent mother does not necessarily stand in the way of future marriage. However, marrying someone other than the natural father of the child may not be possible. Young mothers with two illegitimate children appear to have greater difficulty in acquiring a husband than those with only one child. They also have greater difficulty in attending school and obtaining and holding jobs.

The psychological effects of unwed parenthood seem not to have been studied. However, according to Ladner (1971), Stack (1974), and others, low-income black teenagers often state that having a baby has made them feel more mature and responsible.

The consequences of unmarried motherhood for white females and both white and black adolescents from upwardly mobile blue-collar or upper- or middle-class family backgrounds simply are not known, because there are no satisfactory studies on this subject. In this respect, most of the recent research regarding unwed adolescent childbearing has been overly racist— a situation that is in strong need of correction.

As to the effects of unmarried fatherhood on males, no researcher appears to have studied this topic—another example of the sexism in this field.

It seems important to look at the apparent consequences of unwed adolescent pregnancy compared to the consequences of alternative nonmarital sexual behaviors—abstaining from nonmarital coitus; using contraceptives; or resolving a nonmarital pregnancy through abortion, adoption, or early marriage.

CHAPTER 10

Adolescent Marriage and Childbearing within Marriage

As mentioned earlier, about two-thirds of births to adolescents occur within marriage. Much less attention is given to this group of young people than to those who are unwed parents. However, it is important that married as well as unmarried adolescents be considered.

APPARENT CAUSES OF EARLY MARRIAGE

Although it is frequently assumed that premarital pregnancy is *the* precipitating factor in early marriage, this is only partly true. It should be borne in mind that about 50 percent of early-marrying women are not pregnant at the time of their weddings.

As we have seen, the tendency for women aged 15–19 to marry decreased markedly after the mid-1950s. During the 1950s, however, there was a great deal of alarm about the increase in young marriages during the 1940s and the apparent continuation of this trend. This alarm led to a number of studies of the causes and consequences of these marriages, often with an assumption that they were pathological in origin and problematic in results. The search for causes of early marriage included surveys to assess related demographic charatceristics as well as studies that examined psychological and social factors.

Premarital Behavior

Early marriage (bride age 18 or younger; groom age 20 or younger) was found to be significantly associated with early dating and going steady (Bayer, 1968; Chilman, 1963; Inselberg, 1961; Moss & Gingles, 1959). At least one study found that early marriage was more likely to occur if a girl dated a large number of boys, went steady with a number of them, and considered herself "in love" with her steadies (Burchinal, 1959). As shown in

Chapter 5, these factors are similar to some of those found to be associated with adolescent nonmarital intercourse. At least one study of college students (Chilman, 1963) showed that participation in nonmarital intercourse was associated with early marriage for women, but not for men. Early marriage did not necessarily take place because of nonmarital pregnancy. Rather, at the time of this research (1961), many young women believed that they should not have nonmarital coitus without a marriage commitment. It seems likely that many of them pressed for marriage because intercourse, but not necessarily pregnancy, had occurred.

Psychological Factors

Studies about psychological factors associated with early marriage have yielded conflicting results. It appears that some people marry early partly because they are unusually mature for their age and hold strong family values; conversely, some have had a long history of personality problems, come from unhappy homes, and are looking for the security of an intimate relationship (Chilman, 1963; Moss & Gingles, 1959).

A few studies show that early-marrying girls tend to take a traditional view of the female role, are largely domestic in their interests, and are low in educational and vocational aspirations (Burchinal, 1964; Moss & Gingles, 1959). These characteristics also have been found for adolescent females who engage in early nonmarital intercourse, fail to use contraceptives consistently, and have children outside of marriage. (See earlier chapters.)

A small number of investigators have looked at measured personality differences between early- and late-marrying adolescents. This research has a variety of methodological problems. Therefore, little confidence can be placed in the results. However, in a more rigorous study, Burchinal (1959) assessed the measured personality differences between two small groups of early-marrying girls in Iowa. No significant differences were found for the premaritally pregnant compared with those who were not pregnant, except that the first group had higher heterosexual interests.

Parent–Child Relationships

Some researchers have hypothesized that early-marrying adolescents are particularly apt to come from unhappy homes. Lowrie (1965) found this was especially the case for adolescent girls who married when they were less than 16 years old. Most of this group were premaritally pregnant. (As shown in Chapter 5, there are clues from the research that girls who engage in nonmarital coitus in early adolescence may be especially likely to have social and psychological problems.)

Through intensive clinical interviews, Chilman (1963) found that early-marrying white college students of both sexes tended to divide into two groups with respect to early family relationships. One group of these students came from extremely unhappy families; they perceived their parents' marriages as having been conflict ridden and their own childhood and adolescence as having been "miserable." The second group came from exceptionally strong families in which the relationships between parents and between parents and children were remembered as being "very happy." Perhaps early marriage occurs for two major family relationship reasons: the desire to compensate for, or escape from, an unhappy family life provided by one's own parents or, on the other hand, the desire to emulate one's happily married mother and father.

Moss and Gingles (1959) and Inselberg (1961) learned that parent–child relationships were seen by early-marrying adolescent girls as having been unhappy at the time of the marriage; however, these relationships improved later.

Socioeconomic Status

A number of studies show an association between low socioeconomic status and early marriage (Bartz & Nye, 1970; Burchinal, 1959; Elder & Rockwell, 1976; Rainwater & Weinstein, 1960; Rubin, 1976).

Bartz and Nye (1970), in a review of research on causes and consequences of early marriage, propose "derived theoretical propositions." These propositions emphasize the part played by lower social class membership, with the fewer role and status satisfactions afforded to adolescents and thus the greater attractions that seem to pertain to early heterosexual involvement and marriage.

As Rubin (1976) writes, on the basis of her recent intensive study of a group of blue-collar California families:

> For most working-class girls getting married was, and probably still is, the singularly acceptable way out of an oppressive family situation and into a respected social status and the only way to move from girl to woman. Thus, despite the fact that the models of marriage they see before them don't look like their cherished myths, their alternatives are so slim and so terrible—a job they hate, more years under the oppressive parental roof—that working-class girls tend to blind themselves to the realities and cling to their fantasies (of a perfect marriage) with extraordinary tenacity. (p. 41)

Most of the husbands and wives in Rubin's study married when they were young: an average age of 20 for the men, of 18 for the women. The women usually recalled their courtship in romantic terms, but the men seemed to have drifted into marriage. "Somehow she caught me, I don't know how she did it. But a man has to marry some time, doesn't he?" (paraphrased from Rubin, 1976, p. 52). (Similar findings about blue-collar marriage were obtained by Rainwater & Weinstein, 1960, and Komarovsky, 1964.)

Many of the men and women in the Rubin study had experienced premarital intercourse. Most of the women (now in their thirties) expressed guilt and anxiety about their earlier behavior. Many were pregnant before marriage. For this group, premarital pregnancy automatically meant marriage to both the men and the women: No other choice was acceptable (Rubin, 1976, p. 67).

Elder and Rockwell (1976) carried out an impressive analysis of the causes and consequences of timing of marriage among white women born between 1925 and 1929. Using data from the National Fertility Studies of 1970 and 1965, they identified "early marriers" (under age 19), "on-time marriers" (age 19–22) and "late marriers" (over age 22). They found that early-marrying women were more likely to come from low socioeconomic origins, especially if they failed to finish high school. However, in times of economic depression, women from such backgrounds were especially apt to defer marriage. Regardless of socioeconomic level, early marriers were distinguished by residential separation from parents, a large number of siblings, and birthplace in the South and on a farm.

Late marriers were most likely to be daughters of middle-class Catholics. Non-Catholic, late-marrying women were characterized by advanced education and high occupational status. Late-marrying women of lower socioeconomic origins tended to be exceptionally achieving and ambitious for educational and vocational advancement, to marry men younger than themselves, and to marry men who came from higher social class backgrounds.

The findings cited above from Rubin (1976) and from Elder and Rockwell (1976) apply to people who were in their middle years at the time of the investigations, and similar findings might not be obtained for early-marrying men and women in the 1970s. It appears that no study has been done since 1965 about the causes and consequences of adolescent marriage, aside from Furstenberg's (1976) longitudinal study of a small group of black adolescents. This research will be discussed in the following section on consequences of early marriage.

APPARENT CONSEQUENCES OF EARLY MARRIAGE

Marital Stability and Statistics

Burchinal (1965) reviewed 1950 and 1960 census data and found that divorce and separation rates were two to four times higher for young people who married in their teens, compared with those who married in their twenties. He speculates that age alone is not the determining factor in marital stability. People who marry in their teens are also more likely to be of low socioeconomic origins, have little education, and tend to experience employment problems—all factors associated with divorce and separation in the periods under consideration. Somewhat similar findings were obtained by Glick and Mills (1974) in their analysis of 1960 and 1970 census data. They also report that early marriages are more likely to end in divorce for both white and black females. (Early marriage is defined as occurring at less than age 20 for men and at less than age 18 for women.) They found that in both 1960 and 1970 first marriages were more likely to endure among couples whose incomes were well above the poverty line.

Burchinal (1959) found in his Iowa study of young premaritally pregnant wives compared with other young wives that the premaritally pregnant were more likely to be unhappy in their marriages. Premaritally pregnant couples also had less income than the others. Husbands were younger and more likely to be students or employed at lower occupational levels. More of the premaritally pregnant couples regretted their marriages, and more of these wives wished they had finished high school. These findings are hardly surprising, considering that the premaritally pregnant couples probably entered forced marriages, whereas the others presumably married because of their desires.

Christensen (1958) proposes that the values one holds about premarital pregnancy make an important difference in its effect upon the divorce rate. He found that premarital pregnancy and subsequent marriage was strongly associated with higher divorce rates in Indiana but much less so in Denmark, where norms are more permissive. However, in both Indiana and Denmark, premarital pregnancy and early marriage were more likely to occur among lower socioeconomic groups and more likely to end in divorce than later marriages with postmarital conceptions.

Bacon (1974) analyzed data from a national probability sample in the 1967 Survey of Economic Opportunity. He found that marital instability was markedly related to the age at which married women had become mothers. For those who gave birth before age 15, about 33 percent of the marriages ended in separation or divorce, compared with 10 percent for those who bore their first child after age 22. These findings applied to white women particularly. In general, rates of marital breakdown were over twice as high for black women, and age at first childbearing made far less difference for black than white women.

It should be recognized that Bacon's findings pertained to people at all age levels in 1967 and do not necessarily apply to the impact of early motherhood on adolescents in the 1970s. However, they indicate that early marriage and early childbearing probably make a more distinct difference in marital stability for white than for black couples. This is probably because poverty, with its adverse effects on marriages, is far more pervasive and profound in its overall effects on black people. Racism added to poverty places severe pressure on the marital stability of couples of all ages.

Rosenwaike (1969), in a study of Maryland marriage and divorce data, also found a stronger association between age at marriage and marital dissolution for whites than for blacks. Along with the probable impact of racism and poverty mentioned above, there also may be a cultural norm factor operating, similar to Christensen's findings reported for Indiana compared with Denmark. Because black people at lower socioeconomic levels tend to be more sexually permissive in their attitudes than white people, there is generally less stigma attached to premarital pregnancy, illegitimacy, and early marriage. Thus, fewer sociocultural pressures would be experienced by early-marrying, pregnant black teenagers in low-income families.

For a detailed discussion of the consequences of premarital pregnancy and early marriage on a group of black adolescents, see Chapter 8, in which Furstenberg's Baltimore study is reviewed (Furstenberg, 1976). In brief, teenagers in the Furstenberg study who become premaritally pregnant at less than age 17 and who married early were more apt to experience marital dissolution than those who married later. This was especially true for the late marriers who did not become pregnant either before or soon after marriage. Half of the early marriages dissolved within a few years. This was especially likely to happen if the couple had not established a long-term, mutually committed relationship before marriage.

Factors associated with self-reported marital happiness were analyzed by Chilman (1963) in her study of early- and late-marrying white college students. She found that marital happiness was not associated with such factors as premarital pregnancy, time of marriage, current income, work and student status of husband and wife, and personality characteristics. Two major factors were discerned in the two groups: Significantly more of the unhappy wives saw their parents' marriages as unhappy and rated their own childhood and adolescent years as unhappy (this was also true for unhappy husbands, particularly with respect to their adolescent years), and significantly more of the unhappy husbands and wives had children and more of them had unplanned children. The presence of unplanned children seemed not to be the central problem, however. The difficulty appeared to lie in the husband–wife relationship and its effect on birth planning, because all the married students knew about contraceptives and low-cost contraceptive services were available to all. (See Chapter 6.)

In general, evidence from the studies of Rubin (1976), Chilman (1963), and Furstenberg (1976) provide further credence to similar findings of numerous other studies of marital satisfaction and stability. The large body of research about marital satisfactions and stability is far too extensive to discuss here. However, the following characteristics were found to be conducive to high levels of marital satisfaction (Bowerman, 1957; Burgess & Cottrell, 1939; King, 1952; Kirkpatrick, 1963; Locke, 1951; Locke & Wallace, 1959; Locke & Williamson, 1958; Nye & MacDougall, 1949; Stroup, 1953; Terman, 1938):

1. Happiness of parents' marriage and lack of divorce in family of origin.
2. High level of self-perceived childhood happiness.
3. Mild but firm discipline during childhood, with only moderate punishment.
4. Adequate sex information, especially from encouraging parents.
5. Substantial time of acquaintance before marriage; lower rates of premarital pregnancy.
6. Mutual enjoyment of sex relations.
7. Open expression of affection between sexes, confidence in each other, and equalitarian, free communication.
8. Joint participation in outside interests; friends in common.
9. Stable residence.
10. Education at least through high school.
11. Income above poverty level.

These findings underline the importance of the individual's personal development history and its effects on self-perceived qualities of marital relationships. They also indicate that these personal characteristics interact with situational ones, such as number of children born, education, income, and employment, to affect marital happiness. These findings further suggest that there tends to be a too easy assumption by researchers and others that single factors, such as premarital pregnancy or timing of marriage, make a decisive impact by themselves on marital happiness and stability.

Effects on Income

Early marriers who have a premarital pregnancy are apt to have less money in the first years of marriage, partly because the wife is less apt to work (Burchinal, 1959; Inselberg, 1961). Later, early-marrying women are likely to be forced to take jobs to supplement the meager earnings of their husbands. However, the low income of early-marrying couples is probably heavily affected by the fact that so many of these women came from low-income families in the first place and had relatively little education and few occupational skills (Elder & Rockwell, 1976; Rubin, 1976).

Coombs and Freedman (1970) compared married white urban couples who had experienced a premarital pregnancy with other couples whose children were conceived after marriage. At marriage, the first group of husbands had less education than other husbands in the sample and a lower occupational status. Over time, they tended to catch up to the second group in education, occupation, and earnings. However, those who had married premaritally pregnant women were less likely to accumulate capital assets. They also were less likely to plan the number of children effectively and to realize the child spacing they desired, although their families were not necessarily larger than those in the second group.

The investigators comment that the possible contributions of psychological factors to these different outcomes for the two groups of couples could not be assessed, because measurement of psychological traits was not included in the study. The results of this study are often interpreted as furnishing important evidence that a premarital pregnancy prevents a married couple from building financial security. It seems likely that other factors besides premarital pregnancy played an important part in the obtained findings. It appears that many of these couples were unable (or unwilling) to plan effectively in general and carry out plans in a careful, future-oriented fashion.

The fairly widespread conviction that early marriage usually has adverse effects on family income probably stems from the 1950s and earlier, when it was not customary for wives to hold jobs and when few couples used contraceptives in the early years of marriage. Now that it has become common for wives to work outside the home and for couples to plan for no or few children, marrying at a young age may not have the adverse economic effects that it generally had in earlier times. However, given the high rates of unemployment in the late 1970s and early 1980s for people under age 20, it seems unlikely that most married adolescents would be able to support themselves today. And, as Furstenberg's 1976 study shows, the availability of child care (often through the families of adolescent parents) makes a crucial contribution to the employment of these young people.

Effects on Education

Adolescents who marry early quite naturally tend to have less education at the time of their marriage than those who marry later (Bacon, 1974; Elder & Rockwell, 1976; Furstenberg, 1976). As in the case of income, it has been widely assumed (at least until recently) that early marriage prevents the acquisition of further education for both husbands and wives, especially wives. This was probably true until the late 1940s or so. Before that time, high schools and colleges tended to bar their doors to married students. They seemed to assume that only married students had been sexually initiated and that the purity of the single students would be blemished by their association with those who had carnal knowledge. (Attitudes of these kinds were inherited from the ancient monastic traditions of academia.)

The World War II veterans, returning to school on the GI bill, broke the marital ice in colleges. Most proved themselves to be excellent students, even though married. Their generally fine performance (plus the need of colleges for students in the 1950s) made higher education available to both husbands and wives. It turned out, even more surprisingly than in the case of veterans, that the greater maturity and life experience of married men and women, plus their high levels of motivation, combined to help them turn in a generally excellent record of academic performance. By the end of the 1950s and the beginning of the 1960s, high schools, too, started to be less rigid about insisting that the student body be virginal. As shown in Chapter 9, there was a growing tendency, which has strengthened over the past 15–20 years, to allow pregnant high school girls, and even young mothers, to continue their education.

In general, greater flexibility about the timing of life events has developed since the mid-1940s. We are not as bound as we once were to the Biblical agricultural tradition that "there is a time and season for all things." Old beliefs die hard. It is still difficult for many people to accept that life today can hold many options for most people. It is possible, for instance, to obtain an education and to launch new careers at many stages of the life cycle. It is possible to have children early and enter the labor or education market later. It is less possible, in actuality, to defer marriage and childbearing for many years until educational and vocational goals have been achieved.*

Just as the culture is becoming more flexible about the timing of life events, so is it becoming more tolerant of a wide variety of behaviors. It is quite possible today to enter marriage as a pregnant bride without social condemnation. It is also quite possible to end an unhappy marriage with relative ease and social approval. As recently as 30 years ago, young people were counseled that their lives could be permanently blighted by one false

---

* It is said frequently that young people should not marry before age 25, when presumably they have been able to find their identity and they can choose a marital partner suited to this identity. It might be said with equal cogency that people should not embark on education past high school or on a work career until they are at least 25, so that school and work are in harmony with their adult identity. Supposedly, employment and education experiences particularly help youths find themselves; might not marriage and parenthood also make this kind of contribution, especially in times of increasing equality between the sexes and shared work roles?

step. Today's less puritanical culture allows many false steps and many new beginnings. (See also discussion in Chapter 9 on changing attitudes toward illegitimacy.)

The more flexible and permissive contemporary cultural climate brings its own problems in the demands it makes on people to use their freedom wisely. On the other hand, this climate is less likely to lock people in with such overly simplistic, self-fulfilling prophecies as: "Early marriages end in divorce." "A premarital pregnancy is bound to have negative effects on marital happiness." And "Early-marrying youths shortchange themselves of chances for further education and a successful career."

As shown in the discussion of research related to illegitimacy among adolescents, the social and psychological characteristics of individuals, perhaps especially their educational ambitions, appear to be the major determining factors as to whether unwed pregnant girls finish high school. (Of course, high schools have to be willing to accept them.) Research also shows that high school graduation and future employment of both males and females depends, to a large extent, on their individual social and psychological characteristics (as well as the state of the job market), rather than on their completed years of education per se.

Chilman (1963) found in her study of married and single undergraduates that none of the women who were wives of students (but not students themselves) had left school because of marriage. They left because they felt no need for further education, had low achievement drives, and had largely domestic interests. The married women who remained in school were unusually oriented toward educational achievement and had married men who supported their goals (similar to findings of Furstenberg, 1976).

On balance, it seems that, while both premarital and early marriage (as well as illegitimacy) might temporarily cut short the educational careers of some young people, it does not necessarily prevent further education on the part of those who are highly motivated and academically achieving. The above statement is not likely to be true, however, unless educational opportunities are made available to young marrieds (including pregnant young women) and child-care arrangements can be made by young parents. (See also Chapter 15 on social policy and programs.)

Glick and Mills (1974), in their analysis of census data, provide evidence that the association between early marriage and leaving school early is more complex than is commonly believed. They find that people who drop out of either high school or college have higher rates of divorce than those who graduate from either of these educational programs. They speculate that the kinds of personal characteristics people have tend to increase their chances of dropping out of various kinds of human endeavors, including both school and marriage.

In general, there is growing evidence that America's love affair with advanced education for all is turning somewhat sour. For instance, higher levels of education (including graduation from high school) do not necessarily guarantee better employment chances. Then, too, Campbell, Converse, and Rodgers (1976) present suprising findings concerning the effects of education on marital and overall life satisfactions. They found in their national survey that black females, on the average, were the most dissatisfied group in American society. Those who had graduated from high school were far less satisfied with their lives and their marriages than those who had less education and those who had a college education. Presumably, their aspirations had been stimulated by high school graduation, but their employment situation had not been markedly improved. Higher education for both races of men and women adversely affected their levels of marital satisfaction. This finding is different from earlier ones that usually showed a positive relationship between college graduation and marital happiness. Among other things, it seems likely that today's college graduates (especially women) have higher aspirations for individual fulfillment than other people do and are more likely to question traditional values about the central importance of marriage and family living.

Effects on Fertility

A few studies show that early-marrying young people are likely to have more children than those who marry late. However, this finding needs to be viewed with caution because, as shown in earlier chapters, there is a greater tendency for people from lower socioeconomic backgrounds to marry early and to fail to use contraceptives consistently or to terminate a pregnancy with an abortion. Although early marriage may be associated with larger family size, the timing of the marriage is probably one piece in a much larger life pattern that affects the number of children that people have.

Effects on Child Care

It is not known whether early-marrying couples are any different in their parenthood attitudes, feelings, and behaviors than couples who marry later. As we saw in Chapter 8, Furstenberg's (1976) longitudinal study of adolescent mothers (both married and unmarried) showed that most of them were apparently loving, responsible parents of little children, especially if they shared child care with another adult. In connection with his findings, it was suggested that the extended, cooperative black family kinship network probably gave many important supports to these young mothers and that white mothers might receive less help with child care from their relatives.

It seems likely that adolescent females and males have not yet reached a stage of development in which they are able to meet the many needs of children in a complex, technological society such as that of the United States. It seems that this would be especially true, overall, for girls under ages 18 or 19 and for boys under ages 20 or 21. As discussed in Chapter 2, adolescents around age 16 (about age 15 for girls, 17 for boys) are generally in the early stage of adolescent development and have not yet established psychological independence from their parents. They also are apt to be at immature levels of cognitive, ego, and moral development. According to some theorists, the whole personality is in a stage of disorganization during this period.

By age 16 or so, most young people are at a higher level of development and integration but need more time to assess their values, goals, and heterosexual relationships. Because child care requires the ability to be nurturant to another, to carry a heavy load of responsibility, to control one's impulses, to make wise judgments, and to provide the child with a wealth of experiences and firm guidance,* it seems unlikely that younger adolescents would, on the average, be as effective as older ones in their child rearing. It also seems likely that, on the average, a premarital pregnancy would particularly strain a young marriage.

On the other hand, ages and stages are far from the whole story in human development and the capacity for parenthood. People who have been well parented themselves, whose motivations, values, interests, and experiences have particularly prepared them to care happily and effectively for children, may be excellent parents, regardless of their age, especially if various support systems are available to them in their own families and in the community.

In general, as shown in Chapter 9, the consequences of early marriages are easily confused with the causes that lead to this particular life event. Then, too, the nature of American society and its life-styles have changed so much in recent years, particularly since the early 1960s, that assumptions about the causes and consequences of youth behaviors must be carefully reexamined. As young people often say, "It is a whole new ballgame." However, whether or not a new ballgame is fundamentally different from an old one in how it affects the basic feelings and values of human beings may be another question.

Effects on Parent Generation

Although many young people may take a flexible and experimental approach to the "brave new world" of the present, their seeming ease in doing so may have positive and negative effects on their parents. No studies have looked at the consequences of early marriage and early childbearing on the

* In sober truth, who can do all these things?

parents of the young people involved. To what extent are parents called upon to give financial, child-care, and social-psychological supports to the young family? What effects may the provision of such supports have on relationships between the older and younger generations? What effects may the provision have on the life-styles and plans of older couples? These are all areas that require further serious consideration and research.

IN SUMMARY

The factors most closely associated with early marriage appear to be (or to have been) the following: being premaritally pregnant; dating early and frequently; going steady; "falling in love" at an early age; having premarital intercourse at an early age (for girls); coming from families of lower socioeconomic status; having domestic interests, a traditional view of the female sex role, and a low achievement drive (in the case of girls); and coming from either an unusually happy or unusually unhappy family situation.

The consequences of early marriage are so intertwined with the causes that it is impossible to clearly identify them. Although early marriages are more likely to end in divorce or separation and to be more characteristic of couples with relatively little education and earning ability, it cannot be said with confidence that these results would have been different if the people involved had entered their first marriage at a later age.

CHAPTER 11

The Service Needs of Pregnant and Parenting Adolescents

LORRAINE V. KLERMAN, JAMES F. JEKEL, and
CATHERINE S. CHILMAN

This chapter is concerned with the service needs of pregnant and parenting adolescents. First, however, a warning is important regarding the relationship between presumed causes and consequences of adolescent childbearing and the prevention of unplanned births to teenagers. As discussed in Chapters 8 and 9, the apparent consequences of adolescent childbearing are often confused with underlying causal factors. Poor employment prospects may contribute to early pregnancy rather than result from it. School failures may stimulate behaviors leading to early pregnancy rather than pregnancy being the cause of dropping out of school. Second, association does not prove causation. Many adolescent mothers would face similar problems if they became pregnant after age 18, and many of their children would be exposed to poor parenting even if their births had been delayed. The problems facing these adolescents and their children are often due to malnutrition, inadequate medical care, unimaginative educational systems, and other factors frequently associated with poverty, racial prejudice, and sexism. An early pregnancy undoubtedly worsens the effect of these factors, but these underlying issues also contribute heavily to the problems.

It would logically follow that if society wanted to prevent adolescent pregnancy or its unfortunate sequelae, it should target its programs on the institutions responsible for the underlying issues (e.g., the school system, the labor market, and welfare programs). However, most attention has been focused on the casualties of these institutions—pregnant and parenting adolescents. Given early pregnancy and parenthood, what can be done to minimize the consequences for mother, child, male partner, families, and society? This chapter will follow society's lead and focus on what can be accomplished working directly with adolescents and their children, families, and male partners in the absence of broader social welfare approaches, which are discussed in Chapter 15. Specifically, this chapter will examine needed services in the areas of health care, education, financial support, child care, living arrangements, and counseling.

GENERAL PRINCIPLES OF SERVICE DELIVERY

Before proceeding to examine each specialized service, some general principles of service delivery need to be underscored because of their particular relevance for pregnant and parenting adolescents. For example, those planning services should not act as though all females who become pregnant under age 20 belong in the same category. Rather, each human service worker who assists a pregnant or parenting adolescent should conduct a careful assessment of needs. Contrary to common assumptions, not all pregnant or parenting adolescents require special services. For instance, many of these young people are married, many receive help from family members, and the majority of "adolescent" parents are 18 or 19 years old.

Looking at pregnant teenagers individually rather than as a statistical group helps to determine not only who is most in need of services but also what services these clients are likely to need. Reviews of needed services for pregnant adolescents tend to degenerate into laundry lists of all possible services, with little attention to fiscal realities or the differences among individuals. Several social welfare programs already require that services be individualized for clients—for example, the Individual Service Plan of the Supplementary Security Income (SSI) program or, better known, the Individualized Education Program (IEP) of Public Law 94–142, the Education for All Handicapped Children Act. Rather than have a package of prepared services into which a pregnant woman is placed without regard for her particular needs, each young woman should be studied carefully in terms of her socioeconomic characteristics, her aspirations, the needs she expresses, and the unspoken needs perceived by the human service workers. The young mother's resources should be examined, both financial ones and such potential social and psychological support systems as members of the immediate family, relatives, friends (both female and male), and involved agencies. On the basis of this information, an individualized service plan should be developed.

An individualized service plan should not be made *for* a pregnant adolescent but *with* her. This is usually easier to accomplish with a 17 year old than with a 13 year old, but it is urgent and frequently difficult regardless of age. A very young adolescent often is unable to project herself into the future, to see clearly the impact of what she does or does not do today, this week, next month, or at age 20 or later. Even with middle or late adolescents, long-range planning may be a problem. Many social agencies that attempt to serve a select sample of especially troubled pregnant teenagers report that only a small percentage of their clients are future oriented in the sense of being able to plan their lives in a realistic way. Many lack information about financial needs and resources. Some are passive, accustomed to having decisions made for them by their mothers, fathers, boyfriends, or school systems. They tend to let things happen and accept what comes, rather than trying to manipulate their environments in order to produce the outcomes they desire.

Human service workers serving pregnant adolescents (young women and their partners) would do well not to reinforce their psychological dependency through planning for them. Rather, it is better to encourage both young mothers and young fathers to participate in the decision-making processes. This is difficult for both the professionals and the young people with whom they work. It may be frightening for pregnant adolescents to realize they are expected to think ahead and grow in self-reliance, especially at a time when they are stressed with an unplanned and possibly unwanted pregnancy. Clearly, these young people should not be encouraged to make decisions in the absence of needed information. This is the appropriate role of the professional: to inform, to advise, to support, and to guide.

The family of the pregnant adolescent, and possibly of her male partner, should also be encouraged to participate in planning for the future of the young woman and the others involved. In almost any family, the pregnancy of an unmarried daughter is likely to create a crisis. Many adolescents exhibit avoidance–delay tactics and flight reactions because they expect negative reactions from their parents. Thus, they resist informing their parents about the pregnancy. But frequently adolescents misjudge their fathers and mothers. They anticipate feelings of hurt and unforgiving anger by family members that may not materialize, or they fail to realize early tempers may soon fade. A more objective assessment of the situation by skilled counselors often reveals underlying warm family feelings toward the daughter, parental guilt about possible contributions to her predicament, and, in some cases, positive anticipation of a grandchild.

It is important to encourage pregnant teenagers to communicate with family members and their partners regarding the pregnancy, if such communication is at all possible. Counseling sessions that include family members of the young woman and perhaps her partner, as well as other crucial members of his family, may be particularly helpful in establishing clear communications between the persons involved in the total family system. A sense of family unity and a set of possible realistic plans may be developed through such sessions. Though often difficult and stormy, at least in their earlier phases, these sessions can be extremely helpful, especially when guided by a skilled counselor or team of counselors.

In the past, family members and male partners were often excluded from planning by professionals who worked with young unmarried mothers, sometimes because of the adolescents' desire for secrecy. In general, family attitudes have become more tolerant in recent years, and, if the young woman consents, it has become common to include family members in counseling. Because beliefs and feelings vary enormously, individual assessment of each situation is again advised.

Of course, neither family nor group counseling is best in all circumstances. The situation and preferences of the adolescent may recommend individual counseling or a combination of approaches. Whatever methods are used, both the counselor and the young woman need to realize that the quality of her family life and her relationships with both her family members and her boyfriend contributed to her present situation. Moreover, in the months and years to come, family members, and perhaps the baby's father, will be important people in her life and probably the major sources of assistance. It is crucial, therefore, that a young pregnant woman and the professionals who work with her consider these significant others when making plans for the future (Fox, 1978; Furstenberg and Crawford, 1978. Also see the counseling section in a later part of this chapter and in Chapter 12.).

HEALTH CARE

The health services needed by pregnant and parenting adolescents cover a wide spectrum from pregnancy testing through prenatal care, labor, and delivery, to the postpartum care of mother and infant for several years. Numerous studies have shown that specialized health services, particularly in the prenatal period, can be successful in preventing many of the negative health consequences of at least the first adolescent pregnancy for the young mother and her infant. It is crucial to emphasize the importance of health services from the beginning. Social agencies, schools, welfare departments, and other organizations assisting pregnant adolescents should urge their clients to receive early and appropriate health services.

Pregnancy Testing

The health care needs of pregnant adolescents usually begin with pregnancy testing. Easy availability of this service is crucial regardless of the test's outcome or the adolescent's decision about her pregnancy. If she is not pregnant and did not want to be, the fright frequently will lead to effective contraception. The excellent opportunity for contraceptive guidance offered when a negative test is reported should not be wasted.

If the test is positive, the adolescent faces an important series of decisions: To abort or to carry to term? To surrender the baby for adoption or to raise it herself? To raise the child as a single parent or to plan to marry? If the decision is to abort, the earlier the procedure is performed, the safer it is. If the decision is to carry to term, the earlier prenatal care is instituted, the greater the likelihood of a healthy pregnancy.

For all these reasons, young women who suspect pregnancy should be encouraged to present themselves for pregnancy tests as early as possible. This requires that there be a sufficient number of testing facilities and that they be easily accessible, confidential, and free or low cost. Not many teenagers are likely to seek confirmation of a pregnancy in the office of their family physician. Public facilities are obviously needed. Many family planning clinics offer pregnancy testing without charge. School health rooms would be convenient sites to leave urine specimens for pregnancy testing, but few school systems seem willing to undertake this service. An exception is the high school-based health program in St. Paul, Minnesota. Pregnancy testing is only one of the services offered, many of the others being more socially acceptable, such as athletic examinations, immunizations, and weight control (Edwards et al., 1980). When pregnancy testing is not available on the premises, school nurses and guidance counselors should at least know where such services are available and be able to refer students to the sites. They also should know how a pregnancy test is done so they can explain it to hesitant and frightened young people.

Adolescents should be cautioned against trusting the do-it-yourself pregnancy tests that can be obtained from pharmacies. Teenagers are possibly more likely than adults to make an error in performing the test. A false negative test will delay considerably the time when a pregnant adolescent first seeks care for a pregnancy, and a false positive test could lead to unnecessary panic and perhaps rash actions. Two existing home pregnancy test kits are Predictor and E.P.T. (Early Pregnancy Test). Both claim low false positive and false negative rates if the tests are done correctly, but it is easy to make a mistake. For example, at least 9 days after the most recent period was expected to begin, one must collect the *first* morning urine, put a specified amount into a small bottle with tablets *without touching the bottle,* add the contents of a small vial, shake for at least 10 seconds, and then place in a vibration-free place for at least 2 and no more than 3 hours. The test must be read from an attached mirror within that time period or the test is invalid, and the appearance of the reaction may be less clear than on the enclosed instructions. Although these tests may be useful for some women, it is probably unwise for a teenager to trust them. Also, they are not cheap, in the range of $12 per test.

Abortion

Abortion is another health service that should be available to those who choose this alternative. The latest statistics of the Alan Guttmacher Institute (Henshaw et al., 1981) indicate that some teenagers will have easier access than others to abortion. The Institute reported that in 1978 there were 2753 abortion providers: 1626 hospital and 1127 nonhospital. These facilities, however, were not evenly distributed geographically; they were especially lacking in nonmetropolitan areas.

Financing is another problem faced by pregnant adolescents seeking abortions. Since late 1977, when the Hyde Amendment was first enforced, federal funds have not been available to finance abortions through Medicaid. Although the total number of abortions has continued to rise, the increase has been smaller than projected. As of 1981, only 16 states and the District of Columbia still paid for abortions from public funds.

Abortion is not a medical procedure exclusively. Before deciding to have an abortion, a young woman should be given an opportunity to discuss whether or not it is the best option for her from the physical, social, psychological, economic, and familial points of view. (See also Chapters 7, 13, and 14.) If she decides to proceed with the abortion, comprehensive follow-up services are essential, including contraceptive assistance and other educational and counseling programs directed toward treatment of the problems that may have led to the early unwanted pregnancy and toward the prevention of such pregnancies in the future.

Prenatal Care, Labor, and Delivery

For adolescents who choose parenthood, whether single or married, many health services are required both for the prenatal and the postpartum period. During the prenatal period pregnant adolescents need medical care both for pregnancy-related problems and for other health problems they may have brought to the pregnancy, such as dental caries, inadequate nutrition, or allergies. Each community must decide where and by whom prenatal care is to be delivered, and how it is to be financed. Many adolescents probably will seek medical attention in the office of an obstetrician or general practitioner. Payment for such care may be a problem. Often the family does not have adequate financial resources. The family medical insurance policy may not cover maternity services for dependents. Moreover, the family may have rejected the adolescent and may refuse to be responsible for her medical care expenses. Unfortunately, in many states Medicaid will not pay for prenatal care and delivery for young women who are not on welfare, even though the mother and child may be eligible for Aid to Families with Dependent Children (AFDC) once the child is born. Clearly this is a shortsighted policy.

Adequate prenatal care can prevent prematurity and other forms of infant morbidity. If the absence of funds causes an adolescent to delay seeking care, or not to receive any care prior to delivery, the risk of a less than perfect outcome increases, and it is the welfare department that probably will assume a large share of the financial burden.

Some communities offer several alternatives to the private physician's office, including hospital ambulatory care centers, health department clinics, Maternity and Infant Care Projects, and community health centers. In the early days of adolescent pregnancy programs, the providers at some facilities were insensitive to the special needs of adolescents. They saw both teenagers and older pregnant women during the same clinic periods and conducted clinics during school hours. They did not prepare young women for pelvic examinations or provide opportunities for adolescents to discuss their problems and anxieties. And they were frequently judgmental.

Most experts in the field today recommend that there be clinics exclusively for adolescents under age 18 or 20, that such clinics be operated after school hours, and that they employ only obstetricians, nurse-midwives, nurses, social workers, and clerical personnel who enjoy young people and who are not judgmental. Such facilities should not be organized on the schedule that might be used for older pregnant women. Sufficient time must be allowed for explaining procedures before and after they are done and for sensitive listening to the adolescents' doubts and fears.

It is crucial that clinics or private practitioners make appointments for prenatal care soon after the pregnant adolescent contacts them. Not only may the young woman have problems that need immediate attention, but a long delay between the initial contact and first appointment may be perceived as a rejection, and she may delay still further before actually obtaining care.

Educational programs are essential to help an adolescent understand her body's needs and changes during pregnancy, the process of labor and delivery itself, and what she can expect in the immediate postpartum period. These programs may be offered by the same institution that provides the medical care or collaboratively with a school or social agency. Nutritional information and counseling certainly should be part of such an educational program.

Unfortunately, even the best medical program is of little assistance to adolescents who do not seek care. Eliminating financial barriers, making facilities easily accessible in terms of time and place, and making them inviting by employing sympathetic personnel are essential steps in reducing the present high rates of late care seeking among adolescents. But more is needed: a program of aggressive outreach. This can be accomplished in many ways. For example, the March of Dimes/Birth Defects Foundation has attempted to make all pregnant women, particularly adolescents, aware of the need for prenatal care. Its spot announcements are carried on many radio stations, and its literature is often available in public facilities.

However, communities should not depend on the media alone; an individual approach to case finding also is needed. Pregnancy should be suspected when a young woman indicates that she wishes to drop out of school, and questions should be asked discreetly, with assurance of confidentiality. Pregnancy should also be suspected when there is an increase in absences or trips to the nurse's office. The schools, moreover, are not the only organizations that can detect early pregnancy and guide a young woman into care. Youth-serving organizations, such as neighborhood centers, youth groups, and religious organizations, also can play a role. In addition, information may be received from the young man involved, if the youth worker is sensitive to changes in attitudes and actions of young men and is available to listen sympathetically and with assurances of confidentiality.

Postpartum Care

After the baby is delivered, health services are needed for both the new mother and her child. A routine postpartum checkup is recommended at approximately 6 weeks postpartum, or earlier if there were complications during the pregnancy or in the labor and delivery period, in order to assure that the mother has recovered physically from the delivery and also to initiate family planning if she is willing to accept contraceptives. Actually, family planning and contraceptive use should have been discussed with the adolescent during the pregnancy or at discharge in individual counseling sessions with the physician, nurse, or counselor or in group meetings; however, the postpartum checkup is usually the time when a contraceptive program is decided upon by the adolescent with the help of the health care provider. A schedule of periodic checkups can be established at this point, if the provider believes these are needed because of gynecological problems or for contraceptive regulation.

Soon after birth, health care for the infant must be started. The infant should be taken to see a pediatrician, pediatric nurse-practitioner, or family physician at about 1 month of age, or sooner if there are any problems. The child should receive a complete physical examination, including a check for developmental milestones. The well-child visits continue at about one per month for the first 6 months, and the immunizations begin at 2 months of age, unless there are complications. During the second half of the child's first year, the well-child visits come less often, about every other month, depending on the needs of the child and the young mother, as well as the practitioner's judgment.

Some studies suggest that teenage mothers are relatively diligent in caring for their infants, at least initially. They tend to take the infant to private physicians or to clinics regularly and have the child immunized (Kinard et al., 1980). The literature also suggests that a young mother may rely on her mother for advice when the infant is sick (Zuckerman et al., 1979). The task of the young mother is made easier if pediatric care is available from the same hospital or agency that provided her with prenatal care or other services. The continuity of personnel apparently makes her less hesitant to seek care than if she had to contact a new agency or organization and explain her need, particularly when she expects negative reactions because of her youth, and possibly her unmarried status. When the agency that provided services during the prenatal period is unable to care for the child, as a minimum it should offer adolescent parents the names of child health care providers and call the personnel at other agencies to prepare them for the arrival of the young mother.

Public health or visiting nurses should be considered an important resource in the care and support of adolescent parents. Often they will be involved in prenatal care and health classes for the adolescents, but even if not, they should be scheduled to visit homes soon after babies are born to determine the basic strengths and weaknesses in the child-care patterns. They can assist new mothers by suggesting methods of infant stimulation, examining the infant from a health viewpoint, and making appropriate referrals, if needed. Most important, they should be easily available for help on an ongoing basis. Because of their training, which emphasizes social and physical factors, public health nurses can be depended on to be an important asset to educational and social programs for adolescents.

Suggested Guidelines

In 1978 the Committee on Maternal Health Care and Family Planning, Maternal and Child Health Section, American Public Health Association, issued a volume entitled *Ambulatory Maternal Health Care and Family Planning Services; Policies, Principles, Practices.* Its chapter on adolescent pregnancy included the following guidelines for the health aspects of programs for pregnant and parenting adolescents.*

> Adolescents are individuals and should be treated with respect and a nonjudgmental attitude in an atmosphere of privacy and confidentiality.
> Adolescents must be provided access, without parental consent, to sex and family life education, contraceptive advice and treatment, pregnancy testing, abortion, and prenatal and postpartum care.

---

* In 1979, the American College of Obstetricians and Gynecologists issued a booklet that also described the service needs of young women. Entitled *Adolescent Perinatal Health: A Guidebook for Services,* it can be obtained from ACOG at 600 Maryland Ave., SW, Washington, DC 20024.

Adequate financial support should be available so that access to services is not restricted.

Provisions should be made for the early detection of pregnancy in adolescent women, and information concerning the availability of this service should be emphasized.

All alternatives for dealing with the pregnancy must be presented as viable solutions.

An interdisciplinary, comprehensive approach should be utilized in dealing with adolescent pregnancy.

Where appropriate and possible, services should be offered to the father of the child and to the adolescent's parents.

Early and consistent prenatal care should be available and accessible for those young women continuing their pregnancies to term.

The nutritional status of the adolescent should be assessed to ensure that appropriate counseling and services are provided.

Adequate preparation for the hospital and childbirth experience should be provided.

Postpregnancy care should be provided and should emphasize family planning.

A program of consistent counseling and health education should be provided to the pregnant adolescent during and after pregnancy.

The pregnant adolescent should be encouraged to continue her regular education and be provided with the appropriate support services needed to do so.

Special classes in family life education should be provided for all adolescents, especially those pregnant adolescents who continue their pregnancy to term.

Programs for pregnant adolescents should undergo systematic, ongoing evaluation.

EDUCATION

One of the most publicized consequences of adolescent pregnancy is the interruption or cessation of secondary education (Card & Wise, 1978; Moore, 1978). Historically, and well into the 1970s, pregnant school-age women were forced out of their regular schools during pregnancy, or even permanently. Clearly, this was a consequence of adolescent pregnancy that was difficult for a teenager to overcome, and society's response was often part of the problem.

In the 1960s, many school systems began to provide alternative forms of education, such as homebound instruction (Holmes, 1970), or detached, special schools for pregnant school-age students. The theory behind the special efforts was that, if one could help a teenager continue her education during pregnancy, she could return to her regular school after delivery with a minimum loss of learning and could then proceed to finish high school, at least. This view was partly correct, but it was also somewhat naive for at least two reasons. First, many school-age mothers were in academic difficulty before the pregnancy and might not have finished school even in the absence of a pregnancy (Foltz et al., 1972). Second, there was insufficient appreciation of the difficulties many school-age mothers would face in finding the child care essential to school completion or the time needed to do school assignments and still care for a young child.

Although the educational system's reasons for creating separate, special schools were often negative—to avoid "contamination" of the other students or to reduce the potential for injury to pregnant adolescents and the possibility of lawsuits—those responsible for the creation of these schools viewed them as the best solution to the real needs of pregnant adolescents and adolescent mothers. Special schools permitted pregnant adolescents to be surrounded by others in a similar situation and by teachers and counselors with the special interests and skills essential to help these young people handle their problems. In such a setting, it was easier to develop comprehensive educational and counseling services and often to integrate medical services as well.

Special schools also provided opportunities for intensive remedial educational efforts for pregnant adolescents who were below grade or doing poorly in school. Many found these special efforts such a boost that they were able to improve their interest and performance in school.

Despite these assets, the special schools have not proved to be panaceas. They are expensive. Also many young women preferred to stay in their regular schools rather than be cloistered with other pregnant teenagers, away from their friends and usual activities. Third, those using the special schools often faced reentry shock upon returning to the regular school postpartum.

A Rand study of school responses to teenage pregnancy and parenthood (Zellman, 1981a) revealed the problems in attempting to integrate special and regular schools, with regular schools usually assuming little if any responsibility for the reentry of young mothers. For this and other reasons, the study reviews favorably several school programs that use a supplementary curriculum approach. Pregnant students in these schools attend regular classes and are offered additional relevant courses, such as classes in homemaking and child care. In addition, specialized services are available at the school, such as counselors who put pregnant students in contact with the community agencies that can provide the services they need. Released time is given for medical appointments.

No clear conclusions can be drawn at this point regarding the regular school–special school controversy. Current wisdom suggests that most older pregnant schoolgirls, especially those with more self-confidence and involvement in school activities, may do better in regular schools. However, for younger or more timid adolescents, especially if they are having academic problems, the detached programs may provide important assistance.

Another group of pregnant adolescents who may particularly benefit from the services provided by the special school are those who already have children. The primagravida is more mobile and independent and can more easily keep appointments and handle errands, appointments, and so on. For adolescents carrying a second or third child, transportation and child-care services become crucial if they are to attend school or go to clinics. In addition, it may be more difficult for a regular school to meet the emotional and educational needs of older adolescents who still have not completed their education. If they are behind in grade, they may feel out of place or stupid. Without the support of close friends and family members, they are likely to drop out. However, this does not mean they can never finish high school. Many young mothers obtain their high school equivalency through night classes, or by passing the General Educational Development (GED) examination. They may also secure vocational training (Klerman & Jekel, 1973; Moore & Caldwell, 1977). Such findings reinforce the view that increasing their options enables a higher proportion of young mothers to complete secondary education.

Educational programs for pregnant or parenting adolescents should be viewed in the context of Title IX of the Educational Amendments of 1976, which prohibit discrimination in a school's educational program because of pregnancy or childbirth. A pregnant or parenting student may not be forced to enter a special program, nor can any of the resources available to other students be denied her. Some schools ignore these provisions, and many adolescents, parents, and educators seem unaware of them. Nevertheless, Title IX provides a way to protect the rights of this vulnerable population. Human service professionals should be aware of this legislation and take active steps, if necessary, to see that it is implemented in their communities (Zellman, 1981b).

LIVING ARRANGEMENTS

Human service professionals may also be asked to help make decisions about the living arrangements for pregnant and parenting adolescents. What kind of arrangements are best, and where can resources be found for these arrangements? A variety of plans should be examined with a flexible, experimental attitude. What might seem like a good arrangement at one time, for example, may not work well later. Among the factors that need consideration are the psychological characteristics of the young woman and her male partner; the characteristics of the family members, and the support they provide to the young mother; the sociocultural patterns of the people involved; the physical condition of the young mother and, in the postpartum period, of the baby; the financial resources of the young parents; the actual kinds of housing available; and the perceptions and wishes of the persons involved. Community organizations that may assist with planning living arrangements for pregnant and parenting adolescents include departments of public welfare, child and family service associations, medical social service departments in clinics and hospitals, child welfare programs, and special programs for adolescent parents.

Possible living arrangements include: at home with the young woman's own family; with the family of the young woman's male partner; with another young woman in an apartment; with the male partner (either in a married or a cohabiting relationship); in a foster home; and in a center for pregnant adolescents or unmarried mothers. Each of these arrangements has advantages and disadvantages. For example, it may seem to be practical and desirable for the young woman to live with her own parents. Furstenberg's longitudinal study of adolescent mothers showed that often parents not only provided homes for the young women but also helped care for the children so the mothers could either continue high school or obtain employment (Furstenberg & Crawford, 1978). In some instances, however, the pregnancy may be a pathological response to a family situation. Remaining in such a situation could increase the social and psychological problems of the young mother and her children.

Living with the family of the male partner also may have positive aspects. Such an arrangement, however, could represent a deeper commitment by the young couple than they are ready to make. Also, whenever family living arrangements are made, the two sets of older parents may become embroiled in competition over the "possession" of the young parents and the child. These counseling and treatment issues are discussed in greater detail in Chapter 13.

Under almost no circumstances should a young mother live alone. Especially if she is less than 18 or 19 years old, she may well be frightened and lonely in such a situation. Also, it can be very expensive. Moreover, studies show that child development is enhanced when there are at least two adults in the home rather than only one parent or parent substitute. Sometimes young mothers decide to live with girlfriends. This may or may not work out well, depending on the characteristics of the friends and the resources available to them.

The young mother might prefer to live with her boyfriend away from both families. Such an arrangement would have been considered totally unacceptable in an earlier time, but now that cohabitation is more prevalent, it may occasionally be a viable arrangement, depending on the maturity of the young parents and their financial resources. Although counselors might be tempted to encourage marriage instead of such an arrangement, the separation and divorce rate for marriages between teenagers is extremely high. Also, early marriages often lead to rapid subsequent pregnancies.

In the past, agencies often arranged foster home placement for expectant unmarried mothers. Although data on the costs and benefits of such a plan are not available, impressionistic evidence tends to recommend it, at least in some cases. However, in recent years, high quality foster homes have become much more difficult to locate because so many potential foster mothers are in the work force. Also, foster home living arrangements have become increasingly expensive as the cost of living has risen.

Until recently, institutions for unmarried expectant mothers were often the living arrangement of choice. Frequently, these institutions were in another city to provide secrecy for the young woman and adoption arrangements for her baby. The greater social acceptability of unmarried parenthood and the resultant decline in the choosing of adoption by adolescent mothers has led to a decline in the number of these institutions. More recently, centers for pregnant high school girls that provide institutional living arrangements have been set up in a number of cities. Unfortunately, these arrangements have proved to be extremely expensive and their presumed benefits, such as prevention of future pregnancies and completion of high school, did not occur to a significant extent.

COUNSELING

At many times during her pregnancy and for several years after delivery, the young woman, as well as her male partner and both of their families, may need counseling. Since Chapter 13 is devoted to this subject, it will not be treated in detail here, except to review some of the areas in which counseling was recommended in earlier sections and to describe needs in two areas not previously discussed: adoption and the male partner.

Sexually active adolescents, or those considering becoming sexually active, need counseling about sexual feelings, the consequences of unprotected intercourse, and the types of family planning methods most suited to their life-styles. If pregnancy occurs, the adolescent and significant others in her life may need advice and guidance regarding the options of abortion, adoption, single parenthood, and marriage and parenthood. Those who decide to carry to term will need help in making decisions about education, living arrangements, and financial support during the prenatal period. Expectant adolescents need supportive counseling to encourage them to continue their prenatal care and to deal with such feelings as anxiety and fear regarding the pregnancy and approaching childbirth.

After the child's birth, adolescent parents should be offered counseling assistance in respect to such issues as child care, family and couple relationships, consistent use of contraceptives, continuing education, employment, living arrangements, and sources of financial aid. The young woman's new status as a pregnant female and later as a young mother will require redefinitions of roles and relationships with her male partner, peers of both sexes, and her family. If these negotiations are handled well, the young woman can enter motherhood with a stronger support network than existed prior to her pregnancy. For instance, Furstenberg (1980) has reported that a new baby sometimes pulls a family together, even if the baby is that of an unwed adolescent. If these negotiations go poorly, however, the young woman may become isolated, confused, and belligerent. Not only is she likely to suffer, but her child is apt to be denied the advantages of other adults in the environment, and the male partner as well as the two families involved may feel guilt and remorse.

Many pregnant adolescents and young parents can profit from counseling assistance that goes beyond the need for information but does not require intensive therapy or highly specialized guidance. They may profit from the continuing encouragement, supporting warmth, and sensitive understanding that should be available from a range of human service professionals with whom pregnant teenagers and adolescent parents may naturally come in contact. More specialized counseling, such as family therapy, psychotherapy, psychological assessment, and educational and vocational guidance, may be needed by some young parents. It seems unlikely that most communities need a specific adolescent service to meet these needs. Competent counseling specialists, such as child and adolescent psychiatrists and psychologists, social workers, and certified family therapists, are often available in both public and private settings. Costs of these services are often minimal for low-income persons or may frequently be met through Medicaid or health insurance.

As discussed earlier in this and other chapters, the factors associated with becoming an expectant mother or father are many and complex and vary from person to person. For some, the pregnancy may seem at least partly desirable or rather easily acceptable. For others, it may reflect serious psychological disturbances in the young parents-to-be and/or their family sys-

tem. Also, individual and familial reactions to an early unplanned pregnancy may vary from a calm, realistic acceptance to denial, rage, hysteria,
guilt, and anxiety.

Whether or not the persons involved should be referred for psychotherapy or intensive personal counseling depends on such factors as their desire
for or willingness to accept such a referral, the quality and costs of services
available, the depth of personal or familial disturbances, and the assessment
by a skilled diagnostician as to whether or not intensive individualized counseling or psychotherapy is likely to be helpful. This last decision usually
cannot be made until the therapist has worked with individuals or families
for at least several sessions. Some pregnant adolescents actively resist one-
to-one counseling. An illegitimate birth is not seen as deviant behavior by
many. It may have happened to their mothers or sisters, as well as to other
people they know. Many pregnant girls view their pregnancy as normal
(Clines, 1979).

Compared to individual counseling, group sessions seem to meet with
less resistance from pregnant and parenting adolescents. Unless these groups
are skillfully led, however, they may accomplish little except an exchange
of experiences, misinformation, and unhappy feelings. If group sessions are
to have positive effects, they need to have specific objectives and skilled
leadership. (See Chapters 12 and 13.)

Adoption

Although in the past many unwed pregnant young women released their
babies for adoption, today's adolescents seldom select this plan. It has been
suggested that most young women today who do not feel ready to take on
the responsibilities of parenthood decide to have abortions. Nevertheless,
young women should be encouraged to consider the alternative of adoptive
placement, particularly if abortions become more difficult to obtain because of restrictions on federal funding. Young parents-to-be interested
in exploring the possibility of adoption should be referred to professional
social agencies. Application to such an agency does not imply that the young
parents have chosen to relinquish their child. These agencies can provide
skilled counseling services that help parents explore the choices open to
them, with adoption being one of the informed decisions they may wish to
make. Adoption is a highly technical and serious matter and should be
handled only by people who have training in this area. Careful, specialized
services are needed, which require a full knowledge of adoption laws, of the
family that wishes to adopt the child, and of the parents who are giving up
the baby for adoption.

If young parents decide to place the baby for adoption, they probably should relinquish the child legally either before birth or immediately afterward. Taking a baby home and then relinquishing it later is much more difficult than giving up the baby initially. It also is better for the child to be placed in the adoptive home as soon as possible after birth. Leaving a child in limbo, such as in a foster home or an institution, for even a month can have adverse effects on the infant, and parents should be discouraged from prolonging the decision process. Far too many children have been lost in foster homes and institutional placements awaiting possible adoption because the natural parents have been indecisive. Over time, the child can be so psychologically damaged by this situation that eventual adoption becomes very difficult, if not impossible.

A Special Look at Male Partners

There is a need to revise common images and fallacious assumptions about the male partners of pregnant or parenting adolescent women. A number of these assumptions reflect earlier attitudes toward male and female sexual behavior. Counseling couples and male partners requires understanding, empathy, skill, and knowledge of the current situation. Studies show that most of the male partners of adolescent unmarried mothers also are very young. They tend to have low educational goals and inadequate academic achievement, poor self-esteem, defective interpersonal skills, feelings of alienation from much of society, and distrust of many of its middle-class organizations. (See Chapters 15 and 16.) Contrary to a frequent image of the male partners as irresponsible, many have positive attitudes toward the young women, and later the child. Attitudes toward the self as a father vary a good deal by race, ethnicity, and socioeconomic status. For example, low-income, black males tend to value fertility highly, to take pride in themselves as fathers, to want to be helpful to mothers and to the children, but to shy away from commitments to marriage or long-term legal obligations for financial support. In part, their wariness concerning marriage and continued support is rooted in lack of good employment opportunities.

Many blue-collar working-class white families tend to believe that a premarital pregnancy is acceptable but requires the expectant mother and her partner to marry. Further variations in attitudes have been discussed elsewhere in this book. Attitudes and behaviors of adolescents in these situations are heavily affected by their cultural patterns as well as by other factors.

Studies (Komarovsky, 1976; Rainwater, 1970; Rubin, 1976) of low-income males (who are more likely than other young men to become adolescent fathers) report the following characteristics:

Rigid sex role differentiation, with males being seen as having little to do with child rearing, homemaking tasks, and interpersonal relationships within the family.

Distrust of verbal communication and lack of knowledge and skills in respect to discussing one's feelings and personal behaviors.

A fatalistic attitude, with the belief that one's life is determined far more by luck than by one's own efforts.

Alienation from the middle-class community and its organizations.

Distrust of intellectualism and of persons in authority.

Such values and attitudes create barriers to efforts at counseling by middle-class human service professionals. They might also lead to communication and relationship difficulties between the young man and young woman. Skilled and sensitive counseling with the young couple as a pair might help them gain a better understanding of each other and some of the skills needed to improve their style of communicating and planning.

A number of studies suggest that males may be more negatively affected than females by being brought up in a one parent family. (See Chapters 2 and 8.) Many adolescent fathers have such a background. They may particularly need acceptance and reassurance about their potentialities as young men. In this context, it is important to recognize that most adolescent men are less knowledgeable about sexuality and family planning than most adolescent girls, because they are less likely to have had education on these subjects, either at school or in the family. They may be disturbed about their lack of knowledge, because society expects them to be competent in a whole range of sex behaviors and to take leadership with their female partners.

In conclusion, it should be noted that many communities fall short of providing all the kinds of high quality counseling that pregnant adolescents and teenage parents, male and female, may need. In situations of serious service deficits, human services personnel should act as advocates for their young clients and participate in community development activities to obtain needed resources.

FINANCIAL SUPPORT

Most pregnant teenagers and adolescent parents are likely to need some help with finances. This is partly because many come from low-income families in the first place and partly because of the expense of medical services, child care, and maintaining a household that includes a young child. Professionals who work with these young people may need to help them assess their financial situation and possible resources from their families and their own employment as well as their anticipated expenses. These professionals should be aware of other sources of financial assistance, both public and private, and the regulations concerning them. These may include special projects for pregnant teenagers and young parents; government programs that require monetary support from the putative father and family members; AFDC and other governmental assistance programs; child-care allowances; Medicaid; educational and employment programs that provide work for unemployed youths; vocational rehabilitation services; and private health and social agencies. Sources of information about these matters are often available through welfare departments, social service departments of hospitals and clinics, and the United Way.

The Male Partner

The male partner is the most traditional source of financial help. By law in most states, the male who has contributed to the pregnancy must support the infant regardless of whether he and the mother are married. In many states, when a pregnant adolescent or young mother applies for welfare she is asked for the name of her male partner. Many hesitate to divulge this information because the partner may have urged against it. He may not want to be legally obligated to make payments or to have his parents know about his predicament. If the couple's relationship is important to the young woman, she usually will not want to risk impairing it by taking legal action or making such action possible. Or a young woman may decide not to give her partner's name because she may receive less money by this action. Usually the money putative fathers officially contribute goes to a state account and is not reflected in the mother's welfare payment, whereas if the young mother does not reveal his name, he may pay her directly.

This is just one of many instances where welfare regulations may have a negative impact. In this case, they not only encourage falsification but deter the male from publicly assuming responsibility for his child. Although federal and state governments are now involved in a large-scale program of child support enforcement under Title IV-D of the Social Security Act, reports on this program do not analyze the data by age of mother or father or by legitimacy status. Research is essential to determine what proportion of the male partners currently are or have the potential to become sources of financial support. Many of them are teenagers and are unemployed or working at very low wages, and come from low-income families.

According to studies of black unmarried mothers (Furstenberg, 1976; Sauber and Corrigan, 1970; Bowerman, Irish and Pope, 1966; Ewer & Gibbs, 1975; Lorenzi, Klerman and Jekel, 1977) (research about other groups is unavailable), most young fathers give what financial and child-care help they can, at least for a limited period. Moreover, at least in the populations and at the times researched, the majority of young fathers tend to continue a helping relationship with their children and the mothers over a period of time. Official efforts to legally identify these young men and extract support payments from them are likely to be costly, to result in meager financial returns, and to have adverse effects on positive informal helping relationships. (Most of the available studies were done before the late 1970s, and the situation may have changed since that time.)

Even if the adolescent mother marries, AFDC policies may have an adverse effect on the young family. In 22 states, assistance payments will not be made if the child's biological father is present in the home. This policy, based on the fallacious assumption that any man, even a teenager, can find steady employment at adequate wages, penalizes couples who marry and establish a home together. This policy overlooks the high unemployment rate for youths, particularly for those in the inner city.

The Woman's Family

Most pregnant women and young mothers receive many types of support from their families. If they live at home during the pregnancy and for a short or long period after the child is born, their families will be providing shelter, food, clothing, and other necessities either from household earnings or from their welfare allotment.

Several studies have suggested that young mothers who live with their parents in the first few years of their child's life are more likely to finish school and less likely to become pregnant again quickly. However, welfare policy does not always provide incentives for this living arrangement. Policies should encourage more young mothers to remain in their parents' homes until they have the maturity and financial ability to establish an independent household, or an opportunity for a supportive and lasting marriage. This should include supplemental assistance, if needed, to family members who provide a home for pregnant teenagers or young parents and their children.

Present policies generally provide separate grants for welfare-eligible teenage mothers and their children. These grants may be a source of friction between the various members of the extended family. In some cases, this policy may also create a larger or more complicated assistance grant than is actually necessary. These issues are difficult matters of policy. An extended-family grant, for example, might give parents too much control over adolescent mothers and fathers and the grandchildren. Also, in some cases, living apart from an extended family might be a better arrangement for adolescents than living within it. Flexible policies in this regard seem most useful, but, of course, they are difficult to administer equitably.

Although there is no clear federal policy, there seems to be a general consensus that women with children under age 6 years should have the option of staying home with their children, rather than seeking outside employment. For example, an AFDC mother is required to register for the Work Incentive Program (WIN) when her youngest child reaches age 6. However, there is less reason to expect young mothers to work, because the majority have not yet finished school. Their education, plus child care, should be the major tasks for most of them.

Adolescent mothers usually go off and on the welfare rolls according to the state of the job market for themselves and their male partners and the availability of low cost child care. Given women's low earnings, it is the rare woman of any age who is so fortunate as to hold a job that pays enough for her to support her family and meet the costs of child care (Keniston & the Carnegie Commission on Children, 1977; Ross & Sawhill, 1976). The inescapable conclusion is that a large number of single mothers, both teenagers and older women, are likely to be welfare dependent unless wages for women are vastly improved and free or low cost high quality child care is made available.

Medicaid policies further complicate the problem. In many states, Medicaid is available only to those on AFDC. Many young mothers who can earn sufficient money to enable them not to need AFDC—and thus often to raise their own self-esteem—choose either not to earn the money or to conceal the amount in order not to lose Medicaid benefits. Although they might be able to support themselves and their children, they cannot cover unexpected physicians' or hospital bills. A Medicaid program for the medically needy, a Medicare-type program for children, or national health insurance is needed to solve this problem.

The entire issue of whether single parenthood causes poverty and unemployment, or results from poverty and unemployment, is extremely complex and beyond the limits of this book. However, it can be briefly stated that both sets of factors might be termed causative and interact in numerous ways in a variety of life situations. Nevertheless, because a large percentage of adolescent mothers are welfare dependent, and possibly because of society's anger over the high rate of out-of-wedlock births in this group, economic self-sufficiency is frequently given as a goal for programs designed for pregnant and parenting adolescents. Full economic self-sufficiency can be only a long-term goal for many of these young women—at least 6 years after delivery if only one child is involved, and more if there are other, later children. The other route to avoiding welfare dependency is marriage to a gainfully employed male. However, it is probably more realistic to establish intermediate goals for financial independence, such as vocational training and part-time employment.

CHILD CARE

The young mother who wishes to further her education or to work full or part-time must find someone to care for her child. This problem is particularly acute with the infant and young toddler. By the time the child reaches age 4 or 5, such public programs as Head Start or kindergarten may be available for part of the day.

Services and Financing

The problem has two dimensions: first, to find someone or some institution to care for the child; and second, to secure funds to pay for the service. Many young mothers leave their children in the care of their parents, siblings, male partners, or male partner's family. This solution may bring with it several problems. The chosen baby-sitters may be employed and may wish to continue to support themselves and their families. They should not be forced to make a choice between their own needs and wishes and the needs and wishes of the young parent. When the grandmother agrees to care for the child, another problem may be conflict about how the child is to be raised. The grandmother may assume the role of parent, and the real mother may resent this. A third problem is the potential for neglect, if not abuse, when the care provider is forced to assume a task he or she may not want.

Alternatively, care may be purchased from unrelated individuals, family day-care providers, or day-care centers. Family day-care settings that shelter more than a specified number of infants or children and all day-care centers are usually licensed by states. Individual baby-sitters are not. Family day-care providers usually care for two or three infants or a slightly larger number of toddlers in their own homes. Day-care centers usually care for larger numbers in agency or institutional settings.

Although family day care and day-care centers seem to overcome some of the problems associated with the use of relatives, they also are not perfect solutions. First, in most communities, there are fewer day-care openings, especially for infants, than there is demand. Second, these services must be purchased. In some communities, the welfare department will pay for day care if the adolescent mother attends school or works, but in others, different categories of individuals receive first priority for welfare-provided day care. Third, many young mothers or their families are reluctant to leave children, especially young infants, with strangers. Then, too, some agencies report some grandparents may insist that their daughters stay home and care for their infants even if it means a temporary or permanent end to the adolescents' education. Finally, the real hazards to health and safety when many young children are housed together for long periods of time means that continual surveillance of day-care programs by public health and safety officials is essential.

On the positive side, family day care and day-care centers may offer advantages that relatives cannot. Often the staff members have received training in child health and development. Not only can they use such education directly in their interactions with their charges, but they can also share this information with young parents, helping them to understand their children's needs. Some providers, especially day-care centers that may be affiliated with a hospital, social agency, or school, may also help young parents obtain services for themselves and their children.

The Child's Well-Being

The well-being of the child should not be neglected when the adolescent parent's desire for substitute child care is considered. Adequate child care is an important issue in and of itself, regardless of parental age. Such care may be especially important, however, for teenage parents, because both the young parents and their children are particularly vulnerable, not only because of their youth and marital status, but because so many are also victims of poverty, racism, and unstable family backgrounds.

Caring, consistent, competent parenting is one of the central components of a child's development, especially in the early years of life. Although it was thought until recently that only a mother could provide the kind of loving, dependable care that a baby and toddler needs, more recent research indicates that other people can be adequate parent substitutes and that parenting can be shared by two or three people, at least. In fact, evidence is emerging that children, especially boys, with only one adult caretaker may suffer developmental and cognitive deficits and display disturbed social behavior. (See discussion in Chapter 8 and Clarke-Stewart, 1977.)

Research has also shown that most young children aged 3 and older benefit from high-quality preschool programs. This is especially true when the parents are heavily involved in the programs. This finding challenges earlier assumptions that young children need the security of staying home with their own mothers until they begin kindergarten or elementary school. Research supporting high-quality day-care programs for preschoolers, however, does not necessarily support the concept that substitute care in a family day-care setting or a formal day-care center is beneficial for infants and toddlers. The needs of babies and toddlers for protective, individualized, consistent care are quite different from those of preschoolers who seek independence, social interaction, and environmental exploration (Harmon & Brim, 1980; Ziegler & Valentine, 1979).

Concern for the sound development of children, especially their cognitive development, has been another source of popular enthusiasm for encouraging adolescent mothers to place their infants in licensed day-care centers. Especially during the late 1960s and early 1970s, it was thought that such centers, administered by highly trained personnel, could make a significant positive contribution to the infant's cognitive development that might lead to greater academic success in later years. Evaluative studies of some of these programs, however, yielded somewhat disappointing results (Clarke-Stewart, 1977).

Options

A variety of child-care arrangements should be available to adolescent parents, as well as to older ones. Decisions about arrangements should be based on the characteristics of both the parents and their children. Some infants and young children require much more individualized care than others because they are tense, anxious and irritable, hyperactive, or frequently ill. Clearly, substitute day care is harder to arrange for such infants and, in fact, is probably not in their best interest.

Human service professionals working with adolescent parents should bear in mind these principles and help young parents explore various options for themselves and their children. It is important to know child-care resources in the community. This includes parenting classes, support groups, and counseling as well as substitute day-care programs. When essential resources are lacking, concerned professionals should join with others to advocate the development of a range of options for high-quality substitute day care of children, as well as educational and other support programs for young parents.

COMPREHENSIVE SERVICE PROGRAMS

Pregnant teenagers and parenting adolescents often need a large array of services. In 1978, Congress, in authorizing a grant program to organizations that served pregnant and parenting adolescents, specified 10 core services that had to be provided by all grantees:

1. Pregnancy testing, maternity counseling, and referral services.
2. Family planning services.
3. Primary and preventive health services, including pre- and post-natal care.
4. Nutrition information and counseling.

5. Referral for screening and treatment of venereal disease.
6. Referral to appropriate pediatric care.
7. Educational services in sexuality and family life (including sex education), and family planning information.
8. Referral to appropriate educational and vocational services.
9. Adoption counseling and referral services.
10. Referral to other appropriate health services.

Supplemental services that are encouraged but not required include child care, consumer education and homemaking, counseling for family members, and transportation. This list suggests the services that experts in the field considered crucial to meet the needs of pregnant teenagers and adolescent parents.

Various organizations offer a package of services to pregnant and parenting adolescents. Some were created expressly for that purpose; others are subunits of such larger organizations as social service agencies, maternity homes, hospitals, health departments, or schools. Many offer some services on site and rely on referrals for other services, other organizations offer many services under one roof. Some have provided services to the adolescent during pregnancy and the immediate postpartum period only, but increasingly agencies realize that, to reach their goals, it is important to make services available to young parents for a number of years after a child's birth.

EVALUATION OF SERVICES AND PROGRAMS

Although considerable effort and funds have been invested in multiple-service programs for pregnant and parenting adolescents, evidence concerning both the costs and effectiveness of such programs is limited. First, there are relatively few programs compared to the need. In general, programs are found in large urban areas (Goldstein & Wallace, 1978; Wallace et al., 1973), leaving adolescents in smaller communities or in rural areas with few or no resources. Second, even where such programs exist, they often do not reach a large segment of those in need (Forbush & Jekel, 1978).

Relatively few well-designed studies have been conducted of program outcomes. Those that are available suggest that such services have a positive influence on maternal and infant health. On the other hand, their impact on such desired outcomes as improved contraceptive practice, steady employment, and reduced welfare dependency has been less than anticipated.

Many programs appear to assist pregnant adolescents to remain in school during pregnancy and to return to school in the immediate postpartum period. Some report success in the delay of subsequent pregnancies and in encouraging vocational training. Few have long enough follow-up periods or sufficiently powerful evaluation components to measure long-term impact on educational attainment, economic self-sufficiency, marital success, or subsequent fertility, and these outcomes are closely related. A redefinition of program goals (making them more realistic) plus further careful, longitudinal evaluation projects seems to be indicated (Klerman, 1979).

One important finding of the research is that, although with good medical care the mother and infant usually do well during the first pregnancy, the same cannont be said for rapid subsequent pregnancies (i.e., second or third pregnancies to women still in their teens). Both national statistics and specific studies (Jekel et al., 1975) indicate that these subsequent pregnancies are at higher risk for prematurity and infant death or illness. And yet, too often the program emphasis is greatest for the first teenage pregnancy, and the older adolescent experiencing a subsequent pregnancy must seek care by herself, despite less adequate nutrition, more personal stress, and reduced mobility due to problems with both baby-sitting and transportation. Medically speaking, adolescents with second or higher order pregnancies should be considered at especially high risk.

The same general principle applies to education. If a teenager has only one child, the chances are good she will return to school and will remain in school for a considerable period of time, often until graduation. With rapid subsequent deliveries, the chances of high school graduation drop drastically.

CONCLUSIONS

The service needs of pregnant and parenting adolescents are many and varied. Meeting them can place a strain on families and communities. Clearly, it would be less expensive if pregnancy could be delayed until education was completed and a source of economic support for a child was developed. But the methods for accomplishing this are not certain. Some believe it can be accomplished through sex education and easy availability of family planning and abortion. Others either see no proof of the effectiveness of these measures or are unwilling to use them regardless of their effectiveness.

While this debate continues, 4 in 10 of today's teenagers are likely to become pregnant before their twentieth birthday. Some will choose abortions, and many will not need specialized services because they are 18 or 19, are vocationally prepared, and have a source of economic support in a husband or family. A large number, however, will need help if they are to reach their potential and help their children do the same. Some argue that the easiest solution is to place the child for adoption, thus allowing the adolescent to return to more usual life and the infant to be reared by an intact, economically solvent family. Few adolescents appear willing to choose this option.

Thus, in many cases, the burden of providing the services essential for the development of mother, child, and sometimes the father is placed on society. It is an expensive burden, but it may be less expensive, and surely it is more responsible, to provide the services necessary to increase the possibility that these young parents become competent self-supporting mothers and fathers. At a more basic level, the prevention of adolescent pregnancy and parenting will require reforms in fundamental social and economic systems, including education, employment, and income maintenance.

CHAPTER 12

Adolescent Sexuality and Education: Principles, Approaches, and Resources

PETER SCALES

This chapter is organized into four sections. In the first, the possible goals and content of sexuality education programs are discussed. The second section describes the principles that guide various types of sexuality education. The focus of the third section is on approaches for effectively implementing sexuality education programs in the community. The chapter concludes with a brief list of selected resources that will assist the professional in developing, implementing, and evaluating sexuality education.

ADOLESCENT SEXUALITY IS MORE THAN SEX

Sex Education versus Sexuality Education

In the summer of 1979, a group of professionals from around the world gathered in Uppsala, Sweden, to define a series of principles basic to sexuality education (Hawkins, 1980). For too long, "sex education" has been misunderstood to mean learning about the physical aspects of sexual behavior or being presented with a few basic facts about puberty, reproduction, pregnancy, and childbirth. It has been misunderstood to consist of a lecture, a film, or a single talk between parent and child. Opponents of sex education have used this misunderstanding to represent sexuality education programs as mere instruction in the mechanics of sex. Calling it how-to-do-it education, some have charged that such instruction encourages children to practice what they learn in the classroom, even to the point of raping their sisters (Anchell, 1970). Even supporters of sexuality education have focused on the physical acts of sexual relating and the possible dangers associated with these behaviors (e.g., unplanned teenage pregnancy and sexually transmitted diseases). Sexuality education, however, is couched in a much broader context; a context that includes not only discrete acts or behaviors but the entire process of relating to the world as a man or a woman. Sexuality education includes an understanding of the motives for and meanings found in relationships. It includes our ability to be intimate and loving.

At the Uppsala conference, the participants noted that human sexual functioning actually begins before birth, in the uterus, and that "sexuality reflects our human character," manifesting itself in "every dimension of being a person" (Hawkins, 1980: 7). The development of gender identity, the sense of maleness or femaleness, is an inevitable process related fundamentally to our overall sense of self-identity, personal security, and emotional well-being. The further development of gender roles throughout life, the processes of learning about intimacy, the ability to establish caring, loving relationships with people of all ages, and the necessity of coming to terms with a wide range of possible expressions of sexuality all either add to the firm foundation of security from which we relate to the world or heighten the uncertainty and suspicion with which we function. These experiences, so intimately connected to our sexual selves, contribute heavily to a sense of basic trust or mistrust, a sense that affects our relationships and ultimately the societies we create (Scales, 1981a).

As the foregoing indicates, adolescent sexuality is more than sex, and education for sexuality must involve a consideration of more developmental, emotional, psychological, and social issues than are usually included in sex education. For example, as discussed in Chapter 5, the following factors are shown by research to significantly influence participation in nonmarital intercourse before age 18: levels of self-esteem, ego strength, a sense of personal competence, anxiety reactions, interpersonal attitudes and skills, family relationships, personal and familial values and expectations, stage of development, attitudes toward society, social reference groups, life situation, quality of same- and other-sex relationships, and availability of contraceptive services.

What is Effective Sexuality Education?

Given this context, it is clear that effective sexuality education should be guided by a broader range of goals than sex education as it is usually defined. Specifically, it is educationally misleading and overly limiting, as well as unrealistic, to judge the effectiveness of education for sexuality solely on the basis of reduced rates of teenage pregnancy or sexually transmitted diseases. Certainly, these are among the appropriate long-term outcomes to hope for, but they are both improbable short-term goals and also too narrow as criteria of program effectiveness.

Even the most comprehensive programs of sexuality education take up but a small proportion of a young person's time and attention, and a program is only one of many influences on sexual behavior. It is useful to consider that sexual learning actually consists of four types: (1) formal (e.g., school sex education classes); (2) nonformal (e.g., a church youth group discussion); (3) informal (e.g., parental reinforcement or discouragement of certain behaviors, the peer group, or an educational TV show that is watched primarily because it is entertaining); and (4) incidental (e.g., TV commercials, overheard parental conversations, or any other situation in which neither the "teacher" nor the "learner" has educational intentions). Clearly, incidental sexual learning is the most pervasive. As Simpson, Aptekar-Litton, and Roberts (1978) observed in developing these types, "When the school is compared with the family, the peer group, the mass media, and the subtle learning which is inherent in the social structure, one can begin to see that its role as an influencer of sexual learning is not as primary as we sometimes assume" (p. 13).

Nevertheless, formal programs can have an impact, and thus, it is appropriate to consider the kinds of goals that should guide these programs. Some of the goals that have been proposed in the literature (Kirby et al., 1979; Kirkendall, 1965) include:

To promote equalitarian relationships between the sexes.

To provide accurate information about sexuality.

To facilitate insights into personal sexual behavior and the sexual behavior of others.

To reduce fears and anxieties about personal sexual development and feelings.

To encourage more informed, responsible, and successful sexual decision making.

To encourage students to question, explore, and assess their sexual attitudes and values.

To develop more tolerant attitudes toward the sexual behavior of others.

To facilitate communication about sexuality with parents and others.

To reduce sex-related problems, such as unplanned teenage pregnancy.

To integrate sex into a balanced and purposeful pattern of living.

To facilitate rewarding sexual expression.

To encourage protection against exploitation.

In order partially to answer the questions about program content raised by noting such goals, Kirby and Alter (1980) specified two major goals for sexuality education: (1) the reduction of unplanned adolescent pregnancy; and (2) the facilitation of positive and fulfilling sexuality, including the improvement of social, sexual, and psychological health. In 1978, 100 professionals working in sex education were mailed a survey in which they were asked to rate the importance of a series of possible program features and outcomes in attaining those two goals. These features and outcomes were identified through reviewing the literature and holding discussions with both professionals and students taking human sexuality courses. Figure 12.1 displays the results of their research.

Thus, the major intermediate goals of sexuality education as viewed by these professionals involve changes in knowledge, understanding of self, values, self-esteem, interaction skills, and confidence in sex-related activities. Program content and activities should be selected on the basis of their contribution to the attainment of these intermediate goals.

There are several advantages to this framework. For instance, it recognizes that facts alone are clearly insufficient as influences on behavior. One of the central concerns of adolescents, for example, is whether they are "normal." Often, their self-esteem is predicated upon a seriously distorted view of what normal adolescent sexual behavior is like ("Everybody's doing it but me"). Programs based on communicating that there is indeed a broad range of normal behavior can reduce the need for young people to grade themselves on the basis of their sexual experience. Relieved of this anxiety, they may be freed to improve their ability to make rational and ethical decisions. Moreover, the framework shown in Figure 12.1 acknowledges that a key aspect of an effective sexuality education program is the development of various skills (e.g., the ability to communicate about sex and to assert oneself in a sexual situation). Then, too, in focusing on understanding of self and appreciation of one's values, this framework helps students become more aware of how their environment influences them (i.e., it raises their awareness of informal and incidental sources of sexual learning) and what their particular personal standards mean as guideposts for choices and behavior.

This framework also addresses the needs of both sexually experienced and sexually inexperienced youths. Programs that concentrate on pregnancy prevention and avoidance of sex-related problems do not deal effectively with the basic issues that all young people face, whether currently sexually involved or not. These issues include developing a sense of independence by integrating, not rejecting, the need for dependence on others; developing a sense of what is important and meaningful in their lives; identifying areas of their special competence; learning how to establish and maintain satisfying interpersonal relationships; coming to terms with the enormous changes in their bodies; and coming to terms with the expectations that society has for them as young women or men.

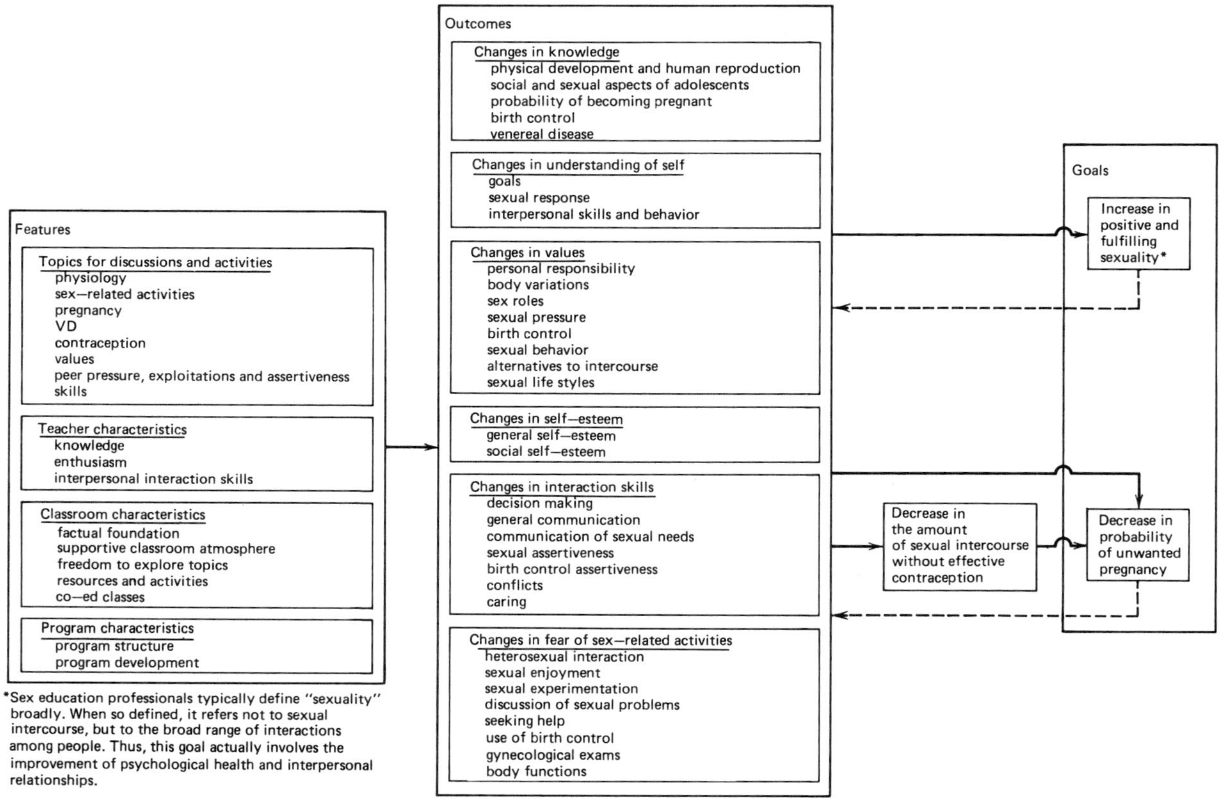

Features
Topics for discussions and activities
physiology
sex–related activities
pregnancy
VD
contraception
values
peer pressure, exploitations and assertiveness
skills
Teacher characteristics
knowledge
enthusiasm
interpersonal interaction skills
Classroom characteristics
factual foundation
supportive classroom atmosphere
freedom to explore topics
resources and activities
co–ed classes
Program characteristics
program structure
program development
Outcomes
Changes in knowledge
physical development and human reproduction
social and sexual aspects of adolescents
probability of becoming pregnant
birth control
venereal disease
Changes in understanding of self
goals
sexual response
interpersonal skills and behavior
Changes in values
personal responsibility
body variations
sex roles
sexual pressure
birth control
sexual behavior
alternatives to intercourse
sexual life styles
Changes in self–esteem
general self–esteem
social self–esteem
Changes in interaction skills
decision making
general communication
communication of sexual needs
sexual assertiveness
birth control assertiveness
conflicts
caring
Changes in fear of sex–related activities
heterosexual interaction
sexual enjoyment
sexual experimentation
discussion of sexual problems
seeking help
use of birth control
gynecological exams
body functions
Decrease in the amount of sexual intercourse without effective contraception
Goals
Increase in positive and fulfilling sexuality*
Decrease in probability of unwanted pregnancy

*Sex education professionals typically define "sexuality" broadly. When so defined, it refers not to sexual intercourse, but to the broad range of interactions among people. Thus, this goal actually involves the improvement of psychological health and interpersonal relationships.

Figure 12.1. Features, outcomes, and goals of sex education. (From D. Kirby, and J. Alter. "The experts are important features and outcomes of sex education programs." *The Journal of School Health* **50**(9), November 1980, pp. 498–99. Copyright 1980, American School Health Association, Kent, Ohio 44250.)

Implications for Staff and Teacher Training

In order to conduct this kind of sexuality education, teachers or leaders need to become sophisticated concerning emotions and understanding values and interpersonal skills. They must know about adolescent development, both physical and emotional, and have a good sense of typical adolescent concerns, awareness of the influences on decision making about sexuality, and a sense of the wide variety of values that accompany sexual issues. (See Chapters 1–7.) Teachers should have a variety of classroom skills, such as the ability to lead exercises and discussions that help students examine their own values and that communicate respect for that wide range of values. In other words, group process skills are important.

Accumulation of information, however, cannot substitute for important human qualities in a teacher. Genuine respect for and enjoyment in being with young people (or whomever the audience might be) is a fundamental quality for teachers in general, perhaps especially for those who teach human sexuality. Other important teacher qualities include warmth and sensitivity, a willingness to learn as well as to teach; a readiness to admit ignorance or discomfort; skilled capacity for sensitive, two-way teacher–student communication; an ability to share personal experiences without parading them; a commitment to freedom of speech and diversity of values; a belief that an important goal of education is to help people think clearly; and a good dose of natural, unforced humor in putting life's tragic and ecstatic experiences into perspective. With these attributes as a foundation, professional sexuality education and training can enrich teachers with factual knowledge, enhanced self-awareness and ease with one's own sexuality, greater appreciation of educational and counseling techniques, and more awareness of resources for sexuality education. But without these qualities, the human connection central to education for sexuality is apt to be lost to the mere mechanics of sex education.

Formal classroom teachers are not the only teachers with whom young persons will interact in relation to sexuality. School nurses, librarians, religious leaders of youth groups, social workers, physicians, and many others are important, too. It is desirable that these human service professionals also enhance these qualities and their knowledge and skills as sexuality educators and counselors. Knowing how to use the "teachable moment" is a particularly important aspect of effective education for sexuality that may be provided by professionals in these roles.

Leaders of sexuality programs are called upon to handle a variety of situations, from a simple imparting of information through lectures and group discussions, to group and individual counseling on specific problems, to furnishing consultation with other concerned adults, such as parents and human service professionals. Particularly when leading the discussions, leaders should be sensitive to individual differences in both values about the ethics of sexual issues and the ability to comfortably hear challenges to these values. Effective discussions should not single out one individual's values as being either right or wrong. Rather, the more effective discussion leader illustrates the variety of legitimate values that exist on any issue, helps people learn about the sources of their own values, and underscores the fact that, regardless of one's values, there are implications for behavior and behavioral outcomes based on those values. Equal consideration needs to be given to those values that support abstinence and those that are more permissive.

Certainly the degree of skill required to conduct such sessions is considerable. There is no substitute for role playing or rehearsing such teaching behaviors as preparation for dealing with them in an actual situation. Many excellent teacher training opportunities are available each year. Selected issues of *SIECUS Report,* the journal of the Sex Information and Education Council of the United States, are basic sources of information about numerous workshops offered throughout the country. (See section on resources for sexuality education, later in this chapter.)

PRINCIPLES OF EFFECTIVE SEXUALITY EDUCATION PROGRAMS

Although there are many possible formats and approaches for sexuality education, ranging from weekend retreats to semester-long courses, the best programs share some basic principles and content.

Programs Must Be Based on Youth Needs

One of these principles is that programs must be based on the actual needs of youths, not on the needs as imagined by adults or as determined by what the leader wishes to teach. For example, teachers are often most at ease simply providing information or facts about sex, yet students are frequently more interested in the social and emotional aspects of sexuality. It is rare that youths are involved in planning these programs. For instance, in a major study of 23 U.S. communities, only a few communities minimally involved young people in planning their sexuality education (Scales, 1981c). At the very least, the professional should try to collect and analyze questions about sex asked by young people in the age groups the program will include. For example, here are some questions collected by the author in recent years (all written anonymously on index cards):

Fourth grade

> Why do girls grow faster than boys?
> How come you have wet dreams?
> Why do we have sex?
> Why are the breasts important?
> Why does everyone laugh when we talk about sex?

Seventh grade

> How good a relationship should you have to have sex?
> What if saying no doesn't work?
> What should you feel while you're having sex?
> When do most people first have sex?

Eighth grade

> Does God always forgive you?
> What if you get pregnant and don't know how to tell your parents?
> Does the relationship differ after a sex act?
> How can you tell when you really love someone and are ready for sex?
> Is there anything wrong with oral sex?
> Why do guys drop girls who haven't for girls who have?

Ninth through twelfth grades

> What is the best contraceptive?
> Do most people masturbate?
> If your religion doesn't allow contraceptives, what options do you have?
> If a girl refuses to have sex until she's married, is that stupid?
> If a girl is raped and gets pregnant, what should she do?
> If the boy wants sex and the girl doesn't, what will happen to the boy?
> Can you get pregnant if the penis goes in, but not all the way?
> What is VD?
> How can I make my girlfriend forget her old boyfriend?
> Is abortion OK?
> How and where do you go to get treated for VD?
> How do you put a rubber on?
> When are you ready for sex?
> What is a fantasy?
> Is it bad to tell boys you have your period?
> Whose fault is it if the child is gay?
> Do you think frenching is gross?

Ask yourself how you would respond to such questions, paying particular attention to concerns that might underlie a given question. It is clear that programs offered in the absence of soliciting these kinds of questions are far less likely to deal with the actual needs of young people. Equally clear is the fact that young people's questions reflect the broad framework described already; they are certainly not limited to anatomical, social, or psychological concerns, but include all these. The freedom young people have to raise these questions, and the comprehensiveness with which teachers feel free to respond, may well be important determinants of the effectiveness of sexuality education.

Youths Can Be Leaders Too

A primary goal of sexuality education programs is to increase youths' responsibility, yet few programs offer experiences with responsible behavior. Responsible sexual behavior requires attitudes and skills similar to those required by responsible behavior in other areas of life. Yet throughout our society, young people are rarely challenged and helped to be responsible regarding their sexual behavior (although they are often admonished to be responsible). Increasingly, however, programs are being created in which young people themselves take the lead in designing workshops, writing scripts for plays on sexual responsibility, planning and running conferences, and even conducting basic research. This more complex approach aims to affect fundamental growth concepts, such as self-esteem, personal competencies, assertiveness skills, decision-making ability, job skills, and responsibility. These projects go beyond merely admonishing young people to be responsible, by offering them the chance to learn how. Sometimes, teenagers are paid for the experience or receive school credit. For the teenagers involved as leaders, an opportunity for self-discovery is provided. For the teenagers reached by the projects other young people help develop, the likelihood is greater that actual rather than simply imagined needs are being met. Some of these cases of youth involvement and leadership include:

Planned Parenthood of Washington, D.C., involved peer counselors in planning and conducting a research study on teens' perceptions of teenage problem pregnancies; one of their interesting recommendations was to hold rap groups for parents and *other* parents' children (H. David & Johnson, 1979).

Teenage Health Consultants in Minneapolis trained groups of 10–12 teenagers in all facets of health care, and the teenagers then made formal presentations, did one-to-one counseling, implemented workshops for parents, developed information and referral centers and health curricula, and even produced a weekly radio show by and for teenagers (Scales, 1979).

Cleveland YWCA had a peer-advocate program in which teenagers received 200 hours of training and were then placed in social and health agencies to work directly with other teenagers and adult staff. Using this approach, another local YWCA held discussions on sexuality, in the smoking room during its Friday night dances (Holloway, 1980).

In each of these cases, a group of well-motivated and competent teenagers is identified. These teenagers (usually with parental consent) are then provided with more advanced sexuality education, including knowledge and skill development comparable to the teacher training discussed earlier. In consultation with an adult advisor, these trained teenagers may then serve as peer counselors or work on projects similar to those just mentioned. At least 30 hours of training is needed to prepare young people for such tasks. In addition, an adult who is willing to allow considerable time for planning, brainstorming, and learning is essential, since several months of after-school work are required to organize many of these projects.

Sexuality Is Just One Aspect of Youth Development

The foregoing indicates that sexuality education focuses on more than sex. Sexuality education is most effective when it promotes knowledge, attitudes, and skills that are also important traits in all aspects of life. Sexuality education ideally is education for living in a complex world. For instance, in teaching about different sexual values and the importance of accepting these differences, messages are also being communicated about understanding and accepting cultural, racial, and religious differences. In learning how to talk about sexuality, youths may also learn transferable skills that help them talk about other emotionally laden subjects. In studying the influence of family life on development of values, students can learn how they might influence their own children someday (if and when they become parents) and can begin to develop opinions about the role of the family and other social institutions. In increasing their sense of competence in dealing with sexuality, young people are also being provided with experiences that might increase their feeling of confidence in dealing with other significant issues.

Sexuality Education Is Really Relationship Training

Effective sexuality education also helps participants enhance their relationships, in part by increasing their self-esteem. Self-esteem can be significantly fostered by promoting acceptance of each individual's values and by stressing the wide range of behaviors that are normal. In this context, sexuality education increases self-esteem while simultaneously increasing esteem and regard for others. Sexuality education, to be effective, should stress the importance of being aware, not only of one's own values, needs, and motives regarding sexual behavior, but also of the other person's values, needs, and motives. The other person may be a parent, a sibling, a religious leader, or a boyfriend or girlfriend. The important message is that the person is as significant and worthy as the self.

Because of their preoccupation with the changes of adolescence and its accompanying challenges, many young people are far less able than older adults to recognize the impact of their behavior on others. Good sexuality education helps young people consider the consequences of their behavior. In part, this is accomplished by helping young people learn to take the other person's perspective in a given situation. One technique for doing this is to have students role play or behaviorally rehearse a particular situation, such as how to say no to a partner who is aggressively forcing him- or herself sexually on the other. An alternative technique, and one perhaps more acceptable to some parents and some students, is to have teams of male and female adults provide the role play or modeling situation, and then lead a discussion in which they stay in their roles and talk about what they were thinking and what their motivations were. A Denver-based group, Project RAM (Reaching Adolescent Minds), had the adult team perform the role play, but asks the students to suggest the words and role each character will take.

Another example of teaching about relationships is a technique used to illustrate the responsibilities of parenthood. In this exercise, students are assigned to "take care of" a raw egg for a week. If they go out, an "egg-sitter" must be found. If they drop the egg, they lose points for "abusive" parenting. In one school, there were not enough students to pair as parents, and when one female student was left to care for her egg alone, this prompted a class discussion of the additional challenges of single parenting!

Different Sexes and Even Ages Should Participate Together

It is clear that part of an effective sexuality education program should be to learn how to relate respectfully with people who are different from oneself. Yet, the separation of the sexes during sexuality education, still practiced in some communities, promotes only myths and misunderstandings. Most boys and girls do not have structured opportunities to hear what the other sex feels and thinks about sexuality. Consequently, it is more difficult to take the other person's feelings into account in an actual sexual encounter. This is especially true for boys, who are often not rewarded for empathetic behavior. When boys hear girls tell them how they feel when a boy forces himself on someone sexually, or when boys tell girls how they feel when a girl "teases," each sex becomes less ambiguous and more personal to the other. In this way, exploitative behavior may be discouraged, and the dignity, equality, and worth of each individual can be promoted.

Similarly, there may be occasions when providing a program to people of different ages is especially effective. Many communities, for example, are offering programs for parents and their children together. Such programs are meant to increase family communication about sexuality and to enhance parents' ability to promote their own sexual values in the home. Research clearly shows that such increased communication results in teenagers delaying their first intercourse and being more likely to use contraception when they do have intercourse (Fox, 1981; S. Gordon et al., 1979).

One such program has been offered by the Family Planning Department of the Family Guidance Center, St. Joseph, Missouri. This community health center offers the program on its own premises as well as through outreach to churches, schools, YWCAs, and other youth organizations. One parent attends with a child (modules have been developed for children as young as 9 years of age), and, insofar as possible, mothers attend with daughters and fathers attend with sons. Basic content includes anatomy and physiology, pubertal changes, health and hygiene, pregnancy, and childbirth. For older children and their parents, there is a greater emphasis on values clarification, communication skills, and birth control. A question box allows parents and children to ask questions anonymously. In fact, every participant after each session must drop a question or comment into the box, thus making it impossible to know who has asked a question about sex. This anonymity helps promote free discussion and information seeking. Games and films are also used, such as a "Dear Abby" game that requires participants to answer typical advice-column letters and thus enhance their decision-making skills and their appreciation for their own values (L. Peterson & Kirby, 1981).

Leaders Must Respond to Differences among Adolescents

As shown in Chapter 2, young people reach puberty at different ages, with girls being ahead of boys in their level of physical development. Younger adolescents (those under age 16 or so) are apt to be particularly concerned with establishing their independence from their parents (and all authorities). In terms of cognitive abilities, they may well lack the ability at this stage to reason in abstract principles and to anticipate the long-range consequences of their behavior. Older adolescents will be further along in their cognitive development and are apt to have reached the stage in which they are interested in examining their moral values and their commitment to a particular partner, and in sorting out clearer vocational goals. (This superficial sketch should be amplified by a thorough review of Chapters 2 and 4.) Moreover, careful attention should be given to the varieties of family backgrounds, life experiences, and cultural backgrounds (ethnic, racial, religious, and social class) that characterize the adolescents for whom the programs are being planned.

Additional differences exist between adolescents in general and still younger children, and these too should be reflected in the content of the program. For example, here are a few content suggestions based on age differences as proposed by S. Gordon and Dickman (1980) and modified by the author:

Grades K-3

Everyone is part of a family.
Everybody is either male or female.
How babies are born.
Correct terms for body parts.
Getting along with other people.
The importance of privacy in sexual behavior.
Pregnancy and childbirth.

Grades 4–6

Basic information about puberty.
Dispelling myths about masturbation.
Our main values about sexuality come from family life.
Family life can undergo changes.
Becoming aware of individual differences in rate and timing of physical changes.

Junior high school

Incest.
Secondary sex characteristics.
Male and female reproductive systems.
Meaning of self-esteem.
Nature of sexual intercourse.
Risks involved in sexual intercourse.
Basic understanding of boy–girl relationships.
Basic understanding of birth control.
Dealing with family relationships.

Senior high school

Child development and parenting.
Love, dating,

Problems associated with teenage pregnancies.

Detail on sexually transmitted diseases and birth control.

Pros and cons of early marriage, including single parenting and community resources.

Concept of sexual equality and training in assertiveness skills.

Emerging sex role changes.

Social and emotional problems related to sex.

Homosexuality.

Rape

Tolerance for sexual differences.

Intimacy and trust.

Factual and Attitudinal Myths Should Be Countered

Effective programs focus on myths that make it difficult for young people to behave effectively and responsibly. Some of these common myths include: various reasons why "I can't get pregnant"; the confusion of sex with love; the equating of sex with intercourse; the belief that "everyone's doing it but me"; and the belief that a sexual experience "just happens"; (Scales, 1981b). For example, the fear that everyone else is more sexually active can lead to boasting about sexual exploits that never occurred or to exploitive behavior intended to gain peer acceptance as one who is sexually active. Yet, most young people and many adults are unaware that there are far more virgins than they imagine—almost half of young people have not had intercourse by the time they graduate from high school (Zelnik & Kantner, 1980b)—yet the nonexperienced think they are the last of a dying breed! An effective way of introducing such material is for the leader to generate a few such myths, some humorous, and then to ask the group to continue generating and discussing the myths.

Brief Educational Experiences May Have Little Effect

Although a brief unit or course might indeed be a catalyst for changes in such profound constructs as self-esteem, it is unlikely that a brief educational experience will produce dramatic and permanent changes in such basic personality constructs. Changes in life orientation, in viewing oneself as worthwhile or worthless, as capable or incapable, require time to test learning in relation to other people and time to integrate learning into the life situation outside the classroom. More limited and realistic objectives should be set for the usual sexuality education program. In a few hours of interaction, for example, it is probably best to hope for knowledge gain and perhaps a slight attitudinal change. Behavioral change is hardly likely. In a program that consists of 20–30 hours of experiential exercises, small group discussions, didactic presentations, and opportunities for exploring values and enhancing communication skills, more significant attitudinal and some behavioral change might be expected. Content and activities should always be carefully geared to plainly stated, simple objectives. (See Chapter 13 on counseling.)

Programs Should Be Evaluated

Plainly stated, simple, concrete objectives both foster appropriate selection of curriculum and resources and also encourage clearly focused evaluation. Evaluation of sexuality education is often neglected or poorly conducted, but it is crucial both for planning and assessing a program and for communicating results to the community to ensure community acceptance of a program. A well-designed pretest, for example, provides not only an indication of the students' knowledge, attitudes, and behavior but also direction regarding content and approaches. Clearly, if a high percentage of students scores well on a reliable and valid test of knowledge, then less time needs to be devoted to this area. In this way, adequate evaluation also functions as an assessment of needs.

Adequate evaluation also requires a control group. (Preferably, students will be randomly assigned to the sexuality program or the control group.) If the program is more than a few sessions in duration, a second posttest to measure longer-term effects of a program is recommended. Young people should obtain permission from their parents to participate in the course, and this permission should explicitly cover evaluation activities. Students should also retain the right not to participate in all or part of the evaluation (i.e., it should be entirely voluntary). No grade or other penalty should be given to those students who choose not to participate. Of course, responses should be anonymous and confidentiality of responses should be protected. Students themselves should be involved in developing questionnaires, in order to remove or modify poorly worded, repetitious, or threatening items. Alternatively, since questionnaire development is costly and time consuming, leaders may choose to use existing measures (cf. Kirby et al., 1979), but even these should be carefully pretested and modified if necessary for each intended audience.

STRATEGIES FOR OFFERING SEXUALITY EDUCATION

Extent and Kind of Opposition and Support

Regardless of the program approach used, and particularly if the public schools or a family planning agency is involved, some community opposition to sexuality education can be expected. Although over 80 percent of Americans support sex education in the schools, including the teaching of contraception (Gallup Poll, 1980; Smith, 1980), a vocal minority (often calling themselves "profamily") frequently succeeds in derailing or limiting such programs. It is useful to remember that typically only 1 percent of parents refuse permission for their children to enroll in a human sexuality course or program, that many parents enroll in sexuality education courses themselves, and that popular support for sexuality education is overwhelming, according to both nationally representative and local studies (Scales, 1983). Given this support, program organizers should focus upon strategies that effectively use and mobilize favorable public sentiment, in order to preserve a climate in which the kind of sexuality education described here can flourish.

Not all people with reservations about sexuality education are opponents, by any means. It is reasonable for parents and other community members to wonder about the teachers' qualifications, the kinds of values that underlie a program, the age appropriateness of certain topics, and so on. These questions offer opportunities for improving sexuality education, and program developers should respond to them openly and honestly. For example, many communities hold meetings at which parents can raise their concerns. In other communities, parents are involved in small committees that help establish goals for a sexuality education program, review films and other course materials, and perform other tasks. In Minneapolis, for instance, teams of a parent, a teacher, a school health staffperson, and a school administrator were given 9–12 hours of training so that they could then map out curricula specific to the schools in which they worked. In the Archdiocese of Minneapolis, parents must take the human sexuality course themselves before their children are allowed to enroll (Scales, 1983).

While most opposition is responsible and reasonable, there are undeniably some extreme opponents of sex education. These people have attempted to ban a variety of books and teaching materials, completely abolish all types of sexuality education outside the home and church, and require that absolute standards of right and wrong, rather than respect for a variety of values, be depicted in school textbooks (Scales, 1981c). Usually, if careful work is done in meeting with important parent and other community groups (such as religious and youth organizations), so much support can be mobilized for a program that the minority of citizens with extreme objections are not able to have a serious impact on the program. It is no accident that a study of 23 U.S. communities found the communities that most significantly involved parents and other groups had the most comprehensive and unrestricted sexuality curricula (Scales, 1983). Involving such key people and groups is especially effective if program planners are sensitive to the important values and beliefs of influential people in the community and if the content of the program avoids sharp conflict with prevalent community norms.

Some Principles of Community Organization for Sexuality Education

Although the following principles cannot be fully detailed in this chapter, they are intended to accomplish three tasks. First, they are intended to enhance the ability of sex education supporters to become a more visible and timely constituency. Second, they are meant to encourage broad-based community, and particularly parental, involvement. Finally, they are offered in order to increase supporters' ability to respond respectfully and clearly to opponents' basic concerns while at the same time combating their extreme polemics.

The most important principle is that controversy cannot be avoided. Often, sexuality education programs are planned with the hope of being completely acceptable to everyone in the community. Even with the degree of community involvement described above, some opposition can be expected. Controversy can be managed and minimized, however, and the approaches that are offered here are intended to accomplish that goal.

Another basic principle is that sexuality education is not value free. Some program planners have tried to insist that their program teaches no particular values, but this is hardly likely. When supporters are able to clearly articulate their values, the great majority of the community can more readily recognize their own beliefs embodied in the goals of contemporary sexuality education. For example, it might be helpful to list and have available for parents and others the key values that underlie a program. Each program and community will stress somewhat different values, and the following are only suggested by the author as common values that most people share. They may be a beginning for a more complete statement of values.

Knowledge and information are helpful, not harmful.

Adequate self-esteem is essential for making healthy and responsible sexual decisions.

In a democratic society, a wide range of values should be respected and tolerated.

It is usually preferable for adolescents to refrain from sexual intercourse.

Each sexual decision has an effect or consequence.

It is important to examine and become aware of one's own values about sexuality.

It is wrong to exploit or force someone into an unwanted sexual experience.

Assertiveness and communication skills are needed in order to tell another what decision has been made.

Each person is worthy, and sexual decisions should support the dignity, equality, and worth of each individual.

It is best if adolescents can discuss sexual matters with their parents and other important adults.

Parenthood requires many responsibilities that adolescents are usually unable to assume.

Finally, long-term commitment and persistence are required in order to plan and offer good sexuality education programs. Once a curriculum has been accepted, program planners should still regularly evaluate the appropriateness of the program, based in part on community feedback. In addition, it can take a year or more of steady meeting and negotiating to develop an approach that seems to satisfy both the needs of the students and the concerns of the community.

Primary Strategies

As noted above, in a study of 23 U.S. communities, it was found that those communities in which parents were significantly involved in the planning of sexuality education had the most comprehensive curricula and the most open policy regarding teachers' answering questions in the classroom. Parents should be involved, not simply at the stage of giving permission for a child to attend a class, but rather at the earliest points, when consideration is given to the kinds of subjects that will be covered, the ages of students to be reached, and the nature of the materials to be used. Parents might be offered a back-to-school night to meet the sexuality education teachers, or a newsletter might be developed to keep them informed of various health education activities. Some parents might even welcome sexuality education programs available to fathers and mothers.

Another way of involving parents is having some mothers and fathers serve on a community committee that is formed for the purpose of representing varied opinions of important community groups. These committees should also include clergy, health professionals, school teachers and administrators, members of opposing parent groups, and adolescents themselves. Tasks can be divided among subcommittees; they often involve setting standards for the teacher's qualifications, determining appropriateness of various materials, reviewing films, developing possibilities for parent involvement, and helping propose a statement of values, as described earlier. Committees of about 15–20 people seem to be the most workable.

Two other tasks that can be partially or fully performed by such a committee are assessing community opinion and establishing realistic goals and objectives. Community surveys usually show about 80 percent support for sexuality education. It is helpful to construct these surveys so as to assess opinion about specific subjects to be offered, coed or single-sex classes, appropriate ages for certain topics, and other issues. Such information is helpful for program planners. In addition, the committee can discuss goals and come to the realization that it is unreasonable to expect a brief educational experience to have dramatic effects on such phenomena as rates of adolescent childbearing and nonmarital coitus. Developing and publicizing realistic objectives for the program helps the rest of the community keep this educational experience in perspective as just one of many influences on the complex behaviors of teenagers.

Through establishing a community committee and thereby increasing the understanding and support of key community members, the first steps are taken toward building an essential coalition for the programs. Circulating a small newsletter and holding regular informational meetings open to an expanding group of interested and concerned citizens can broaden the community coalition supportive of high quality sexuality education in the schools. Such a coalition can be important in many ways, including active involvement in school board elections. Such involvement may well be essential to offset the possibly strong political influence of a small but highly articulate group of citizens who organize to censor educational programs dealing with human sexuality.

It is essential that the community committee, working with the professional staff and school administrators, develop written policies that support sexuality education teachers. Teachers may sometimes err in judgment in their conduct of sexuality classes or their remarks may be misunderstood. Such events can create a storm of protest, especially by parents who are already doubtful about, or opposed to, the program. If written policies supportive of teachers are already available, and teachers are careful to work within these policies, the protests can be handled effectively through referral to the guidelines developed and approved by a citizen committee.

RESOURCES FOR SEXUALITY EDUCATION

The resources presented in the next few pages constitute selections from hundreds of good to excellent materials. These resources should help educators increase their own knowledge and skills. They also furnish suggestions for various audiences. New resources are being developed rapidly. Reviews are carried regularly in the professional and scholarly journals listed below. These journals should be consulted for current information and critical analyses.

It is important that each resource be previewed by the program leader and at least a small group of parents and adolescents before it is used. The reader who wishes more detailed lists of resources should consult the excellent bibliographies included in the list that follows.

GENERAL REFERENCES FOR PROGRAM LEADERS

Carrera, Michael. *Sex: The Facts, The Acts, Your Feelings.* NY: Crown, 1981. Wide-ranging reference also useful for parent workshops.

Gagnon, John H. *Human Sexualities.* Glenview, Ill.: Scott, Foresman, 1977. College text focusing on sexuality as learned conduct.

Gordon, Sol, Peter Scales, and Kathleen Everly. *The Sexual Adolescent: Communicating with Teenagers about Sex.* North Scituate, Mass.: Duxbury Press, 1979. Stresses adolescent sexual behavior and development, covers political issues, and contains appendix of references.

Katchadourian, Herant A., and Donald T. Lunde. *Fundamentals of Human Sexuality* (3rd ed.). New York: Holt, Rinehart & Winston, 1980. Basic, college-level text.

Kirby, Douglas, Judith Alter, and Peter Scales. *An Analysis of U.S. Sex Education Programs and Evaluation Methods.* Springfield, Va.: National Technical Information Service, 1979. Five-volume study, covers state guidelines, characteristics of exemplary programs, methods of evaluation, and overview of the effects of sex education.

Morrison, Eleanor S., and Mila Underhill Price. *Values in Sexuality.* New York: A and W Publishers, 1974. Exercises for examining values and feelings.

Otto, Herbert A. *The New Sex Education.* Chicago: Association Press, 1978. Useful as a supplement, it contains curriculum suggestions from the view of practitioners in different fields. Much of the material, however, is dated.

Rosenzweig, Norman, and F. Paul Pearsall (Eds.). *Sex Education for the Health Professional: A Curriculum Guide.* New York: Grune and Stratton, 1978. Highly informative collection of articles on various curriculum approaches.

Scales, Peter. *The Front Lines of Controversy: Sex Education and Public Action in America.* Forthcoming 1983. Handbook of practical suggestions for offering sex education by effective community organizing, also covers key opposition arguments and how to respond. (Available from author.)

Uslander, Arlene, and Caroline Weiss. *Dealing with Questions about Sex.* Belmont, Calif.: Pitman Learning, 1975. Fascinating collection of children's questions and ways of responding.

MODEL CURRICULA FOR USE WITH ADOLESCENTS

Bignell, Steven. *Family Life Education: Curriculum Guide.* Santa Cruz, Calif.: Planned Parenthood of Santa Cruz County, 1979. Models for a 10-session program at the junior and senior high level are presented. Also available is a companion teacher's guide. Highly recommended.

Dodds, Jane M. *Human Sexuality: A Curriculum for PreTeens.* Rochester, N.Y.: Planned Parenthood, 1980. Excellent curriculum for use with Grades 5–8, it contains suggestions for 12 different units.

Planned Parenthood of Monterey County. *Peer Education.* Monterey, CA: Author, 1980. Both training curricula and curricula for peer presentations in school are included.

U.S. Department of Health and Human Services. *A Decision Making Approach to Sex Education.* Washington, D.C.: Bureau of Community Health Services, 1979. Meant for professionals who work with parents and children but not necessarily sex educators, this excellent curriculum guide includes suggestions for 10-session adolescent *and* parent programs. Staff training guidelines are also given.

U.S. Department of Health and Human Services. *Family Life Education: A Problem-Solving Curriculum for Adolescents.* Washington, D.C.: Bureau of Community Health Services, 1980. Excellent curriculum guide for 15–19 year olds, concentrating on skill development and self-esteem building.

FOR ADOLESCENTS TO READ

Junior High

Changes: You and Your Body. Philadelphia: CHOICE, Family Planning Council of Southeastern Pennsylvania, n.d. Basic review of anatomy and relationships.

Gordon, Sol. *Facts about Sex for Today's Youth.* Syracuse, N.Y.: Ed-U Press, 1980. Excellent overview of basic physiology with clear drawings, especially good for those who don't like to read.

Johnson, Eric. *Love and Sex in Plain Language.* Philadelphia: Lippincott, 1977. Just what it says; this book is a classic.

Mayle, Peter. *What's Happening to Me?* Secaucus, N.J.: Lyle Stuart, 1975. Graphic and humorous coverage of puberty; this excellent but liberal book may be found offensive by some.

Senior High

Bell, Ruth. *Changing Bodies, Changing Lives: A Handbook for Teens.* New York: Random House, 1980. Explicit and readable, with many statements by teenagers on the problems they deal with.

Chiappa, Joseph, and Joseph Forish. *The VD Book.* New York: Holt, Rinehart & Winston, 1976. Complete paperbook for those with average to good reading skills.

Gordon, Sol, and Mina Wollin. *Parenting.* New York: Oxford, 1975. Highly recommended book covering responsibilities of parenting, child development, and sex education as the parent's role.

Hanckel, Frances, and John Cunningham. *A Way of Love, a Way of Life: A Young Person's Introduction to What it Means To Be Gay.* New York: Lothrop, Lee and Shepard, 1979. Excellent introduction for young people and their parents.

McCoy, Kathy, and Charles Wibbelsman. *The Teenage Body Book.* New York: Pocket Books, 1978. Thorough coverage of psychological and physiological issues of adolescence. Many comments from teenagers are included.

Todd, Kay Rodenberg, and Nancy Abbey-Harris. *The Birds, the Bees, and the Real Story.* Santa Cruz, Calif.: Planned Parenthood, 1980. Excellent book with fact sheets and self-help quizzes; it is most useful for highly motivated teenagers. Also available is a companion parents' volume.

RECOMMENDED FILMS FOR ADOLESCENTS

Acquaintance Rape Prevention Series. New York: ODN Productions, 1978. Four brief films that stimulate discussion about physical and nonphysical pressure to have intercourse, these films are believable and come with teachers' guides and students' materials.

A Matter of Respect. Boston: Blackside Films, 1980. Fifteen minutes focusing on the male role in sexual decision making. Some scenes are very stereotyped, however, and preview is especially recommended.

Am I Normal? Boston: Momentum Media, 1979. A brief film that examines a young boy's concerns about entering puberty. Some humorous scenes.

Dear Diary. Companion film about young girls (1981).

Hope Is Not a Method II. New York: Perennial, 1977. Update of an earlier film, it focuses upon contraceptive methods. Excellent, objective information.

Running My Way. Los Angeles: Children's Home Society of California, 1982. By the producers of *Teenage Father,* this excellent film about teenage sexual decision making depicts the story of a high school track star who must decide whether to become sexually involved with her boyfriend or not.

What Can A Guy Do?. Oakland: Serious Business Company, 1982. A semi-documentary format shows male teen attitudes toward birth control, and covers the pressures that inhibit young men from making responsible decisions.

Teenage Father. Los Angeles: Children's Home Society of California, 1979. Superb, Academy Award winner, this believable half-hour film traces the story of a teenage couple and their families as they struggle with decisions about an unplanned pregnancy. Highly recommended for audiences of parents as well as adolescents.

Mother May I? New York: Shared Future Films, 1981. A dramatic film that covers parent-child communication about sexuality, and that deals with the difficulties of making responsible sexual decisions.

IMPORTANT PROFESSIONAL JOURNALS

Family Life Educator. ETR Associates, 1700 Mission, #203, Santa Cruz, Calif. 95060.

SIECUS Report, Sex Information and Education Council of the United States, 80 Fifth Avenue, N.Y., N.Y. 10011.

Journal of Sex Education and Therapy. American Association of Sex Educators, Counselors and Therapists.

Journal of School Health. American School Health Association, Kent, Ohio 44240. (See especially the April 1981 special double issue on sex education.)

Family Relations. National Council on Family Relations, 1219 University Avenue SE, Minneapolis, Minn. 55414. (See October 1981 issue on family life education.)

Voice of Youth Advocates. PO Box 6569, University, Ala. 35486. (Always contains reviews of films and books for young people, for use in sexuality and other classes.)

IMPACT. Institute for Family Research and Education, 760 Ostrom Avenue, Syracuse, N.Y. 13210. (Contains helpful ideas for community programming.)

Emphasis Subscriber Service. Education Department, Planned Parenthood Federation of America, 810 7th Avenue, NY, NY 10019. (Variety of resources published annually.)

BIBLIOGRAPHIES

Basic bibliographies on sex education, for professionals and nonprofessionals as well, can be obtained from SIECUS, Planned Parenthood Federation of America and the Institute for Family Research and Education, addresses listed above. In addition, the following will be helpful:

Beckstein, Douglas. *An Annotated Guide to Men's Sexual Health Resources.* 406 Dakota Avenue, #D, Santa Cruz, Calif. 95060.

Scales, Peter. *The Politics of Sex Education: Bibliography of Useful Resources.* NY: Education Department, Planned Parenthood Federation of America, 810 7th Avenue, NY, NY 10019.

Wilson, Pamela. *An Annotated Bibliography of Selected Curriculum Materials.* MATHTECH, Inc., 4630 Montgomery Avenue, Bethesda, Md. 20014.

CHAPTER 13

Counseling with Adolescents about Their Sexuality

LEWAYNE D. GILCHRIST and STEVEN PAUL SCHINKE

INTRODUCTION

Given the importance of sexuality in the lives and maturation of adolescents, surprisingly little research documents effective techniques for counseling with youths about their sexual development. This lack is unfortunate. Few professionals dispute the need for such counseling. In the growth from childhood to full adult status, young people must adjust to formidable changes in their own bodies, drastically altered social roles and expectations, new feelings, and new behavioral opportunities. Though adolescents sometimes experience these changes with pride, often sexual feelings and physiological growth are sources of embarrassment and confusion.

Certain concerns involving sexuality emerge again and again in counseling relationships with young people. In the midst of sweeping physiological, hormonal, social, behavioral, and psychological changes, almost all adolescents need reassurance that what is happening to them is normal. Many struggle with accepting their own masculinity and femininity and with the disturbing question "Will I be successful as a man? As a woman?" When dating begins, adolescents must deal with the issue of sexual relationships: "Should I neck, pet, or have intercourse with my boy/girlfriend? How far should I go, when, with whom? How will I know when I am ready for these things? What do these kinds of touching feel like? Will I be good at sex? Will I like it?" Adolescents who are having intercourse often agonize about "What if my behavior results in pregnancy? Does my partner really care about me? What if my parents find out what I am doing?" On a broader level, adolescents in counseling often need assistance with the meaning and purpose of sex in interpersonal pair relationships. Though they may engage in the act of intercourse, adolescent sexual partners may not achieve psychological or emotional closeness. Biological growth equips them for physical but not psychological intimacy. Petting and coitus without exchange of deep feel-

230

ings and commitment is frequently experienced as mechanical or exploitative. Often, enjoyment does not enter into such relationships. In sum, adolescents who have not yet become sexually involved in necking, petting, or intercourse may be anxious, apprehensive, and fearful that they are in some way abnormal and not like their peers. More experienced adolescents may feel disillusioned with sex, guilty about their behavior, worried about possible pregnancy or venereal disease, and fearful that they may be abnormal. Moreover, many adolescents are concerned about such topics as their appearance, masturbation, sexual fantasies, menstrual problems (girls), nocturnal emissions (boys), and homosexual or lesbian interests.

Much research shows that a great many adolescents suffer in silence through the uncertainties and discomforts connected with becoming a mature sexual person (Fox, 1980; Pocs et al., 1977; Rothenberg, 1980; Zelnik & Kantner, 1977). Few young people have open, in-depth discussions about their sexual development or sexuality in general with relatives, teachers, ministers, doctors, social workers, psychologists, or other sources of adult assistance and support. Reasons for this lack of communication are many. Some researchers argue that, for pressing psychological reasons, parents cannot serve as sexuality counselors during their children's adolescence. Many parents have great difficulty accepting their sons and daughters as sexual individuals. Adolescents, on the other hand, may be equally reluctant to recognize the sexual experience of their parents. (See also Chapters 2 and 4.) Even at times of great distress over sexual behavior, many young people do not turn to their parents. Rosen (1980) estimates that only 14 percent of teenage women seek parental advice when they believe they are pregnant. Adults in nonparental roles who might offer sexuality counseling to adolescents fail to raise the topic because they believe they lack requisite information, training, and skills. Many embarrassed adolescents, out of fear of revealing naiveté or self-perceived abnormality, or because they simply do not trust a relationship far enough, do not broach their sexual concerns even with adults they consider sympathetic.

Much of the literature offering guidelines for sexuality counseling with adolescents provides limited assistance. Too many writers appear to view sexual development as separate and distinct from other aspects of young people's growth and daily life. Thus, the clinical procedures and programs they describe tend to be unnecessarily narrow in scope. Goals for counseling adolescents about their sexuality are not different from the goals of counseling generally. No one argues that a major task of adolescence is solidifying a sense of personal identity. Since sexuality is central to identity, the task of separating sexual concerns from other aspects of life and growth is not merely fruitless but impossible and undesirable. Counseling with adolescents clearly should touch all areas of development, including sexuality.

The aim of any counseling is to promote well-being and maturity, to provide resources and support during periods of growth and change, and to allay anxiety, confusion, and uncertainty. Whether explicitly limiting their work to sexual concerns or not, counselors of adolescents are called upon to help young people make sound decisions about present and future behavior, to help decrease family conflicts generated by adolescents' individuation and growing independence, and to locate, provide, or mobilize resources of benefit to their young clients. Such resources may include job training or referral, academic tutoring, help with an alcoholic parent, special medical care, and the like. When counseling focuses specifically on sexual behavior, other resources outside the traditional counseling relationship may also be needed, such as provision of contraceptive information and services, referral for pregnancy testing, abortion counseling, or arranging treatment for venereal disease. Many programs ostensibly treating sexuality, however, simply begin and end with the provision of these specific services. By not addressing broader emotional and interpersonal components of sexuality, these programs do nothing to help young people incorporate sexual functioning in satisfying ways into their sense of who they are and into their daily choices and behavior.

COUNSELING WITH ADOLESCENTS— A LIFE-SKILLS APPROACH

Puberty profoundly affects adolescents' interactions with the environment. Young people need new information and new ways of thinking and interacting with others to function effectively in new roles that are often radically different from those of childhood. Sensitive counseling can certainly assist this growth process. Traditional "talking cure" counseling techniques, however, have limited usefulness (Kraus, 1980). Many adolescents do not willingly involve themselves in counseling, especially about their sexuality. They exhibit an unwillingness to disclose themselves or to appear unsure or different from their peers. Many dislike appearing unable to handle any situation (C. Shapiro, 1981). They are preoccupied with the present and usually do not see the value of examining past behavior or future possibilities. Further, virtually all adolescents prefer action and experiential learning to formal didactics of "just talk" (Gilchrist, 1981). They are impatient for answers and may break appointments or terminate counseling if they perceive the sessions as a waste of time.

The authors are engaged in developing methods for counseling adolescents that take into account adolescents' cognitive and social development, their widely differing growth rates and individual values, and their preference for time-limited, focused, concrete assistance. Our approach, called life-skills enhancement, is grounded in social learning theory and is based on the proposition that coping with sexuality consists, in large part, of a set of acquired skills. These skills involve specific thinking processes and social abilities critical to mature functioning. In counseling, adolescents learn cognitive skills to manage both positive and negative emotions, to make important decisions independently, and to use problem-solving techniques effectively when a decision or course of action is not clear. The life-skills approach also emphasizes improving young people's interpersonal communication. Communicating assertively and honestly with others has long been recognized as important for healthy functioning and essential to the achievement and regulation of intimacy. Thus, the life-skills approach includes structured practice in such behavioral skills as disclosing positive and negative feelings, making effective refusals, negotiating, resolving conflicts verbally, initiating difficult conversations, and asking for needed information.

The final area emphasized in the life-skills approach is helping adolescents apply information about sexual growth and behavior to themselves and their own lives. Often information—so freely provided in many clinic and sex education settings—is of little value to adolescents, who, though they may be adults physiologically, cannot yet think of themselves in terms of adult sexual behavior. According to Piaget and others (Flavell, 1974; Piaget & Inhelder, 1969), adolescents are in transition between concrete (childlike) and abstract (adult) modes of thinking. Younger adolescents, in particular, tend to believe only what they experience. They have difficulty projecting themselves into the future and do not consider abstract possibilities. Their own experiences and those of their friends are usually far more powerful educational influences than any formal didactic efforts. Counselors in one family planning program, for example, reported that despite extensive information provision, their adolescent clients simply refused to believe facts that ran counter to their experiences. "If one friend had a condom break, then condoms were perceived as unreliable. If another friend had sex for a while without using birth control, then it didn't seem necessary to use birth control either" (Office for Family Planning, 1979, p. 283). If information about physiological changes and human sexuality is to be of value, adolescents must make the transition from passively being aware of this information to applying it to themselves and actively using it in planning, decision making, and personal behavior (Schinke et al., 1979). This knowledge application process, called relational thinking by cognitive theorists (M. Mahoney, 1974), may be critical to the formation of a sense of identity that includes sexuality. Certainly it is critical to assuming independent responsibility for personal sexual behavior.

Group Counseling and Life-Skills Enhancement

Life-skills enhancement sessions may be conducted in groups or with individuals. Groups have several advantages. They allow learning from a variety of models and make good use of peers as aids in the counseling process. Groups constitute a microcosm of adolescents' normal social milieu and therefore a more realistic setting than individual sessions for practicing interpersonal skills and methods for overcoming embarrassment or anxiety. Groups also make efficient use of counselors' time. On the other hand, adolescents mature at greatly varying rates. Rarely is a group homogeneous in terms of needs, interests, abilities, or values. Group leaders must exercise extra care to individualize group procedures or the sessions will remain impersonal and ineffective. Also, many adolescents will not reveal their true concerns to a group. The deep, long-term relationship possible in individual or private counseling sessions may be necessary, especially for more troubled youths. Counselors should be aware, however, that adolescents often have great difficulty translating the content of private sessions to the real world outside. Special provisions must be made for such transference to occur. The following discussion will treat, first, a group counseling format and, second, the extension of that format to work with individual adolescents.

A life-skills group is led by a pair of counselors—one male, one female. Initially, through role play and use of both humorous and serious examples, leaders demonstrate a sensitivity to typical adolescent concerns about sexual development and behavior. They explain the goals, experiential focus, and time-limited nature of the group. They may also ask group members to state anonymously, on 3 inch by 5 inch cards, situations or topics they want covered during group sessions.

The first group session is usually spent in get-acquainted exercises, rapping, and building group cohesion. In following sessions, leaders present a series of strategies drawn from problem-solving, self-control, and assertion training literature to help group members control anxiety and maximize their chances of choosing and implementing the best course of action when faced with situations they define as difficult. One such strategy is self-talk or self-instruction (Kendall & Finch, 1979). Leaders demonstrate how to talk to yourself when feeling anxious or confused. Self-talk can be in the form of instructions ("Wait! Stop and think this through.") or self-praise ("Hey, I'm doing fine."). Leaders also cover deep breathing and other self-relaxation techniques (see Rose, 1972). One whole session is devoted to a specific paradigm for solving problems (D'Zurilla & Goldfried, 1971; D'Zurilla & Nezu, 1980). The paradigm includes recognizing when a choice needs to be made, identifying the best possible outcome for the given situation, generating a list of possible actions that will make that outcome happen, and developing a detailed plan for implementing the actions that are most feasible and consistent with personal values.

Using films, demonstrations, and discussion, leaders also cover information about the physiology of sexual behavior and human reproduction. Through in-class exercises and homework, adolescents practice incorporating this information into problem-solving thinking to arrive at optimal solutions for situations involving sexuality. The following exercise is an example:

> You and your boy/girlfriend are alone together after a party. You've had a good time and nobody is around. You've been kissing and touching and, if things go any further, your clothes will probably come off soon. What will you do next? What could you do in this situation? What information do you need to help you decide what to do? What do you finally choose to do? What is your partner's reaction? What are the possible consequences of your choice?

Group members write out their responses. These responses form the basis for group discussions, and, when appropriate, for role-played practice in communicating a decision to a partner or other significant person. Leaders offer coaching and instructive feedback to shape effective verbal and nonverbal communication. Practice situations must fit the concerns of the group. They may include problems regarding physical appearance, appropriate sex role behavior, dealing with community health services, or parents. A pregroup questionnaire is often helpful in soliciting appropriate situational targets for group work.

Throughout, leaders structure many opportunities to practice cognitive and communication skills both within and outside of the group setting. Practice outside the group involves contracts to perform or try out certain behavior and report results at the next group meeting. These contracts typically involve such actions as initiating conversation on a difficult topic with an opposite-sex partner or parent, contacting a community vendor for birth control, or explaining a choice of sexual abstinence to a same-sex friend. Group members' experiences implementing these contracts form the basis for additional discussion, instruction, and skills practice. Emphasis throughout the life-skills enhancement program is on making and implementing independent choices that accurately reflect personal needs and values and, in addition, recognize the needs and values of others.

The experiential life-skills approach basically offers a form of reality testing under controlled conditions. As such, it is far more useful to adolescents than more symbolic or less action-oriented techniques. Young people can test a range of beliefs, choices, and behavior. Learning new skills and testing them successfully in the world outside the counseling group increases adolescents' feelings of mastery, leading to increases in self-esteem and self-efficacy (Bandura, 1977). This latter is the inspiriting belief that one has the ability to manage importunate events and tasks satisfactorily— a requirement for healthy, mature functioning. Finally, the skills enhancement orientation aids recruiting young people to participate in counseling. It provides a positive counter to lingering feelings that only losers or the seriously impaired turn to counselors for help. Adolescents are quick to see the value of a program that will help them be in control of real choices and events.

Evaluation of the Life-Skills Method

Four field studies in Seattle with small numbers of adolescents in treatment and control groups provide effectiveness data for the life-skills enhancement approach to sexuality counseling with groups. Findings are consistently positive across all studies in terms of significant gains in sexual knowledge, self-esteem, assertiveness, and ability to communicate effectively regarding sexual issues. Although further experimentation plus evaluation with a larger number of diverse groups and leaders is needed, as well as longitudinal studies, results look promising at this time (Barth et al., 1981; Gilchrist & Schinke, in press; Schinke & Gilchrist, 1977; Schinke et al., 1980, 1981).

Life-Skills Approach with Individuals

Though more rigorously evaluated with groups, the life-skills approach is valuable in counseling with individual adolescents. Contrasted with more structured group work, individual sessions are frequently a greater mix of relationship building and supportive talk, focused skills training with assignment of extrasession homework, and provision of concrete services to meet clients' needs. These services may be in the form of medical care, job referrals, enrollment in special school or public assistance programs, and so on. The following provides an example of life-skills counseling with an older adolescent.

Shy, depressed, 16-year-old Jane revealed after several sessions with her counselor that she had been having unprotected intercourse with her 18-year-old boyfriend, Ray. The counselor provided information about human fertility and birth control. In the midst of planning how and where to obtain contraceptives, however, Jane further revealed that, although she liked Ray, she did not enjoy their lovemaking and did not want to engage in intercourse until she felt more emotionally prepared. Nevertheless, she felt powerless to change the situation without alienating Ray. Using the problem-solving paradigm, Jane and her counselor generated a list of actions Jane could take to effect the change she wanted. One of the options included having Ray attend the counseling sessions with Jane so they could learn to talk to each other about sex and their relationship. Jane liked this option best but believed that Ray would never agree to it. Nonetheless, with the counselor's support, she agreed to work toward making this option a reality. For several sessions, Jane and her counselor planned how and when to approach Ray, what to say, and how to handle his anticipated objections. Jane role played inviting Ray to the counseling sessions until she no longer felt anxious or uncertain. Her counselor provided feedback to improve her assertiveness. Jane contracted with her counselor to approach Ray on a specific day midway between two of her weekly sessions. She arranged to call the counselor for support just before and just after she did so.

In spite of her fears and to her delight, Jane was successful in persuading Ray to come to a counseling session with her. Their first joint session revealed that Ray himself was depressed over his inability to find a job. The counselor arranged his entry in a job training program that began immediately, and Ray agreed to attend two more joint counseling sessions with Jane. These skills enhancement sessions focused on improving interpersonal communication. Jane and Ray practiced disclosing feelings to each other, making clear requests and refusals when they needed to, problem solving, and negotiating to a mutually acceptable solution when disagreement arose. The counselor provided feedback and encouragement. Following the joint sessions and additional individual practice with the counselor, Jane discussed with Ray her feelings about having intercourse. This resulted in a mutual decision that each would begin to look for other dating partners. Because she had anticipated this possibility, Jane was saddened but not upset by this decision. She and her counselor began work on new goals to improve her grooming and social skills and to increase her social interactions with young men. On termination from counseling 8 months later, Jane was no longer depressed and was involved in two satisfying friendships with boys her own age. She no longer felt powerless in these relationships and was comfortable discussing her values and preferences with her dating partners. She still did not feel ready for sexual intercourse, and her newly acquired social skills and social confidence allowed her to act in a manner consistent with this choice.

In summary, skills enhancement sessions can help young people like Jane achieve such goals as disentangling themselves from unwanted alliances and achieving greater mutuality and satisfaction in their opposite-sex relationships. (Clinicians seeking further information about cognitive and behavioral skills enhancement with adolescents and adults are directed to Gilchrist, 1981; A. Goldstein et al., 1980; Haynes & Avery, 1979; Kendall & Hollon, 1979; Meichenbaum, 1977; Rathjen & Foreyt, 1980; Schinke, 1981; Spivack et al., 1976.)

COUNSELING WITH FAMILIES

Puberty and the changes entailed in the onset of adolescence introduce a period of reactive disequilibrium and readjustment in almost all family systems. Habitual modes of family interaction no longer work. New modes must be found that take into account the adolescent's increasing competencies and shifting needs and expectations.

The Life-Skills Counseling Model for Families

Several recent investigations have successfully applied variations of the life-skills counseling model to teach adolescents and their parents to communicate more effectively with each other on a host of issues, including sexuality. Duehn and Mayadas (1977) designed a sexuality program specifically to enhance parent–adolescent communication about sex. Parents and adolescents met in separate but concurrent groups. Each group received an identical curriculum. Group leaders presented information and demonstrated communication skills. Group members participated in a variety of skills practice exercises. A third group consisting of adolescents whose parents were not involved in the program also received the same information and communication skills training. At posttest, adolescents whose parents were included in the program had retained more accurate information and were significantly more skilled on several measures of communication ability when compared with identically trained adolescents whose parents were not included. "Adolescents in subgroup I [parents included] were fluently discussing complex subject matter in concrete and personal terms. Adolescents in subgroup II [parents omitted] were communicating in much the same manner as they had done during the initial session" (Duehn & Mayadas, 1977, p. 18). Though parents and adolescents had neither met together nor formally practiced communicating with each other, parental participation increased adolescents' ability to incorporate sexual learning into thinking and everyday behavior. Although small sample size (16 adolescents, 14 parents) mitigates generalization, findings from this study are consistent with those of other investigators who also stress the importance of sexuality education for parents that goes beyond mere information giving. (See, for example, C. Shapiro, 1981.)

The life-skills counseling approach has also been successfully applied with whole family units. Often sexuality and sexual behavior is but one concern among many for young people and their parents. Several investigators have taught conflict resolution skills to enhance family relationships and cohesion in general. Robin, Kent, O'Leary, Foster, and Prinz (1977) taught families to define the present problem clearly, list numerous possible solutions, evaluate each of these solution options, and plan implementation of the best (i.e., most mutually satisfying) option. The counselors also provided feedback on families' negative communication patterns (teasing, put-downs, interrupting, sarcasm, lack of eye contact) and instruction in more effective patterns, such as reflective listening, visual attention, nonverbal attention, appropriate voice tone, and clarification of meaning. This counseling program resulted in several statistically significant changes in family relations. (Practitioners interested in the skills training approach to family counseling are directed to Guerney, 1979; Kifer et al., 1974; Robin, 1980.)

Some Special Needs of Parents and Adolescents

As many practitioners recognize, conflict and family disequilibrium caused by a child's entry into adolescence is complicated and augmented by the fact that most parents of adolescents are between the ages of 35 and 50 and are coping with so-called midlife transitions (Gould, 1978) and developmental changes of their own. Thus, most families experience the vicissitudes of adolescence and middle age simultaneously. Steinberg (1980) describes some effects of this developmental clash: "Just as the adolescent finds a new way of looking at the world, a viewpoint that involves a broadening of possibilities and endless hypothetical situations to consider, the mid-life parent undergoes a shift in perspective, a shift toward limits and boundaries, toward the feeling that time is running out" (p. 10). Practictioners may begin counseling with an adolescent but soon find parents or a whole family system the most appropriate target for intervention and help. Parents may need help in coping with such stressful events as loss of a job, career change, divorce, or death of a spouse. They may need concrete services in the form of employment counseling, job training, or treatment for depression, alcoholism, or other chronic disorders. Parents may ignore their adolescents' emerging sexuality and maturing abilities and rigidly maintain outmoded family rules and practices formulated when their children were young. Other parents may wish to shield adolescents from the often difficult realities of adult life, including sexuality. They tend to resist dating experiences or any form of sex or contraceptive education for their children. Many are caught in the dilemma of seeking to meet their adolescents' needs for preparation as sexually maturing young adults and the feeling that they may thereby condone such behaviors as nonmarital heavy petting and intercourse. Then, too, some parents are so focused on their own needs and interests that they provide far too little support and guidance for their sons and daughters.

Special problems may arise in single-parent families with adolescents. The resumption of dating makes single parents' sexuality explicit.

> There may be feelings of competitiveness or rivalry between the parent and the adolescent as both strive to be sexually attractive, socially at ease, and respected in a caring relationship. Single parents may be uncertain how much of their own sexual behavior should be discreet or whether they dare impose values upon the adolescent that they do not observe in their own sexual relations. (C. Shapiro, 1981, p. 49)

Adolescents living with opposite-sex parents often have no model or support for learning appropriate behavior related to expression of sexuality.

An important goal of counseling with parents is to increase parent–adolescent communication and understanding. Assertion and communication training are often required. Counselors should provide information on normal adolescent and midlife developmental changes. Useful, too, is the technique called role reversal (Kraus, 1980). Parent and adolescent exchange roles (or identities) to discuss a current conflict or unresolved issue. The counselor shapes the discussion to illuminate previous misunderstandings. The counselor can also temporarily assume one role in the discussion to model alternative ways of thinking and responding. Socially isolated or conflicted parents may need to learn new social skills, relaxation, or problem-solving techniques to enhance the quality of their own lives and relationships. This is especially important when parents have trouble setting consistent limits for adolescents because they secretly receive vicarious pleasure and excitement from the teenager's sexual adventures (C. Shapiro, 1981).

Incest and Sexual Abuse

In cases with serious parental dysfunction, counselors may need to serve as sources of long-term support and assistance for adolescents. When parents sexually abuse their children, counselors may need to use strong intervention techniques, such as skilled intensive counseling with all family members, provision of substitute care for children, and emancipation of older adolescents.

Counselors working with adolescent victims of sexual abuse, incest, or rape often must advocate for understanding and sensitive treatment for their clients from police, medical personnel, parents, and siblings. Victims, paradoxically, often feel guilty for somehow causing the event or, especially in the case of incest, for upsetting and disrupting their families (Giarretto, 1976). In cases of incest, the entire family is the appropriate target for counseling and intervention. (Practitioners wishing more information about treatment programs for sexually abused adolescents and their parents are referred to Giarretto, 1976, and McMillen-Hall, 1977.)

Counseling Adolescent Parents

Counseling and skills training to enhance family relationships take on added importance when counseling with pregnant adolescents. In a longitudinal study, Furstenberg and Crawford (1978) found that the life chances of low-income young mothers and their children were often enhanced if, after giving birth, young mothers did not marry and lived, instead, at home. Families in the process of absorbing a new member—particularly an infant requiring time-consuming care—often need new skills to negotiate new roles, settle disagreements, and meet new requirements and new strains on family resources. When this is accomplished, the results can be salutary. (See also Chapter 11.)

When adolescents marry either before or after a birth, the couple's ability to form a stable, continuing relationship may be enhanced by counseling that stresses empathic and honest communication, and negotiation, conflict resolution, and problem-solving skills. Adolescents face an enormous challenge when they marry. They must suddenly cope with independent adult status, 24-hour intimacy, financial worries, jobs, a new household and lifestyle, and oftentimes an infant as well. Counselors often need to draw upon a full range of resources, including life-skills training to help young couples with the many problems they usually encounter.

Parenting skills and child development information should definitely be provided to *both* parents. Equity and power imbalances in the marital relationship can often be improved if each member of the couple has the opportunity to examine and adjust, if necessary, stereotyped beliefs about adult sex roles and parenting behavior.

A counselor may need to act as an advocate for the new couple with welfare and child care agencies, landlords, potential employers, parents, and health care resources. Obviously, it is important that the counselor have in-depth information about community resources or know how to obtain this information. (See, for example, the community health and welfare department, United Way, Legal Aid, and the yellow pages of the telephone book.)

SPECIAL TOPICS

Abortion Counseling

Abortion counseling is characterized by clear time constraints and a focus on making and implementing a single decision. Often, what to do about a pregnancy is the first large decision an adolescent is called upon to make independently. This can be a frightening and difficult experience, particularly if the young woman or couple has no support from parents or friends. Young people often delay acting when they suspect a pregnancy. Thus, the counselor's first concern is to arrange for tests that will confirm or deny that conception has occurred and determine when the baby is due. When tests are positive, counseling sessions turn to examination of options. Abortion is one among several pregnancy resolution alternatives: having the baby and rearing it alone or with the help of her parents and boyfriend, marrying and having the baby, placing the child for adoption, or abortion. Counseling can help adolescents understand what their options are (see Chesler & Davis, 1980; Mace, 1972). The ultimate decision, however, should be made by the pregnant young woman herself, preferably in consultation with the baby's father and family members. To make the decision that is best for her, she needs to view each option in the context of her present skills, resources, values, goals, emotions, important interpersonal relationships, and future plans. Her counselor's role is to support and shape her realistic selection of the most feasible pregnancy resolution alternative.

Although this rational decision-making process is the accepted model for abortion counseling, it is often extraordinarily difficult to implement, especially with adolescents. In one recent study of 40 adolescent women seeking abortions, Cain (1979) found that pregnancy was often the symptomatic expression of a host of chronic problems with parents, peers, and school that preoccupied these young women. These adolescents were resistant to counseling, often refusing responsibility and trying to pressure counselors into making the abortion decision for them. Many of them were engaged in power struggles with their mothers, and their actions regarding resolution of the pregnancy were more a reflection of this battle than of any informed or sincere personal decision.

Additional problems implementing the decision-making model remain even when young women have enough emotional maturity to make a rational, informed choice. Although there is less chance of subsequent emotional problems and repeat pregnancies when the decision to abort is uncoerced and freely made (Perez-Reyes & Falk, 1973), adolescents often do not feel free to choose. Most of them are living at home at the time they become pregnant.

> Whereas the emancipated woman in her 20s or 30s can go against her family's wishes, the young teenager is dependent on her parents for emotional and financial support. A 14- or 15-year-old might find it almost impossible to bring an unwanted baby into a hostile household or, if she had an abortion that her parents had strongly opposed, to remain there herself. (Cain, 1979, p. 54)

Because parents are adolescents' primary sources of support and assistance, parents should, if at all possible, be involved in the abortion counseling and decision-making process. The family's joint problem-solving behaviors regarding the pregnancy, especially when guided by a counselor skilled in enhancing family communication patterns, can result in growth for all family members.

Male sexual partners of pregnant adolescent women are ignored by most human service professionals in discussions of abortion and pregnancy resolution. Though data regarding young men's feelings about impending fatherhood and abortion are sparse, there is evidence that a partner's abortion can be profoundly disturbing for many men (Rappaport, 1981; Rothstein, 1978). Practitioners should attempt to involve both members of the adolescent couple in all aspects of counseling about an early pregnancy. (Interested practitioners are directed to Rappaport, 1981, for a helpful account of how one family planning clinic successfully included males in preabortion counseling.)

If the decision to abort is made, counselors should prepare young women and their families and partners for the procedure itself. Many adolescents, especially males, know almost nothing about the abortion process. Information provision and reassurance can significantly increase an adolescent's ability to cope with this potentially unnerving medical procedure. For help with the technical aspects of abortion, counselors are referred to the valuable compendium by R. Hatcher, Stewart, Stewart, Guest, Schwartz, and Jones (1980). (For information on the legal issues involved in abortion for minors, see Paul & Pilpel, 1979. Also, see Chapters 7, 11, and 14.) Follow-up counseling appointments should be scheduled 1–3 weeks after the abortion. If the young woman's sexual partner and parents were involved initially, they should be included in the follow-up.

Counseling Adolescents about Homosexuality

A small number of adolescents come to counseling with either self-suspected or self-confirmed preferences for sexual relations with members of their own sex. Sometimes this preference is not well established but merely suspected or feared. For example, peers may call a male adolescent "fag" or "queer" if he engages in styles of behavior usually thought of as feminine. The client's acceptance or confusion about the accuracy of such labels can touch off a reaction akin to panic. Several studies report the therapeutic power of helping young men who are basically heterosexual in orientation gain social- and self-esteem through learning more traditional masculine social skills and mannerisms (see Barlow et al., 1979; Hay et al., 1981;

Rekers, Lovaas, & Benson, 1974). Social competence and assertive training literature are helpful for this task (see Schinke, 1981).

When an adolescent's homosexual orientation seems clear, counseling should include an emphasis on open communication, acceptance, and anxiety and guilt reduction as well as help with specific social or interpersonal problems that may arise. For example, McKinley, Kelly, and Patterson (1977) helped a passive, depressed homosexual 17–year–old become more assertive. This young man had no desire to change his sexual preference; he simply wanted to interact more successfully in a variety of social situations. Because of his stereotypically effeminate behavior, peers frequently ridiculed him at school and at work. He learned to respond decisively and effectively to taunts and to firmly refuse unwanted demands.

Other adolescents may need help with coming out, especially to parents (Malyon, 1981). Role play and behavior rehearsal can be valuable aids in planning for this event. It is important to anticipate parental reactions and to practice in advance how to cope with them. Even with such anticipatory planning, parental reactions may be highly emotional. Parents as well as young people are apt to need counseling help in gaining an understanding of homosexuality, coming to terms with it, and communicating with their adolescent and other significant persons about the topic.

Regrettably, many parents will accept only their teenager's conversion to heterosexuality as a reason for continuing counseling (Malyon, 1981). The truly homosexual adolescent, on the other hand, is rarely in sympathy with this treatment goal. The counselor should stress that the most important reason for counseling is to help the young person develop a positive self-concept and a genuine capacity for intimacy, irrespective of sexual orientation (Davison, 1976). This goal is a challenging one for homosexual youths. As one clinician states, "Social attitudes militate against feelings of self-acceptance. Few, if any, institutional and/or ritualized social activities, support groups, or agency services exist for the homosexual minor . . . gay adolescents are alienated from their peers as well as from the larger heterosexual culture" (Malyon, 1981, p. 328). Many critical developmental experiences, including extensive social involvements and interpersonal attachments with peers, are not available to homosexual youths. The counselor may, for some time, be an adolescent's main source of personal validation and support. Since gay bars and other aspects of adult homosexual society are closed to adolescents, counselors may wish to collaborate with church organizations or other community groups to provide discussion, support, and socialization groups for homosexual young people. (See also Chapter 4. Professionals dealing with homosexual behavior in residential treatment facilities, group homes, boarding schools, or other institutions may wish to consult Shore & Gochros, 1981, for additional information.)

Though virtually no treatment studies focus on teenage lesbian attachments, Loewenstein (1980) provides useful general information about such relationships. Many of the points made above may be fairly readily adapted to working with lesbian adolescents.

Though not specifically attracted to same-sex partners, some adolescents may be highly anxious, constricted, or fearful when dealing with opposite-sex peers. Such young people may well be heterosexual in orientation but unskilled in social relationships. Counseling should focus on lessening anxiety, improving communication and social skills, and increasing dating opportunities. A reassuring counselor can help examine fears and provide accurate information about both heterosexuality and homosexuality and the development of sexual identity. Same-sex crushes are fairly common in adolescence. Sensitive counseling should help anxious adolescents and their parents see such emotional attachments as rehearsals for intimacy or attempts to fulfill natural needs for warmth, understanding, and assistance or guidance, and not necessarily as confirmation of lifelong homosexual preferences.

Fear of Sexuality

Adolescents who are fearful or ashamed of their sexual interests are frequently shy, ill at ease, socially constricted, and withdrawn. Their faulty or irrational beliefs are often a large part of this problem. Goldfried's work (Goldfried & Sobocinski, 1975) shows that unrealistic beliefs about oneself and the consequences of one's behavior are positively correlated with anxiety and social avoidance. For a variety of reasons, young people may appraise sexual feelings as threatening or dangerous. Inaccurate information and strong parental or religious prohibitions can be one reason. In an example from the authors' practice, a father's frightening exhortation against venereal disease led one 15-year-old boy to reject not only his own sexual feelings but all opportunities to interact socially with young women. He became increasingly distanced from male peers as well. Provision of accurate information on both VD and normal adolescent development was beneficial to both father and son. Goldfried's technique of systematic rational restructuring (Goldfried et al., 1974) helped the boy reappraise his father's warnings as evidence that his father cared about him, not, as he had previously thought, that his father feared that his son would lose control of sexual impulses and be harmed. Counseling also focused on increasing the young man's problem-solving skills in order to decrease his overdependence on his father. Communication skills training improved his interactions with peers of both sexes and with his father.

Many adolescents—particularly intellectual, high-achieving youths—reject their sexual feelings because they fear losing control. They often hold an unrealistic view of themselves as superior or successful only when they reject unpredictable emotions and maintain a sense of rational objectivity. Often, these young people are using intellectualization to defend against their equally unrealistic appraisal of themselves as fundamentally unattractive; they must perform rationally, perfectly, with no uncertainty or loss of control or they will be rejected. Small wonder that many of these young people protect themselves by steering clear of sexuality and dating. Again, a cognitive skills approach such as systematic rational restructuring can be valuable. Counselors can help adolescents examine inhibiting irrational beliefs and assumptions, recast negative self-appraisals, reevaluate previously misinterpreted situations and unrealistic standards, and overcome pervasive self-criticism by learning how to self-praise. More experiential social and communication skills training is also helpful in decreasing social anxiety and increasing self-confidence. (Clinicians interested in more complete descriptions of these cognitive techniques are directed to Beck, 1976; Berlin, 1980; Goldfried & Goldfried, 1980; M. Mahoney & Arnkoff, 1978; Meichenbaum, 1977.)

Adolescent Sexual Offenders

Literature describing well-evaluated techniques for counseling with adolescent sexual offenders is sparse. Several investigators report successful treatment of adolescent male exhibitionists (Callahan & Leitenberg, 1973; Lowenstein, 1973; MacCulloch et al., 1971). These studies, however, all relied on technical behavior modification procedures and, because clients' long-term incarceration was imminent, electroshock. These procedures should be employed only as a last resort and only by highly trained specialists. They are not recommended for general counseling practitioners.

Less radical humanistic treatment approaches appear to be more useful. According to one extensive study (James, 1980), female juvenile prostitution increased 183.3 percent between 1968 and 1978. James (1980) identified three key elements in the backgrounds of adolescent women who turn to prostitution: unstable and volatile family life, a history of physical or sexual abuse, and early negative labeling, especially in the area of sexuality. Often lacking in self-esteem and involved in drug use, larceny, and other self-destructive activities, young prostitutes appear in need of counseling. They are, however, a mobile and elusive population reluctant to voluntarily engage in treatment.

Schroeder (1981) reports success in a pilot study testing the feasibility of cognitive and behaviorally based life-skills counseling for groups of young female prostitutes. During the first get-acquainted group, the young women participated in planning subsequent sessions. They requested instruction in grooming and self-defense. Counseling sessions covering these issues were interspersed with sessions on such cognitive skills as analyzing irrational beliefs, replacing self-criticism with self-praise, and problem solving. Other sessions contained assertion training and information on health care. Preliminary analyses of results indicate that "client enthusiasm for and participation in the treatment is high. As this population is known to be generally uncooperative about participating in most psycho-social interventions, it is noteworthy that there was such a high degree of positive involvement" (Schroeder, 1981, p. 10).

Chronically Ill and Mentally Handicapped Adolescents

Little research beyond clinical impressions exists documenting effective sexuality counseling with chronically ill and physically handicapped youths. Their chance to gain self-knowledge, self-esteem, and a mature sexual identity through intensive interpersonal relationships with peers is complicated and difficult. Further, parents are more likely to shield these adolescents, thus increasing their social isolation and delaying maturation. The goal of counseling is to solve unique interpersonal problems and to promote self-acceptance, self-esteem, and the capacity for intimacy. Some emphasis on changing parental attitudes may be necessary. (Interested practitioners may consult Robinault, 1978, and C. Shapiro, 1981.)

Sexuality counseling with mentally retarded adolescents generally has had an emphasis on personal safety and on discrimination of appropriate times and settings for sexual behavior. To avoid exploitation, some mildly to moderately retarded youths need to learn who may touch them, when, and where, and what to do about inappropriate advances from strangers. Most retarded youths have little or no accurate, useful information about human physiology or sexuality. Large posters, 3-D models, and sometimes mirrors are helpful for teaching young people about their own bodies and about the varieties of public and private touching. (See, for example, Livingston & Knapp, 1974; Ryerson, 1979.)

Mentally handicapped youths have "sexual feelings, are exposed to sexual messages and experiences, and are, indeed, sexual people" (Kempton & Carelli, 1981, p. 213). Often, however, these adolescents express sexual behavior in socially problematic or unacceptable ways. Counselors working with mentally handicapped youths often receive complaints about youths' public masturbation. Masturbation is an important source of sexual satisfaction, and counselors may need to advocate for retarded youths' right to enjoy their own bodies in privacy. Counselors must also employ ingenuity in helping especially institutionalized young people learn about private times and places for such sexual activity. Dickerson (1981) contains many illustrations of sensitive sexuality counseling with retarded adolescents and adults.

Birth control for mentally handicapped youths is a frequently raised issue. "Not everyone in the field is willing to make a blanket statement that the retarded can use anything that the nonretarded use. Much depends on the method, the level of the user's intelligence, *and* the supportive guidance of a responsible adult" (Robinault, 1978, p. 63). Counselors must carefully assess the capabilities and life-style of a mentally retarded person in order to select the contraceptive method that best fits that individual. If they are to use a particular method reliably, retarded persons need a great deal of preparation and initial assistance. Kempton (1975) provides an excellent background for this type of counseling. (Interested practitioners may also wish to consult J. P. Edwards & Wapnick, 1979; Hamre-Nietupski et al., 1978; Shore & Gochros, 1981.)

SOME GENERAL GUIDELINES

Counseling with adolescents about their sexuality involves skills and expertise in a number of areas. Counselors should have a thorough knowledge of and comfort with their own sexuality and sexual values, as well as the sexuality and sexual values of others. Young people are quick to detect conscious or unconscious hypocrisy, moralizing, or value confusion regarding sexual behavior. The presence of these elements is detrimental to the counseling relationship. Prospective counselors can benefit greatly from meeting together in groups to explore attitudes and values that inhibit their ability to counsel effectively about sexuality.

To be successful, counselors need a broad knowledge of adolescent development, social milieu, and the socialization experiences of a wide variety of young people from varying religious, racial, ethnic, and social class backgrounds. Effective sexuality counseling with young men, for example, may be difficult unless the counselor recognizes the influence of male sex role stereotypes. As C. Shapiro (1980) states, "Adolescent boys often have been socialized to believe that stoicism is equivalent to masculinity." Many young men are invested in living up to stereotyped standards of manliness that prohibit discussing fears or uncertainties—particularly about sexuality.

Rappaport (1981) describes an imaginative program to improve sexuality counseling with young men:

> When we started our program, we simply talked to the young man about the need for good information regarding sexuality and the importance of

being free to ask about sexual concerns. It is not surprising, given all that we have said about the male role, that the usual response to this was a long silence. (p. 26)

Reacting to this resistance, the counseling staff developed a set of 3 inch by 5 inch cards, each containing a brief and usually false statement designed to promote discussion. For example, "You have to be 18 to buy condoms" and "Women mean yes when they say no." The young man is given a stack of these cards and asked to read them and put each into one of three boxes. The boxes are marked "true," "false," or "don't know." The counselor then goes over the cards in each box, correcting misinformation and validating what accurate knowledge the young man has. This "myth card game" allows the counselor to "ask the question *for the client* while respecting his need not to appear naive. It gives some guidance about which areas need more discussion, but mainly it breaks the ice and lets the questions flow" (p. 26). Responses of male clients to this approach have been consistently positive.

Such mechanical icebreakers are often valuable for raising the topic of sex in individual counseling sessions. (See also Bedrosian, 1981.) Use of such devices depends greatly on the setting, the length of time the counselor and client have known each other, and the nature of the client's problems. When a warm relationship has been established, opening a discussion about sex may be done with proper timing, a warm smile, and the counselor's direct statement, "Let's talk about sex for a while. How's it going for you?" or "You may want to talk about sex later on in our meeting." Sometimes adolescent clients will test a counselor's willingness to discuss sexuality by mentioning the sexual experiences or problems of friends. Counselors may find it helpful to respond to these cues with a general statement of their own, such as "Interesting. Several young people I've talked to have had the same experience." Focusing can then occur with follow-up questions to the present client, such as "Has that ever happened to you? How would you handle it if it happened to you?"

The best sexuality counseling is tailored to young people's immediate concerns and present level of skill. It is important for counselors to recognize differing abilities and stages of cognitive development and not to expect young adolescents to use problem-solving techniques fluently or immediately grasp the future consequences of their current behavior.

In conclusion, though sexual counseling often contains an educational component, a counselor's main concern should not be imparting information but structuring sessions to meet the needs of individuals. If required, counselors should be willing and able to serve as advocates for adolescents in a variety of situations. Extensive knowledge of such community resources as health services, special school and job training programs, welfare offices, and day-care centers is extremely valuable. Good counseling also entails providing adolescents with emotional support and permission to explore difficulties and fears regarding sexuality. Counselors often can reassure, relieve fears and anxieties, dispel myths and misinformation, provide accurate facts, teach needed social and cognitive skills, and help young people realign distorted expectations.

ACKNOWLEDGMENT

The authors were financed by Maternal and Child Health Training Project 913 from the Bureau of Community Health Services (Health Services Administration), and by Mental Retardation and Developmental Disabilities Branch Grant HD 0227 and Center for Population Research Grant HD 11095 from the National Institute of Child Health and Human Development (National Institutes of Health), all administered through the United States Public Health Service, Department of Health and Human Services, and awarded to the University of Washington Child Development and Mental Retardation Center, Seattle, Washington.

CHAPTER 14

Contraceptive and Abortion Services for Adolescents

MARGARET FELDMAN and CATHERINE S. CHILMAN

Social workers, nurses, teachers, and other human service workers have important roles to play in helping adolescents cope with the birth control aspects of their sexuality. In their contact with young people, these workers are important sources of referral to a family planning services. They also may provide direct service to adolescents and their families through counseling and education concerning various aspects of birth control. Moreover, they may perform important functions in community resource development and mobilization for support of needed programs through legislation. All these functions will be discussed in this chapter.

CONTRACEPTIVE SERVICES

Legal Issues

In 1977 the U.S. Supreme Court established the right of adolescents, either single or married, to obtain contraceptives without the necessity of parental consent. This decision established that condoms and other nonprescription contraceptives should be openly available for sale in drugstores and similar outlets. Moreover, public clinics were prohibited from refusing contraceptive services on the grounds of either age or marital status. These provisions apply to all states but are not followed consistently in some of them.

Earlier, in 1966, federal funds had been made available to states through Medicaid for the provision of family planning services to low-income women who desired them. By the early 1970s, this provision was gradually expanded to include services to adolescents.

The issue of parental consent for contraceptive services to adolescents has been a thorny one. Difficulty arises over the fact that many teenagers feel they cannot tell their parents they are engaging in intercourse or planning to do so in the near future. Parents may be hesitant to discuss the topic partly because many think that by doing so they imply consent to behavior that they, or others, may think is immoral or at least inappropriate.

Then, too, as shown in earlier chapters (especially Chapters 2 and 4), the development of more mature sexuality during adolescence is an important aspect of the youngster's growing autonomy and sense of separate identity as a person who is moving away from a dependent attachment to parents. Sharing with parents information about love–sex attachments outside the family may be inhibiting to the young person's growth. Although research has shown that communication about intercourse and contraception between mothers and daughters is associated with more effective contraceptive use, we need to know more about these communication processes and conditions under which they may be either positive or negative in their total effect. This is one of the important and sensitive areas in which counselors and educators will need to work in a skillful, individualized manner in respect to sons and daughters, mothers and fathers.

To return to the legal issue of parental consent, it can be seen that a requirement that parents must be informed and give consent before a teenager can obtain contraceptives might well impose severe damaging constraints on many young people as well as on their families. (After all, a number of parents either do not want to become involved in such issues or feel they are unable to cope with these behaviors.) A higher number of unwanted, untimely adolescent pregnancies would be the most likely outcome of increased parental consent barriers to contraception for sexually active teenagers.

Although some people apparently believe that fewer adolescents would engage in coitus if parental consent were required to obtain contraceptives, it is unlikely that such would be the case. As shown in Chapter 5, many social, psychological, and biological factors are interactively associated with teenage participation in early intercourse. Furthermore, over half of the adolescent girls who are participating in coitus do so for at least a year before seeking contraceptives. Clearly, contraceptive availability is not a primary cause of sexual activity for a large proportion of young people.

Trends in Development and Use of Services

Federal subsidy of family planning programs has been widely (though not universally) accepted as an essential element in public health services to assist low-income persons achieve their own goals in respect to the number and spacing of their children. Since many adolescents in need of these services cannot pay for them from their own funds and since so many believe they cannot ask for assistance from their parents, it seems especially important that free or low-cost contraceptive services be available. These services are primarily medical, but most programs also offer educational and counseling components. Organized family planning programs are supported by private and public funding from state and local resources as well as from the federal government.

Table 14.1 shows that Title X of the Public Health Services Act was the main funding source for family planning programs in 1981 (Nestor, 1982). The stated objectives of this legislation were to provide family planning and related reproductive health services to all women with incomes below 150 percent of the poverty level. This legislation included family planning services for adolescents. Although this legislation came under attack from conservatives in 1981, its funding was continued by the Congress at least through 1984.

Title V of the Social Security Act furnishes grants to state departments of health, which in turn fund specialized services to low-income mothers and their babies. These have included contraceptive services.

Titles XIX and XX of the Social Security Act (Medicaid and selected social services) have provided federal reimbursement on a patient-by-patient basis for services rendered. A 1974 amendment to the Title XX social service legislation required states to offer family planning services and supplies to women of childbearing age, including minors.

By the early 1980s, federal provision of specialized Title XX social service programs had come under attack. Proposed legislation recommends, instead, that more power be given to states to design their own health and social services programs through block grants—the return of federal tax revenues to states in general block funding rather than in program-specific grants.

At the local level, services for family planning have been provided in a number of settings. Virtually all public family planning programs have served some adolescent patients, and about 33 percent of all patients in these

TABLE 14.1. Federal and State Sources of Family Planning Funds for Contraceptive Services, 1981 (in thousands of dollars) (Adapted from Nestor, 1982.)

152,186	Title X of Public Health Services Act
22,185	Title V of Social Security Act (Grants-in-aid funds to states)
90,136	Title XIX of Social Security Act (Medicaid), 90 percent federal matching
60,470	Title XX of Social Security Act for social and related services
49,847	State legislated funding
3,300	Other health agency funds
378,124	TOTAL

programs have been age 19 or less. About 40 percent of adolescent patients have attended health clinics; 30 percent, Planned Parenthood programs; 19 percent, other centers for women or special neighborhood clinics; and 11 percent, hospitals (Alan Guttmacher Institute, 1981).

Use of organized family planning services on the part of adolescents increased after 1969. This was partly because of the passage of Title X of the Public Health Services Act and the subsequent establishment of family planning clinics nationwide. From 1969 to 1979, the number of both new and continuing adolescent patients in these programs doubled.

In spite of the expansion of contraceptive services available to adolescents and in spite of increased adolescent use of these services, serious problems have remained. As we saw in earlier chapters, many thousands of adolescents become pregnant each year even though most of them do not intend to. A 1979 national survey (Zelnik & Kantner, 1980b) showed that, unfortunately, the contraceptive behavior of adolescent women was *less* effective in 1979 than in 1976. In both years, only 45 percent of sexually active young women said they used contraceptives at their first intercourse, 33 percent said they had never used contraceptives, and another 33 percent said they always used this protection. However, the proportion of young women who relied on the risky method of male withdrawal increased to 19 percent and the rate of use of the more effective pill decreased from 48 to 41 percent in 1979 (Zelnik & Kantner, 1980b). These developments are particularly disturbing because the proportion of adolescents participating in nonmarital coitus increased between 1976 and 1979, so that more of them were at risk of untimely pregnancy in 1979 than in 1976.

As we have seen, demographic characteristics, life situations, and social-psychological variables all play a part in the contraceptive behavior of teenagers. These variables point to the fact that the characteristics of birth control programs play an important, though not an all-important, part in whether or not teenagers use contraceptives effectively.

Characteristics of Effective Contraceptive Services for Adolescents

A 1976 study by the then U.S. Department of Health, Education, and Welfare (Urban and Rural Systems Associates, 1976) undertook to identify the characteristics of contraceptive clinics that adolescents said were important to them. According to this survey, three major characteristics of successful programs were identified: ready availability, low cost, and confidentiality. Adolescents preferred locations that were unobtrusive so that they would not be observed entering or leaving the clinic. Confidentiality was a central issue because many adolescents were fearful of parental involvement. For example, even those who said their parents knew they were getting birth control indicated such attitudes as: "I don't want to keep reminding them of what I am doing."

Four programmatic features made it most likely that adolescents would continue coming to a clinic after a first visit:

1. Availability of pregnancy tests. One-third to one-half of first visits to clinics were the results of a pregnancy scare. Those patients with negative pregnancy tests often became motivated to accept contraceptives, at least for a while.
2. Responsive scheduling of clinic appointments. Delayed appointments of more than a week were correlated with no-shows.
3. Convenience of hours and location. Clinics should be available by public transportation at convenient after-school or evening hours.
4. Simplified admission and payment procedures. Some specific service should be provided the first day the person appears, and charges should be reasonable, with an opportunity for small payments over time.

According to the respondents, three conditions were related to their continued participation in the clinic.

1. Staff treatment. Adolescents want to be treated with warmth and understanding, as "people."
2. Physician treatment. Young women are fearful of the pelvic examination and want a physician or nurse-practitioner to be understanding and gentle and to explain procedures to them. The younger the patients, the greater their preference for young female practitioners and those wearing white coats, which give a feeling of professionalism. Competence is valued by all.
3. Clinic efficiency. Services should be provided without excessive delay, and there should be privacy from the first to the last encounter.

The study also discusses the conditions deemed (but not proven) necessary to become an effective teenage contraceptor:

To be an effective contraceptor, a teenager should have a clear understanding of the consequences of sexual activity without contraception; an understanding of the cycle of fertility; sufficient information to choose an appropriate method; a thorough knowledge of how to use her method properly; and information about any potential side effects related to her particular "method of choice." In addition to knowledge, teenagers—and other women as well—also have to be motivated to use their method on a consistent basis. The support of the teenage patient's sexual partner, the extent of his understanding of how and when pregnancy occurs, and his willingness to accept joint responsibility for the use of contraception may be a very important factor in motivating a teenager to use contraception regularly. In the case of some methods such as condoms, foams, or diaphragms, the active involvement and commitment of the teenager's sexual partner may be even more important (p. 11, Urban and Rural Systems Associates, 1976).

This survey also found that it would be extremely difficult for many adolescents to obtain payments for contraceptive services either through Medicaid or health insurance because, in most cases, this would mean that the youngsters would be forced to inform their parents about the kind of medical help they needed. The great majority of teenagers who were questioned felt they could not talk to their parents about this matter.

It has been suggested that adolescents pay what they can for these services out of their own allowances or earnings. This is an appealing idea, although the staff time and record keeping that such a procedure might entail could cost more than the income obtained.

Private physicians are urged to incorporate the subject of adolescent sexuality and contraception within their service to adolescents. Although this is an excellent idea and such a service should be useful to some teenagers, it does not solve the problem of financing the service without the involvement of parents.

It is to be hoped that, in time, more parents will become accustomed to the changing sex norms for young people in our society and will be able to discuss comfortably and honestly the possible needs of their sons and daughters for help with contraception and, in some cases, abortion. Even if this change occurs, there will still be the need for subsidized birth control services for those people who cannot otherwise afford them.

The survey revealed, further, that teenagers particularly like the informal rap sessions that many special adolescent clinics have; such sessions were much preferred by the study respondents to formal educational lectures. When skillfully led, these sessions allow young women to share their fears and anxieties with other sexually active adolescents and with the group leader. Some adolescents need individual counseling besides the group sessions for help with special problems. All need staff procedures that are sensitive to their desires for privacy and anonymity.

The investigators also comment that retrenchment of funds for birth control (or family planning) programs often results in a sharp reduction in, or elimination of, educational and counseling services. This seems unwise in light of the research evidence we have concerning the particular difficulties teenagers encounter within themselves in seeking birth control help and in maintaining contraceptive practice after it has been initiated. Careful evaluation of the educational–counseling component of birth control services is indicated in order to assess how effective this component is. Evaluations also are needed for the program suggestions that follow.

Education and counseling as well as medical services of a birth control program can be made far less expensive than is often the case. The paramedical staff, if suitably trained, can carry out many of the functions often reserved for the physician. Individual and group counseling can be performed, in many cases, by family planning specialists who have had specialized in-service training and are not necessarily psychologists or social workers. (However, supervisory personnel and consultants drawn from these professions are indicated.)

Unfortunately, poor treatment is generally accorded to males in most birth control clinics. These clinics tend to be almost completely oriented toward serving females, although it has been found that many young women would welcome the inclusion of their partners at least in rap sessions. Some have expressed interest in also including their partners in the physical examination. Would it not be a good idea to provide a physical examination for the males, especially perhaps in reference to venereal disease, and give them instruction in techniques of withdrawal and use of the condom?

Because so few adolescents use effective contraceptives consistently and the great majority participate in coitus for at least a year before seeking formal assistance with contraceptives, a number of strategies, besides those discussed above, seem indicated. Continuing effort appears to be necessary to make contraceptive education, counseling, and supplies available to adolescents where they are, such as in schools and recreation centers. This recommendation particularly applies to providing instruction in coitus interruptus, condoms, foams, and jellies. It is recognized that a more specialized service is needed for female prescription methods. Condoms, foams, and jellies should be available to adolescents in convenient locations, such as in public restrooms, gas stations, and the like. Although these methods are not as effective as the orals or the intrauterine device, much of the research shows that many young people fail to use the more effective methods, especially if they are young and not in a long-term, steady relationship.

Public anxiety about the possibility of encouraging adolescent coitus by making contraceptives available has to be countered through educational efforts that help citizens realize that adolescent nonmarital intercourse is on the rise in many parts of the world as well as in this country. This rise is most likely a result of the growing complexity, mobility, urbanization, and industrialization of society, as well as younger ages at puberty, rather than availability of contraceptives per se. In all probability, many, if not most, adolescents will become sexually active by ages 15 or 16—many by age 12.

It may be impossible to halt this trend. It seems tremendously important, therefore, to make contraceptives and abortion available to teenagers in an appropriately sensitive and humane way rather than have them run the risk of early, unwanted pregnancies.

It is especially important to reach parents with messages of this kind, with the hope that secrecy, distance, and conflicts between the generations can thereby be reduced. Young people need support, understanding, and guidance from their parents in all aspects of their lives as they assay the difficult task of moving from childhood to adult maturity in a complex, often frightening and hostile world.

Problems regarding the acceptance and consistent use of effective contraceptives by young people as well as adults is partly a matter of the failure of the culture (its values, understandings, norms, and goals) to adapt with sufficient rapidity to the enormous changes that have shaken American and other societies. A new, more adaptive culture is struggling to be born. Cultural leaders, such as policymakers and program builders, need to help in its birth and development. Some in the field of birth control services for adolescents are already doing this, most notably the Planned Parenthood Federation of America and its research arm, the Alan Guttmacher Institute.

Because birth control services for adolescents have been established quite recently as a matter of public policy (about 1968), it will take time for many young people, as well as adults, to become accustomed to the concept of birth prevention and use the services readily. This is apt to be especially true for people from those socioeconomic, racial, and ethnic groups that have traditionally held high fertility values and have been suspicious of the mainstream culture.

It should be helpful, therefore, to employ both males and females of various backgrounds to perform outreach as well as other staff functions in a family planning (or birth control) service for adolescents. Such personnel would ideally include members of the major racial, ethnic, and religious groups of the area. A personnel mix of this kind far from guarantees that staff people will understand and empathize with the values, norms, goals, and beliefs of the young people with whom they work. For instance, an ambitious, well-educated black professional from a middle-class family may well have little sympathy for, or understanding of, a sexually active teenager from the inner city. This suggests staff development training and use of a variety of lecture, discussion, audiovisual, and group participation techniques to enhance staff knowledge, skills, and insights. Such training would include attempts to promote deeper understanding about the sexual and contraceptive needs, behaviors, and values of adolescents and parents of varying cultural backgrounds.

This training also would be useful to help staff members develop furuther knowledge and skills in methods of individual and group counseling, as indicated above. Such counseling also might be carried out profitably with parents. It should be helpful to work with both adolescents and parents as *whole persons* with their own particular life histories, stages of development, personality structures, life situations, and goals. All too often the focus of counseling programs in family planning clinics is solely on the use of contraceptives. Important as this may be, it seems overly narrow and likely to have limited effectiveness.

Groups can be profitably used in education and counseling, partly because of the importance of a peer support system and the development of a peer "contraceptive culture." This is especially true for adolescents but is also true for parents in times of rapid change. Group members who have used contraceptives successfully and parents who have been able to handle this issue wisely with their sons and daughters can be helpful role models and advisors to other group members.

The anxiety of parents tends to be high concerning the sexual behavior of their teenagers. Many feel that the larger society will hold them responsible for whatever their youngsters do. This is less true than it once was. Although parents play an important part in the developmental outcomes of their sons and daughters, society takes a very large hand in child rearing today from the moment children are born. By the time they reach adolescence, young people have been exposed to a veritable flood of societal influences. Thus, the larger society cannot hold parents solely accountable for the behavior of their teenagers. Parents can be helped to realize that they are still responsible for their youngsters, but not *totally* responsible; that both contemporary conditions as well as the youngster's developmental stage call for loving parental support and clear guidance, but not parental overprotection and attempts to control or assume responsibility for all the young person's behavior.

Both individual and group counseling may help teenagers and parents gain better communication skills. Ideally, males and females from both age groups would be included. The group process itself may develop communication skills. Beyond specific role-playing experiences, techniques can be used to help people learn how to talk about their personal feelings, sexual relationships, and use of contraceptives. (See also Chapters 12 and 13.)

A sole focus on contraceptive technology can depersonalize and dehumanize partner relationships. It seems important, therefore, to assess the knowledge, attitudes, and behaviors of family planning personnel (medical, social work, paraprofessional, and clerical) toward adolescents (both male and female) of differing socioeconomic, racial, and ethnic backgrounds. This assessment should particularly include areas related to the young person's sexual and contraceptive behavior. Many staff people in these settings are not comfortable about their own sexuality, not to mention that of the people with whom they work. They are unable to discuss the topic easily, with real insights about, and acceptance of, the sexuality of adolescents and differing attitudes and values about sex, their sexual and contraceptive experiences, problems with lack of sexual satisfaction, physical pain (often owing to the female's failure to lubricate adequately), and fears and anxieties about many forms of sex behavior, including contraceptive use.

Sexually active boys and girls need more than an intellectual understanding of contraception. They need a chance to share their feelings about these techniques, gain reassurance, and acquire communication and behavior skills regarding contraceptive use in a sexual relationship. (How do you say, "Are you using a contraceptive? What kind? Do you need time to apply it?") (See also Chapter 13.)

In order to help adolescent (and older) patients with these matters effectively, staff people are very likely to be in need of in-service training regarding all aspects of human sexuality for people of different ages and different psychosocial characteristics. It is not essential that all staff people be able to deal intensively with the many aspects of human sexuality. Certain staff members (often the social workers and sex educators) have particular knowledge and skills about this. Other personnel can use these staff resources more frequently than they often do and refer patients for both individual and group counseling.

The family planning service offers a unique opportunity to help people in the very sensitive and often troublesome area of human sexuality. The application of adolescents for contraceptive help usually indicates they are sexually active (or at least plan to be in the near future); this, in itself, offers the opportunity for expert assistance that is rarely available in our society.

One might wonder how to reach the parents of adolescents in a family planning clinic. An easy place to start would be with the women patients already served by a clinic. It would be highly appropriate to discuss the developing sexuality of the children of these women, including that of young children. Of course, such a discussion might well start with the woman's values, understanding, and feelings about her own sexuality.

Ideally, a family planning service might be a multiservice agency dealing with a whole range of human needs, including those of overall health care, educational–vocational concerns, employment problems, and financial need. The connection between these factors and contraceptive use has been shown earlier in Chapter 6. However, such a service is often impractical in communities where a network of specialized programs already exists. It would be useful, then, for family planning personnel to have in-depth information about these services plus the skills to help people get the services they need—a role often appropriate for staff social workers. Among other possible beneficial outcomes, programs of this sort would make the family planning center seem more relevant and humanely concerned with the total well-being of people, both male and female, especially those who are most in need of contraceptive and many other forms of help.

The foregoing is written as if contraceptive services were offered only through family planning clinics. Of course, this is not the case. Many of the remarks apply as well to other kinds of medical settings. Many of them also apply to other human services, such as those offered through the schools and social agencies. It seems important that these organizations deal, in an enlightened way, with the sexual and contraceptive needs of the young people with whom they work and refer them as indicated to the more specialized family planning services.

Frequent mention has been made above concerning the importance of including males as well as females in birth control programs for adolescents. The usual focus on females as being *the* person responsible for contraception is a flagrant example of sexism. This focus is frequently excused by such statements as "It is the female who gets pregnant," or "Male methods of contraception are less effective; besides, males don't like them." (What female ever said that she *liked* her methods?) It also is said, "You can't trust a male to use a contraceptive." This very attitude is apt to become a self-fulfilling prophecy.

All the above attitudes would seem to undermine the male's sense of responsibility as a copartner in reproduction control. When his sense of partnership in this endeavor is undermined, his sense of significance and competence as a male also may suffer. With the female in sole charge of reproductive outcomes, he can be further threatened in his sense of power and masculinity—and many socioeconomic trends already present him with a multitude of these threats.

A Model Contraceptive Program

A high school clinic sponsored by the St. Paul Maternal and Infant Care Project has had many desirable features. The project has offered comprehensive, multidisciplinary health care to adolescents since 1968. At first the service was offered in an inner-city junior–senior public high school. The school was closed at the end of the 1975–1976 school year, but by that time the clinic was being used by about 66 percent of the twelfth grade students and by more than 90 percent of the pregnant students. During the years the clinic was in operation, the birthrates of adolescents in the school had fallen from 79 births per 1000 adolescent girls to 35 per 1000.

When the school was closed, the project opened clinics in the two senior high schools to which the students transferred. These clinics, like the others, included a range of physical and health services for both men and women students: athletic, job, and college physicals; immunizations; a weight control program; and contraception. The service thus provided anonymity to the students who came for contraceptive services and also, since this service was located in the school, allowed the nurse to follow up easily on problems of contraceptive use.

Staff members included a family planning nurse-practitioner who took health histories, performed lab tests (including pregnancy tests), and gave individual and group contraceptive counseling. A social worker routinely saw all family planning patients to talk with them about their relationships with their parents and their partners in order to help work out a birth control program that would be satisfactory to their needs. An obstetrician-gynecologist came one morning a week to do birth control examinations, evaluations of students who were pregnant, and follow-up of all abnormal findings from previous examinations. A pediatrician provided the physical examinations for jobs and college, and this service was an important referral source to the birth control clinic for sexually related problems or contraceptive needs. Those students who wished contraceptive supplies and devices were referred to an after-school and evening clinic at a nearby medical center, since the school board thought these services should not be provided on school grounds.

The program also included a nutritionist, dental hygienist, and a day-care director who supervised care for the children of students. The objective of this service, to which a student could bring her baby at 6 weeks of age, was to allow students to continue their schooling through graduation and also to learn good parenting skills. Students were provided services until they were 18 years of age and then transferred to another clinic for adult care.

The clinic was very well accepted in the school community and was used for one or more of its many services by 75 percent of the students. During 1978–1979, about 25 percent of the young women students came for contraceptive services, and they had a high continuation rate.

Not every school system will allow the kind of clinic found in St. Paul. However, a staff member working with adolescents in a Planned Parenthood affiliate in Ithaca, New York, organized a network of social workers, nurses, and teachers who referred young women to an adolescent service. This staff member was willing to go immediately to a school in order to perform a pregnancy test or to confer with an adolescent with a serious problem. She developed a program with the acronym of SEARCH (Sexuality Education Around Responsibility, Contraception and Health). Printed cards with the phone number and no further identifying information were given to the teenagers, to help them preserve confidentiality in respect to their activities in obtaining contraceptive services.

At this Planned Parenthood clinic, as in many others, a teenage rap group meets every week. The rap group discusses such topics as responsible decision making, including the right to say no, and the types of contraceptives and their effectiveness as well as their advantages and disadvantages. Following the group education meeting, those who want to obtain physician-prescribed contraceptives are scheduled for an appointment. The young women are told there is a $10 medical fee, which they can pay in a lump sum or in small payments within a 3-month period. Free services are also provided to those who have no financial resources.

Contraceptive Methods

Table 14.2 gives a summary of the different kinds of contraceptives and their effectiveness.

Research shows that early sex activity is apt to be sporadic before a young person becomes committed to a partner or fully accepts the idea of being a sexual person. For these young people, the condom is probably the contraceptive method of choice. The condom is not only effective when used correctly but the only method that protects both the male and the female from sexually transmitted diseases (STD, the new term preferred by many professionals, instead of VD, venereal disease). A high level of safety is provided by the combined use of the condom by the man and foam by the woman. This combination provides both a mechanical and chemical barrier to impregnation. Most inexperienced adolescents may not have the communication skills, knowledge, and motivation to use both condom and foam, but discussions with young people can help clarify these two types of nonprescription contraceptives and should promote their effective use. (See also Chapter 13 regarding the developing of contraceptive communication skills.)

It is important for all human service professionals who work with adolescents to have a good general knowledge about the various kinds of contraceptives, where they may be obtained, their costs, their methods of use, their possible side effects, and their reliability. It is usually not adequate simply to tell a teenager to attend a family planning service or to see a physician for help with contraceptives. Since many teenagers are embarrassed and fearful about this matter, it can help in a referral to give them some idea of what to expect and what kinds of options are open to them. In this connection, if an adolescent girl is planning to visit her doctor or a birth control clinic, it is probable that she will have a pelvic examination. The pelvic examination is necessary in order for the doctor to determine if there is any abnormality in the uterus or cervix (mouth of the uterus), or any disease that needs treatment. If the woman has decided to use a diaphragm, the doctor needs to determine the size she will need. Most Planned

TABLE 14.2. Major Contraceptive Methods: Their Effectiveness, Advantages, and Disadvantages

Characteristic	Method		
	Orals	IUD	Diaphragm with Jelly/Cream
Effectiveness	Combination: 90–96% Minipills: 90–95%	95%	83%
Advantages	Gives most protection Regulates menstrual cycle May lessen menstrual cramps and flow Usage does not intrude on lovemaking	Nothing to do just before intercourse String easily checked Inexpensive Plastic IUDs one-time insertion only	No side effects Jelly acts as lubricant No medical supervision after fitting Can be used as part of sexual fore-play, thus sharing responsibility with partner
Disadvantages	May cause some unpleasant side effects especially during first few months Requires medical supervision Long-term effects still being researched	Insertion may cause temporary discomfort May increase menstrual cramps and flow Uterus may reject it Requires medical supervision May aggravate pelvic infection	Requires planning May interrupt lovemaking for insertion
Risks	Relationship to blood clot problems and heart attack, especially in women over 35 and heavy smokers Continuous use 5 years or more related to circulatory disease Possible absence of periods several months after stopping	Rare possibility of tubal pregnancy Possible increase of pelvic infection Rare possibility of uterine perforation	Pressure may aggravate bladder and cause cystitis in some women Occasional woman allergic to jelly or cream

Reasons for failure			Contraceptive foam and suppositories	Condom	Periodic Abstinence
Reasons for failure	Missing pills Minipill may not have enough hormone to prevent ovulation for occasional woman	Not checking string to be sure IUD is still in place Occasional pregnancy with IUD in place; reason not yet known	Putting too little cream or jelly on diaphragm Having a second intercourse without adding more jelly Gaining or losing a lot of weight and not being refitted Not using it every time Not refitted after each pregnancy Not leaving diaphragm in place for 6–8 hrs after last intercourse		
Effectiveness			75–80%	90%	80% variable
Advantages			No prescription needed Inexpensive No side effects Provides lubrication Highly effective if condom is also used	No prescription needed Man can be responsible for birth control Inexpensive No side effects Helps prevent spread of venereal disease	No hormonal or mechanical device No cost No side effects

TABLE 14.2 (*Continued*)

Characteristic	Method		
Disadvantages	Use may intrude on lovemaking Can be messy Must be used every time May provide too much lubrication	Use may intrude on lovemaking Some men report decreased sensation Requires planning	Requires careful monitoring of basal temperature, vaginal mucus, and menstrual cycles Instructions must be given by a professional or successful experienced user May require many days of abstinence each cycle
Risks	Occasional man or woman may have allergic reaction	None	None
Reasons for failure	Putting foam in more than ½ hr ahead of intercourse	Not using it every time	Not keeping careful track of cycles

Characteristic	Sterilization	Condom and foam used together
Effectiveness	Nearly 100%	95–99%
Advantages	Permanently unable to conceive or impregnate Nothing to think about One-time only cost for surgery Available to either man or woman	Mutual responsibility of partners
Disadvantages	Cannot change mind about fertility later Possible risks of surgery (more detailed information available)	Takes communication skills
Risks		None
Reasons for failure	Rarely, tubes may reconnect	Poor techniques

Less effective methods

Withdrawal	Man withdraws penis from vagina just before ejaculation. This method is cost free, is always available, and has no side effects. But man may forget, may mistime, or may impregnate with lubricating fluid before ejaculating. Theoretical—85%. Actual—60%.
Breast feeding for 12 months	A woman usually does not ovulate while nursing. But she may be fertile before menstrual periods resume.
Chance—no contraceptive	10% effective.

Ineffective methods (myths)

Douching	Sperm travel faster into the uterus and tubes than a woman can travel to her douche. Also, the force of the douche spray may help propel the sperm into the uterus.
Holding back	Having an orgasm or climax has nothing to do with getting pregnant.
Virginity	If sperm are deposited near the vaginal opening they may get inside even if the woman has never had intercourse.
Positions	Any position where there is penis–vagina contact can result in pregnancy whether sitting, standing, or lying down.

Parenthood affiiliates and other clinics have an informative slide show or film or at least informative pamphlets that will help young women understand what will happen when they have their pelvic examinations.

Although the medical–biological aspects of contraceptives are beyond the purview of this report, a continuing effort is indicated to find better contraceptive methods for both males and females. It is well recognized that all the present methods have their liabilities. Although the improvement of contraceptives would be helpful, especially for adolescents whose patterns of sex behavior are apt to be different from those of older people (infrequent coitus, unplanned intercourse, sex relations in secret, and so on), such improvement would be unlikely to solve the birth control problems of teenagers. As we have seen in Chapter 6, many psychosocial difficulties, such as anxiety about one's own sexuality, egocentric thinking, and risk-taking attitudes are still likely to remain.

ABORTION

Trends in Legislation

Various issues concerning abortion became highly publicized and politically salient during the 1970s following the 1973 Supreme Court decision that declared unconstitutional all state laws that prohibited or restricted abortions during the first trimester of pregnancy. In this decision, the Court also limited state intervention in second-trimester abortions to the "regulation and medical practices involved insofar as they affect the woman's health." The Court left the prohibition of third-trimester abortions to the separate states. Several other issues, including the rights of minors to abortion without consent of their parents, were also left to state discretion. In 1974 the Massachusetts Supreme Court ruled that a husband does not have the right to prevent his wife from having an abortion. The attorney general of California, in the same year, issued an opinion that an unmarried girl under age 18 does not need her parents' consent for an abortion (Katchadourian & Lunde, 1975).

Despite these federal and state legal developments, antiabortion (so-called prolife) groups in many states and localities continued attempts to limit the availability of abortion, especially for teenagers. For example, a number of states enacted laws in 1974 and 1975 that required that teenagers be barred from abortions unless they obtained parental consent. This legislation was declared unconstitutional by the Supreme Court in a 1976 decision that stated that a minor should have free access to sex-related health care and that a third party (that is, a parent) could not give an absolute veto over a decision made by a physician and his or her patient to terminate pregnancy (Paul & Pilpel, 1979). Through this decision, parental consent statutes were invalidated in 13 states. However, in defiance, some states kept the laws on the books, even though such laws were unconstitutional.

In 1976, the Supreme Court invalidated a state law to the effect that parents must be notified in all cases before an abortion was performed on a minor daughter. The court declared that "mature minors" had the right to seek and obtain abortions without informing their parents. Many states and localities had passed laws requiring parental notification. The Supreme Court decision created considerable confusion in the lower courts as to the definition of a "mature minor." This issue is viewed by Paul and Pilpel (1979) as being important, especially because very young pregnant teenagers are at particular childbearing risk and especially apt to need and desire an abortion. In March 1981, the Supreme Court seemed partly to reverse an earlier decision by upholding a state law in Utah that required parent notification but not necessarily consent before an abortion could be performed.

The Hyde Amendment, passed by Congress in 1976, struck a blow at the availability of federal funds to defray abortion costs for low-income women. After the 1973 Supreme Court decision, such funding had been available to the states through Title XIX of the Social Security Act (Medicaid). The constitutionality of the Hyde Amendment was challenged by prochoice (pro-abortion) groups, but it was upheld by the Supreme Court in 1980 with the argument that the federal government was not obligated to provide funds for abortion costs, although the option of individuals to obtain abortions with the agreement of their physicians remained a basic constitutional right.

Despite the withdrawal of virtually all federal funds for abortion services in 1979, 17 states continued making Medicaid funds available for abortion through state monies and 20 more states provided such funds for abortion services only when physicians attested that a woman's health was seriously endangered if she could not obtain an abortion (Granberg & Granberg, 1980).

The issue of legalized abortion in general, as well as for adolescents, remains highly controversial, with extremely strong emotional positions being taken on both sides of the issue. "Prolife" organizations are pushing for a constitutional convention to amend the federal constitution so as to make abortions illegal except perhaps for pregnancies that are life threatening or that result from rape or incest.

Perhaps the opposition to legalized abortion comes about partly because changes regarding this matter have been so rapid and pervasive in recent years. The developments sketched above that followed the 1973 Supreme Court abortion decision were preceded by a long period in which it was impossible to obtain a legal abortion in the United States. It was not until 1967 that legalized abortions first became available in a small number of states, and then only when continuing the pregnancy might seriously endanger the woman's health or the child might be born with serious defects or conception was the result of rape or incest. In 1970, Hawaii, New York, Alaska, and Washington enacted more liberal laws that removed such restrictions on abortion, as long as it was performed within 24 weeks of conception.

Legalized abortions are now available in many parts of the world. Numerous countries took this step during the 1960s; however, Japan legalized abortion in 1948 and most of the socialist countries acted during the 1950s. Earlier, antiabortion attitudes and legislation had developed in Western Europe and the United States during the nineteenth century. Before this, little official attention seems to have been paid to the matter (H. David, 1972). However, it should be recalled that before the nineteenth century and its medical advances, a low value was generally placed on human life, especially on the lives of infants and young children.

Trends in Abortion Rates and Services for Adolescents

The rates of legal abortions obtained by pregnant teenagers increased each year in the United States between 1973 and 1978. This followed a trend for older groups, but the rates of pregnancies terminated by means of abortion were as high or higher for teenagers than for all other age groups except for women over age 40. One-third of all reported abortions were for teenagers in 1977: This proportion was similar to that in the immediately preceding years. Almost half of all adolescent pregnancies ended in abortion in 1978, and this was the case for more than half of pregnancies occurring among young women less than age 16. In 1977, nonwhite, low-income, single adolescents were especially apt to have abortions (Forrest et al., 1979; Tietze, 1981).

As detailed in Chapter 8, the availability of abortion services was an important factor in lowering the adolescent birthrate in the late 1970s. (See especially Table 8.2.)

It is estimated that well over one-fourth of pregnant, low-income women who wanted an abortion in 1978 were unable to get one because of lack of public funds to defray the cost as a result of the Hyde Amendment. In general, women who live far from large urban centers have found it difficult to obtain abortions because 95 percent of such services are located in metropolitan areas, with the most heavy concentration being in the big cities on the East and West Coasts (Forrest et al., 1979).

Since the mid-1970s, the trend has been for abortion to be offered in free-standing clinics rather than hospitals partly because abortion tends to be a new and controversial service that many hospitals are not eager to offer and many doctors are not psychologically ready to provide (Nathanson & Becker, 1980).

Methods of Abortion

Up until about 12 weeks of pregnancy, abortions can be done in clinics as an outpatient procedure. Early abortions are usually done by the vacuum procedure, in which the products of conception are removed by suction. Curretage (scraping) is another method. Some doctors may insert a laminaria (a stick of a special seaweed) into the cervix, which is left there for 24 hours and gradually enlarges the opening so there is less danger of injury to the cervix during the vacuum procedure.

After the early weeks of pregnancy, when suction or curretage is no longer possible, abortions are performed by injections of saline solutions or prostaglandins, which require an interval of several hours or a day before the fetus is expelled. Abortions in the sixth month of pregnancy are either by hysterotomy (opening of the uterus) or hysterectomy (removal of the uterus). Any of these later procedures are far more dangerous than early abortion but may be less dangerous than a full-term difficult birth.

Abortion Risks

No attempt is made here to discuss the medical risks of abortion in any detail. However, generally speaking, abortion is considered a safe procedure, with only 1 percent of those legally performed in the United States resulting in complications. Procedures are the safest if they are performed before the thirteenth week of pregnancy; methods become more complex at later dates, as shown above. Teenagers are more likely than older females to delay taking action regarding their pregnancies. This is probably a result of ignorance, anxiety, fear, and a frequent need for secrecy. Blacks are more likely to delay action than whites. Thus, abortion complications are more apt to occur for black adolescent girls.

Fewer than 10 percent of all U.S. abortions in 1978 were in the second trimester. These later abortions are far more physically dangerous and emotionally upsetting than earlier ones. However, owing to improved techniques, the death rate from second-trimester abortions has dropped markedly since 1976. Despite this improvement, medical specialists strongly recommend prevention of these later abortions through improved contraceptive services plus early diagnosis of pregnancy, skilled pregnancy counseling, and early decision making if the pregnancy is to be terminated (Benditt, 1979).

Trends in Public Attitudes

Trends in public attitudes toward abortion are shown in analyses of the results of nine national opinion polls conducted between the early 1960s and the late 1970s. Approval of legalized abortion increased dramatically between 1965 and 1973, rising from acceptance by 43 percent of the adult population to acceptance by 68 percent over a span of 8 years. The 68 percent approval figure remained stable from 1973 to 1977, decreased slightly in 1978 (a time of intense political action against abortion), but rose again to 68 percent in 1980 despite highly organized and continued antiabortion agitation nationwide.

An analysis of the characteristics of persons opposed to legalized abortion shows that, in comparison to those who favor this service, those who oppose it have a somewhat lower level of education (for Protestants and Jews but not for Catholics), are more apt to have somewhat authoritarian child-rearing attitudes, and tend to be opposed to nonmarital intercourse, small family size, equal rights for women, and euthanasia. Despite these attitudinal differences, differences are not found in respect to political or religious affiliation, gender, or social class status.

Senators opposed to aborton have been found to be also opposed to gun control and to a range of social services that support women and children, such as the Maternity and Infant Care Programs of the Public Health Service.

As might be expected, the broadest consensus of approval of abortion is found for the so-called hard reasons: to terminate a pregnancy that would seriously endanger the woman's health, that would result in the birth of a defective child, or that is the result of incest or rape. In 1980, 90 percent of respondents in a national opinion poll approved of the right to a legalized abortion for reasons of these kinds.

However, there was only 50 percent approval in 1979 for the so-called soft reasons: single marital status, poverty, or married women who already had children and wanted no more. According to Granburg and Granburg (1980), analyses of the results of these national surveys reveal considerable ambivalence and confusion among the respondents. Results vary somewhat depending on the wording and ordering of questions. This is particularly true in respect to the soft reasons for abortion as well as for items concerning the rights of parents of pregnant adolescents and of spouses of pregnant women.

Most, if not all, pregnant women find it difficult to decide to obtain an abortion and actually follow through with the necessary steps. These difficulties are usually magnified for adolescents for a number of reasons such as lack of requisite information and understanding, inexperience in obtaining medical services, fear of rejection by medical personnel or lack of confidentiality, limited financial sources, and guilt and anxiety.

Human services professionals (including the clergy) can be very helpful to young men and women who are faced with a problem of an early, unplanned pregnancy. Adults who work with adolescents are often in contact with teenagers in a special way. They should try to be easily available for personal counseling regarding pregnancy-related issues as well as other adolescent concerns. It is imperative that such personnel keep the confessions and questions of troubled young people totally confidential and that they be adequately informed regarding the resources to which teenagers with problem pregnancies can be easily referred.

An ideal resource is a professionally qualified, objective counseling service (usually a nondenominational social agency is preferable) to help pregnant adolescents (hopefully the fathers as well as the mothers) explore the various options open to them: (1) pregnancy continuation and keeping the child, with or without marriage; (2) placing the child for adoption; or (3) abortion. If abortion is the decision, it may well be the best plan for the young woman to attend the abortion service with her male partner, a family member, or close friend, assuming that she has felt able to take one or more of these people into her confidence. Studies show that abortion processes and outcomes are less traumatic if the young patient has this kind of personal support.

However, studies suggest that about one-fourth of pregnant adolescents would not attend a legalized abortion service if parental notification were required (Alan Guttmacher Institute, 1981). Even though the Supreme Court has ruled otherwise, some private physicians and clinics may require parental notification and, in some cases, parental consent for an abortion. This is especially apt to be true in respect to youngsters who are age 15 or less. However, medical facilities have been less likely to require parental involvement for youngsters over age 16. Then, too, clinics tend to be more flexible than hospitals in this matter.

Legalized, low-cost but high-quality abortion for women of all ages in need of this procedure seems to be an important public health service. If such a service is not available, it is likely that the physical and emotional well-being of many young people and their children will be seriously endangered.

MANY ROLES FOR HUMAN SERVICES PERSONNEL

As we have seen, professionals concerned with adolescent family planning and abortion services are apt to have many roles: counselor, educator, administrator, and so on. Community organization and advocacy functions are also important. Beyond the development of referral networks of the types described earlier, work within the community at large is necessary to provide facts about family planning services and needs of adolescents. It is important that discussions be held with parents and other interested people in the community. Moreover, it may be important to act as lobbyists to advocate adequate programs and funding of family planning and related services for all age groups, including adolescents. This point applies to abortion services as well as those for contraception.

Then, too, family planning personnel and other concerned citizens can monitor the availability of condoms and nonprescription foam products in their local stores to make sure they are easily visible. Condoms are usually found near the check-out counter. Examination of the shelves in a local drugstore may show that products for female contraception are grouped with feminine hygiene in a way that makes it difficult for an inexperienced adolescent shopper to find the contraceptives she actually wants. Store managers can be encouraged to group contraceptive products together and market them in a readily accessible manner.

CHAPTER 15

Some Implications for Public Policies

"Pure" social scientists would probably say that not enough is known from research to make any recommendations about public policies concerning adolescent sexuality. Although this may be fairly true in the absolute sense, it seems to this writer that enough is now known to make some suggestions, although a few of them are offered tentatively and in the vein of recommendations for experimental programs that require formal evaluation to test their effectiveness. (For specific program suggestions, see Chapters 11–14.)

SOCIAL AND ECONOMIC CONSIDERATIONS

The research points to the adverse effects of poverty, racism, youth unemployment, poor family relationships, and inadequate human services on the healthy development of adolescents as young women and men. Because most of the research about adolescent sexuality is tied to specific topics of sex behavior, the probable full effects of these factors are only partially revealed. We have seen, however, that early nonmarital intercourse, poor use of contraceptives, late use of needed abortions, illegitimacy, and teenage marriage are all more likely to occur when these adverse socioeconomic, community, and familial factors are present. We also have seen that the supposedly adverse consequences of both out-of-marriage births and early marriage are intertwined with more fundamental problems in the society— problems that initially deprived many adolescents of the full development of their potential during childhood and that continue to undermine their life chances.

Improved family, community, school, employment, and human services environments for children and youths have been advocated many times. Such advocacy is a familiar prescription for the prevention of a host of social ailments: delinquency and crime, drug and alcohol abuse, poor physical and mental health, family breakdown, illegitimacy, and child neglect and abuse. It is clear that these problems are not completely caused by environmental deficits, but individualized treatment approaches are apt to have relatively little effect without concomitant changes in the environment in which people live. We also have seen that both specific environmental and individual characteristics are not the whole story of current shifts in social behavior, including the rise in teenage childbearing outside of marriage. Society is in the throes of cultural upheaval as a result of basic socioeconomic trends. These trends are causing many dislocations in the lives of individuals, their beliefs and values, and their adaptation to an urban, technological society.

We have seen, too, that unemployment and underemployment of youths tend to produce low self-esteem, alienation, and fatalism. Such attitudes appear to be linked to early nonmarital intercourse and contraceptive risk taking. Furthermore, research shows that unwed motherhood and dissolution of early marriages are associated with the poor employment prospects of young people. Then, too, the earnings of employed young men (especially minority group youths from poverty or otherwise troubled backgrounds) are generally so low that young women who have children tend to be better off financially if they receive welfare benefits than if they marry their mates.

In 1981, most of these programs aimed at the root causes of poverty were sharply cut back by the Reagan administration. A full detailing of these cuts and the evasion of federal responsibilities for meeting the needs of poor people is far beyond the scope of this book. However, the ending of CETA (a federal–state work experience and training program for the unemployed, including unemployed minority youths) is apt to escalate the severe employment and economic problems of many youths, especially those from low-income families. It seems likely that such an action, combined with others, would increase the rate of illegitimate births to young people, since marriage would become less feasible than it was in the recent past.

WELFARE REFORM AND FAMILY SUPPORT SYSTEMS

This situation calls for not only improved employment opportunities for youths (both male and female) but reform of welfare policies. As discussed in Chapter 9, the major public assistance program, Aid to Families with Dependent Children, operates in such a way in many states as to make families ineligible for benefits if the mother is married to the natural father of the children and the father is present in the home. A full discussion of needed welfare reforms is far beyond the scope of this book. However, it seems clear that federally aided income support programs are needed to help families in which the natural father is in the home, whether or not the couple is married. Also, these programs should provide supplemental assistance for wages that are not adequate to meet the budgeted needs of the family, including the costs of child care, if both parents are either employed or going to school.

Although research shows that a two-parent family is not essential to the healthy development of the child, it does suggest that a two-parent family, involving the natural parents of the child, tends to provide the best family environment for the youngster if the parents are in a happy, stable relationship. This implies that the larger society would be well advised to provide a variety of support systems to young families to help them achieve and maintain stability. These support systems include high-quality, affordable medical care (including contraception and abortion services, as needed); continuing education and vocational training; availability of jobs; adequate housing; income maintenance; child-care availability; and family counseling and educational service.

Recommendations for support systems to young families are not limited to two-parent families. As several studies indicate, unwed mothers who marry are often in a far worse situation than those who do not. At least one small study shows that mothers tend to have more children, are less likely to continue their education, and end up in a worse financial situation than if they had not married. These findings may (or may not) particularly apply to low-income black women. The research findings to date are far too fragmentary to make any definite statement about these matters. They do suggest, however, that marriage is not necessarily a solution to the difficulties that young unwed mothers and their children may face. The decision of many young mothers not to marry may indeed be a wise one. Such young women and their children may often constitute highly vulnerable families. These one-parent families also may require a variety of support systems of many kinds. Because a number of small investigations indicate that the extended family may provide important assistance to the young single-parent families, there is a need to take into account the extended kinship network, including the contribution this network may make to child care.

On the general subject of child care, H. Ross and Sawhill (1975) make an interesting recommendation when they write that public child-care services might well be extended beyond the formal child-care center. Because their data analysis and other studies indicate that the great majority of parents favor leaving their children with relatives or neighbors rather than placing them in day-care centers, and because in the early 1980s the cost of quality day-care centers appears to be about $3600 per year per child, it seems wise to go further than present programs generally do and provide income assistance, as needed, to parents who have their children cared for by persons other than day-care center personnel. (This, too, is a large topic that is too complex for adequate discussion here. See also Chapter 11.)

As of this writing, the chances of welfare reform along the lines suggested seem dim, indeed. Moreover, federal funding for income assistance and child care has been cut sharply. Decisions about welfare programs are to be made largely at state levels, with the resulting administrative chaos, following almost 50 years of federal policymaking in these areas. Then, too, programs will probably vary sharply from state to state, with the plight of poor people becoming heavily dependent on local politics in each state. It is likely that social problems, including child neglect, family breakdown, illegitimacy, delinquency, and racial conflicts will increase under these conditions, especially in those states that will give minimal assistance to poor families.

INCLUSION OF MALES

Returning to the subject of young parents, it appears that human service and income support programs for unwed mothers far too often overlook fathers as young people who may also need a variety of services. Age-old cultural norms tend to cast the young man as the "villain in the piece." There is a tendency to see him as irresponsible at best and an exploitative, promiscuous Don Juan (or pimp) at worst. Unwed mothers may find comfort in picturing themselves as helpless victims of seductive, noncaring males. All too often the male is seen only in terms of the financial support that he might provide. Yet, the few available studies that include young fathers (almost all these studies have black, low-income fathers as their subjects) show that a large number of these fathers would like to marry their partners. Even if marriage does not occur, they tend to give what financial, social, and psychological support they can to the young mothers and children.

Most researchers and human services (including family planning) personnel have found it difficult to reach and work with young fathers. Their elusiveness is probably a result of the way in which society has tended to treat males from early childhood onward. As others have commented, there is a need for male, as well as female, liberation. The apparent toughness, self-sufficiency, aggressiveness, egocentrism, and relative lack of interpersonal skills and responsibilities of many males is very largely a result of their socialization and the way they have been treated in their families, schools, community programs, and work places. It is well known that males, compared to females, have higher rates of school retardation, emotional problems, deviant behavior, and suicide. As shown in Chapter 2, the prenatal sexual development of males is far more vulnerable than that of females. These difficulties tend to be exacerbated in the boy's developmental experiences within the family because the mother is usually the major person in the boy's life. Even if the father is present in the home, his own socialization plus his preoccupation with making it in the outer world tend to prevent a close father–son relationship. The young boy's struggles to develop a clear male identification and escape from female controls are further hampered by the fact that most of his teachers from preschool through at least the eighth grade are females.

The women who tend to be the dominant figures in the young male's life often have ambivalent responses to his sexuality, probably being both attracted to it and fearful of it. Their complex reactions, also affected by their other experiences in male–female relationships, are likely to make them unable to accept the boy as a sexual person.

These are probable reasons, among others, that boys, more than girls, tend to take to the streets and join groups of other boys, groups in which the rituals of tough masculinity are acted out in numerous ways, including proving one's proficiencies as a virile male who can score with females without becoming trapped by them and without being exposed to possible rejection by them.

This sketchy discussion may seem rather far afield from suggestions for programs and policies related to adolescent sexuality. However, the implications should be clear that boys and young men need to be treated with far more enlightened and sensitive understanding than is generally the case. As many others have pointed out, there is a serious need for more men teachers and recreation leaders to work with young children. The present trend toward advocacy of part-time jobs for both fathers and mothers so that parents can share equally in child care is also welcome, as is the push for changing social norms that allow men to be more fully human, rather than supermen. These changing patterns appear to be essential in a technological society, which puts a premium on technical, interpersonal, communication, and rational planning skills rather than on skills requiring physical strength, aggressiveness, and autonomy.

IMPROVEMENT IN SCHOOL PROGRAMS

It is striking that educational achievement and clear educational–vocational goals seem to be so important in reducing the tendencies of young teenagers to participate in nonmarital coitus. A number of studies point to this factor for girls and at least one study does so for boys. Education also seems to promote the consistent use of effective contraceptives among sexually active teenagers, to affect positively the choice of abortion to terminate an adolescent pregnancy, and to reduce the likelihood of teenage marriages.

Numerous research studies indicate that educational achievement is closely related to the socioeconomic status of the parents of students. Educational achievement also is affected by the physical and emotional well-being of the child; this well-being, in turn, is deeply affected by the child's early experiences within the family. Moreover, the employment outcomes of educational achievement are dependent on a host of interacting factors, such as ready entree into jobs through the influence of the young person's family and close associates, the conditions of the labor market, the youth's psychological and physical characteristics, and his or her level of education.

Racism, with its frequent adverse effects on the socioeconomic status of parents, family life, the overall development of young people, and their educational–vocational opportunities, creates a network of difficulties for many black adolescents. Studies show that black youngsters (especially males) are more likely than whites to be retarded in school, beginning in the early grades, and that this retardation, as might be expected, becomes more severe in high school. Then, too, the unemployment rates of black youths are at least twice as high as they are for young whites, partly because educational deficits so negatively affect the lives of young people.

Programs that seek to give very young children a head start in their education would seem to deserve stronger public support than these programs now receive. The same might be said for special programs in the public schools, particularly in the early grades. The tendency to mount intensive and expensive intervention projects for high school students who are in trouble, rather than concentrate these projects on younger children, is a case of far too little, far too late. This comment applies to school programs for pregnant teenage girls, as well as to other programs.

It is fortunate that the Head Start programs remain chiefly a federal responsibility and that they escaped the general budget cutting of 1981. However, it is highly possible that their funds will be reduced in the immediate future, if present trends continue. Other educational programs fared far less well. Many special programs, especially those directed toward low-income students and those with learning disabilities, were subjected to severe fund reductions. School lunch programs, aimed at improving the nutrition of poor children were sharply cut. Federal support of school integration dwindled, and the entire enterprise of federal participation in the strengthening of public education came under attack.

ANTIPOVERTY PROGRAMS: SOME SUCCESS AND FAILURES

It is claimed that antipoverty programs are being abandoned because they "didn't work." This is an inaccurate statement. It is true that they did not fulfill the claims of their enthusiastic supporters of the 1964–1968 war against poverty. The claim that "we shall wipe out poverty from this land" should not have been made. It was a political statement, aimed at winning congressional and public support. No nation has been able to wipe out poverty as economic dependency, despite a series of strenuous efforts. Poverty, in the sense of dependency on economic assistance from others, is inevitable in most, if not all, societies. It is inevitable because some people are too young, too old, too ill, or too handicapped to work and earn enough to support themselves.

Economic dependency is also inevitable in an industrial–technological society, which inevitably has periods of unemployment related to such factors as the overall state of the economy (see present high rates of unemployment in the United States and most of the Western World); economic slowdown in certain industries (see the U.S. automobile industry); high rates of inflation; and seasonal unemployment, such as that found in agricultural occupations, among others.

The war on poverty did not wage war on the basic employment, pricing, and wage problems of our economic system. A *real* war on poverty would need to try to correct the system. Instead, the war attacked such individual problems as the lack of educational and vocational training. Supposedly, if all adolescents could be kept in high school through graduation, their employment problems would vanish. In actuality, the school dropout rate was markedly decreased in the years 1964–1979. Thus, one part of the program "worked" to a certain extent. However, youth unemployment rates remained high, largely because there simply were not enough entry-level jobs for the large numbers of young people who needed and wanted them. (One difficulty was the huge numbers of youths as a result of the 1948–1958 baby boom.) CETA (the work placement and training program mentioned earlier) was designed to meet the problem, but, among other things, it was not large enough to make a great difference in youth unemployment.

This complex topic cannot be discussed in further detail here. However, the main point is that the antipoverty programs *did* mitigate the poverty problem. Recent reevaluations of Head Start programs showed that real educational gains associated with high-quality programs were obtained by a cohort of youngsters over a 12-year period; a larger proportion of young people graduated from high school (well over 80 percent); and the rate of poverty among families was reduced from about 18 percent in the late 1950s to 11 percent in the late 1970s, owing largely to two factors: increases in income maintenance programs and the large increase of women, including wives and mothers, in the work force.

The war on poverty certainly was not a great victory, but it was not a great failure either. It should not be abandoned with the fallacious statement that "it did not work." Few human programs work completely.

PROGRAM EVALUATION

Certain policies have survived the general recent rollback in programs for poor people. It is noteworthy that well-designed evaluation components that can show positive program results with economic benefits outweighing economic costs are particularly apt to survive budget cuts (e.g., the survival of Title X, Public Health Services Act, and its provision for federal funding of family planning programs). Thus, human services professionals are well advised to plan for sophisticated evaluations of a sampling of their programs, especially those programs that are somewhat controversial. They also need to plan for effective dissemination of favorable evaluation results and participation in the political lobbying process.

There are a host of programs that seek to help adolescents with respect to their sexual development and behaviors. It is likely that more programs will develop as a result of growing public concern about such issues as relatively high rates of illegitimacy and the greater prevalence of nonmarital intercourse among teenagers.

Programs concerned with adolescent sexuality per se include sex education and counseling for young people and parents, contraceptive and abortion services, treatment centers for venereal diseases, special services for unwed parents and their children, public assistance programs, and comprehensive service centers for the prevention and treatment of adolescent pregnancy. Very little is known about the relative effectiveness of many of these models or of the programs themselves.

There is a need for better evaluation of these programs and of the various models they use. Evaluation needs to be directed, of course, to outcome objectives. The objectives of such programs as sex education and counseling and services to unwed parents are frequently not clearly defined. This is an unfortunate oversight that calls for better explication of specific goals.

The objective of contraceptive and abortion services is generally stated as the prevention of unwanted births. Important as this objective is, it appears to be overly narrow. Prevention of unwanted births often is claimed to have a number of benefits for adolescents, such as promoting educational achievement, self-support through employment, avoidance of welfare dependency, more stable marriages at a later date, and smaller family size. Are these objectives actually reached? Measurement of whether programs obtain objectives of these kinds calls for long-range research and the use of sophisticated research design, which includes a careful description of program methods, use of appropriately matched experimental and control groups, comparisons of various program strategies, and analyses of the comparative costs and benefits of these programs.

A number of program and policy recommendations are made in Chapters

11–14. Some of them are in operation in various localities. They provide natural experiments that might be carefully described and evaluated as possible models to be used elsewhere if program evaluation suggests their probable effectiveness. It seems unnecessary to evaluate the effectiveness of every operating program. Rather it would be more economical and useful to evaluate samples of a variety of programs.

A special word is in order about sex education, which has been widely endorsed as an essential part of the school curriculum. A number of studies show that sex education has had no measurable impact on the prevention of nonmarital intercourse, promotion of contraceptive use, or reduction in the incidence of illegitimacy. Before such programs are advocated for widespread adoption, they should be launched as pilot projects, clearly described, carefully monitored, and tested for their effectiveness. (See also Chapters 12 and 13.)

Some programs (such as family planning services) are evaluated by asking their users what they like and do not like about them. (See, for example, the report of the Urban and Rural Systems Associates 1976, cited in Chapter 14.) Although such a study may provide useful clues, it fails to tackle the more important issues of why some adolescents do not use the program at all or, having obtained contraceptives from the service, discontinue contraceptive use or use contraceptives only sporadically. Moreover, the statements people make concerning their likes and dislikes about a program constitute an expression of opinion that may not be reflected in their actual behaviors in using or not using the program.

CHAPTER 16

Clues and Illustrations from Clinical Studies

INTRODUCTION

Purpose

This chapter provides illustrations of different patterns of adolescent sexual behavior as exemplified by a number of selected individual cases. These illustrations yield numerous clues as to the etiology of these behaviors and carry rich implications for education and counseling. Before illustrations are given, some tentative generalizations are suggested as drawn, in part, from an overall analysis of the cases under discussion. The tentative generalizations may be helpful to practitioners as well as to those researchers who are interested in suggested directions for further investigations.

These case illustrations might also be useful for lectures and discussions in training programs for human services personnel. They humanize the rather arid data drawn from more formal research. They illustrate the enormous complexity of individual human behavior and the need in counseling and educational programs for careful individual assessment of each person in his or her family and total life situation. They might well be used in discussions of a number of chapters of this book (including Chapters 2, 4–10, 12, and 13).

Methods

The case illustrations presented later in this chapter are derived from over 50 clinical interview studies of adolescents who volunteered for the project. The studies were carried out in the late 1970s by advanced graduate students in social work under the present author's supervision. All of these students were mature men and women with considerable experience in social work or such related fields as education and nursing. All had taken courses in both human sexuality and adolescence. Many were parents themselves.

Adolescents—and often their parents and siblings—were interviewed following a general guide that had been developed on the basis of the research findings regarding adolescent sexuality presented in this and an earlier book (Chilman, 1978). The guide called for such information as age, sex, religion (and religiosity), race, ethnic background, education and occupation of parents, family size and structure, feelings about the self (such as levels of self-esteem, locus of control perceptions, feelings of competence in many life areas), perceptions about the self as a female or male, communication patterns of self and of family, attitudes toward family members, attitudes of rebellion or conformity, major interests and goals, use of alcohol and drugs, school progress, age at puberty and attitudes toward it, values and beliefs concerning sexuality, recollections of sexual behaviors and understandings during early childhood, main sources of sex information, and sexual behaviors of recent years, including interpersonal relationships with both sexes, dating, "being in love," necking, petting, intercourse, use of contraceptives, pregnancy, abortion, early marriage, and adoption.

Interviewers also gave their clinical judgments of the major personality characteristics of the persons they interviewed. Such characteristics as the following were especially noted: apparent sense of ease or tension during interview, style of self-presentation and communication, levels of defensiveness and typical use of certain defense mechanisms, indications of anxiety and of impulsivity, seeming openness or withholding in interview, style of self-presentation, and expressions of affect. In all instances, the purpose, method, and general content of the interviews were explained in advance and consent was gained from both the adolescent and his or her parents (or parent).

Interviews were written up in considerable detail, with careful alterations to preserve anonymity. A number of these cases were discussed and analyzed in a graduate seminar and were further analyzed by the author.

Limitations

A major limitation of this clinical approach was the nonrandom method of case selection and the small sample size. Students used a sample of convenience (i.e., they studied adolescents who were readily available to them). Students working in mental health clinics or medical social service departments of hospitals chose teenagers known to these agencies. As might be imagined, particularly troubled teenagers came from the mental health centers and pregnant teenagers came from the hospital clinics. At the other extreme, students selected adolescents who were known to them through religious organizations, their neighborhoods, and recreational programs. Thus, the sample ran the gamut, so to speak, from lower socioeconomic levels to the upper middle class, from urban to suburban to village, from exceptionally troubled youngsters to those who were exceptionally achieving and well adjusted, from sexually promiscuous young people to those who had never had a date. Although many ethnic backgrounds and religions were represented, unfortunately too few black and Hispanic youngsters were in the sample and none of the interviewees were Asian or Native American. This bias was probably because nearly all the student interviewers were white Anglos and because they studied the teenagers to whom they had ready access.

Aside from a lack of racial and ethnic diversity, the convenience sample had certain advantages. It provided illustrations of seriously disturbed teenagers as well as illustrations of those who were well adjusted, responsible, and, in some cases, of upper socioeconomic status. Since most social-psychological studies deal with clinic populations of problem-laden youngsters, the cases that derived from this project provide a broader than average view of adolescent sexual behaviors and their correlates.

Other criticisms of the reliability and validity of clinical studies have been made many times and cannot be satisfactorily explored here. The studies and discussion that follows are presented as a supplement to (not a substitute for) more formal research—research that has been discussed particularly in Chapters 2–10.

For purposes of overall analysis and later illustrative presentation, the cases were divided into behavioral categories as follows:

Coitus with a number of partners in brief relationships; no contraceptives used; pregnancy and abortion in a few cases.

Coitus with one to three partners; primarily in a going-steady relationship; no contraceptives used, but no pregnancies had occurred.

Coitus with one to three partners; primarily in a going-steady relationship; contraceptives used at least part of the time; pregnancy and abortion or early marriage in some cases.

No coitus, but heavy petting experiences.

No coitus, but necking and light petting experiences.

No dating; no sexual experiences with a partner.

Males and females were considered separately in developing these types and classifying each of the adolescents. There were at least a few cases of each sex in all the categories.

GENERAL OBSERVATIONS

As one perceptive student interviewer wrote:

The most striking finding from my case studies is that the sexual behaviors of a person so clearly express her/his total personality and life history.

These behaviors do not grow out of a particular set of intellectual under-standings, a particular event, a particular group of friends, a particular set of values and beliefs; they are not behaviors that "just happen." Rather, these behaviors are an expression of the total person in terms of her/his total life experience within family, school, and community.

This observation is similar to the longitudinal research findings concerning adolescent sexual behaviors, as reported by R. Jessor, Costa, Jessor, and Donovan (in press, 1983).

It is possible to observe further that the social, psychological, and physi-cal aspects of a person can be seen, in each of our clinical studies, to interact in a unique fashion and in complicated ways, different for each individual, but in a discernable overall pattern. In brief, case analyses and observations lead to the tentative conclusion that many clinicians and theorists, including Freud and the neo-Freudians, were correct in observing that emotionally disturbed people also tend to have emotionally disturbed sex lives. Although Freud proposed that sexual disturbances were the root cause of other emo-tional or psychosocial problems, later clinicians have seen that sexual dif-ficulties are often an expression or consequence of more pervasive diffi-culties.

Extremes of sexual problems were found in some of the cases studied in the project. Some young women and men, for instance, were promiscuous and self-destructive (as well as destructive toward others) in their sexual behaviors. Some had intercourse only when drinking or under the influence of drugs. They also had intercourse only with pickups. At the other extreme, there were 19 or 20 year olds, both male and female, who had never had a date and were depressed and anxious about their situation. Between these extremes were more moderate, one might say normal, forms of behavior.

No one individual characteristic or set of characteristics could be ob-served to be clearly associated with any of the behavioral categories ana-lyzed. For some adolescents, early physical maturation seemed to be central to the onset of dating; for others, the association seemed minimal. High religiosity, in some cases, was associated with highly controlled sexual be-havior, but in other instances, the opposite association seemed to occur. If any one factor or cluster of factors seemed to be of fundamental importance in shaping sexual behaviors at adolescence, it was the nature of interper-sonal relationships within the family along with the characteristics of the family system. The relationships between the young person and his or her parents from infancy onward seemed to be of central importance. The na-ture of the parents' marital relationship, including nonmarital parenthood, separation, divorce, and remarriage, and the death of a parent also appeared to have striking effects. Such other factors as religion and religiosity, ethnic-ity, social class, school adjustment, community involvement, physical and cognitive development, peer group membership, employment experiences, and activities of parents at work, at home, and in the community were of varying degrees of importance for different youngsters, but none seemed to be so important as the influence of family behaviors and relationships.

Of course, this observation is hardly new. It tends simply to further support theories held by many clinicians and academics. Although the salience of the family to child and adolescent development has been questioned frequently, especially in recent years (see, for example, Chapters 2–4), the present cases seem to reaffirm the importance of early family relationships to the individual's sense of self, capacity for relating to others, concepts of sexuality, style of communication with the same and opposite sex, capacity for impulse control (including sexual impulses), levels of anxiety, mechanisms of defense, self-esteem, and the nature and salience of personal values and goals.

With regard to values and goals, as folk wisdom has long claimed, it is not so much what parents say that matters, it is what they *do* that counts. For example, a number of parents stated that they had given their youngsters a thorough sex education and had taught them that sex was a good, natural part of living. But some of them had teenagers who were anxiously overcontrolled in many aspects of their lives, including sex. They appeared to be behaving like their parents and disbelieving the intellectualized "natural–normal" sex talks they received from parents who had many sexual anxieties themselves.

Along these lines, it was found that many of the upper-middle-class parents gave their children a great deal of sex education, through answering questions, providing books, and arranging for them to go to sex education classes. None of these youngsters (ages 14–19) was involved in nonmarital coitus. Intercourse outside of marriage seemed *not* to be a product of sex education provided by parents. (Research shows that adolescents are less likely to have early nonmarital coitus if they receive sound sex education at home.) However, we observed that parents who provided such education also were controlled in the expression of their own sexuality and high in educational and occupational achievements. They provided their children with a generally prosperous and intellectually enriching environment that gave the young person considerable security and status as well as the stimulus for high levels of career achievement.

These youngsters, when queried, actually knew very little about sex: the nature of intercourse, time of ovulation, kinds and functions of contraceptives, and how contraceptives might be obtained. This was true even for a number of outstandingly bright students, both female and male. Many had not achieved a sufficiently separate identity to develop a love–sex dating relationship. They often said they had too many long-term goals to risk involvement beyond the necking and light petting stage. They tended to comment that they had read or heard a lot about sex but could not remember details and that they would learn more about intercourse and contraception when this knowledge had practical uses for them.

Their assertion seems to be highly cogent—few people actually retain information they consider useless, but they may be able to retrieve it, or relearn it, when it seems important to them (perhaps a generalization that applies for most education). Thus, sexuality education that anticipates later behavioral developments (such as intercourse and contraceptive use) may seem to have little meaning for youngsters who have not yet become sexually involved. However, the educational program might alert them to resources—people, medical services, publications—that they might use later when they perceive the need.

The analyses of these cases show, as others have, that sexual behaviors, for most adolescents, have little to do with intellectual understandings or rational decision making. Rather, as indicated above, these behaviors grow out of a person's total developmental history and life experiences. In fact, it can be observed that the young persons (both female and male) who are most rational and intellectual in their approach to sexuality are often the least likely to have had any sexual or dating experiences, even by age 19 or 20. This is not chiefly because they have decided not to become involved in dating and sex, but seemingly because their intellectual defenses against feelings of social inadequacy are so strong that they are unable to relate openly and warmly to other people, including their opposite-sex peers. Some may then rationalize their lack of involvement by reciting high academic goals and long-range career plans as a deterrent to dating and love–sex involvement. (See also the similar findings of R. Jessor et al., in press, 1983, as cited in Chapter 5.)

Of course, parents gave their youngsters no sex education in many cases. They often sternly ordered their children to "stay out of trouble," to refrain from dating, drinking, and drug use. However, parents often failed to explain these rules or to live by them in their own lives. Such double messages did not of themselves, *cause* precocious sex behavior on the part of teenagers, but they were one factor in a complex network of family relationships that often failed to provide needed supports and limits for developing adolescents.

A few more tentative generalizations follow. Problematic acting-out sexual behavior does not seem to come about because a person is adolescent. Adolescents in the cases studied who had such problems as promiscuity, exploitative sexual relationships, unprotected intercourse, and coitus under the influence of drugs or alcohol appear to have been troubled youngsters *before* they reached puberty. Most had had difficulties in school and in the neighborhood and were difficult within the family. When such youngsters became adolescents, sexual acting out seems to have become a readily available way to express such feelings as anger, inadequacy, loneliness, needs to control others (mainly for males), and dependency (mainly for females). To the extent that these cases are representative, they provide striking illustrations of the point that the roots of the problematic consequences of early marriage and/or early childbearing lie deep in the total developmental history of the adolescents who become wives and husbands, mothers and fathers at an early age.

These illustrative cases appear to lead to a general principle to be explored through further research: Development and expression of sexuality is difficult no matter what pathway is followed, although some pathways may be more stressful than others. Perhaps for humans (at least for teenagers) in a society such as ours, there is no such thing as easy, safe, joyous sex with few or no negative aspects. This seems to be true, at least to some degree, for most people—for those who are freely expressive of their sexuality and use virtually no restraints, for those who are married as young teenagers and have ready access to "legal sex," for those who use contraceptives and those who do not, for those who have resolved an early pregnancy through an abortion and those who have not, for those who are young parents, for those in a love–sex relationship, for those in steady or casual petting relationships, and for those who have had no sex experiences with another person.

For example, adolescents who have a number of sexual partners without steady relationships seem to have little capacity, in general, for interpersonal relating and appear to be essentially lonely and afraid. All the couples who married early (age 17 or less) in the sample studied were premaritally pregnant and hampered by financial, employment, and other problems. Many singles who had been in steady love–sex relationships had experienced the stresses of a broken affair; some had experienced unplanned pregnancies and abortions or forced marriages. Those who were in their late teens and had not become involved in petting or coitus tended to have a variety of personality difficulties ranging from mild to extreme manifestations. Denial, repression, guilt, anxiety, and obsessive–compulsive behavior were frequently observed in seemingly overcontrolled or even moderately controlled youngsters. Several young men who had severe personality disturbances and were known to mental health clinics appeared to be struggling with panic reactions to their seeming, but repressed, homosexual orientations.

One further major point should be made: Human services professionals who work with teenagers may become so concerned about the possibility of early, unplanned pregnancies that they tend to forget that adolescent sexuality has a number of manifestations and that the pathways from the immature sexuality of childhood to the relatively mature sexuality of the adult years are apt to be arduous, no matter what route is taken. Probably *all* adolescents need our enlightened empathy and general support, if not specialized individual services, as they traverse these rocky roads.

These comments should not be interpreted, however, as a conclusion that sexuality for adolescents constitutes a *unique* developmental crisis. Obviously, sexuality is apt to be an important, difficult issue for girls and boys, women and men at many points in the life cycle. The issues are apt to vary somewhat from time to time, but they are beyond the scope of this book, even though people of all ages deserve sensitive understanding of their behaviors and feelings as sexual beings. This includes a humane understanding of human services professionals.

CASE ILLUSTRATIONS

Identifying information about all the cases that appear below has been altered so that the anonymity of the persons involved is preserved. They are selected as representing the behavioral typologies described above and as providing clear illustrations from our larger sample.

No Dating, No Sexual Experiences: Jean

Jean, white, age 16, Protestant, Swedish descent, upper-middle-class family in a small city, has never had a date. She is an intellectually outstanding A+ student at school and church, where she is also an acknowledged leader of many activities. Her father is the minister of a liberal church, and her mother is a successful career professional.

Family unity is strong; relationships are warm and equalitarian; communication is easy and fairly open; many activities are shared.

However, Jean's older sister, Laura, is mentally retarded and now placed in a special school. Her brother is far too young to understand much about the situation. Earlier, Jean and her sister went to the same school and Jean felt she should be responsible for protecting her sister. On several occasions, her sister was the object of mild sexual exploitation, which Jean tried to solve without "burdening her parents."

At age 15, Jean had a severe illness of headache and vomiting, eventually diagnosed as a "nervous breakdown." Her sister was placed in another school, and Jean improved. Jean said she had been embarrassed by her sister and yet felt responsible for her.

The family had lived in San Francisco for some years before coming to a small midwestern city a few years ago. Jean feels out of place in the new setting. She has few friends and says she does not like the partying that most of her peers enjoy, nor does she care for drugs or alcohol. She also feels that people put pressure on her to be "perfect" because she is a minister's daughter. Also, she is teased for being a Protestant by neighbors, most of whom are Catholic.

Jean says she wishes she could learn to be less assertive, less achieving, and a more accepted part of her community. She yearns for a boyfriend but doubts whether most modern boys can be trusted. She has an excellent intellectual understanding of sex, since her liberal parents are ardent supporters of enlightened sex education for teenagers.

Basically, Jean is fairly typical of those adolescents in the sample studied who, by age 16 or 17, had never had a date; that is, an important maturation-inhibiting factor could be observed in nearly all these cases. For Jean, the most crucial factor seemed to be the problems of her mentally retarded older sister and her guilt feelings of both rejection of and responsibility (including sexual responsibility) for that sister. Then, too, there were such problems as the family's recent arrival in a tightly knit, conservative, culturally different community; the pressures of being a "preacher's kid" and, possibly, the isolating influence of having an exceptionally bright mind that was used, perhaps a bit too aggressively, in part to compensate her highly educated parents for the disappointments of their mentally retarded older child.

Slight Sexual Involvement, No Petting or Coitus: Sam

Sam, age 17, white, upper middle class, small town, Protestant, Dutch descent, has been going steady for a year. He and his girl neck and have been tempted to go further but have decided not to because they love each other and want to keep their relationship within bounds. They both plan to go to college and, perhaps, on to graduate school. They think they should not marry until after college because they want to be "mature enough to succeed." They want to follow the teachings of their church and "save sex for marriage."

Sam comes from a remarkably warm, closely knit family, marked by open communication, expressed love, and firm, mild discipline. Both parents are professionals, but while the five children were growing up, they arranged their employment so that one parent would always be at home.

The family undertakes many joint activities: work sharing at home, camping trips, community involvement, church attendance. All the children achieve well at school, have numerous hobbies, and are active in school affairs.

Sam has high professional goals for himself and says he would like to "turn out just like his parents someday, with a good job and a nice wife who is an equal companion."

Although he finds it difficult to control his sexual feelings, he thinks he should and can. He uses masturbation as an outlet and says he views this as normal, though he actually seemed anxious about it and even more guilty about his enjoyment of pornography, which he views occasionally. His mother says his obsession with cleanliness, neatness, and order are a trial for every member of the family. However, she was observed to possess similar characteristics herself.

Sam is an excellent example of a well-adjusted, competent, effective young person who has a rewarding interpersonal heterosexual relationship that is under good impulse control. Yet these controls are not easy for him. They exact a price in a certain amount of repression, substitution, guilt, and anxiety. This again supports the point that, even under supposedly ideal conditions, sexual maturation is not easy.

Some Petting, No Coitus: Sandy

Sandy, age 16, white, upper middle-class, Protestant, English-Norwegian descent, is an extremely popular girl who has numerous dates but only mild petting experience. She says she is fearful of deep involvement with boys because she has so many long-range educational–vocational goals and is so busy at the moment going to high school and holding a half-time job.

It seems likely that she is also afraid of intimate sexual involvements because her parents divorced (when she was 5 years old) and at present she lives in a reconstituted family—a family that seems full of contradictions. Her mother, who has a graduate professional degree, holds a highly responsible position and is intensely religious. On the other hand, she openly conducted an affair with her present husband while still married to the first; the affair precipitated the divorce.

Sandy's first father is a conservative, inhibited, shy person, who is guilty and fearful about sex. After years of single living, he recently married a much younger woman. Sandy's stepfather takes a stern, authoritarian, conventional stance with the children but continues to drink heavily and have extramarital affairs. Nevertheless, he is a successful businessman and community leader. Sandy is his favorite.

Sandy also has two socially conservative older brothers, who "adore and pamper" her. She says she has such a good time with them that she often prefers her brothers to her dates.

Despite the complexities and stressful events in the family, there is a good deal of family unity and strength. Many would give Sandy a high rating on such criteria as school achievement, competency as an employee, loyal family membership, social skills, and realistic controls over her own behavior.

She seems to be an example of positive development within a family context that appears to have enough positives for her so that the negatives are balanced. She is also an example of sexual behavior that appears to be healthy, in that she has a number of pleasant dating relationships, apparently enjoys her femininity, seems not to be concerned about her ability to attract the opposite sex, and appears to have realistic controls over her own sexual behaviors. On the other hand, it is possible to be concerned about her attachment to her "mixed up" stepfather, her dependence on her brothers, and her (perhaps) basic fear of love–sex relations originating in the marital disturbances of her biological parents and the inhibited personality of her own father.

The above observations are an illustration of what is meant by comments made earlier to the effect that, even for the well-adjusted, sexually moderate adolescent, growth into sexual maturity is neither simple nor easy.

Involvement in Petting but Not Coitus: John

John, age 16, white, upper middle-class Jewish family, is a handsome, superficially poised, glib person. The interviewer knew that he had been adopted at age 2, but John did not reveal this fact. He had reached puberty at age 14 and had been dating frequently since that time. He said girls always liked him at first, but he soon ended the relationship after heavy petting to climax had taken place. He also remarked that he did not want to become really involved with a girl, because he had many years of education before him.

He stated he was essentially a "loner" with many solitary interests, such as reading and playing musical instruments. His intellectual, late middle-aged, generally lonely parents are very ambitious for him, but he is not sure he can perform at the required level. According to his reports, they had given him a thorough, rational sex education, but he seemed vague on such subjects as a woman's fertile period and contraceptives.

John struck the interviewer as being extraordinarily neat and fundamentally anxious, remote, and depressed. His difficulties in forming close, satisfying relationships with girlfriends seemed similar to the difficulties he had in relating to other people. His intellectualized sex education left him with little information that he could apply to himself and a partner in a real-life, emotionally laden situation. In general, his intellectualization of his essentially solitary life probably serves as a defense against his own inadequacies in the realm of interpersonal relationships and his anxieties about being an adopted child.

Adolescent Pregnancy and Early Marriage:
Peg, Her Mother, and Grandmother

Peg, age 18, white, Catholic, lower-middle-class, German background, is 6 months pregnant and has been married for 3 months. She had been going steady with Bob, who took responsibility for contraception and used a condom, but it "failed." At 3 months of pregnancy, she had a hemorrhage and was rushed to the hospital, where the pregnancy was saved. Following this, Peg lost 40 pounds and much of her strength but was gradually improving at the time of the interview. (Had this been a self-induced attempted abortion?)

Like her mother and grandmother before her, Peg had numerous physical ailments, including an ulcer, "nerve problems," eczema, and many allergies. Also, like these older women, she did outstanding work at school and had many intellectual interests in literature, music, and art.

All three generations of women seemed to be torn between the traditional female roles of marriage and motherhood versus achievement and employment in the larger world. For example, the grandmother had been burdened with five children and a dominating husband. After 20 years of confining domesticity, she made a "break for freedom" with a job outside the home, where she was highly successful and socially popular. Threatened, her husband insisted that she give up the work. Returning to full-time homemaking, she became pregnant and bore her sixth child. Three months later, she was in a mental hospital with a severe depression from which she never totally recovered.

Her daughter, Peg's mother, sought to escape a similar fate. She married a weak, crippled man and, out of necessity, worked full-time outside the home. However, her early marriage (at 18 and pregnant) forced her to turn down a college scholarship she had been offered. Peg's mother also had six children, with Peg being the oldest. Peg carried out many of the child-care and domestic duties her employed mother escaped, especially because her mother suffered from so many physical problems.

Although Peg's mother said, in an interview, that she had always resented the preferential treatment given to her brothers by *her* mother, she carried out the same pattern with her three sons, partially seeing them as compensation for her poor marriage. Peg expressed the view that men always got the better deal in any situation. Like her mother and grandmother, she grew up in a family in which sons were preferred.

Soon before Peg became pregnant, she too was offered a college scholarship. After she became pregnant, she expressed regret over not being able to accept the scholarship but took a passive, fatalistic attitude toward her helplessness as a woman. She was pleased that, through marriage, she had escaped her poor home situation and said she anticipated few problems in her new role as wife and mother. However, her tense, anxious manner throughout the interview suggested that she actually perceived many past, present, and future problems about which she thought she could probably do nothing. Although she hoped to have no more than two children in her family, she said "Well, you probably have to take what the Lord sends. Besides, Bob wants a lot of kids."

This three-generation case history provides a striking illustration of the difficulties some women experience as they seek to resolve conflicts between the traditional and contemporary female roles. Peg's grandmother rebelled ineffectually against a strong, authoritarian husband and was badly defeated. Peg's mother sought to solve the problem by marrying a weak, passive man but was then overwhelmed by her traditional childbearing attitudes (and the results), plus her heavy employment and financial responsibilities. These, combined with her poor health, seemed to be creating defeat for her, too. And Peg looks as if she is well on *her* way to creating defeats for herself in a self-destructive, familial pattern.

These defeats seem even more ironic in the face of three generations of women who appear to have been exceptionally intelligent and to have held wide-ranging intellectual interests. The physical problems experienced by all three generations (ulcers, eczema, allergies) are generally believed to have large psychosomatic components. However, they also may signal special biological sensitivities and suggest that these women may have struggled with serious physical problems that surely affected the social and psychological aspects of their functioning.

Early Promiscuity, No Contraceptives; Later, Sex with Commitment and Contraception: Joan

Joan, age 18, is from a white, blue-collar, German-Irish, Protestant-Catholic family. During the year that she was 16, Joan had a number of sexual affairs with casual dates; no contraceptives were used. However, by the time she was 17, she was going steady with a young man, using contraceptives, and following her goal of attending both college and graduate school. She is an excellent student now and may be able to achieve this goal, partly because her boyfriend has similar ambitions.

Joan was a poor student, however, from ages 13 to 16. During these years, her father, a machinist, became a heavy drinker, removed her from her parochial school, and sent her to a public school—despite her mother's pleas. Her father was suspended from his job, and her mother went to work full time in a factory to support the family.

During this period, Joan gained 60 pounds and became a social recluse. Her isolation was increased by the fact that her father forbade her to have any dates until she was 16. Fortunately, during her sixteenth year, the entire family entered therapy, which proved to be successful. The father quit drinking and returned to his former job; marital harmony was restored; the mother took part-time work; and Joan lost a great deal of weight and began a more stable, contraceptively protected dating relationship.

In discussing the past, she commented that her usually family-centered, dependable father had "gone off the track" for a few years but then seemed to recover fully. This case seems to be a prime example (and there were others) of the adverse impact of stressful family events on an adolescent's sexual behavior and the improvement of that behavior when the family stress is reduced, especially if the earlier years of the person's life have provided a sound foundation for healthy development.

A Promiscuous Boy, No Contraceptives: Dave

Dave, age 17, a member of a white, urban, blue-collar, Polish Catholic family, has been having intercourse with a number of partners for the past 2 years. All his affairs terminate as soon as he has had coitus. After intercourse, he feels that his partner is a "no-good whore." He prides himself in having a good "line" and being able to "sweet-talk" girls into having sex. He does not believe he should be bothered about using contraceptives: That's a woman's problem. He has a group of adolescent male friends, most of whom are school dropouts and unemployed. Together, they seek young women and often brag to each other about their sexual exploits.

Dave says he has not thought about whether he ever wants to marry. At present, he is failing in school and bothered with a problem of "shaky nerves," for which he is receiving psychotherapy. His "shaky nerve" problem began when he was 15, soon after his first coitus, but he fails to see a connection between the two events. Interviewed by an experienced male graduate student, Dave, with much agitation, "confessed" that he masturbates frequently. He was deeply relieved to learn that masturbation was normal for young men. With even more confusion, Dave then asked if masturbation was a sign of homosexuality and was even more relieved when informed that both heterosexuals and homosexuals masturbate.

Dave is the third of three brothers and also has a younger sister. The oldest brother, regarded as the family success, graduated from a technical school and has a well-paying job as a machinist. The second brother is the family "black sheep," a high school dropout, unemployed, father of several illegitimate children. The sister, like her mother before her, is quiet, submissive, and a fair student at a parochial junior high school.

Dave is very close to his father, who is a hard-working, semiskilled, nonunion construction worker. The father is a dominating person of few words, with a primary interest in mechanical things. Dave frequently works with his father and shares his interests. However, he is afraid of his father's hot temper and rigid controls over the family.

The parents have always had a poor marriage, with little sharing and almost no verbal communication. The mother has sought her main solace in the church and her children before they reached adolescence.

Even more so than most of the other adolescents in the case studies, Dave expressed deep gratitude to the interviewer for an opportunity to discuss subjects you *"never* talk about, and worry about all the time." After this discussion, his progress in treatment at the mental health clinic moved forward rapidly, following a prior period of stagnation. Among other things, the case seems to illustrate the value of a professional counselor's deliberate raising of the topic of sexual experience with troubled adolescents and (probably) the value of having a competent male professional, well trained in the area of human sexuality, working with adolescent boys.

A Promiscuous Girl, No Contraceptives: Susie

Susie, white, middle-class, urban, age 15, Scotch-English, Protestant, first had intercourse at a teenage drinking party when she was 13, a year after her first menstruation. Between the ages of 13 and 15, she had a large number of partners, often when under the influence of drugs or alcohol. She "ran with" a group of girlfriends who enjoyed skipping school and "cruising" the shopping malls together. At age 15, she began to go steady and says she now mostly limits coitus to her boyfriend. She does not use contraceptives because she would "just as soon get pregnant because my grades at school will force me out anyhow," and "I'll probably die young, so what difference does anything make?" Susie says she likes sex because it makes her feel cared for, at least briefly.

Despite the fact that she seems very intelligent, her schoolwork has been poor since she was age 8, when her parents divorced after a year of bitter conflict and a period in which both parents openly had extramarital affairs.

Susie's mother, a college graduate, had always been active in the community, trying to "save the world" for freedom and self-expression. She reared both of her children with such statements as "I can't tell you what to do because you'll do what you want anyway," and "Make up your mind what you like but don't let me catch you doing wrong!"

Susie's older sister began to deal in drugs at the time of the parents' divorce and started Susie smoking marijuana in the fifth grade. The sister also had an explosive temper and often beat Susie mercilessly, with no intervention from the mother.

The mother married an unskilled laborer with an eighth-grade education when Susie was 13. The whole family moved to a farm, but Susie was so miserable that she ran away to her father's city home, where he lived with his new wife and her five children. Susie's father gave her small welcome; he appeared to have shifted his paternal affections to his stepdaughter Betsy, also age 15, but an achieving student at school and "cooperative" family member at home. Susie's stepmother, a well-organized, competent person, tried to help Susie with her problems but found it difficult to establish anything but a superficial relationship with her.

The above case clearly shows the interaction of a large number of factors in creating Susie's present familial, educational, interpersonal, and sexual problems. Among other things, it also indicates the importance of early intervention into the family system, if at all possible, together with a consideration of the complexity of the several interlocking family systems at the present time. Other service needs can (or should) be readily identified by professionals who work with young women whose problems are similar to Susie's.

IN CONCLUSION

The cases sketched briefly here should illustrate the point that adolescent sexual behaviors are one expression of an adolescent's total self in the context of his or her family, school, and community. They dramatize the points revealed by research regarding social, psychological, and physical factors associated with nonmarital intercourse and poor contraceptive use. (See Chapters 5 and 6.) They also illustrate the practice and program principles discussed in Chapters 11–14 regarding the importance of working with the whole person in the context of a total life situation.

These cases also provide a vivid demonstration of the extreme importance of giving teenagers, and frequently their parents, an opportunity to discuss openly their sexual thoughts, experiences, and feelings with a trained, experienced human services professional.

All the adolescents who were interviewed spontaneously expressed their deep appreciation of the experience. This was also true of participating parents. From toddler days, most children and adolescents are told by their parents and other adults that sex talk is forbidden, especially with adults. Thus, few, if any, youngsters will readily raise a sexual topic with an older person on their own initiative. The initiative must often come from the professional and should come only from a professional who has the training and ability to handle the subject. It is hoped that this book will be of real assistance in this training process and that the cases given here will provide further insights into the complexity and sensitivity of adolescent sexual development. (See also Chapters 12 and 13, especially.)

References

Abramson, P. The relationship of the frequency of masturbation to several aspects of personality and behavior. *Journal of Sex Research,* 1973, **9** (2, May), 132–142.

Adelson, J. The development of ideology in adolescence. In S. Dragastin & G. Elder (Eds.), *Adolescence and the life cycle.* New York: John Wiley & Sons, 1975.

Alan Guttmacher Institute. 11 Million Teenagers. New York: Planned Parenthood Federation of America, 1976.

Alan Guttmacher Institute. *Characteristics of women served by organized family providers.* Preliminary Report, March 1981. (Mimeo)

Anchell, M. Classroom for perversion. *Education,* 1970, **90**, 241–244.

Arafat, I., & Cotton, W. Masturbation practices of males and females. *Journal of Sex Research,* 1974, **10** (4, Nov.), 293–307.

Arafat, I., & Yorburg, B. Drug use and the sexual behavior of college women. *Journal of Sex Research,* 1973, **9** (1, Feb.), 21–29.

Bacon, L. Early motherhood, accelerated role transition and social pathologies. *Social Forces,* 1974, **52** (March), 331–341.

Baldwin, W. Adolescent pregnancy and childbearing—growing concerns for Americans. (Population Reference Bureau) **31** (2, Sept.). Washington, D.C., 1976.

Baldwin, W. Adolescent pregnancy and childbearing—growing concerns for Americans. (Population Reference Bureau) **31** (2). Washington, D.C., Jan. 1980, updated reprint.

Baldwin, W., & Cain, V. The children of teenage parents. *Family Planning Perspectives,* 1980, **12** (Jan/Feb.), 34–43.

Baltes, P., & Schaie, K. *Life-span development psychology: Personality and socialization.* New York: Academic Press, 1973.

Bandura, A. Self-efficacy: Toward a unifying theory of behavioral change. *Psychology Review 84:* 191–215, 1977.

Bandura, A., & Walters, R. *Social learning and personality development.* New York: Holt, Rinehart, and Winston, 1963.

Bardwick, J. *Psychology of women.* New York: Harper & Row, 1971.

Bardwick, J. Psychological factors in the acceptance and use of oral contraceptives. In J. Fawcett (Ed.), *Psychological aspects of population.* New York: Basic Books, 1973.

Barglow, P. Some psychiatric aspects of illegitimate pregnancy in early adolescence. *American Journal of Orthopsychiatry,* 1968, **38,** 672–687.

Barglow, P., & Weinstein, S. Therapeutic abortion during adolescence psychiatric observations. *Journal of Youth and Adolescence,* 1973, **2** (4, Dec.), 331–342.

Barlow, D., Abel, G., & Blanchard, E. Gender identity change in transsexuals, follow-up and replications. *Archives of General Psychiatry,* 1979, **36,** 10001–10007.

Barth, R., Schinke, S., Liebert, M., & Maxwell, J. Distressing situations and coping responses for school-age mothers and mothers-to-be. Paper presented at the Biennial Western School-Age Parenthood Conference, Portland, Oregon, 1981.

Bartz, K., & Nye, I. Early marriage: A propositional formulation. *Journal of Marriage and the Family,* 1970, **32** (2, May), 258–268.

Bauman, K., & Udry, R. Powerlessness and regularity of contraception in an urban Negro male sample. *Journal of Marriage and the Family,* 1972, **33** (1, Feb.), 112–114.

Bauman, K., & Wilson, R. Sexual behaviors of unmarried university students in 1968 and 1972. *Journal of Sex Research,* 1974, **10** (4, Nov.), 327–333.

Baumrind, D. Early socialization and adolescent competence. In S. Dragastin & G. Elder (Eds.), *Adolescence and the life cycle.* New York: John Wiley & Sons, 1975.

Bayer, A. Early dating and early marriage. *Journal of Marriage and the Family,* 1968, **30** (4, Nov.), 628–32.

Beck, A. *Cognitive therapy and the emotional disorders.* New York: International University Press, 1976.

Bedrosian, R. The application of cognitive therapy techniques with adolescents. In G. Emery, S. D. Hollon, & R. C. Bedrosian (Eds.). *New directions in cognitive therapy, a casebook.* New York: The Guilford Press, 1981.

Benditt, J. Second trimester abortions. *Family Planning Perspectives,* 1979, **11** (Nov./Dec.), 357–362.

Bell, R., & Chaskes, J. Premarital sexual experience among coeds, 1958 and 1968. *Journal of Marriage and the Family,* 1970, **32** (1, Feb.), 81–84.

Benedeck, T. *Psychosexual functions in women.* New York: Ronald Press, 1952.

Berlin, S. A cognitive-learning perspective for social work. *Social Service Review,* 1980, **54,** 537–555.

Bernard, J. *Marriage and the family among Negroes.* Englewood Cliffs, N.J.: Prentice-Hall, 1966.

Bernard, J. Adolescence and socialization for motherhood. In S. Dragastin & G. Elder (Eds.), *Adolescence and the life cycle.* New York: John Wiley & Sons, 1975.

Bernard, J. *The Female World.* New York: The Free Press, 1981.

Bieber, I. *Homosexuality: A psychoanalytic study.* New York: Basic Books, 1962.

Billingsley, A. Illegitimacy and the black community. In *Illegitimacy: Changing services for changing times.* New York: National Council on Illegitimacy, 1970.

Block, J. Issues, problems, and pitfalls in assessing sex differences: A critical review of *The psychology of sex differences* (E. Jaccoby and C. Jacklin). *Merrill-Palmer Quarterly,* 1976, **24** (4, Oct.), 283–308.

Blos, P. *The young adolescent.* New York: Free Press, 1970.

Bowerman, C. Adjustment in marriage: Over-all and in specific areas. *Sociology and Social Research,* 1957, **41,** 257–263.

Bowerman, C., Irish, D., & Pope, H. *Unwed motherhood: Personal and social consequences.* Chapel Hill, NC.: Institute for Research in Social Sciences, University of North Carolina, 1966.

Bracken, M., & Suigar, M. Factors associated with delay in seeking induced abortions. *American Journal of Obstetrics and Gynecology,* 1972, **113** (3, June), 301–309.

Bracken, M., et al. The decision to abort and psychological sequelae. *Journal of Nervous and Mental Disease,* 1974, 158 (2, Feb.), 154–162.

Broderick, C. Social heterosexual development among Negroes and whites. *Journal of Marriage and the Family,* 1965, **27** (2, May), 200–203.

Broderick, C., & Bernard, J. *The individual, sex and society.* Baltimore, Md.: Johns Hopkins University Press, 1969.

Bromley, D., & Britten, F. *Youth and sex.* New York: Harper, 1938.

Brown, S., Lieberman, J., & Miller, W. Young adults as partners and planners: A preliminary report on the antecedents of responsible family formation. Paper presented at 103rd Annual Meeting of the American Public Health Association, Chicago, 1975.

Bumpass, L., Rindfuss, R., & Janosik, R. Age and marital status at first birth and the pace of subsequent fertility. *Demography,* 1978, **15,** 75–86.

Burchinal, L. Adolescent role deprivation and high school age marriage. *Marriage and Family Living,* 1959, **21** (4, Nov.), 373–377.

Burchinal, L. The premarital dyad and love involvement. In H. Christensen (Ed.), *Handbook of marriage and the family.* Skokie, Ill.: Rand McNally, 1964.

Burchinal, L. Trends and prospects for young marriages in the U.S. *Journal of Marriage and the Family,* 1965, **27** (2, May), 243–254.

Burger, G. *The reactions of adolescents to birth control and abortion.* Chicago: Crittenden Comprehensive Care Center, 1974.

Burgess, E., & Cottrell, L. *Predicting success or failure in marriage.* Englewood Cliffs, N.J.: Prentice-Hall, 1939.

Burgess, E., & Wallin, P. *Engagement and marriage.* New York: J. B. Lippincott, 1953.

Cain, L. Social worker's role in teenage abortions. *Social Work,* 1979, **24,** 52–56.

Callahan, E., & Leitenberg, H. Aversion therapy for sexual deviation: Contingent shock and covert sensitization. *Journal of Abnormal Psychology,* 1973, **81,** 60–73.

Campbell, A., Converse, P., & Rodgers, W. *The quality of American life.* New York: Russell Sage Foundation, 1976.

Campbell, A. *The sense of well-being in America.* New York: McGraw Hill, 1980.

Cannon, K., & Long, R. Premarital sex behavior in the 60's. *Journal of Marriage and the Family,* 1971, **33** (1, Feb.), 37–49.

Card, J. *Long-term consequences for children born to adolescent parents.* Palo Alto, Cal.: American Institute of Research, 1978.

Card, J., & Wise, L. Teenage mothers and teenage fathers: The impact of early childbearing on the parents' personal and professional lives. *Family Planning Perspectives,* 1978, **10,** 199–205.

Carns, D. Talking about sex: Notes on first coitus and the double standard. *Journal of Marriage and the Family,* 1973, **35** (4, Nov.), 677–688.

Chesler, J., & Davis, S. Problem pregnancy and abortion counseling with teenagers. *Social Casework,* 1980, **61,** 173–179.

Chilman, C. A study of married and single undergraduates at Syracuse University. Unpublished report to Office of Education, U.S. Department of Health, Education and Welfare, Washington, D.C., 1961.

Chilman, C. The educational–vocational aspirations and behaviors of unmarried and married undergraduates at Syracuse University. Unpublished study, 1963.

Chilman, C. *Growing up poor.* Social and Rehabilitation Service, U.S. Department of Health, Education, and Welfare. Washington, D.C.: U.S. Government Printing Office, 1966.

Chilman, C. Fertility and poverty in the United States: Some implications for family planning programs, policy and research. *Journal of Marriage and the Family,* 1968, **30** (2, May), 207–228.

Chilman, C. Programs for disadvantaged parents. In Ricciuti, H. & Caldwell, B. (Eds.), *Child development research* (Vol. 3). Chicago: University of Chicago Press, 1973.

Chilman, C. Some psychosocial aspects of female sexuality. *The Family Coordinator,* 1974, **23** (2, April), 123–131.

Chilman, C. Interpersonal relationships over the life-span. *Encyclopedia of Social Work.* New York: Columbia University Press, 1977.

Chilman, C. *Adolescent sexuality in a changing American society: Social and psychological perspectives.* National Institutes of Health, U.S. Department of Health, Education, and Welfare. Washington, D.C.: U.S. Government Printing Office, 1978.

Chilman, C. Parent satisfactions–dissatisfactions and their correlates. *Social Service Review,* 1979, **53** (2, June), 195–213.

Chilman, C. Social and psychological research concerning adolescent childbearing: 1970–1980. *Journal of Marriage and the Family,* 1980, **42** (9, Nov.), 793–805. (a)

Chilman, C. *Adolescent pregnancy and childbearing: Findings from research.* U.S. Department of Health and Human Services. NIH Publication No. 81–2077. Washington, D.C.: U.S. Government Printing Office, 1980. (b)

Christensen, H. Value variables in pregnancy timing: Some intercultural comparisons. In R. Anderson (Ed.), *Studies of the Family* (Vol. 3). Gottingen, Germany: Vandenhoek and Ruprect, 1958.

Christensen, H., & Gregg, C. Changing sex norms in America and Scandinavia. *Journal of Marriage and the Family,* 1970, **32** (4, Nov.), 616–627.

Clarke-Stewart, A. *Child care in the family.* New York: Academic Press, 1977.

Clausen, J. The social meaning of differential physical and sexual maturation. In S. Dragastin & G. Elder (Eds.), *Adolescence and the life cycle.* New York: John Wiley & Sons, 1975.

Clayton, R., & Bokemeier, J. Premarital sex in the seventies. *Journal of Marriage and the Family,* 1980, **42** (April), 750–775.

Clines, F. Children of desire. *The New York Times Magazine,* 1979 (30, Sept.), 36–48.

Cobliner, G., Schulman, H., & Romney, S. The termination of adolescent out-of-wedlock pregnancies and the prospects for their primary prevention. *American Journal of Obstetrics and Gynecology,* 1973, **115** (3, Feb.), 432–444.

Coleman, J. C. Friendship and the peer groups in adolescence. In J. Adelson (Ed.), *Handbook of adolescent psychology.* New York: John Wiley & Sons, 1980.

Conger, J. *Adolescence and youth.* New York: Harper & Row, 1973.

Coombs, L., & Freedman, R. Premarital pregnancy and status before and after marriage. *American Journal of Sociology,* 1970, **75** (5, March), 800–820.

Croake, J., & James, B. A four year comparison of premarital sexual attitudes. *Journal of Sex Research,* 1973, **9** (2, May), 91–96.

Cutright, P. Illegitimacy: Myths, Causes, and Cures. *Family Planning Perspectives,* 1971, **3** (3, Jan.), 26–48.

Cutright, P. The teenage sexual revolution and the myth of an abstinent past. *Family Planning Perspectives,* 1972, **4** (1, Jan.), 24–31.

Cutright, P. Illegitimacy: The prospect for change. *American Journal of Public Health,* 1973, **63** (Sept.), 765–766. (a)

Cutright, P. Timing the first birth: Does it matter? *Journal of Marriage and the Family,* 1973, **35** (4, Nov.), 585–595. (b)

Cvetkovich, G., & Grote, B. Antecedents of responsible family formation. Progress report paper presented at a conference sponsored by the Population Division, National Institute of Child Health and Human Development, Bethesda, Md., 1975.

Cvetkovich, G., & Grote, B. Psychological factors associated with adolescent premarital coitus. Paper presented at the National Institute of Child Health and Human Development, Bethesda, Md., May 1976.

Cvetkovich, G., & Grote, B. Towards a theory of psychosocial development and fertility control. Paper presented at the annual meeting of the American Psychological Association, Montreal, Canada, 1980.

David, D., & Brannon, R. The male sex role. In A. Skolnick, & J. Skolnick, (Eds.), *Family in transition*. Boston: Little, Brown, 1980.

David, H. Abortion in psychological perspective. *American Journal of Orthopsychiatry*, 1972, **42**, 61–68.

David, H., & Johnson, R. *Teen problem pregnancies: Peer counselors' perceptions about community concerns and solutions*. Bethesda, Md. Transnational Family Research Institute, 1979.

Davis, E. Health service use in the inner city. Unpublished paper, 1974.

Davis, K. *Factors in the sex life of twenty two hundred women*. New York: Harper, 1929.

Davison, G. Homosexuality: The ethical challenge. *Journal of Consulting and Clinical Psychology*, 1976, **32** (Feb.), 316–321.

DeLameter, J., & MacCorquodale, M. *Premarital sexuality: Attitudes, relationships, behaviors*. Madison: University of Wisconsin Press, 1979.

Deutsch, H. *The psychology of women* (Vols. 1 and 2). New York: Grune & Stratton, 1945.

Dickerson, M. *Social work practice with the mentally retarded*. New York: Free Press, 1981.

Douvan, E., & Adelson, J. *The adolescent experience*. New York: John Wiley & Sons, 1966.

Dragastin, S., & Elder, G. (Eds.). *Adolescence and the life cycle*. New York: John Wiley & Sons, 1975.

Dryfoos, J., & Belmont, L. The intellectual and behavioral status of children born to adolescent mothers. Final report to the Center for Population Research, National Institute of Child Health and Human Development, Bethesda, Md., 1978.

Duehn, W., & Mayadas, N. Integrating communication skills with knowledge: A conjoint adolescent/parent format in sex education. *Journal of Sex Education and Therapy*, 1977, **3** (Feb.), 15–19.

D'Zurilla, T., & Goldfried, M. Problem-solving and behavior modification. *Journal of Abnormal Psychology*, 1971, **78**, 107–126.

D'Zurilla, T., & Nezu, A. A study of generation-of-alternatives process in social problem solving. *Cognitive Therapy and Research*, 1980, **4**, 67–72.

Edwards, J. P., & Wapnick, S. Being me . . . A social/sexual training guide for those who work with the developmentally disabled. Portland, Oreg.: Ednick Communications, 1979.

Edwards, L., Steinman, M., Arnold, K., & Hakanson, E. Adolescent pregnancy prevention services in high school clinics. *Family Planning Perspectives,* 1980, **12** (1, Jan./Feb.), 6–14.

Ehrmann, W. *Premarital dating behavior.* New York: Holt, Rinehart & Winston, 1959.

Eichorn, D. Asynchronization in adolescent development. In S. Dragastin & G. Elder (Eds.), *Adolescence and the life cycle.* New York: John Wiley & Sons, 1975.

Elder, G. Adolescence in the life cycle: An introduction. In S. Dragastin & G. Elder (Eds.), *Adolescence and the life cycle.* New York: John Wiley & Sons, 1975.

Elder, G. Adolescence in the life cycle: An introduction. In J. Adelson (Ed.), *Handbook of adolescent psychology.* New York: John Wiley & Sons, 1980.

Elder, G., & Rockwell, R. Marital timing in women's life patterns. *Journal of Family History,* 1976, **1** (1, autumn), 34–53.

Elkind, D. Conceptual orientation shifts in children and adolescents. *Child Development,* 1966, **37,** 393–448.

Elkind, D. Egocentrism in adolescence. *Child Development,* 1967, **38** (4, Dec.), 1025–1034.

Erikson, E. *Identity: Youth and crisis.* New York: W. W. Norton, 1968.

Evans, J., Selstad, G., & Welcher, W. Teenagers: Fertility control behavior and attitudes before and after abortion, childbearing or negative pregnancy test. *Family Planning Perspectives,* 1976, **8** (4, July/Aug.), 192–200.

Evans, R. Parental relationships and homosexuality. *Medical Aspects of Human Sexuality,* 1971 (April), 164–177.

Ewer, P., & Gibbs, J. Relationship with putative fathers and use of contraception in a population of black ghetto adolescent mothers. *Public Health Reports,* 1975, **90,** 417–423.

Faust, M. Developmental maturity as a determinant in prestige of adolescent girls. *Child Development,* 1960, **32,** 173–184.

Ferrell, M., Tolone, W., & Walsh, R. Maturational and societal changes in the sexual double standard. *Journal of Marriage and the Family,* 1977, **39** (May), 225–271.

Finger, H. Sex beliefs and practices among male college students. *Journal of Abnormal and Social Psychology,* 1947, **42,** 57–67.

Fingerer, M. Psychological sequelae of abortion: Anxiety and depression. *Journal of Community Psychology,* 1973, **1** (2, April), 221–225.

Finkel, M., & Finkel, D. Sexual and contraceptive knowledge, attitudes and behaviors of male adolescents. *Family Planning Perspectives,* 1975, **7** (6, Nov./Dec.), 256–250.

Fisher, W., Byrne, D., Edmonds, J., Miller, C., Kelley, K., & White, L. Psychological and situation-specific correlates of contraception among university women. *Journal of Sex Research,* 1979, **15** (Jan.), 38–52.

308   References

Flavell, J. *The developmental psychology of Jean Piaget*. Princeton, N.J.: Van Nostrand-Reinhold Books, 1963.

Flavell, J. *Cognitive development*. Englewood Cliffs, N.J.: Prentice-Hall, 1974.

Foltz, A. Pregnancy and special education: Who stays in school? *American Journal of Public Health*, 1972, **62**, 1612–1619.

Forbush, J., & Jekel, J. A survey of programs for pregnant adolescents in the United States. Presented at the annual meeting of the American Public Health Association, Washington, D.C., 2 November, 1978.

Ford, S., & Beach, F. *Patterns of sexual behavior*. New York: Harper, 1951.

Foreit, K., & Foreit, J. Correlates of contraceptive behavior among college students. *Family Planning*, 1978, **9**, 169–174.

Forrest, J., Sullivan, E., & Tietze, C. Abortion in the United States. *Family Planning Perspectives*, 1979, **11** (Nov./Dec.), 329–341.

Fox, G. Sex role attitudes as predictors of contraceptive use. Paper presented at the annual meeting of the National Council on Family Relations, Salt Lake City, August 20–23, 1975.

Fox, G. The family's role in adolescent sexual behavior. Paper presented at Family Impact Seminar Consultation for Teenage Pregnancy. Washington, D.C., 1978.

Fox, G. The mother–adolescent daughter relationship as a sexual socialization structure: A research review. *Family Relations*, 1980, **29**, 21–28.

Fox, G. The family's role in adolescent sexual behavior. In T. Ooms (Ed.), *Teenage pregnancy in a family context: Implications for policy*. Philadelphia: Temple University Press, 1981.

Fox, G., & Inazu, J. Patterns and outcomes of mother–daughter communication about sexuality. *Journal of Social Issues*, 1980, **36** (winter), 7–29.

Freedman, M. The sexual behavior of American college women: An empirical study and a historical survey. *Merrill Palmer Quarterly*, 1965, **11** (1, Jan.), 33–47.

Freedman, M. *Homosexuality and psychological functioning*. Belmont, Calif.: Brooks-Cole, 1971.

Freud, A. Adolescence. In Winder, P., & Angus, D. (Eds.), *Adolescence: Contemporary studies*, New York: American Books, 1969.

Freud, S. *The ego and the mechanisms of defense*. New York: International Universities Press, 1946.

Freud, S. Three essays on sexuality. In *Complete psychological works* (Vol. 7, Std. ed.). London, Eng.: Hogarth, 1953.

Furstenberg, F., Jr. *Unplanned parenthood: The social consequences of teenage childbearing*. New York: Free Press, 1976.

Furstenberg, F. The impact of early childbearing on the family. *Journal of Social Issues*, 1980, **36** (winter), 64–87.

Furstenberg, F., & Crawford, A. Family support: Helping teenage mothers to cope. *Family Planning Perspectives*, 1978, **10**, 322–333.

Gabrielson, I., Goldsmith, S., Potts, L., Mathews, N., & Gabrielson, M. Adolescent attitudes towards abortion: Effects on contraceptive practice. *American Journal of Public Health,* 1971, **61** (4, April), 730–738.

Gagnon, J. Sexuality and sex learning in the child. *Psychiatry,* 1965, **29,** 212–228.

Gagnon, J. *Human sexualities.* Glenview, Ill.: Scott, Foresman, 1977.

Gagnon, J., & Simon, W. Youth, sex, and the future. In Gottlieb (Ed.), *Youth in contemporary society.* Beverly Hills, Calif.: Sage Publications, 1973.

Gallup, G. Attitudes of Americans on sex seen undergoing profound change. *Family Planning Digest,* 1974, **3** (Jan.), 3.

Gallup Poll. *American Families—1980.* Princeton, N.J.: The Gallup Organization, 1980.

Gebhard, P., Pomeroy, W., Martin, C., & Christensen, C. *Pregnancy, birth, and abortion.* New York: Harper, 1958.

Gendell, M. Illegitimacy ratios in large U.S. cities: Determinants and implication. *American Journal of Public Health,* 1974, **64** (July), 724–725.

George Washington University Medical Center, Department of Medical and Public Affairs, Adolescent fertility-risks and consequences. *Population Reports,* 1976, Series J (10, July), J–157–175.

Gessell, A., Ilg, F., & Ames, L. *Youth: The years from ten to sixteen.* New York: Harper & Row, 1956.

Giarretto, H. Humanistic treatment of father–daughter incest. In R. Helfer & C. Kempe (Eds.), *Child abuse and neglect, the family and the community.* Cambridge, Mass.: Ballinger, 1976.

Gilbert Youth Research. How wild are college students? *Pageant,* 1951, **7,** 10–21.

Gilchrist, L. Social competence in adolescence. In S. P. Schinke (Ed.), *Behavioral methods in Social Welfare.* New York: Aldine, 1981.

Gilchrist, L., & Schinke, S. Coping with contraception: Cognitive and behavioral methods with adolescents. *Cognitive Therapy and Research,* in press.

Glenn, N., & Weaver, C. Attitudes toward premarital, extramarital and homosexual relations in the U.S. in the 1970's. *Journal of Sex Research,* 1979, **15** (May), 108–118.

Glick, P. A demographer looks at American families. *Journal of Marriage and the Family,* 1975, **37,** 15–26.

Glick, P., & Mills, K. Black families: Marriage patterns and living arrangements. Paper presented at W. E. B. Du Bois Conference on American Blacks, Atlanta, October, 1974.

Glick, P., & Norton, A. Marrying, divorcing and living together in the U.S. today. *Population Bulletin,* 1979, **32** (5).

Goldfried, M., Decenteceo, E., & Weinberg, L. Systematic rational restructuring as self-control technique. *Behavior Therapy,* 1974, **5,** 247–254.

Goldfried, M., & Goldfried, A. Cognitive change methods. In R. Kanfer & A. Goldstein (Eds.), *Helping people change: A textbook of methods.* New York: Pergamon, 1980.

Goldfried, M., & Sobocinski, D. Effect of irrational beliefs on emotion arousal. *Journal of Consulting and Clinical Psychology*, 1975, **43**, 504–510.

Goldsmith, S., Gabrielson, M., & Gabrielson, I. Teenagers sex and contraception. *Family Planning Perspectives*, 1972, **4** (1, Jan.), 32–38.

Goldstein, A., Sprafkin, R., Gershaw, N., & Klein, P. *Skill-streaming the adolescent, a structural learning approach to teaching prosocial skills.* Champaign, Ill.: Research Press, 1980.

Goldstein, H., & Wallace, H. Services for the needs of pregnant teenagers in larger cities of the U.S., 1976. *Public Health Report*, 1978, **93**, 46–54.

Gordon, C. Social characteristics of early adolescence. In Kagan, J., & Coles, R. (Eds.), *Twelve to sixteen: Early adolescence.* Toronto: George J. MacLead, 1972.

Gordon S., & Dickman, I. R. *Schools and parents—partners in sex education.* New York: Public Affairs Committee, 1980.

Gordon S., Scales, P., & Everly, K. *The sexual adolescent: Communicating with teenagers about sex.* North Scituate, Mass.: Duxbury Press, 1979.

Gould, R. *Transformations, growth and change in adult life.* New York: Simon and Schuster, 1978.

Granburg, D., & Granburg, B. Abortion attitudes from 1965 to 1980: Trends and determinants. *Family Planning Perspectives*, 1980, **12** (Sept./Oct.), 250–261.

Grinder, R., & Schmitt, S. Coed and contraceptive information. *Journal of Marriage and the Family*, 1966, **28** (4, Nov.), 471–479.

Griswold, B. Illegitimacy recidivism among AFDC clients. *Unmarried parenthood: Clues to agency and community action.* New York: National Council on Illegitimacy, 1967.

Guerney, B., Jr. *Relationship enhancement.* San Francisco: Jossey-Bass, 1979.

Hamilton, G. *A research in marriage.* New York: A and C Boni, 1929.

Hammond, B., & Ladner, J. Growing up in a Negro slum ghetto. In C. Broderick & J. Bernard (Eds.), *The individual, sex and society.* Baltimore, Md.: Johns Hopkins Press, 1968.

Hamre-Nietupski, S., Ford, A., Williams, W., & Gruenwald, L. Sex education and related home and community functioning skill programs for severely handicapped students: Toward appropriate functioning in less restrictive environments (Vol. 3, P. 2). Madison: University of Wisconsin Press, 1978.

Haney, A., & Michielutte, R. *Social and psychological factors affecting fertility, family planning and clinic utilization.* Behavioral Sciences Center of the Bowman Gray School of Medicine, Wake Forest University, Winston-Salem, N.C., 1974.

Harmon, D., & Brim, O. *Learning to be a parent.* Beverly Hills, Calif.: Sage, 1980.

Hartley, S. F. *Illegitimacy.* Berkeley: University of California Press, 1975.

Hatcher, R., Stewart, G., Stewart, F., Guest, F., Schwartz, D., & Jones, S. *Contraceptive technology 1980–81* (10th rev. ed.). New York: Irvington, 1980.

Hatcher, S. The adolescent experience of pregnancy and abortion: A developmental analysis. *Journal of Youth and Adolescence,* 1973, **2** (1, March), 53–102.

Hawkins, R. The Uppsala connection: The development of principles basic to education for sexuality. *SIECUS Report,* 1980, **8** (March), 1–2, 12–16.

Hay, W., Barlow D., & Hay, L. Treatment of a stereotypic cross-gender motor behavior using covert modeling in a boy with gender identity confusion. *Journal of Consulting and Clinical Psychology,* 1981, **49,** 388–394.

Haynes, L., & Avery, A. Training adolescents in self-disclosure and empathy skills. *Journal of Counseling Psychology,* 1979, **28,** 526–530.

Heltsey, M., & Broderick, C. Religiosity and premarital sexual permissiveness: Reexamination of Reiss's traditionalism proposition. *Journal of Marriage and the Family,* 1969, **31** (3, Aug.), 441–443.

Henshaw, S., Forrest, J., Sullivan, E., & Tietze, C. Abortion in the United States, 1978–1979. *Family Planning Perspectives,* 1981, **13,** 6–18.

Hetherington, M. Effects of father–absence on personality development in adolescent daughters. *Developmental Psychology,* 1972, **7,** 313–326.

Hoffman, M. Moral development in adolescence. In J. Adelson (Ed.), *Handbook of adolescent psychology.* New York: John Wiley & Sons, 1980.

Holloway, B. *Sexuality education by youth-serving agencies: An evaluative study.* Lafayette, Calif.: Pacific Institute for Research Evaluation, 1980.

Holmes, M. Parenthood in adolescence. *Sharing Supplement,* 1970, 10–17.

Hornick, J., Doran, L., & Crawford, S. Premarital contraceptive behaviors among young male and female adolescents. *Family Coordinator,* 1979, **28** (April), 181–190.

Hunt, M. *Sexual behavior in the 1970's.* Chicago: Playboy Press, 1974.

Inselberg, R. Social and psychological factors associated with high school marriages. *Journal of Home Economics,* 1961, **53** (9, Nov.), 766–772.

Jackson, E., & Potkay, C. Pre-college influences on sexual experiences of coeds. *Journal of Sex Research,* 1973, **9** (2, May), 143–149.

James, J. *Entrance into juvenile prostitution.* Unpublished final report. Grant No. MH 29968. The National Institute of Mental Health. University of Washington, 1980.

Jekel, J., Harrison, J., Bancroft, D., Tyler, N., & Klerman, L. A comparison of the health of index and subsequent babies born to school-age mothers. *American Journal of Public Health,* 1975, **65,** 370–374.

Jessor, R., Costa, F., Jessor, L., & Donovan, J. The time of first intercourse: A prospective study. *Journal of Personality and Social Psychology,* in press, 1983.

Jessor, S., & Jessor, R. Transition from virginity to nonvirginity among youth: A social-psychological study over time. *Developmental Psychology,* 1975, **11** (April), 473–484.

Joint Commission on Mental Health of Children and Youth. *The crisis in child mental health.* New York: Harper & Row, 1972.

Jorgenson, S., King, S., and Torrey, B. "Dyadic and Social Network Influencing an Adolescent Exposure to Pregnancy Risk." *Journal of Marriage and the Family,* 1980, **42** (Feb.), 141–155.

Josselyn, I. *The ego in adolescence.* Report to the Joint Commission on Mental Health of Children and Youth, Washington, D.C., 1968.

Jurich, A., & Jurich, J. The effect of cognitive moral development upon the selection of premarital sexual standards. *Journal of Marriage and the Family,* 1974, **36** (4, Nov.), 736–741.

Kaats, G., & Davis, K. The dynamics of sexual behavior of college students. *Journal of Marriage and the Family,* 1970, **32** (3, Aug.), 390–399.

Kagan, J., & Moss, H. *Birth to maturity.* New York: John Wiley & Sons, 1962.

Kanin, E. An examination of sexual aggression as a response to sexual frustration. *Journal of Marriage and the Family,* 1967, **29** (3, Aug.), 428–433.

Kantner, J., & Zelnik, M. Sexual experiences of young unmarried women in the U.S. *Family Planning Perspectives,* 1972, **4** (4, Oct.), 9–17.

Karlen, A. *Sexuality and homosexuality.* New York: W. W. Norton, 1971.

Katchadourian, H., & Lunde, D. *Fundamentals of human sexuality* (2nd ed.). New York: Holt, Rinehart & Winston, 1975.

Kellam, S. Consequences of teenage motherhood for mother, child and family in an urban black community. Progress report to Center for Population Research, National Institutes of Health, Bethesda, Md., 1979.

Keller, R., Sims, J., Henry, W., & Crawford, T. Psychological sources of resistance to family planning. *Merrill-Palmer Quarterly,* 1970, **16** (March), 286–302.

Kempton, W. *Sex education for persons with disabilities that hinder learning: A teacher's guide.* North Scituate, Mass.: Duxbury, 1975.

Kempton, W., & Carelli, L. Mentally handicapped. In D. Shore & H. Gochros (Eds.), *Sexual problems of adolescents in institutions.* Springfield, Ill.: Charles C. Thomas, 1981.

Kendall, P., & Finch, A. Developing nonimpulsive behavior in children: Cognitive–behavioral strategies for self-control. In P. Kendall & S. Hollon (Eds.), *Cognitive–behavioral interventions, theory, research and procedures.* New York: Academic Press, 1979.

Kendall, P., & Hollon, S. (Eds.). *Cognitive–behavioral interventions, theory, research and procedures.* New York: Academic Press, 1979.

Keniston, K., & the Carnegie Commission on Children. *All our children: The American family under pressure.* New York: Harcourt Brace Jovanovich, 1977.

Kifer, R., Lewis, M., Green, D., & Phillips, E. Training predelinquent youth and their parents to negotiate conflict situations. *Journal of Applied Behavior Analysis,* 1974, **7**, 357–364.

Kinard, E., Klerman L., Levy, J., Bonanno, R. Teenage mothers and their use of pediatric care for their children. *Massachusetts Journal of Community Health,* Fall/Winter 1980, 12–16.

King, C. The Burgess-Cottrell method of measuring marital adjustment applied to a non-white southern urban population. *Marriage and Family Living,* 1952, **14** (284), 5–12.

Kinsey, A., Pomeroy, W., & Martin, C. *Sexual behavior in the human male.* Philadelphia: W.B. Saunders, 1948.

Kinsey, A., Pomeroy, W., Martin, C., & Gebhard, P. *Sexual behavior in the human female.* Philadelphia: W.B. Saunders, 1953.

Kirby, D., & Alter, J. The experts rate important features and outcomes of sex education programs. *Journal of School Health,* 1980, **50** (9), 497–502.

Kirby, D., Alter, J., & Scales, P. *An analysis of U.S. sex education programs and evaluation methods.* Springfield, Va.: National Technical Information Service, 1979.

Kirkendall, L. A. *Sex education.* New York: Sex Information and Education Council of the United States, 1965.

Kirkpatrick, C. *The family as process and institution.* New York: Ronald Press, 1963.

Klerman, L. Evaluating service programs for school-age parents: Design problems. *Evaluation and the Health Professions,* 1979, **2**, 55–70.

Klerman, L., & Jekel, J. *School-age mothers: Problems, programs, and policy.* Hamden, Ct.: Linnet Books, 1973.

Kohlberg, L. Development of moral character and moral ideology. In L. Hoffman & M. Hoffman (Eds.), *Research* (Vol. 1), New York: Russell Sage Foundation, 1964.

Kohlberg, L., & Gilligan, C. The adolescent as a philosopher: The discovery of self in a post conventional world. In Kagan, J., & Coles, R. (Eds.), *Twelve to sixteen.* Toronto: George J. McLead, 1972.

Kohn, M. *Class and conformity.* Homewood, Ill.: Dorsey Press, 1969.

Komarovsky, M. *Blue collar marriage.* New York: Random House, 1964.

Komarovsky, M. *Dilemmas of masculinity: A study of college youth.* New York: W. W. Norton, 1976.

Konopka, G. *The teenage girl.* Albany, N.Y.: State Division for Youth, 1967.

Kraus, L. Therapeutic strategies with adolescents. *Social Casework,* 1980, **61**, 313–316.

Ladner, J. *Tomorrow's tomorrow: The black women.* Garden City, N.J.: Doubleday, 1971.

Lake, A. Teenagers and sex: A student report. *Seventeen,* 1967, **26** (7, July), 88–131.

Landis, J., & Landis, M. *Building a successful marriage.* Englewood Cliffs, N.J.: Prentice-Hall, 1953.

Laws, J. Toward a model of female sexual identity. *Midway,* 1970, (summer), 39–72.

Lewis, R., & Burr, W. Premarital coitus and commitment among college students. *Archives of Sexual Behavior,* 1975, **4** (Jan.), 73–79.

Liebow, E. *Tally's corner*. Boston: Little, Brown, 1967.

Lindemann, C. *Birth control and unmarried young women*. New York: Springer, 1974.

Livingston, V., & Knapp, M. *Human sexuality portfolio*. Seattle: Planned Parenthood of Seattle-King County, 1974.

Livson, N., & Peskin, H. Perspectives on adolescence from longitudinal research. In J. Adelson (Ed.), *Handbook of adolescent psychology*. New York: John Wiley & Sons, 1980.

Locke, H. *Predicting adjustment in marriage: A comparison of a divorced and a happily married group*. New York: Holt, 1951.

Locke, H., & Wallace, K. M. Short marital adjustment and prediction tests: Their reliability and validity. *Marriage and Family Living*, 1959, **21**, 251–255.

Locke, H., & Williamson, R. Marital adjustment: A factor analysis study. *American Sociology Review*, 1958, **23**, 562–569.

Loevinger, J. Meaning and measurement of ego development. *American Psychologist*, 1966, **21** (3, March), 195–206.

Loevinger, J. *Ego development*. San Francisco: Jossey-Bass, 1976.

Loewenstein, S. F. Understanding lesbian women. *Social Casework*, 1980, **61**, 29–38.

Lorenzi, M., Klerman, L., & Jekel, J. School age parents: How permanent a relationship? *Adolescence*, 1977, XII, **5** (spring), 68–76.

Lowenstein, S. F. Understanding lesbian women. *Social Casework*, 1973, **61**, 28–38.

Lowenthal, M., Thurnher, M., & Chiriboga, D. *Four stages of life*. San Francisco: Jossey-Bass, 1974.

Lowrie, S. Early marriage: Premarital pregnancy and associated factors. *Journal of Marriage and the Family*, 1965, **27** (1, Feb.), 49–56.

Luckey, E., & Nass, G. A comparison of sexual attitudes and behavior of an international sample. *Journal of Marriage and the Family*, 1969, **31** (2, May), 346–379.

Luker, K. *Taking chances: Abortion and the decision not to contracept*. Berkeley: University of California Press, 1975.

Maccoby, E., & Jacklin, C. *The psychology of sex differences*. Stanford, Calif.: Stanford University Press, 1974.

MacCulloch, M., Williams, C., & Bortles, C. The successful application of aversion therapy to an adolescent exhibitionist. *Journal of Behavior Therapy and Experimental Psychiatry*, 1971, **2**, 61–66.

MacDonald, A., Jr. Internal–external locus of control and the practice of birth control. *Psychology Report*, 1970, **27** (1, Aug.), 206.

Mace, D. *Abortion: The agonizing decision*. New York: Abington Press, 1972.

Macklin, E. Non-marital heterosexual cohabitation: A review of research. *Marriage and the Family Review*, 1978, **4** (1, March/April), 1–12.

Macklin, E. Review of research on non-marital cohabitation in the United States. In B. Murstein (Ed.), *Current and future intimate life styles,* forthcoming, 1983.

Mahoney, E. Gender and social class differences in attitudes toward premarital coitus. *Sociology and Social Research,* 1979, **62** (Jan.), 279–286.

Mahoney, M. *Cognition and behavior modification.* Cambridge, Mass.: Ballinger, 1974.

Mahoney, M., & Arnkoff, D. B. Cognitive and self-control therapies. In L. S. Garfield & A. E. Bergin (Eds.), *Handbook of psychotherapy and behavior change* (2nd ed.). New York: John Wiley & Sons, 1978.

Maracek, J. Economic, social and psychological consequences of adolescent childbearing. Report to Center for Population Research, National Institutes of Health, Bethesda, Md., 1979.

Marcia, J. Identity in adolescence. In J. Adelson (Ed.), *Handbook of adolescent psychology.* New York: John Wiley & Sons, 1980.

Malyon, A. The homosexual adolescent: Developmental issues and social bias. *Child Welfare,* 1981, **60,** 321–330.

Martin, C. Psychological problems of abortion for the unwed teenage girl. *Genetic Psychiatric Monograph,* 1973, **88** (Aug.), 23–110.

Masters, W., & Johnson, V. *Human sexual response.* Boston: Little, Brown, 1966.

Masters, W., & Johnson, V. *Human sexual inadequacy.* Boston: Little, Brown, 1969.

Matteson, D. *Adolescence today: Sex roles and search for identity.* Homewood, Ill.: Dorsey Press, 1975.

McCormick, E. *Attitudes towards abortion.* Lexington, Mass.: Lexington Books, 1975.

McCarthy, J., & Menken, J. Marriage, remarriage, marital disruption and age at first birth. *Family Planning Perspectives,* 1979, **11** (Jan./Feb.), 32–40.

McKinley, T., Kelly, J., & Patterson, J. Teaching assertive skills to a passive homosexual adolescent: An illustrative case study. *Journal of Homosexuality,* 1977, **3,** 163–169.

McMillen-Hall, N. The focus of group treatment with sexually abused children. In *Child abuse: Where do we go from here?* Conference Proceedings, Children's Hospital National Medical Center, Washington, D.C., February, 1977.

Mead, M. *Male and female.* New York: William Morrow, 1939.

Mead, M. Marriage in two steps. *Redbook,* 1966, 48–49.

Meichenbaum, D. *Cognitive–behavior modification: An integrative approach.* New York: Plenum, 1977.

Menken, J. The health and social consequences of teenage parenthood. In Furstenberg, F., Lincoln, R., & Menken, J. *Teenage sexuality, pregnancy and childbearing.* Philadelphia: University of Pennsylvania Press, 1981.

Miller, W. Psychological vulnerability to unwed pregnancy. *Family Planning Perspectives*, 1973, **5** (4), 199–201. (a)

Miller, W. Sexuality, contraceptives, and pregnancy in a high school population. *California Medicine*, 1973, **119** (2, Aug.), 14–21. (b)

Miller, W. Relationships between the intendedness of contraception and wantedness of pregnancy. *Journal of Nervous and Mental Disease*, 1974, **59** (6, Dec.), 396–406.

Miller, W. Some psychological factors predictive of undergraduate sexual and contraceptive behavior. Paper presented at the 84th Annual Convention of the American Psychological Association, Washington, D.C., September, 1976.

Millman, S., & Hendershot, G. Early fertility, and lifetime fertility. *Family Planning Perspectives*, 1980, **12** (May/June), 139–149.

Milwaukee Journal, Washington Bureau, Report of Bureau of Labor Statistics, Oct. 8, 1982, p. 3.

Mirande, A. Reference group theory and adolescent sexual behavior. *Journal of Marriage and the Family*, 1968, **30** (4, Nov.), 572–577.

Modell, J., Furstenberg, F., Jr., & Hersberg, T. Social change and the transition to adulthood in historical perspective. *Journal of Family History*, 1976, **1** (autumn), 7–32.

Money, J. *Sex errors of the body: Dilemmas, education, counseling.* Baltimore, Md.: Johns Hopkins Press, 1968.

Money, J., & Ehrhardt, A. *Man and woman, boy and girl.* Baltimore, Md.: Johns Hopkins Press, 1972.

Money, J., Hampson, J. C., & Hampson, J. L. An examination of human hermaphroditism. *Bulletin of Johns Hopkins Hospital*, 1955, **97**, 301–319.

Money, J., & Tucker, P. *Sexual signatures.* Boston: Little, Brown, 1975.

Monsour, K., & Stewart, B. Abortion and sexual behavior in college women. *American Journal of Orthopsychiatry*, 1973, **43** (5, Oct.), 804–814.

Moore, K. Teenage childbirth and welfare dependency. *Family Planning Perspectives*, 1978, **10**, 233–235.

Moore, K., & Caldwell, S. Out of wedlock childbearing. Washington, D.C.: The Urban Institute, 1977.

Moore, K., & Hofferth, S. *Consequences of age at first childbirth: Final research summary.* Washington, D.C.: The Urban Institute, 1978.

Morrison, P. Consequences of late adolescent childbearing. Preliminary report to the Center for Population Research, National Institute of Mental Health, Bethesda, Md., 1978.

Moss, J., & Gingles, R. The relationship of personality to incidence of early marriage. *Marriage and Family Living*, 1959, **21** (4, May), 372–377.

Napier, A., & Whittaker, C. *The family crucible.* New York: Harper & Row, 1978.

Nathanson, C., & Becker, M., Obstetrician's attitudes and hospital abortion services. *Family Planning Perspectives,* 1980, **12** (1, Jan./Feb.), 26–33.

Nestor, B. Public funding of contraceptive services. *Family Planning Perspectives,* 1982, **14** (4, July/August), 198–203.

Nye, I., & MacDougall, E. The dependent variable in marital research. *Pacific Sociological Review,* 1949, (2), 67–70.

O'Connell, M., & Moore, M. The legitimacy status of first births in U.S. women age 15–24, 1939–1978. *Family Planning Perspectives,* 1980, **12** (Jan./Feb.), 16–25.

Offer, D., Marcus, D., & Offer, J. A longitudinal study of normal adolescent boys. *American Journal of Psychiatry,* 1970, **126** (7, Jan.), 41–48.

Offer, D., & Offer, J. *The psychological world of the teenagers.* New York: Basic Books, 1969.

Offer, D., & Offer, J. *From teenage to young manhood.* New York: Basic Books, 1975.

Office for Family Planning. *A decision-making approach to sex behavior.* Washington, D.C.: U.S. Government Printing Office, 1979.

O'Neil, W. *Coming apart: An informal history of America in the 1960's.* Chicago: Quadrangle Books, 1971.

Ooms, T. (Ed.). *Teenage pregnancy in a family context: Implications for policy.* Philadelphia: Temple University Press, 1981.

Osofsky, J., & Osofsky, H. The psychological reaction of patients to legalized abortions. *American Journal of Orthopsychiatry,* 1972, **42** (1, Jan.), 48–60.

Packard, V. *The sexual wilderness.* New York: David McKay, 1968.

Pakter, J., Nelson, F., & Svigir, M. Legal abortion: A half decade of experience. *Family Planning Perspectives,* 1975, **7** (6, Nov./Dec.), 248–255.

Pannor, R. *The unmarried father.* New York: Springer, 1971.

Paul, E., & Pilpel, H. Teenage pregnancy: The law in 1979. *Family Planning Perspectives,* 1979, **11** (Sept./Oct.), 297–300.

Perez-Reyes, M., & Falk, R. Follow-up after therapeutic abortion in early adolescence. *Archives of General Psychiatry,* 1973, **28,** 120–126.

Perlman, D. Self-esteem and sexual permissiveness. *Journal of Marriage and the Family,* 1974, **36** (3, Aug.), 470–474.

Peterson, A., & Taylor, B. The biological approach to adolescence. In J. Adelson (Ed.), *Handbook of adolescent psychology.* New York: John Wiley & Sons, 1980.

Peterson, L., & Kirby, D. A successful parent–child sex education program. *Child Welfare,* 1981.

Peterson, R. Early sex information and its influence on later sex concepts. Unpublished master's thesis, College of Education, University of Colorado, Boulder, 1938.

Piaget, J. The intellectual development of the adolescent. In Caplan, G., & Lebovic, P. (Eds.), *Adolescence: Psychological perspectives*. New York: Basic Books, 1969.

Piaget, J. Intellectual evaluation from adolescence to adulthood. *Human Development*, 1972, **15**, 1–12.

Piaget, J., & Inhelder, B. *The psychology of the child*. New York: Basic Books, 1969.

Playboy. Playboy's student survey. *Playboy*, 1970, **17** (9, Sept.), 182–240.

Playboy. Playboy's student survey. *Playboy*, 1971, **18** (9, Sept.), 118–216.

Playboy. What's really happening on campus. *Playboy*, 1976, **23** (10, Oct.), 128–169.

Pocs, D., Godow, A., Tolone, W., & Walsh, R. Is there sex after 40? *Psychology Today*, 1977, **11** (87), 54–56.

Pope, H. Unwed mothers and their sex partners. *Journal of Marriage and the Family*, 1967, **29** (3, Aug.), 555–567.

Population Reference Bureau. Family size and the black American. *Population Bulletin*, 1975, **30** (4).

Porterfield, A., & Ellison, S. Current folkways of sexual behavior. *American Journal of Sociology*, 1946, **52,** 209–216.

Presser, H. Early motherhood: Ignorance or bliss? *Family Planning Perspectives,* 1974, **6** (2), 8–14.

Presser, H. Some consequences of adolescent pregnancies. Paper presented at the National Institute of Child Health and Human Development Conference, Bethesda, Md., 1975.

Presser, H. Role and fertility patterns of urban mothers. Contract No. 1-HD-2038. Final report presented to the National Institutes of Health, U.S. Department of Health, Education, and Welfare, Bethesda, Md., 1976. (a)

Presser, H. Social factors affecting the timing of the first child. Paper presented at the Conference on the First Child and Family Formation, Pacific Grove, Calif., March 1976. (b)

Presser, H. Guessing and misinformation about pregnancy risks among urban mothers. *Family Planning Perspectives,* 1977, **9** (March/June), 234–236.

Presser, H. Age at menarche, socio-sexual behavior and fertility. *Social Biology,* 1978, **2** (summer), 94–101.

Presser, H. Social and demographic consequences of teenage childbearing for urban women. Final report to Center for Population Research, National Institutes of Health, Bethesda, Md., 1980.

Rains, P. *Becoming an unwed mother*. Chicago: Aldine, 1971.

Rainwater, L. *Family design*. Chicago: Aldine, 1965.

Rainwater, L. Some aspects of lower-class sexual behavior. *Journal of Social Issues*, 1966, **52** (2, April), 96–108.

Rainwater, L. *Behind ghetto walls: Black families in a federal slum*. Chicago: Aldine, 1970.

Rainwater, L., & Weinstein, K. *And the poor get children.* Chicago: Quadrangle Books, 1960.

Rappaport, B. Helping men ask for help. *Public Welfare,* 1981, **39** (2), 22–27.

Rathjen, D. P., & Foreyt, J. P. (Eds.). *Social competence: Interventions for children and adults.* New York: Pergamon, 1980.

Reeder, L., & Reeder, S. Social isolation and illegitimacy. *Journal of Marriage and the Family,* 1969, **31,** 451–461.

Reichelt, P. Psychosexual background of female adolescents seeking contraceptive assistance. Paper presented at the American Psychological Association Convention, Washington, D.C., September 3–7, 1976.

Reiss, I. *Premarital sexual standards in America.* Glencoe, Ill.: Free Press, 1960.

Reiss, I. *The social context of sexual permissiveness.* New York: Holt, Rinehart & Winston, 1967.

Reiss, I. Premarital sex as deviant behavior: An application of current approaches to deviance. *American Sociological Review,* 1970, **35,** 78–87.

Reiss, I. *Heterosexual relationships: Inside and outside of marriage.* Morristown, N.J.: General Learning Press, 1973.

Reiss, I. *Family systems in America* (2nd ed.). Hinsdale, Ill.: Dryden Press, 1976.

Reiss, I., & Miller, B. Heterosexual permissiveness: A theoretical analysis. In W. Burr, R. Hill, I. Nye, & I. Reiss (Eds.), *Contemporary theories about family.* (Vol. 1). New York: Free Press, 1979.

Rekers, G., Lovass, O., & Low, B. The behavioral treatment of a transsexual preadolescent boy. *Journal of Abnormal Child Psychology,* 1974, **2** (2), 99–116.

Ricketts, S. *Contraceptive use among teenage mothers.* Unpublished doctoral dissertation, University of Pennsylvania, 1973.

Robbins, M., & Lynn, D. The unwed fathers: Generation recidivism and attitudes about intercourse in California youth authority wards. *Journal of Sex Research,* 1973, **9** (4, Nov.), 334–341.

Robin, A. Parent–adolescent conflict: A skill-training approach. In D. Rathjen & J. Foreyt (Eds.), *Social competence: Interventions for children and adults.* New York: Pergamon, 1980.

Robin, A., Ken, R., O'Leary, K., Foster, S., & Prinz, R. An approach to teaching parents and adolescents problem-solving communications. *Behavior Therapy,* 1977, **8,** 630–643.

Robinault, I. *Sex, society, and the disabled: A developmental inquiry into roles, reactions, and responsibilities.* New York: Harper & Row, 1978.

Robinson, I., King, K., & Balswick, J. The premarital sexual revolution among college females. *Family Coordinator,* 1972, **21** (2, April), 189–194.

Rodgers, D., & Ziegler, F. Social role theory, the marital relationship, and the use of ovulation suppressors. *Journal of Marriage and the Family,* 1968, **27,** 59–64.

Rose, S. *Treating children in groups.* San Francisco: Jossey-Bass, 1972.

Rosen, R. Adolescent pregnancy decision-making: Are parents important? *Adolescence,* 1980, **15,** 44–54.

Rosen, R., Hudson, A., & Martindale, L. Contraception, abortion and self-concept. Paper presented at the American Sociological Association, Washington, D.C., September 1976.

Rosen, R., Martindale, L., & Grisdela, M. Pregnancy study report. Wayne State University, Detroit, March 1976.

Rosenwaike, I. Differentials in divorce in Maryland. *Demography,* 1969, **6** (2, May), 151–159.

Ross, H., & Sawhill, I. *Time of transition: The growth of families headed by women.* Washington, D.C.: The Urban Institute, 1975.

Ross, R. Measures of the sex behaviors of college males compared with Kinsey's results. *Journal of Abnormal and Social Psychology,* 1950, **45,** 753–755.

Rothenberg, P. Communication about sex and birth control between mothers and their adolescent children. *Population and Environment,* 1980, **3,** 35–50.

Rothstein, A. A. Adolescent males, fatherhood and abortion. *Journal of Youth and Adolescence,* 1978, **7,** 203–214.

Rubin, L. *Worlds of pain.* New York: Basic Books, 1976.

Russ-Eft, D., Springer, M., & Beever, A. Antecedents of adolescent parenthood and consequences at age 30. *Family Coordinator,* 1979, **28** (April), 173–178.

Ryerson, E. Special education curriculum on sexual exploitation (Level II). Seattle: Comprehensive Health Education Foundation, 1979.

Sandler, H. Effects of adolescent pregnancy on mother–infant relations: A transactional model of reports to the Center for Population Research. National Institutes of Health, Bethesda, Md., 1979.

Sarrel, L., & Sarrel, P. The college subculture. In M. Calderone (Ed.), *Sexuality and Human Values.* New York: Association Press, 1974.

Sarrel, P. The university hospital and the teenage unwed mother. *American Journal of Public Health,* 1967, **58** (8), 308–319.

Sauber, M., & Corrigan, E. *The six year experience of unwed mothers as parents.* New York: Community Council of Greater New York, 1970.

Scales, P. The context of sex education and the reduction of teenage pregnancy. *Child Welfare,* 1979, **53** (4), 263–273.

Scales, P. The forefront of controversy: Sex education and public action in America, Manuscript in progress, 1982.

Scales, P. The moral basis of education for sexuality. *Free Inquiry,* 1981, **1** (3), 1–6. (a)

Scales, P. Myths about sex that mislead young people. *Medical Aspects of Human Sexuality,* 1981, **15** (4), 132–148. (b)

Scales, P. The new opposition to sex education: A powerful threat to a democratic society. *Journal of School Health,* 1981, **51** (4), 300–303. (c)

Schinke, S. (Ed.). *Behavioral methods in social welfare.* New York: Aldine, 1981.

Schinke, S., Blythe, B., & Gilchrist, L. Interpersonal skills training with teenagers with high risk for unwanted pregnancy. *Health and Social Work*, 1980, **5** (3), 54–59.

Schinke, S., Blythe, B., & Gilchrist, L. Cognitive–behavioral prevention of adolescent pregnancy. *Journal of Counseling Psychology*, 1981, **28**, 451–454.

Schinke, S., & Gilchrist, L. Adolescent pregnancy: An interpersonal skill training approach to prevention. *Social Work in Health Care*, 1977, **3**, 159–167.

Schinke, S., Gilchrist, L., & Small, R. Preventing unwanted adolescent pregnancy: A cognitive-behavioral approach. *American Journal of Orthopsychiatry*, 1979, **49**, 81–88.

Schroeder, E. The development of cognitive–behavioral group treatment for adolescent prostitutes and young women at risk. *Behavioral Group Therapy*, 1981, **3**, (2), 23–28.

Schulz, B., Bohrnstedt, G., Borgatta, E., & Evans, R. Explaining premarital intercourse among college students: A causal model. *Social Forces*, 1977, **56** (Sept.), 148–165.

Schulz, D. *Coming up black*. Englewood Cliffs, N.J.: Prentice-Hall, 1969.

Sex Information and Education Council of the United States (SIECUS). *SIECUS Newsletter*, 1970, **6** (2, Dec.), 3–12.

Shah, F., Zelnik, M., & Kantner, J., Unprotected intercourse among unwed teenagers. *Family Planning Perspectives*, 1975, **7**, 39.

Shapiro, C. *Adolescent pregnancy prevention: School–community cooperation*. Springfield, Ill.: Charles C. Thomas, 1981.

Shapiro, C. Sexual learning: The short-changed adolescent male. *Social Work*, 1980, **25**, 489–493.

Shapiro, D. Attitudes, values, and unmarried motherhood. In *Unmarried parenthood: Clues to agency and community action*. New York: National Council on Illegitimacy, 1967.

Sheehy, G. *Passages*. New York: E. P. Dutton, 1976.

Sherfey, M. J. The evolution of female sexuality in relation to psychoanalytic theory. *Journal of American Psychoanalytic Association*, 1966, **14** (1), 28–128.

Shore, D., & Gochros, H. (Eds.). *Sexual problems of adolescents in institutions*. Springfield, Ill.: Charles C. Thomas, 1981.

Simon, W., Berger, A., & Gagnon, J. Beyond anxiety and fantasy: The coital experience of college youths. *Journal of Youth and Adolescence*, 1972, **1** (3), 203–222.

Simpson, J., Aptekar-Litton, K., & Roberts, E. *Harmonizing sexual conventions*. Cambridge, Mass.: Project on Human Sexual Development, 1978.

Skinner, B. F. *The behavior of organisms: An experimental analysis*. New York: Appleton-Century-Crofts, 1938.

Skolnick, A. *The intimate environment*. Boston: Little, Brown, 1980.

Smith, T. *A compendium of trends in general social survey questions.* Chicago: National Opinion Research Center, 1980.

Sorensen, R. *Adolescent sexuality in contemporary America.* New York: World, 1973.

Spanier, G. Sexualization and premarital sexual behavior. *Family Coordinator,* 1975, **24** (1, Jan.), 33–41.

Spence, J., & Helmreich, R. *Masculinity and femininity: Their psychological dimensions, correlates and antecedents.* Austin: University of Texas Press, 1978.

Spivack, G., Platt, J., & Shure, M. *The problem-solving approach to adjustment.* San Francisco: Jossey-Bass, 1976.

Stack, C. *All our kin: Strategies for survival in the black community.* New York: Harper & Row, 1974.

Staples, R. *The black woman in America: Sex, marriage and the family.* Chicago: Nelson-Hall, 1973.

Steinberg, L. *Understanding families with young adolescents.* Carrboro, N.C.: Center for Early Adolescence, 1980.

Steinhoff, P. *Premarital pregnancy and first birth.* Paper presented at the Conference on the Birth of the First Child and Family Formation, Pacific Grove, Calif., March 1976. (Report of larger study, Hawaii pregnancy, birth control, and abortion study, University of Hawaii.)

Stoller, R. *Sex and Gender.* New York: Jason Aronson, 1968.

Stroup, A. Predicting marital success or failure in an urban population. *American Sociological Review,* 1953, **28,** 560.

Tanner, J. Physical growth. In Carmichael, E. (Ed.), *Manual of child psychology* (Vol. 1, 3rd ed.). New York: John Wiley & Sons, 1970.

Terman, L. *Psychological factors in marital happiness.* New York: McGraw-Hill, 1938.

Tietze, C. Teenage pregnancies: Looking ahead to 1984. In F. Furstenberg, R. Lincoln, & J. Menken (Eds.), *Teenage sexuality, pregnancy, and childbearing.* Philadelphia: University of Pennsylvania Press, 1981.

Trussel, J. Economic consequences of teenage childbearing. In F. Furstenberg, R. Lincoln, & J. Menken (Eds.), *Teenage sexuality, pregnancy, and childbearing.* Philadelphia: University of Pennsylvania Press, 1981.

Trussel, J., & Menken, J. Early childbearing and subsequent fertility. *Family Planning Perspectives,* 1978, **10** (July/Aug.), 209–218.

Udry, J., Bauman, K., & Morris, N. Changes in premarital coital experience of recent decade of birth cohorts of urban America. *Journal of Marriage and the Family,* 1975, **37** (4, Nov.), 783–787.

U.S. Department of Commerce, Bureau of the Census. Number, timing, and duration of marriages and divorces in the U.S. *Current Population Reports,* Series P-20, No. 297. Washington, D.C.: U.S. Government Printing Office, 1975.

U.S. Department of Commerce. Money, income and poverty status of families in the U.S. *Current Population Reports,* Series P-20, No. 103. Washington, D.C.: U.S. Government Printing Office, 1976.

U.S. Department of Commerce. Marital status and living arrangements: March 1976. *Current Population Reports,* Series P-20, No. 306. Washington, D.C.: U.S. Government Printing Office, 1977.

U.S. Department of Health and Human Services. National Center for Health Statistics. Summary reports of final natality statistics: 1978. *Monthly Statistics Report.* Series 29, No. 1. Washington, D.C.: U.S. Government Printing Office, 1980.

Urban and Rural Systems Associates. *Improving family planning services for teenagers.* Washington, D.C.: U.S. Government Printing Office, 1976.

Vener, A., & Stewart, C. Adolescent sexual behavior in middle America revisited: 1970–1973. *Journal of Marriage and the Family,* 1974, **36** (4, Nov.), 728–735.

Vener, A., Stewart, C., & Hager, D. The sexual behavior of adolescents in middle America: Generation and American–British comparisons. *Journal of Marriage and the Family,* 1972, **34** (Nov.), 696–705.

Ventura, S. Recent trends and differentials in illegitimacy. *Journal of Marriage and the Family,* 1969, **31** (3, Aug.), 446–450.

Vincent, C. *Unmarried mothers.* London, Eng.: Free Press, 1961.

Vincent, C., Haney, A., & Cochrane, C. Familial and generational patterns of illegitimacy. *Journal of Marriage and the Family,* 1969, **31** (4, Nov.), 659–667.

Wallace, H., Gold, E., Goldstein, H., & Oglesby, A. A study of services and needs of teenage girls in large cities of the U.S. *American Journal of Public Health,* 1973, **63**, 5–16.

Wallerstein, J., & Kelly, J. *Surviving the break-up: How children and parents cope with divorce.* New York: Basic Books, 1980.

Wolpe, J., & Lazarus, A. *Behavior therapy techniques.* Elmsford, N.Y.: Pergamon, 1966.

Yankelovich, D. *The new morality: A profile of American youth in the 1970's.* New York: McGraw-Hill, 1974.

Yankelovich, D. A world upside down. *Psychology Today,* 1981 (April).

Yankelovich, D., Skelly, & White. *Raising children in a changing American society.* Minneapolis: General Mills, 1977.

Zellman, G. L. The response of the schools to teenage pregnancy and parenthood. Santa Monica: The Rand Corporation, 1981. (a)

Zellman, G. L. A Title IX perspective on the school's response to teenage pregnancy and parenthood. Santa Monica: The Rand Corporation, 1981. (b)

Zelnik, M. Determinants of fertility behavior among U.S. females aged 15–19, 1971 and 1976. Final report to the Center for Population Research, NICHD-NIH, Bethesda, Md., 1981.

Zelnik, M., & Kantner, J. The resolution of teenage pregnancies. *Family Planning Perspectives,* 1974, **6** (2, spring), 74–80.

Zelnik, M., & Kantner, J. Sexual and contraceptive experience of young married women in the United States, 1966–1971. *Family Planning Perspectives,* 1977, **9** (2, Mar./Apr.), 55–73.

Zelnik, M., & Kantner, J. Sexuality, contraception and pregnancy among young unwed females in the United States. *Research Reports* (Vol. 1). Commission on Population Growth and the American Future. Washington, D.C.: U.S. Government Printing Office, 1980. (a)

Zelnik, M., & Kantner, J. Sexual activity, contraceptive use, and pregnancy among metropolitan area teenagers: 1971–1979. *Family Planning Perspectives,* 1980, **12,** 230–237. (b)

Zelnik, M., Kantner, J., & Ford, K. *Adolescent pathways to pregnancy.* Beverly Hills, Ca.: Sage Publications, Inc., 1982.

Ziegler, E., & Valentine, J. (Eds.). *Project head start: A legacy of the war on poverty.* New York: Free Press, 1979.

Zuckerman, B., Winsmore, G., & Alpert, J. A study of attitudes and support systems of inner city adolescent mothers. *Journal of Pediatrics,* 1979, **95,** 122–125.

Index

Middle class:
  boys, 38
  case illustrations of, 291–295, 298–299
  characteristics, 20
Midstage, cycle in families, 33–34
Miller, W., 88, 111–112, 119
Mills, K., 171, 176
Minneapolis, sex education curricula, 222
Miscarriage, rates, 9
Model contraceptive program, 261–262
Money, J., 9, 10, 11, 39, 62, 98
Monsour, K., 119
Moore, K., 137, 151
Moral development, 26–27, 68–69
Moral Majority, 27, 50, 93
Morrison, P., 137
Moss, J., 54, 98, 169
Mother-daughter communication, 34,
  114–115, 120–121, 252
Motherhood, as status, 157
Myths, about sex, 220, 245

N.A.A.C.P., 124
Narcissism, 36, 49, 102
Nass, G., 71
National Fertility Studies, 170
National Health Examination Survey, 142
National Institute of Mental Health Task
  Force, 59
National Panel Study of Income Dynamics,
  137
National Study of the Labor Market Expe-
  rience of Young Women, 137
National Survey of Family Growth, 137
Natural development, view of, 22
New York City, study of childbearing, 138
Nocturnal emissions, 15, 70
Nonmarital intercourse:
  attitudes and views toward, 66–70
  and problems for adolescents, 91, 230–231
  rates and trends in, 47, 86, 92, 257
  reasons for, 65–66, 67, 87, 92, 208
  as research category, 286
  three steps to, 90
Nonvirgins, 75, 89, 90, 92
Normal sexual behavior, 210
Nye, I., 169

Occupational status, and early childbearing,
  140

Oedipal conflict, 28, 30, 55, 61, 153
Offer, D., 38
Offer, J., 38
O'Leary, K., 239
One parent family, 197, 277
Open monogamy, described, 106
Opinion polls:
  on abortion, 272
  on female employment, 48
Orgasm, 58, 100
Osofsky, H., 127
Osofsky, J., 127
Outreach:
  program, 186–187
  staffing, 258

Paramedical staff, for family planning,
  257
Parental marriage, proposed, 104
Parental consent and notification, for con-
  traceptive use and abortion, 251–252,
  268–269, 273
Parent-child relations, 91, 92, 168–169
  and communication difficulties, 114–115,
  120–121, 130, 231, 238, 240, 243, 258
Parent generation:
  lack of studies on, 178–179
  needs and behaviors of, 239, 259
Parenting substitutes, 202
Passivity, female, 111
Path analysis, 137
Paul, E., 269
Peer group, 24, 259
  counseling, 215–216
Pelvic examination, 263–264
Penis, 13, 14
Penis envy theory, 29
  scorned, 31
Perez-Reyes, M., 127
Permissiveness, 19, 68–69, 149
Personal fable, in adolescence, 25, 112
Personality development:
  and male and female traits, 54, 94
  theories, 28–31
  three layers of, 29
Peskin, H., 17
Petting behavior, 70–71, 74, 75, 230–231
  case illustrations of, 293, 294
Philadelphia Collaborative Perinatal Project,
  138